WAR PARTY IN BLUE

War Party in Blue

PAWNEE SCOUTS IN THE U.S. ARMY

MARK VAN DE LOGT

Foreword by Walter R. Echo-Hawk

University of Oklahoma Press : Norman

This book is published with the generous assistance of The McCasland Foundation, Duncan, Oklahoma.

Library of Congress Cataloging-in-Publication Data

Van de Logt, Mark, 1968–
   War party in blue : Pawnee scouts in the U.S. Army / Mark van de Logt.
     p. cm.
   Includes bibliographical references and index.
   ISBN 978-0-8061-4139-8 (hardcover) ISBN 978-0-8061-6923-1 (paper)
   1. Pawnee Indians—History—19th century. 2. Indian scouts—West (U.S.)—History—19th century. 3. Indian soldiers—West (U.S.)—History—19th century. 4. United States. Army—Indian troops—History—19th century. 5. Indians of North America—Wars—1866–1895. 6. Indians of North America—West (U.S.)—Wars. 7. West (U.S.)—History, Military—19th century. I. Title.
   E99.P3V36 2010
   978.004'97—dc22

                                                                         2009051911

The paper in this book meets the guidelines for permanence and durability of the Committee on Production Guidelines for Book Longevity of the Council on Library Resources, Inc. ∞

Copyright © 2010 by the University of Oklahoma Press, Norman, Publishing Division of the University. Paperback published 2021. Manufactured in the U.S.A.

All rights reserved. No part of this publication may be reproduced, stored in a retrieval system, or transmitted, in any form or by any means, electronic, mechanical, photocopying, recording, or otherwise—except as permitted under Section 107 or 108 of the United States Copyright Act—without the prior written permission of the University of Oklahoma Press.

To my mother and father

Kira katu kari rarix[a]
Kira katu kari rarix[a]
Kira katu kari rarix ey ey a
Ti rat pari
Tiras ta kawahat
Kira katu kari rarix[a]
Ti rat pari

Let us see, is this real,
Let us see, is this real,
Let us see, is this real,
This life I am living?
Ye gods, who dwell everywhere,
Let us see, is this real,
This life I am living?

—War song of the Pawnee Iruska Society

He e e e e e e
Yo e yoha eyu eyu eyo
Eru he ee ee ee
A tiras ta kawaha ti rat pari hey
Ero he ee ee ee
Tat ara kitawira
Hawa re ra wira
He e e e e yo

O you who possess the skies,
Am I living?
In you I entrust my fate.
Again I am on the warpath.

—Pawnee war song

Both songs adapted from Clark Wissler, *The American Indian* (New York: Oxford University Press, 1922), 150–51.

Contents

List of Illustrations	x
Foreword, by Walter R. Echo-Hawk	xi
Acknowledgments	xvii
Introduction	3
1 Pawnee Military Culture in the Mid-1800s	11
2 U.S. Military Tactics and the Recruitment of Pawnee Scouts	37
3 On the Powder River Campaign with Connor, 1865	57
4 Guarding the Union Pacific Railroad, 1867–1868	80
5 The Republican River Expedition and the Battle of Summit Springs, 1869	110
6 Freelance Scouting Operations, 1870–1874	157
7 The Powder River Campaign with Crook and Mackenzie, 1876–1877	186
8 Homecoming	225
Conclusion	241
Notes	247
Bibliography	315
Index	335

Illustrations

MAP

Major battles and engagements involving Pawnee scouts, 1857–1876	8

PHOTOGRAPHS

La ta cuts la shar ("Eagle Chief")	141
Te low a lut la sha ("Sky Chief")	142
Coo towy goots oo ter a oos ("Blue Hawk") and Tuc ca rix te ta ru pe row ("Coming Around With The Herd")	143
Major Frank North, 1867	144
Luther North, 1867	145
Loots tow oots ("Rattlesnake")	146
Four Kitkahahki Pawnees and interpreter Baptiste Bayhylle	147
Tuh cod ix te cah wah ("One Who Brings Herds")	148
Ke wuk o we terah rook ("Like A Fox")	149
Ta caw deex taw see ux ("Driving A Herd")	150
As sau taw ka ("White Horse")	151
Echo Hawk	152
Pawnee men during a Union Pacific Railroad excursion, 1866	152
Eagle Chief, Knife Chief, Brave Chief, and Young Chief, about 1890	153
Ki ri ki ri see ra ki wa ri ("Roaming Scout"), 1907	154
A group of surviving Pawnee scouts and interpreter James R. Murie, 1911	155
Rush Roberts, 1905	156

Foreword

WALTER R. ECHO-HAWK

Racing through the thick buffalo grass, the mounted, uniformed Pawnee soldiers blew their war whistles and rode their ponies into American history. Their saga is recounted in these pages. The history of the Pawnee scouts is a stirring tale for soldiers and citizens of any nation, race, place, or age. It is about warriors who answered that age-old call to defend their homeland, their way of life, and the survival of their people. This band of brothers formed a unique military unit. Composed of warriors from the four bands of the Pawnee Nation, the Pawnee scouts fought as cavalry in the United States Army. They became, according to one military expert, "the most capable mobile strike force ever to take the field during the Indian Wars."[1]

Until now, their remarkable military history has been unsung, except in tribal lore. Though much has been written about the Indian wars, the role of the Pawnee scouts is usually presented as incidental sidebar information by historians, who have focused on other combatants in the conflicts that swept the Great Plains during the nineteenth century. Thus it is not surprising that the history of the Pawnee scouts is not widely known, or that it has fallen into the realm of Hollywood fiction, twisted into a popular but false stereotype. Ignorance about the important role of the scouts in the service of the United States can be found even among military historians and career army professionals.[2]

Nonetheless, the scouts' unique history deserves to be told. It is imbued with all the familiar hardships and heartbreaks faced by veterans across the ages, races, and cultures. It tells the story of victories, tragedies, privation, and sacrifice. This is the familiar lot of soldiers who, in this instance, fought with all their might for the survival of their people during the tumultuous decades of the mid-nineteenth century, when the Pawnee homeland was engulfed by war, as Manifest Destiny raged throughout the plains. The Indian wars can be seen in a brand-new perspective when viewed through the eyes of the Pawnee warriors in uniform—the *raaripákusu'*, or, to neighboring Indian tribes, the "Wolf Men."

In those turbulent decades, the Pawnee Nation was under siege at home by several powerful allied confederacies of tribal enemies. The Sioux, Cheyennes, Arapahos, Kiowas, Comanches, Osages, Kansas, and others were bent upon the utter destruction of the Pawnee people and their way of life as one of the oldest aboriginal inhabitants of the Great Plains. Women and children were scalped and slain while working in village gardens; innocents were slaughtered during tribal buffalo hunts; and villagers lived under the constant threat of attack. The beleaguered Pawnee Nation thus became a military ally of the United States and furnished crack troops in the battle against common foes. These mounted soldiers provided the Pawnee Nation with a potent offensive capacity in the defense of its besieged homeland. Those who have maligned the Pawnee Nation for its military alliance ignore the war of annihilation brought against it by more numerous tribal adversaries. In the law of nations, the use of military force to repel aggression is the unquestioned right of any nation.

Violence often follows when proud peoples collide. From at least 1850 to 1890 warfare was virtually constant on the Great Plains as cultures clashed. As the inextricable flood of immigration, settlement, and displacement uprooted tribes and threatened their ways of life in the years following the Civil War, unrest and turmoil were followed, ultimately, by the outbreak of full-scale war. The grassy expanse was occupied by numerous buffalo-hunting nations with proud warrior traditions. They were determined to protect their homelands. For more than 150 years the mounted horsemen of these nomadic Indian tribes barred settlement of the prairie by the Spanish conquistadors, Mexicans, Texans, English, French, and Americans. By the 1860s warriors made immigration through the grasslands downright dangerous, and skittish settlers scurried to more hospitable regions. Similarly, the United States was no stranger to the use of violence. From 1776 to the present, the long, almost continuous history of warfare places ours among the most violent nations on earth.

The resolve and warlike prowess of the indigenous peoples matched that of the warlike Americans.

The Pawnee Nation resided in the epicenter of this storm. Armed by warrior traditions of their own, the Pawnees struggled valiantly to survive the clash between proud peoples. They were a nation adrift in a grassy sea of warring Indian tribes and American invaders, living in a violent time when their domain formed a vast cauldron of war. Times of adversity test the best within us. In this crisis, the Pawnee scouts emerged. As the first line of defense, they became a mobile strike force capable of driving the enemy from the Pawnee homeland. Their exploits carried on a warrior tradition from mythic times and provided a bridge to the present, as displayed most visibly in the many decorated Pawnee combat veterans who today wear the American uniform in distant places such as Iraq and Afghanistan.

In carrying the war into the backyard of their enemies, the Pawnee scouts compiled an impressive string of military victories—winning many horses, trophies, and a Congressional Medal of Honor along the way. As Native soldiers trained from boyhood to pay close attention to the land, they were skilled trackers in the vast expanses of their aboriginal terrain. They were gifted scouts, deeply knowledgeable about their tribal foes, and ferocious warriors always found in the forefront of the fighting. One military commentator observes:

> The Pawnee Scouts were unique in American history. They were the most capable mobile strike force to ever take the field during the Indian Wars. The Pawnee Battalion fought as cavalry for the cavalry. Their forte went far beyond the traditional bounds of Indian peoples functioning as guides and scouts. And they were far more effective in an attack than anything demonstrated by other Indian allies and auxiliaries. The Pawnees served the full gamut of reconnaissance, security, and disciplined effective attack, and they routinely augmented or even replaced white army cavalry units.[3]

As this book shows, the Pawnee scouts played pivotal roles in many crucial military campaigns during the height of the Great Plains Indian wars (1864–77). With war howling at the very doorstep of the Pawnee Nation, these soldiers forestalled the specter of genocide in their homeland and safeguarded the cultural survival of their nation into the present. Those veterans in that urgent time of need became tribal heroes who left an enduring legacy.

Today the Pawnee scouts hold an honored place in Pawnee history and culture. They provide ideals for bravery, instill the values of valor, and inspire patriotism for tribe and country. The scouts are revered in song and memorialized in tribal societies, ceremonies, dances, art, lore, names, and family oral traditions. Their history is taught in the Pawnee Nation College. Every family tree traces back to the Pawnee scouts. The Echo Hawk family lines, with which I am most familiar, afford an example of this pervasive influence. The names of our family's forebears include Kutawi-kucu' tawaaku' ah, or Echo Hawk (Howard Echo Hawk; Powder River campaign, 1876–77); Asawiita, or Male Horse (Powder River campaign, 1864–65); Arusa to-tah-it, or Rides A Captured Horse (Robert Taylor; Republican River campaign, 1869); Resaru siti reriku, or The Heavens See That He Is A Chief (Baptiste Bayhylle; 1867); See-lee-lee-lu-ha-lu tike (Abraham Lincoln; Powder River campaign, 1876–77); and Rahekuts Kiri-patski, or Little Warrior (Ralph Weeks; Powder River campaign, 1876–77).

Like many other tribal members, I have walked the cemeteries where the scouts are buried, danced to Pawnee scout songs, visited the battle-fields where they made their mark in history, and listened to the stories told by our elders. Scout lore in family oral traditions abounds. The Blaine family humorously recounts that the Pawnee scouts noticed that, when wounded, white troopers normally fell to the ground, propped themselves up, and strangely cried, "Wah tuh! wah tuh! wah tuh!" This behavior perplexed the Pawnees, who thought it was more prudent for injured soldiers to lie quietly concealed until the fighting was over.[4] In our family it is said that the Echo Hawk name came from the battle against Morning Star's Northern Cheyennes during the Powder River campaign of 1876–77. My great-grandfather enlisted under the name Tawi Hiisi, meaning Leader Of The Group, but he returned home as Echo Hawk after many scouts changed their names, according to tribal custom, to celebrate that victory in battle. He was part of an unbroken family warrior tradition that reaches into the twenty-first century.

My Aunt Malinda ("Bink") Hadley/Haragara (1910–89) was born in a camp south of Pawnee, Oklahoma, and knew the old-time Pawnee scouts. As a young girl she served them coffee, meat, and bread when they came to visit Echo Hawk. The old scouts would sit and talk about their exploits in Nebraska, and many still dressed in old-time Indian leggings. Some, like

FOREWORD

Ruling His Son, were gruff in the eyes of the young girl, but Echo Hawk told her to treat them with respect. They drank black coffee (*rakits katit*) without sugar, according to Aunt Bink, perhaps because that was the way they drank it on the campaign trail. Many stories told by these scouts at Echo Hawk's camp are contained in these pages. In my mind's eye, they recalled their days in words similar to those of Tahirussawichi (Arrives First). In 1900, while in Washington to make cylinder recordings of ceremonial songs for the Smithsonian Institution, he described the Powder River campaign of 1876–77:

> I think back over my long life with its many experiences; of the great number of Pawnees who have been with me in war, nearly all of whom have been killed in battle. I have been severely wounded many times—see this scar over my eye. I was with those who were sent to the Rocky Mountains to the Cheyennes, when so many soldiers were slain that their dead bodies lying there looked like a great blue blanket spread over the ground. When I think of all the people of my own tribe who have died during my lifetime and then of those in other tribes that have fallen by our hands, they are so many they make a vast cover over Mother Earth. I once walked with these prostrate forms. I did not fall but I passed on, wounded sometimes, but not to death, until I am here to-day doing this thing, singing these sacred songs into that great pipe [the graphophone] and am telling you of these ancient rites of my people. It must be that I have been preserved for this purpose, otherwise I should be lying back there among the dead.[5]

These are their stories. They have been compiled by my good friend, historian Mark van de Logt. It was my privilege to accompany him and family members on a summer camping trip as we retraced the campaign trails of the Pawnee scouts in the Republican River expedition of 1869 and the Powder River campaign of 1876–77. Those war trails, forts, campsites, and battlefields led us through largely unsullied natural landscapes in the prairie grasslands, river valleys, sand hills, and mountains of Nebraska, Kansas, Colorado, and Wyoming, in the heart of the Great Plains of Native North America. This is where our ancestors rode into history and earned their place of honor in the Pawnee world. Their story is the story of our land, of the many conflicts and hardships that for better or worse birthed our country, and of the many proud and colorful peoples who inhabit this part of Mother Earth. Although peace has been achieved in this haunting land, it is important to remember the travails of those who came before, as we look to the future of our diverse peoples now joined together on the land.

Acknowledgments

This book could not have been completed without the help and support of many people. I take this opportunity to express my gratitude to all of them. First, I thank Walter, Pauline, and Myron Echo-Hawk, my companions during trips to visit battle sites and other places in Pawnee scout history. Apart from being great travel companions, they broadened my appreciation and understanding of Pawnee history and culture, and I am forever indebted to them for their kindness, insights, support, and encouragement.

I am also grateful to the members of the Pawnee community who encouraged me to turn my dissertation into a book. They include Ramona Osborn, Elmer and Mattie Fish, and Vicky L. Conklin.

Thanks as well to professors and friends at Oklahoma State University: L. G. Moses, Michael M. Smith, Joseph A. Stout, Donald N. Brown, William S. Bryans, Elizabeth A. Williams, Ronald A. Petrin, James and Teresa Klein, Kevin Sweeney, Stacy Reaves, Shelly Lemons, Lisa Guinn, Stephanie Decker, Carter Mattson, Hong Hyun, and Krista Schnee, as well as the staff of the Edmond Low Library, including John Philips, Helen Clements, David Peeters, Micki White, and Kenda Hill.

At Indiana University, I thank Dennis Christafferson, Raymond J. DeMallie, Douglas R. Parks, Rani Andersson, William Anderson, Heidi Kwon, Noemie Waldhubel, Indrek Park, Brad Kroupa, Deb Speer, and Rebecca Gabriel.

At Benedictine College, I thank my colleagues, especially Everett Dague, Susan Taylor, and Erika Kraus for their insights, support, and comradeship.

Thanks also to the staff of the Oklahoma Historical Society, Oklahoma City, particularly Mary Jane Warde, and the staffs of the Western History Collections of the University of Oklahoma, Norman, and the McFarlin Library in Tulsa, Oklahoma. Also thanks to Terri Raburn and Patricia M. Churray of the Nebraska State Historical Society, Lincoln.

I owe additional thanks to Lynn, Kathy, and Mike Harrison of Stillwater, Oklahoma; Rose and Bob McFarland of Maxwell, Nebraska; Junior and Kitty Sramek of Palisade, Nebraska, who for many years have cared for the Massacre Canyon site, which is located on their land; Tom Buecker, curator of the Fort Robinson Museum, Crawford, Nebraska; John A. Doerner, Little Bighorn Battlefield National Monument, Crow Agency, Montana; and Margot Liberty of Sheridan, Wyoming. Thanks and appreciation also to Ken and Cheri Graves of the Red Fork Ranch near Kaycee, Wyoming. Cheri gave a highly instructive tour of the Dull Knife battlefield, and I greatly value her expertise and defer to most of her interpretations of what happened during the fight, which took place where her property is now located.

Invaluable was my experience at the Military History Summer Seminar at the United States Military Academy, West Point, New York, in 2004. I would like to thank Lance Betros, Gian Gentile, Frederick Black, John Hall, Tom Ryder, Clay Mountcastle, Josh Moon, Melissa Mills, Clifford Rogers, Eugenia Kiesling, Chuck Steele, Sam Watson, Les Jensen, Steve Waddell, Caroll Reardon, and others for their hospitality and for putting together a highly instructive program.

I am also much indebted to Roger C. Echo-Hawk, who reviewed the manuscript, challenged some of my assumptions, and generously offered valuable information on the scouts and their descendants. I also owe thanks to an anonymous reviewer for the University of Oklahoma Press for his useful comments and suggestions.

Finally, I thank Alessandra Jacobi Tamulevich, Charles Rankin, and Ashley Eddy at the University of Oklahoma Press, and copyeditor Jane Kepp, for their encouragement, support, and, above all, their patience.

WAR PARTY IN BLUE

Introduction

In 1867 Colonel Christopher C. Augur defended his use of Indian scouts against criticisms from officials in the Interior Department who believed that military service retarded efforts to "civilize" these Indians. According to Augur, not only were Indian scouts effective military allies, but their service would also prepare them for entrance into white society. "It opens to those people a useful career, [and] renders them tractable and obedient, educating them more effectually than can be done in any other way."[1] Lieutenant General William T. Sherman agreed. "If we can convert the wild Indians into a species of organized cavalry," Sherman mused, "it accomplishes a double purpose, in taking them out of temptation of stealing and murdering, and will accustom them to regular habits and discipline, from which they will not likely depart when discharged."[2]

The Indians to whom Augur referred belonged to Major Frank J. North's famous "Pawnee scout battalion," as it was popularly but never formally known.[3] Between 1864 and 1877 these scouts rendered invaluable military assistance to the United States Army. The Pawnees called them *raaripákusu'*, which means "constant fighters" or "persistent fighters."[4] They joined the army in many operations against resisting Indian tribes, who usually were enemies of the Pawnee people as well. During these operations their duties involved much more than scouting alone. The Pawnee scouts led missions deep into contested territory, tracked resisting bands and spearheaded attacks into their villages, protected construction crews of the Union Pacific Railroad against Indian raiders, carried dispatches through dangerous territory, and, on more than one occasion, saved American troops from disaster on the field of battle. Within a few years the Pawnee scouts established a reputation as a highly effective fighting force.

Sherman's and Augur's pontifications that military service streamlined the scouts' assimilation into white society did not correspond to reality. Although the Pawnee scouts took great pride in scouting for the American army, they never relinquished their Indian heritage. In fact, military service reinforced established Pawnee martial values and customs. As scouts they continued to fight their enemies, the Sioux, Cheyennes, and Arapahos. Military service allowed them to exact revenge on these enemies with the approval and the guns of the Great Father in Washington, and to be paid for doing so. Their mode of warfare, based on stealth and surprise, changed little, if at all. They continued to count coups, take scalps, and practice their war-related ceremonies. Sherman and Augur were well aware that the success of the Pawnee scouts depended largely on their familiarity with Indian warfare, and the army enlisted them, first and foremost, for their skills as scouts, guides, and warriors. As a result, their commanding officers did little, if anything, to discourage the persistence of Pawnee martial traditions. Although the scouts proudly wore the army blue uniform of the United States Cavalry, they never ceased to be Pawnees. The Pawnee battalion was truly a war party in blue.

Most histories of the scouts emphasize the role of Major Frank North in the extraordinary success of the Pawnee battalion. This is not surprising, because most of these studies are based on the writings of Luther North, Frank North's brother. Luther North was troubled by the fact that his brother, who died in 1885, had never received the attention and public recognition he deserved, and he published numerous accounts in newspapers, magazines, and historical journals to correct this ommission. Even though these accounts are invaluable in reconstructing the history of the Pawnee battalion, each must be considered a personal monument to Luther North's older brother. The crucial figure in them is not the Pawnees but Frank North.[5]

Basing their works on Luther North's writings, later authors have echoed the claim that it was North's leadership that turned the scouts into an effective fighting force. Typical of writers taking this view, George E. Hyde, in his classic study *The Pawnee Indians* (1951), criticized Pawnee leaders for past military failures and credited the remarkably successful military record of the Pawnee scouts entirely to Frank North and his staff of white officers. "One must admit that there was something wrong with the Pawnee leaders who went through one disastrous experience after another," Hyde wrote, but under "the command of Frank North, his brother Luther North, and other white officers, these same Pawnee warriors—properly armed and led—were never defeated, and they won a number of handsome victories over their Sioux and Cheyenne enemies."[6]

The actual contributions of the scouts have not received the same praise and attention as those of the North brothers.[7] In this book I try to bring the experiences of the Pawnee scouts themselves to the foreground. I argue not only that the scouts remained distinctly Pawnee, but also that it was exactly their military qualities that made them such effective allies of the United States on the field of battle. The role played by Frank North and his officers was smaller than previously assumed. North may have been nominally in charge, but the tactics, style, and conduct of warfare were decidedly Pawnee. The difference with the past was that the scouts were now armed and mounted by the same government that had previously neglected to provide them with the means to defend themselves adequately.

Besides focusing on the role of the scouts, I attempt to provide a comprehensive history of Pawnee military service in the 1860s and 1870s. Although I rely heavily on the accounts by Luther North and George Bird Grinnell, an ethnologist who knew the North brothers and spent years studying the Pawnees, Cheyennes, and other Plains tribes, I go beyond these to include other, less known accounts and events as well. Wherever possible, I try to correct the factual errors that plague the North and Grinnell accounts. Finally, I attempt to put the actions and behavior of the scouts, both on and off the battlefield, within the context of Pawnee cultural practices and customs. Focusing on the Pawnees, I have paid less attention to the viewpoints of their opponents, such as the Sioux and the Cheyennes.

I treat warfare as a cultural construct. This means simply that different cultures fight wars and view warfare in different ways. When these dissimilar cultural traditions meet on the battlefield, the result is usually confusion, all too often followed by mutual accusations of violations of culturally accepted codes of war. Thus, in North America, both American

Indians and Euro-Americans soon accused each other of committing atrocities. Such accusations frequently led to retaliatory acts that could escalate and intensify conflicts. Europeans and Euro-Americans quickly denounced American Indian warfare as "savage" and used it to justify harsh military and political measures (such as removal of the Indians from their homelands to areas not yet inhabited by white people) as "punishment."

My purpose is not to pass moral value judgments on the ways each side conducted war. Instead, I seek to understand each culture on its own terms. I want to know why men acted on the field of battle in the way they did. The Pawnee way of war was different from the way the Americans fought battles. I believe it was because of their experience with Plains Indian warfare that the Pawnees made such efficient allies. For this reason I refer to them with terms such as "warriors" and "war party" that contrast with European and Euro-American concepts. Regrettably, these are racially charged terms that might be misconstrued to mean that Plains Indian warfare was less sophisticated than or inferior to American warfare. This is not my intention at all. I do not believe that the Western way of war was "superior" to American Indian warfare; it was merely different as a result of different cultural values, experiences, and technologies. I do not view terms such as "warriors" and "war party" in racially charged ways. Indeed, I prefer to use the term "war party" because it more adequately describes the temporary character and relatively fluid composition of typical Pawnee military field organizations. In the same way, the term "raid" (as opposed to the vaguer "expedition") refers more accurately to the type of military tactic the Pawnees typically employed in war. It is a military term that describes a quick but intense surprise attack by a relatively small military unit deep into enemy territory. By the same token, I believe the term "warrior" better expresses nineteenth-century Pawnee cultural values than the term "soldier." For lack of better alternatives, I have also found it difficult to avoid other racially charged terms such as "Indian," "chiefs," "village," and "tribe."

Originally, I intended to provide the proper spellings of Pawnee names in the current orthography. This task proved impossible for two reasons. First, differences exist between the spellings and pronunciations of names as they were used by the Skiri Pawnees, the northernmost of the four Pawnee bands, and by members of the other three bands, known collectively as the South Band Pawnees. In many cases the band associations of the scouts were impossible to determine, and to give the proper spellings in both Skiri and South Band Pawnee was impractical. Second, it is often difficult to ascertain the exact meaning of a name, because mustering officers and other eyewitnesses who left accounts gave very imperfect spellings of Pawnee names. Providing all possible translations of names would have considerably lengthened the manuscript and unnecessarily interrupted the narrative.

The research for this book was based on extensive study of primary, secondary, and archival sources as well as field trips to the various sites where the Pawnee scouts were stationed or battled with their enemies. Among the sites I visited in Nebraska were Fort Kearny, Fort McPherson, Sidney Barracks, Fort Robinson, the Plum Creek battlefield near present-day Lexington, Massacre Canyon, the old Pawnee Agency at Genoa, and the Columbus Cemetery, where many of the officers of the battalion are buried. Field trips to Wyoming included visits to Fort Laramie, Fort Fetterman, Fort Reno, the Connor battlefield, and the Dull Knife battle site. I also spent one day visiting the Summit Springs battlefield near present-day Sterling in northeastern Colorado.

The story of the Pawnee scouts is a tale of triumphs as well as tragedies. Although it is true that they helped to conquer the resisting tribes such as the Sioux, Cheyennes, and Arapahos, they did so because they perceived these tribes as a greater threat to the well-being of the Pawnee people than the mighty power that replaced them—the United States. Unfortunately, the United States government never properly honored the contributions of these men. Not only were many scouts denied pensions, but the government also insisted on eradicating Pawnee native culture. Despite this record of mistreatment by the U.S. government, the Pawnee people today take special pride in the service of their scout ancestors, whom they regard as the first Pawnee-American patriots.

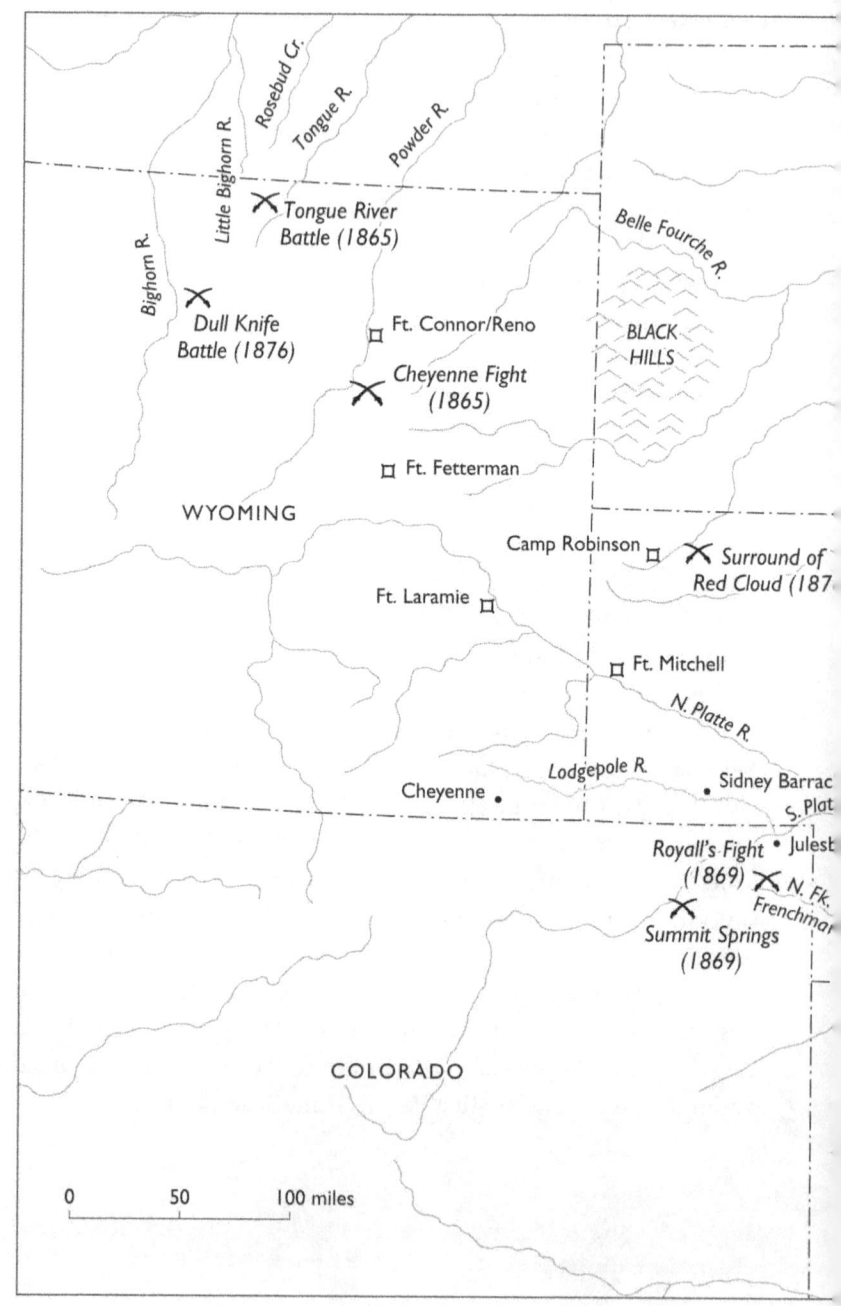

Major battles and engagements involving Pawnee scouts, 1857–1876

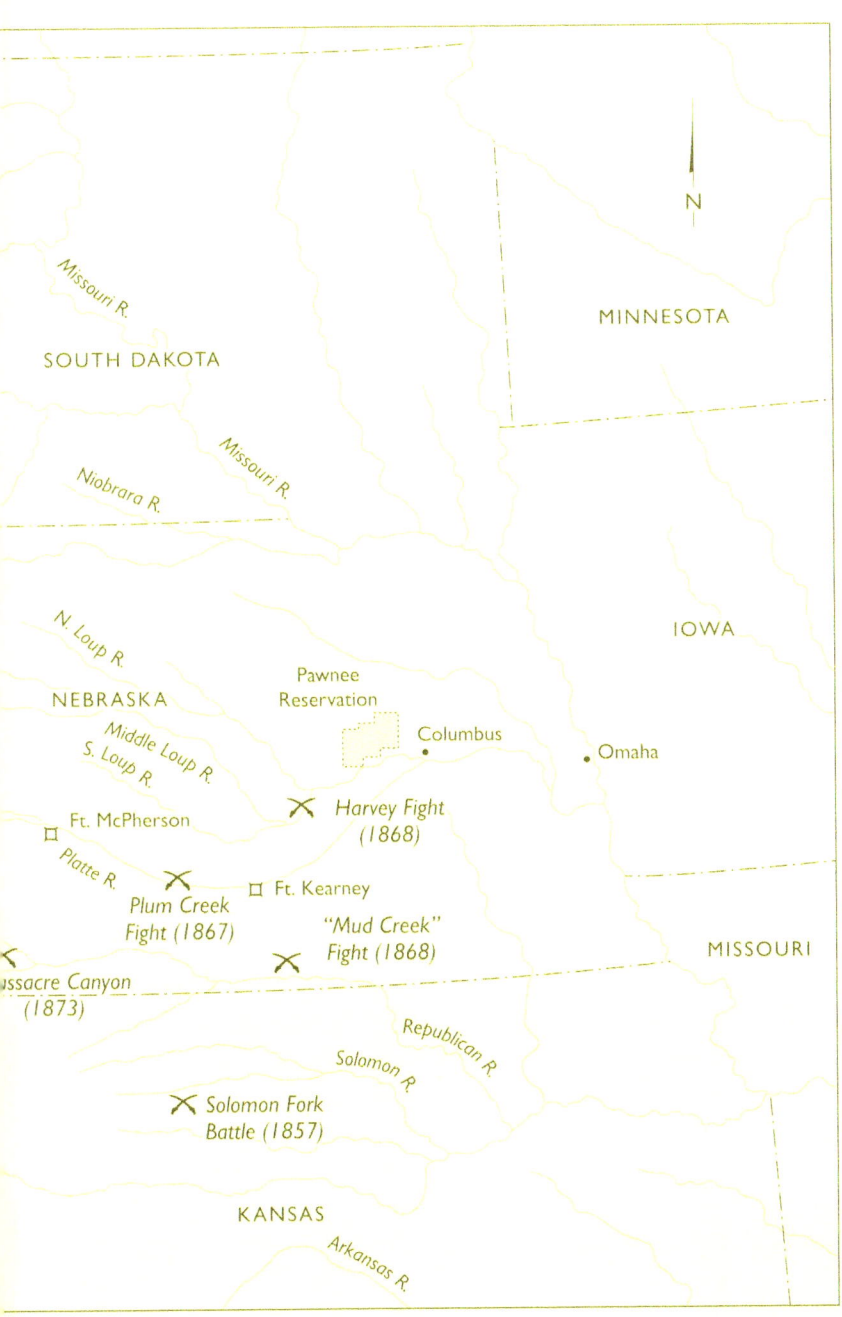

CHAPTER 1

Pawnee Military Culture in the Mid-1800s

Shortly after the birth of Lone Chief, around 1850, his father, a Kitkahahki Pawnee chief, died. Lone Chief's mother took up the responsibility for instructing her son in becoming a successful and important man in the tribe. Among the things she taught him as a child was the following lesson:

> You must trust always in *Ti-ra'-wa*. He made us, and through him we live. When you grow up, you must be a man. Be brave, and face whatever danger may meet you. . . . Your father was a chief, but you must not think of that. Because he was a chief, it does not follow that you will be one. It is not the man who stays in the lodge that becomes great; it is the man who works, who sweats, who is always tired from going on the warpath.
>
> When you get to be a man, remember that it is his ambition that makes the man. If you go on the warpath, do not turn around when you have gone part way, but go on as far as you were going, and then come back. If I should live to see you become a man, I want you to become a great man. I want you to think about the hard times we have been through. Take pity on people who are poor, because we have been poor, and people have taken pity on us. If I live to see you a man, and to go off on the warpath, I would not cry if I were to hear that you had been killed in battle. That is what makes a man: to fight and to be brave. I should be sorry to see you die from sickness. If you are killed, I would rather have you die in the open air, so that the birds of the air will eat your flesh, and the wind will breathe on you and blow over your bones. It is better to be killed in the open air than to be smothered in the earth. Love

your friend and never desert him. If you see him surrounded by the enemy, do not run away. Go to him, and if you cannot save him, be killed together, and let your bones lie side by side. Be killed on a hill; high up. Your grandfather said it is not manly to be killed in a hollow. It is not a man who is talking to you, advising you. Heed my words, even if I am a woman.[1]

This story, recorded by ethnologist George Bird Grinnell in the 1880s, sums up some Pawnee attitudes toward warfare. Only successful men could become prominent members of Pawnee society. In order to be successful, a man had always to put his faith in the sacred powers, without whose supernatural assistance he was destined to fail. Manhood was defined in terms of ambition, hard work, bravery, generosity toward the poor, and loyalty toward friends. One way for a man to satisfy his ambitions was to go to war. Should death come to him while he displayed these virtues on the battlefield, he died with honor, and this honor would then be bestowed on his family. These were the attitudes the Pawnees carried into battle as scouts for the United States Army. Lone Chief, the boy to whom the preceding words were directed, enlisted in the Pawnee battalion in 1867. He distinguished himself in battle against the Arapahos while serving in Luther North's company.[2]

To understand the attitudes, behavior, and tactics of the Pawnee scouts, it is necessary to understand the role of warfare in Pawnee society and culture in the mid-nineteenth century. In this chapter I describe the character of what ethnologist Marian W. Smith called the "war complex" of the Pawnees. I explain why the Pawnee scouts were such effective allies of the United States Army and why the Pawnees formed an alliance with the United States and assisted the army as scouts in the first place. My emphasis is on the nineteenth century, by which time the Pawnees had fully incorporated horses and guns into their military organization.[3]

Because this chapter is focused solely on Pawnee martial values, it may leave the impression that Pawnee culture was highly militaristic. Such an impression would be false. In reality, Pawnee men identified themselves in many different ways: as hunters and providers, doctors, philosophers, teachers, artists and craftsmen, husbands and family men, workers, political leaders, and religious officials. After work, most men enjoyed visiting friends and relatives and attending religious ceremonies or social events and dances. They took part in meetings of one of the men's societies, where they sang songs, challenged each other to games of chance, exchanged stories, and discussed town politics. Pawnee culture was exceptionally rich and offered Pawnee men many ways to express themselves. Warfare was only one aspect of Pawnee life in the mid-nineteenth century, and community expectations of men extended far beyond military matters.

Around 1800, the four bands that composed the Pawnee confederacy—the Skiri, Chawi, Kitkahahki, and Pitahawirata bands—occupied a territory along the Platte, Loup, and Republican Rivers in present-day Nebraska and north-central Kansas. They lived in semipermanent towns of dirt-covered lodges. Their economy was based on corn horticulture supplemented by hunting and gathering. During the summer, while their crops matured, the Pawnees left their earth-lodge towns for several months and traveled west in search of buffalo. During this time they camped in buffalo-skin-covered tepees. The four bands of the tribe were socially and politically autonomous. Indeed, until the late 1700s it is perhaps more accurate to view the northernmost group, the Skiris, as a tribe entirely separate from the three "South Band" Pawnee groups. Still, the four bands shared many of the same basic cultural values and practices.[1]

Religion played a major role in the daily lives of the Pawnee people and formed the basis for their social and political organization. The Pawnees did not clearly distinguish between a "natural" and a "supernatural" world. The "supernatural" was simply part of the natural world. According to Pawnee theology, Tiiraawaahat ("This Expanse" or "The Heavens") had created the universe, the Earth, and everything that existed, both living and nonliving. He was addressed as "father" in prayers and ceremonies. Ranking below him were stars and other celestial objects. Most prominent of these were Evening Star, a female power, and Morning Star, a male power. Morning Star was usually portrayed as a warrior and presented the ideal for any Pawnee man. These celestial powers protected the tribe, band, or town against disease, starvation, and poverty. The power of the celestial beings was represented in so-called sacred bundles called *cu'uhre re ipi ru'* ("rainstorm wrapped up"). Priests were responsible for conducting ceremonies to maintain the covenant with the celestial powers.

Meanwhile, the head chief of a band, town, or village was usually a descendant of the original bundle owner. The positions of priest and band or village chief were hereditary.[5]

The Pawnees also recognized terrestrial powers, manifested in the form of animal benefactors or guardians. The animals appeared to individuals in dreams or visions and instructed the visionary to make a sacred bundle. These personal bundles were called *karu su'* ("sack"). Such bundles and the songs and rituals that accompanied them could be sold to others. Although less powerful than the sky powers, the animal guardians granted individual Pawnees power and fortitude in hunting, doctoring, and warfare. The power bestowed by one of the animal benefactors enabled ordinary people to become doctors and warriors and to accumulate wealth and status in the community. A successful warrior might eventually be raised to the position of subchief and take a seat in the town or village council. Not surprisingly, ordinary Pawnees spent considerable time and effort in acquiring spiritual power.

A man could attain status in Pawnee society in different ways. Doctoring and hunting were both considered important—if not essential—honorable, and noteworthy. Men sought to perfect their skills in these endeavors by obtaining the blessings of the sacred powers.

Another way to attain wealth and status was to go to war. A Pawnee man had plenty of opportunities to do so. By the mid-1700s the Pawnees were surrounded by other tribes. To the east were the Omahas, Iowas, Otoes, and Missourias. To the south were the Kaws, Osages, Kiowas, Comanches, and Plains Apaches. To the west were the Arapahos and the mighty Cheyennes, and to the north were the Poncas and the powerful Lakotas, or Western Sioux. The Pawnees' relations with these tribes were complex. Their interactions with the other sedentary tribes (Omahas, Iowas, Otoes, Missourias, Kaws, and Poncas) fluctuated between war and peace, as did their relations with the more nomadic Kiowas and Comanches. But Pawnee relations with the Sioux and Cheyennes appear to have been poor from the beginning. Certainly by the 1830s, the Sioux and Cheyennes had become the most fearsome enemies of the Pawnees. The Pawnees called the Sioux *paahíksukat*, and the Cheyennes, *sáhi.*

Pawnee men went to war for a variety of reasons: to defend their home territory against invaders, to protect their hunting grounds, to avenge the deaths of relatives, to end the mourning period for deceased loved ones, to gain prestige by accumulating war honors, to accumulate wealth (primarily in horses), to gain social status by giving away the spoils of war, to protect tribal trade interests, to capture (or recapture) women and children, to take scalps, which they sacrificed in honor of the sacred powers, and to prove their readiness to be married.[6]

It is unclear exactly when this particular martial culture developed, but it has roots stretching back to earlier, perhaps even ancient, times. There is little doubt, however, that when new tribes appeared on the Great Plains, having been drawn there from the east as a result of opportunities afforded by horses and guns and pushed there through displacement by Europeans and later Euro-Americans, warfare between the Pawnees and these newcomers broke out and quickly escalated. The immigrant tribes competed with the Pawnees for increasingly scarce natural resources, especially buffalo. Pawnee scholar Roger C. Echo-Hawk believes that Pawnee martial culture intensified in response to Sioux and Cheyenne pressures in the nineteenth century. By the 1830s, warfare had become a reality of life for the Pawnees. It was even sanctioned by their religion.[7]

Warfare with the Sioux and Cheyennes was both defensive and offensive. Two forms of offensive warfare can be distinguished: expeditions in search of horses and loot and expeditions to kill and destroy the enemy. Even though participants in the former of these often sought to avoid battle, it was considered an act of war. The latter was more "noteworthy"—that is, it was recognized by the sacred powers. Such expeditions were ceremonial undertakings and involved elaborate ceremonial preparations, such as the opening of a sacred bundle. The act of going on such a dangerous mission could be regarded as a ceremonial act in itself. Like most other Pawnee ceremonies, it involved a sacrifice. In this case, the sacrifice came in the form of the killing of an enemy. If the expedition was unsuccessful, the Pawnee warrior or warriors themselves might end up being the sacrificial victims. If it was successful, the ceremony was not over until the warriors returned home, shared their victory with the people there, and returned the war insignia to the sacred bundles.

Considering the importance of warfare in Pawnee culture, it is not surprising that Pawnees boys were prepared from an early age to follow the path of the warrior. They were told not to fear death and that it was better to die bravely when young than to live to an enfeebled old age.[8] "For those of us that are men it is unworthy to be buried in a regular grave," Effie Blaine's father, a Pitahawirata headman, told her. "It is far better to lie in the open and be eaten by the birds." For this reason Pawnee families welcomed the birth of a son with a mixture of joy and sadness.[9]

When a young man reached an "age of realization" that his fate was not in his own hands but in those of the sacred powers, he would walk around the town singing, "My spirit rests in the belief that power is in the heavens."[10] This song signified his readiness to go on the warpath and his willingness to give up his life in the defense of his people. Declaring himself no longer afraid of death, he could now pursue the goal of becoming a brave warrior. Of course, declaring oneself brave did not necessarily make one so; the real test remained in facing the enemy in battle.

Bravery was the most highly regarded virtue in a Pawnee warrior. According to John Brown Dunbar, son of a Presbyterian missionary to the Pawnees, it determined a person's status in the afterlife. The Pawnees believed that the spirit of the deceased had to follow a dangerous path beneath falling arrows and cross a deep chasm on a small log. Only the brave passed over this dangerous route to a new country of peace and plenty. Cowardly spirits chose a path free of danger but strewn with hoes, axes, and other implements of labor, indicating that they would spend the afterlife in "an existence of endless toil and servitude."[11] Ethnomusicologist Frances Densmore recorded a Pawnee song that told how, should a person die in battle, the spirits would welcome him to the spirit world and talk of all his great deeds:

Aheru raa heru kitu tix wahe he weta axrau isirit ra tawe
("Beloved, come, Beloved, All the spirits spoke. Here he comes.
It is openly known that he did these generous things.")[12]

Warriors carried songs like these into battle because they gave them comfort on dangerous missions. Although men did not actively seek to die in battle, the songs reminded them that they should not fear death.[13]

Apart from learning to place their fate in the hands of the sacred powers, Pawnee boys learned practical skills that were necessary attributes for a warrior. Among these skills were horsemanship, endurance, stealth, and the manufacture, repair, and maintenance of weapons.

"The Pawnees are expert horsemen," wrote visitor Edwin James in 1820, "and [they] delight in the exhibition of feats of skill and adroitness."[14] Like most other Plains tribes, the Pawnees considered horses great "medicine." Their power allowed a man to outrun the buffalo during the hunt or to make deep forays into enemy territory. The Pawnee term for horse is *aruúsa'*. Another common term is *asaa-*, followed by a descriptive term. Thus, *asaataáka* means "white horse," *asaakaatit*, "black horse," and so forth. The Pawnees obtained the horse in the late seventeenth century. The animal had such a powerful effect on them that they believed it was a gift from Tiiraawaahat to the people.[15] Pawnee warriors often painted and decorated their war horses before going on a war party. The decorations usually represented a higher power that would give the horse strength, endurance, speed, and fearlessness in battle. For example, Echo Hawk, a Pawnee scout, always painted his horse's head with white clay to symbolize an eagle. On his pony's chest was a beaded rosette depicting the skull of an eagle.[16] According to Luther North, one of the officers in the Pawnee battalion, the Pawnees also painted their horses to make them less conspicuous targets and disorient the enemy. Conversely, warriors sometimes fastened colored feathers in the tails and manes of their horses. Warriors might spend several hours preparing themselves and their horses in anticipation of a fight.[17]

Pawnee children learned to handle and care for horses at a young age. When John Treat Irving, who accompanied a U.S. peace commission in 1833, entered a Pawnee town he saw small bands of young men amusing themselves by racing their horses at full speed while attempting to throw each other from their saddles by violently steering their animals into each other. "There is nothing upon which the Indians pride themselves, more than their horsemanship," Irving wrote. "They are as much at ease, when mounted, as when sitting upon the floor of their own lodge."[18]

Indian horses were generally better acclimatized to the harsh conditions of the plains than U.S. Cavalry horses. Unlike grain-fed cavalry mounts, which usually required large quantities of feed that had to be carried along in wagons, Indian ponies subsisted primarily on grass. Although usually smaller and therefore slower than cavalry horses, they had greater endurance. George H. Holliday, who served alongside the Pawnee scouts in 1865, wrote that Indian ponies were "better calculated for the use of cavalry on the plains than 'Americano' horses." According to Holliday, Indian horses could "travel a greater distance and carry a load in a day, or week, or all the time, for that matter, and do it on less rations than any other living animal."[19] Pawnee warriors also had an array of "horse medicines" at their disposal. They applied boiled parts of the "sticky head" plant (*Grindelia squarrosa*) to treat saddle galls and sores and fed the bulbs of sheep sorrel (*Oxalis violacea*) to horses "to make them more fleet." They blew dried and powdered meadow rue (*Thalictrum dasycarpum*) into a horse's nostrils to increase its endurance "when obliged to make forced marches of three or four days' duration in order to escape from enemies."[20]

Just as they did horses, the Pawnees often endowed guns with supernatural power to improve their effectiveness. The Pawnees were successful exploiters of imported technologies. After adopting the gun, they applied to it the name they used for the bow and arrows, *tíraaku'*, and used the diminutive form, *tíraakis*, for the bow. The English traveler Charles Augustus Murray wrote in the 1830s that the Pawnees also called the gun "medicine-weapon." To make guns work more efficiently (for example, to avoid misfires), the Pawnees believed they needed the blessing of the supernatural beings. The successful use of these weapons often depended more on an individual's "medicine" than on his ability as a marksman. Hence, many warriors had special ceremonials with which they prepared their guns for battle.

But just as good spirits helped bullets to find their way, so angry or aggrieved spirits could sabotage a weapon. One such spirit caused the Pawnees much grief in the 1830s. This was the spirit of a young Skiri warrior who had been killed during a Sioux raid. The animal spirits took pity on him and breathed new life into him. His spirit then returned to his people and warned them whenever the Sioux came to attack them. But when the Skiris began to ignore him, he turned against them and began aiding the Sioux instead. The Skiris believed that the angry spirit "caused their guns to flash in the pan and the bullets to roll harmlessly from the muzzles." They also thought this spirit broke their bow strings in battle.[21]

Despite the power of the gun, the Pawnees continued to rely heavily on other weapons such as the bow and arrows. Antoine Deshetres, a French trader who toured the prairies with writer Washington Irving in 1832, believed that "the rifle of the white man was no match for the bow and arrow of the Pawnee." On several occasions Deshetres watched Pawnee archers send their arrows through one buffalo into another. He also wrote that the Pawnees could shoot at their enemies while hanging from the horse's side to shield their bodies, discharging their arrows from under the horse's neck.[22] This latter feat might have been more hyperbole than fact.

Describing a Chawi warrior in 1835, Charles Murray observed that he carried a gun only for "show" and that he relied on his bow and arrows "when the chase-signal or the war-cry was given."[23]

The Pawnees preferred a bow of bois d'arc, a type of wood that grew only on the southern plains. They obtained the wood through trade with the closely related Wichitas, who lived in that area. Pawnee warriors always kept a supply of bois d'arc sticks in their lodges with which to make new bows when their old ones gave out.[24] "As soon as the boys are able to run about," wrote Murray in 1835, "they begin to practice the bow and arrow, [and at] the age of twenty they are allowed to hunt, and seek other opportunities for distinction."[25] Grandfathers usually instructed young boys in the manufacture and use of the bow and arrows.[26] Pawnee boys perfected their skills in the use of arms through games. In the arrow game, one player shot his arrow into the ground between forty and sixty paces away. The other players then shot their arrows as close as possible to the main arrow. The player who lodged his arrow closest won and could claim all the arrows discharged. Another game was a hoop and stick game called *stuts-au'-i-ka-tus*, in which the players threw a lance-like stick at a rawhide hoop. These games perfected hand-eye coordination as well as the use of spears and bows and arrows.[27] It is uncertain whether the Pawnees poisoned their arrows, although they were familiar with the poisonous properties of certain plants such as "snow on the mountain" (*Dichrophyllum marginatum*).[28]

Complementing a warrior's arsenal were a battle ax, a war club, a spear, a shield, and usually one or more knives.[29] According to Edwin James, the circular shield of bison skin was thick enough to ward off an arrow. Such shields offered protection only if they had undergone some kind of ceremonial treatment. Shield covers were often decorated with fantastic designs that symbolized their sacred properties. "Defended by this shield," James wrote, "a warrior will not hesitate to cross the path of an arrow; he will sometimes dexterously seize the missile after it has struck, and discharge it back again at the enemy." Only distinguished warriors were allowed to display their weapons on a special rack in front of their lodge.[30] But as the quality and performance of guns improved, most traditional weapons were discarded or obtained a ceremonial function only. Nevertheless, most of the Pawnees who served in the U.S. Army continued to carry one or more traditional weapons with them.[31]

Physical and mental endurance were also highly valued martial virtues. Pawnee runners had a reputation as remarkable athletes who could travel more than one hundred miles in less than twenty-four hours, without food or sleep. The Reverend John Dunbar, who joined the Pawnees on many travels, recorded many instances in which they went without food for several days without a noticeable effect. They merely wrapped a thong several times tightly around the waist "to still the gnawings of hunger."[32] Charles Murray observed how Pawnee warriors chewed on lead bullets, claiming that it "excites the saliva, and relieves the pains of thirst." Murray said that he himself "more than once used one of my own rifle balls for this purpose, and have experienced much relief from so doing."[33]

Every warrior who entered battle did so only after obtaining the protection of the supernatural. This protection was crucial; without it no man, regardless of his skills and personal strength, could achieve success.[34] The Pawnees believed that at birth, each person came under the influence of an animal spirit.[35] Some of these spirits gave the individual the power to cure certain illnesses, but they could also provide a warrior with good fortune in battle. Pawnee animal symbolism was complex and used in many and various ways. In warfare, animal spirits could symbolize certain martial traits. For example, wolf symbolism represented stealth and craft, the eagle represented courage and fierceness, and the bear symbolized invulnerability.[36] Once a spirit had revealed itself, the Pawnee warrior tried to master its powers. Usually this meant that he had to learn the proper procedures for renewing and handling personal medicine bundles and amulets.[37] He also had to observe certain taboos, one of which was to prevent menstruating women from handling the sacred objects. The attire of each warrior included symbolic representations of these supernatural powers. Some wore bird feathers, bear claws, or other prepared animal parts. Many warriors attached a piece of corn, which represented the power of life, to their clothes.[38]

Warriors kept animal skins, bones, claws, rocks, paints, and other representations of the supernatural in small personal medicine bundles, which they carried into battle for protection and success. Captain J. Lee Humfreville, who met the Pawnee scouts during the Powder River campaign in 1865, wrote that "no Pawnee warrior would think of going into battle or on a hunt without it." The bundle, according to Humfreville, was a warrior's "great protection under all circumstances."[39]

The bundles also contained herbs and other medicines to treat wounds. Puffballs (*Lycoperdon perlatum*), for example, were used as a styptic for wounds. Each warrior had his own special medicines. Often these had been revealed to him in dreams or visions.[40]

A Pawnee warrior generally joined one of the men's societies. Although many of these fraternal orders had a certain recreational character, they also served specific public functions. Special organizations were the various doctors' societies, which were composed of men who had obtained sacred power (usually from an animal protector) that enabled them to cure certain diseases. Some acted as a tribal police force during the annual buffalo hunt. Among the Skiri Pawnees, the nonmedicine societies served military purposes. For example, they took on the defense of the town during enemy attacks.[41]

Two types of nonmedicine societies existed among the Pawnees. The first consisted of the prestigious "lance societies," which were associated with the tribal bundles. Only warriors with distinguished records of achievement were allowed to become members. Once a candidate passed the requirements of the fraternity, he became a member for life. Men could join several orders. Each society had its own origin myth, lodge, ceremonies, dances, songs, dress, paint code, and special objects. The ceremonial life of an order usually revolved around a special lance. Each year these lances were symbolically "renewed" (to restore their powers) in a special springtime ceremony. Often the lance represented or symbolized a specific martial quality. The lance of the Thunderbird

Lance society, for example, had a point of flint, a stone that represented thunder or the power to strike an enemy before he was aware of danger. The lances were not normally taken on expeditions but were used only for defensive purposes. Sometimes during battle, a warrior would plant a lance before the enemy and tie himself to it. This symbolized his determination to stand and fight until death. He could be relieved only by another warrior who, in order to save the lance, carried it away.[42]

Like the standards and colors of modern armies, lances were rallying points for the members of a lance society and served to inspire its warriors. One is reminded of the words of the European tactician Maurice de Saxe, who wrote in 1732 that soldiers should never abandon their standard: "It should be sacred to them; it should be respected; and every type of ceremony should be used to make [it] respected and precious."[43] To the Pawnees, the military society lances performed exactly this role.

Less accomplished warriors were organized into private societies, which constituted the second category of military society. These orders were usually formed by ambitious young men and operated in a manner similar to that of the lance societies. They, too, had their own origin myths, sacred bundles, dances, dress and paint codes, ceremonies, insignia, and objects. Unlike the lance societies, however, they lacked the official sanction of one of the tribal sacred bundles. A private society was usually created by a man who had been instructed to do so in a dream or vision. The supernatural power in the vision promised success and protection to the visionary's followers.

Unlike the established orders, the private organizations were more offensive-minded. Their members often went to war in search of horses, scalps, and war honors, or "coups." Some distinguished themselves through their "reckless" behavior in battle. Members of the Crazy Dog society, for example, sometimes "staked" themselves to the battlefield, signaling their determination to fight until death. The "Children of the Iruska" were so-called "contraries," who behaved opposite to their spoken words. For example, they entered a fight only when told not to. Despite this peculiar behavior, they were among the most aggressive fighters. These societies often competed with each other for the highest military honors. Some, such as the Young Dog and the Mischievous societies, were very successful and highly respected by the other members of the tribe. A few societies disappeared when they were annihilated in battle, their members preferring to perish rather than abandon their society brothers.[14]

When old enough, young men were invited to join one of the military societies. There they received instruction in the art of war. Members prepared for war through drills, sham battles, and other military exercises. The emphasis was on tactics, both defensive and offensive. Societies resembled the company system of modern-day armies. They had their own officers and command structure. Their purpose was, apart from drills and tactics, to instill a sense of brotherhood among their members. For this reason each society had its own regalia, songs, and rituals. The bond between members was often so strong that not infrequently warriors sacrificed their lives to save those of their comrades.[15] It appears that when the Pawnee battalion was organized, this society system continued to operate. Not only were scout companies constituted according to band affiliation (Skiri, Chawi, Kitkahahki, or Pitahawirata), but specially assigned platoons were often composed of members of a specific fraternal order.

Although most war parties consisted of members of a specific society, this did not have to be the case. Noted warriors often drew followers from various societies and sometimes even from different bands. Usually the leader of a party had no difficulty recruiting men, but sometimes he organized a special war dance for this purpose. Depending on whether the purpose was to steal horses or take scalps, war parties varied in size from a single man to several hundred warriors. Horse-stealing parties were usually small, to avoid detection. Expeditions in search of scalps were usually larger and could be composed of several warrior societies under the leadership of an elected chief. The contingent of Kitkahahki warriors that surrounded an advance party belonging to Major Stephen Long's western expedition in 1819 numbered about 130 to 140 men.[16]

Plains Indian warfare has often been characterized as undisciplined and disorganized. In reality, Plains Indians usually spent a lot of time preparing for battle, and the Pawnees were no exception. While on expeditions, Pawnees also maintained discipline rigorously. Discipline was essential in both the hunt and war. According to John Brown Dunbar, chiefs on occasion had taken a life in order to secure obedience. A person "persisting in willful insubordination was pretty sure of at least a sound beating."[17] Before setting out on a military expedition, according to Dunbar, Pawnee warriors spent much time practicing maneuvers. They fought mock battles in which they deployed and reassembled troops. Supervising these maneuvers was the leader of the party, who observed the movements of his men from an elevated position. From his vantage point he also gave signals and directions to the warriors.[48]

After the acquisition of the horse in the late seventeenth century, the Pawnees largely abandoned pitched-battle and formation warfare in favor of raids—usually small-scale, lightly armed incursions deep into enemy territory. Their purpose was to catch the enemy off guard, strike quickly, and retreat before the enemy could reorganize and launch a counterattack. The Pawnees perfected the raid and distinguished between expeditions in search of horses and expeditions in search of scalps.[49]

During the eighteenth century, horse-raiding expeditions became more common than expeditions in search of enemy scalps. Pawnee horse-raiding parties were small (from one to perhaps thirteen men) and usually made their forays into hostile territory on foot in order to escape detection. They sometimes walked for hundreds of miles and ventured as far as Wyoming and Texas. According to some observers, war parties went on foot as a show of their determination to return on horseback. According to Dunbar, such expeditions also had some strategic advantages: "Movements on foot, though not so swift for a sudden dash, could be kept more secret and unerring, [and] in case of a hard struggle . . . they could not then be so easily stampeded, and all developments could be kept better in hand."[50] Warriors on foot often carried extra sets of moccasins, usually filled with so-called corn balls, made of a mixture of corn flour, dried and pulverized beef, dried fruits, and buffalo fat. Loaded with calories, these balls were the MREs ("Meals Ready to Eat") of the Plains Indian warrior.

After locating the enemy, the horse raiders usually held a small ceremony to appeal once again to the supernatural powers for success. After the ceremony, the warriors discussed a plan of attack. If the enemy camp was large, they would make a stealthy attack during the night or at dawn to drive off the horses. A few selected men, usually those designated as scouts and "soldiers," approached the herds quietly on foot, then tried to stampede the animals in the direction of the other party members. Sometimes they screamed and shouted to get the horses moving. Josiah

Gregg, a merchant who traveled the Santa Fe Trail in the 1830s and 1840s, claimed that the Pawnees also used a peculiar whistle to stampede the horses.[51]

Although less common than horse raids, expeditions designed to attack and kill the enemy involved more elaborate ceremonial preparations. Such expeditions were often composed of members of different military societies who, for this occasion, temporarily formed new societies, called *araris taka* ("white wolf societies"). In Pawnee cosmology, the wolf symbolized the god of war (the Morning Star). The Skiri Pawnees, or "Wolf" Indians, adopted this animal as their tribal emblem because of its "intelligence, vigilance, and well known powers of endurance." The wolf had the power to steal up on an enemy and get away without being discovered. Hence, the Pawnees always sought the power of the wolf when they went on the warpath.[52]

Before the war party set out, its leader had to obtain this power for his men. He would go to the village bundle keeper and ask for a number of articles from the bundle that were related to the specific powers of the wolf. A four-day ceremony followed in which the warriors sought the sanction of the supernatural. The party carried these objects with them on the warpath in a special war bundle.[53]

According to James R. Murie, an ethnographer and the son of an officer of the Pawnee battalion, the warriors set out on their mission in two columns. Each line had a leader, two scouts, two "soldiers," the warriors, and some assistants. The scouts surveyed the area in front and on the flanks of the expedition and reported their findings to the leaders. The exact task of the "soldiers" is unclear, but it is possible that they led the warriors like modern-day company sergeants. They also made sure that no man wandered off by himself in search of individual war honors, thereby endangering the entire party. The assistants were inexperienced young men on their first expedition. They usually stayed in the back and learned the art of warfare by observing the more experienced members. All were painted heavily with white clay to imitate the wolf. The scouts also wore wolf-skin caps or white eagle feathers arranged in their hair to resemble a wolf's ears. According to Murie, the idea was that as they looked over the crest of a hill, they would appear to be wolves rather than spying men.[54] Yet by adopting wolf power, a warrior in fact "became" a wolf. He received wolf power not simply by putting on a wolf skin or applying white clay; it was the ceremonial appeal to the sacred bundle that enabled him to be a wolf.[55]

As soon as the scouts discovered an enemy camp, they reported their findings to the war party leader, who called a council to discuss the plan of attack and conduct another ceremony in which he appealed to the sacred powers. The warriors prepared for the attack by removing all superfluous clothing and applying face paint. The leader of the expedition did not necessarily participate in this attack but frequently directed the campaign from a strategic location. He usually remained behind to guard the war bundle. Overlooking the battlefield, he sent scouts to convey his orders or signaled the warriors from his position.[56] Western explorer James Ohio Pattie wrote about this particular tactic in 1824: "Their commander stations himself in the rear of his warriors, seldom taking part in the battle, unless he should be himself attacked, which is not often the case. They show no inconsiderable military stratagem in their marches, keeping spies before and behind, and on each flank, at the distance of a few days travel; so that in their open country, it is almost impossible to come upon them by surprise."[57]

Surprise was of the utmost importance during such attacks. For this reason the Pawnees preferred to attack at dawn, when the unsuspecting enemy was least able to organize quickly. If they succeeded in surprising an enemy, the death toll could become high. In warfare, the Pawnees neither gave nor expected to be given quarter, although women and children were sometimes spared and taken back to the war party's town, where they could be adopted into the tribe. When caught in a desperate situation, Plains Indian warriors such as the Pawnees preferred to fight to the death rather than risk the humiliation of capture and death by torture.

Like most other Plains tribes, the Pawnees took scalps (*paksickuusu'*, literally, "head peeling"). Scalps were more than mere trophies or evidence of military prowess. Contrary to what is sometimes believed, scalps represented not a person's soul, which the Pawnees considered immortal and which would, after death, rise to the "village in the sky," but rather his life force. By scalping an enemy the Pawnees took away this life force and, after some ritual treatment, could use it to their own spiritual advantage. For this reason the Pawnees included scalps in their sacred bundles, placed them in or over the graves of loved ones, decorated shirts and other garments with them, gave them to people in mourning to "wipe away their tears," presented them to friends, and sacrificed them as burnt offerings to the sacred powers. According to Murie, the sacrifice of a scalp was one of the most important acts in the life of a warrior. It served to reaffirm the people's relationship with the sacred powers and ensured the vitality and well-being of the tribe. The Pawnees also believed that a person who had been scalped but "survived" was no longer really human and therefore could not live among them anymore.[58]

The Pawnees also took trophies in battle. In the 1830s, Maximilian, Prince of Wied, observed a Pawnee warrior who wore a valuable Sioux headdress into battle. He had taken it from a distinguished Sioux chief and wore it to taunt and challenge his enemies. This warrior took considerable risks, because the Sioux, recognizing the headdress of their deceased comrade, made great efforts to kill him. Clearly, the Pawnee must have been extremely confident, because he intentionally solicited the wrath of the Sioux.[59]

Horses, scalps, and plunder were not the only objects of desire. Warriors also sought to earn war honors, so-called coups, in battle.[60] Although some historians and anthropologists believe that Plains Indian warfare was first and foremost a struggle between tribes over economic resources and political power, war honors reflected the *individual* performance of a warrior in battle. Such war honors were important because they allowed a successful warrior to recruit men for future expeditions. The crucial measure of his success and prowess was the number of coups he had counted on his enemies. In order to lead future war parties and thus receive a larger part of their spoils, warriors hoped to obtain as many coups as possible. Such acts would win them great prestige.

The Pawnees recognized several deeds that counted as war honors. All of them required great bravery and skill. Among these were capturing enemy horses, taking an enemy's scalp or gun in battle, and taking an enemy prisoner. Among the highest honors was to count coup on an enemy in battle. The word "coup," French for "strike" or "blow," refers to the hitting or touching of an enemy in battle. Unlike killing an enemy from a distance with gun or bow, the act of touching the enemy required that a warrior approach his foe and engage in more dangerous hand-to-hand combat. The honor counted even when the enemy was already dead.[61] Although this last act might not seem daring at first glance, Colonel Philip St. George Cooke, who knew the Pawnees personally, explained that a wounded or dead enemy was still dangerous to approach because his friends were usually nearby. Indeed, Cooke claimed that warriors sometimes pretended to be dead in order to draw an enemy close and kill him.[62]

After a successful raid or attack, the warriors immediately retreated with their plunder, riding continuously for two or three days without sleep or food. Once out of reach of their pursuers, they camped in a secure place. Some members went to hunt and brought back meat to be sacrificed in a thanksgiving ceremony. Two men, selected by the leader, divided the spoils of war among the men according to their rank. After the spoils were divided, it was time for a name-changing ceremony.[63]

According to Pawnee belief, a man was entitled to change his name whenever he performed an act of great significance in war or some other endeavor, such as when a boy killed and consecrated his first buffalo. This custom rested on the idea that life developed in certain stages. Some men rose only a little way along the developmental path, but men who sought the favor of the gods could "climb up" through deeds that indicated great ability or strength of character. Success in battle, such as counting coup on an enemy, was among these accomplishments. By discarding his old name and adopting a new one, a warrior announced that he had reached a new level in the path of life. This process involved a name-changing ceremony, during which the man recounted his deed publicly and in the presence of a priest. Among the Chawi, Kitkahahkis, and Pitahawiratas, the ceremony consisted of reciting a lengthy poem that explained the origin of the custom and related the way the gods took pity on the man and gave him the power to perform the deed. The recital, reproduced here as recorded by Alice C. Fletcher, ended with the disposal of the old name and adoption of the new one:

> *Ra-wa! Ha-wa u-ra-sha-ru we tat-ki-wa-ti.*
> *Hi-ri! Ta-tux ta-pa-ki-a-ho, ha-wa, Ra-ruts-ka-tit! Hi-ri! Ra-ro rik-cha ro re*
> *Hi-ri! A-ki-ta-ro hi-wa we-ra-ta-we-ko.*
> *Hi-ri! Sha-ku'-ru Wa'-ruk-ste. Hi-ri-wa wi-ti ra-ka-wa-ka-ru ko re.*
> (Attend! Once more I change his name.

> Harken! *Ri-ruts'-ka-tit it* was we used to call him by, a name he won long days ago, marking an act well done by him, but now passed by. Harken! Today all men shall say—
> Harken! His act has lifted him. Where all his tribe behold a man. Clothed with new fame, strong in new strength, gained by his deeds, blessed of the gods.
> Harken! *Sha-ku'-ru Wa'-ruk-ste* shall he be called.)[64]

After the name-changing ceremony and sufficient rest, the warriors set out for home. According to Murie, they regularly set the prairie grass on fire from a distance, to announce to the towns their return. They also painted their faces black or covered their white face paint with black dots.[65]

Pawnee men composed songs commemorating their victories in battle. After witnessing an attack by a Cheyenne war party on a Pawnee hunting camp in 1835, Charles Murray heard a Pawnee by the name of Black Wolf sing his victory song:

> I rushed upon my enemy like a buffalo!
> I shouted my war cry aloud!
> Hi-hi-hi-hi-hi!&c.
> I took his scalp!
> His women howl for him in their lodge!
> I am a great war-chief!
> I am called the Black Wolf!
> Hi-hi-hi-hi![66]

The torture of enemy captives was not uncommon among the Pawnees. Usually it was the prerogative of the women in the town. Returning war parties presented captives to the town's women's society, which usually consisted of single women and widows. During the four-day ceremony, the women wore mock war bonnets made of corn husks instead of feathers and carried crude representations of weapons. They made a fire in front of the prisoner and humiliated and tortured him in any conceivable way. According to Murie, women would urinate in bowls and force the captive to drink. Others took up coals of fire with which they scorched the victim's skin. Usually the torture ended with the death of the captive.[67]

All this time the war party was formally still in operation, allowing women and other members of the tribe to share in the glory of the expedition. It did not end until a "homecoming" ceremony had been conducted.

In this ceremony, which took place after a long interval, the leader of the war party returned the objects from the war bundle to the original bundle keeper. The members of the party also presented the bundle keeper with gifts such as horses.[68]

The Pawnees had a number of dances that are usually grouped under the label "war dances." Some of them provided individual warriors with a stage on which to display their bravery. They also allowed the Pawnees to impress guests with the military prowess of the tribe. In the early 1830s, Philip St. George Cooke attended a Pawnee war dance at Fort Leavenworth, Kansas. Each time a dancer moved into the dance circle to recount a coup, he placed a small gift before the chief, who, according to Cooke, acted as a judge and rewarded the bravest deed.[69]

Warriors not only tried to impress visitors with war dances but also displayed their deeds on buffalo robe paintings. "The story of a battle is often depicted in this way," wrote Edwin James in 1820, "and the robe of a warrior is frequently decorated with the narration, in pictures, of some of his exploits." Warriors frequently gave such pictorial records away so that their fame might be carried with the gift.[70]

A warrior who died in the defense of his town or for the greater glory of his tribe received a funeral with all the splendor his sacrifice deserved. After clothing him in his finest garments, a priest covered the body and face with a mixture of sacred red paint and buffalo fat to give the skin a smooth and healthy appearance. If the dead warrior had been a member of a fraternal society, his face was painted according to the style of his society. While uttering prayers, the priest placed offerings of fat in the hands and mouth of the deceased, in order to send his spirit on its way. Then the body was wrapped in a buffalo robe or blanket. Burial took place usually within two days after death. The Pawnees commonly buried their dead in the earth with the head pointing east. They also placed objects in the grave such as scalps, knives, revolvers, bows and arrows, pipes, and personal bundles. Warriors belonging to one of the lance societies were sometimes buried with the group's old lance, which had been discarded after the lance renewal ceremony. After the burial, mourners placed food and other objects on the grave. Occasionally, a horse was slain and placed at the gravesite. The idea behind these funerary gifts was that the objects would be useful in the afterlife. Sometimes the mourners burned enemy scalps at the gravesite. Bodies that could not be recovered were left where they had died. This was not a violation of proper burial procedure. According to Pawnee scholar Roger Echo-Hawk, "such resting places on the open ground were respected as acceptable alternatives to interment in the earth."[71]

The death of a loved one was a cause of much pain and grief among the Pawnees. In their grief, mourners slashed their arms, chests, and legs with knives. Women cut their hair. Charles Murray wrote in 1835 that the "duration of mourning among [them] seems very unfixed: the widow always mourns a year for her husband; but I have sometimes seen squaws mourning . . . for a relative, who had been some years dead."[72]

Still, the Pawnees also believed that death on the field of battle was more honorable and even desirable for a warrior than death of old age or sickness. A warrior who died in the defense of his town or for the greater glory of his nation was showered with honors. His death, while a cause of much grief, was also a source of great pride. Jean Baptiste Truteau, a French trader who lived and traded among the Pawnees in the 1790s, observed this sentiment during the funeral of a Pawnee brave:

> I myself have seen, when I resided for three consecutive years at the home of the nation of *Panis Republicains* [Kitkahahkis] fathers and mothers sing near the bodies of their sons that had been brought back to the village to be interred, sons who had been killed in battle between the *Halitannes* [Comanches] and the *Republicains* on open prairie at some distance from their summer hunting camp, which episode I witnessed. These women, mothers of the young men who were killed, holding a bow in one hand and an arrow in the other, sang near the bodies of their sons an air both gay and martial, thanking them for having given them the satisfaction of seeing them die at the hands of the enemy while fighting valiantly for the defense of their country, a death a thousand times preferable to the fate of him who on a wretched mat expires consumed by some deadly disease.[73]

And so the life cycle of a warrior came to an end. But as his spirit rose to the afterworld, another man would take his place. This warrior carried on the struggle against the enemies of his nation. He fought to preserve the hunting grounds. He stole into enemy camps to secure the horses his people needed for the upcoming annual hunt. He was capable of committing acts of great bravery as well as cruelty in the name of honor and revenge. His objective was always to hurt the enemy, who threatened the lives and well-being of his people. Sometimes he fought as part of a war party with his brothers of his lance society. In the 1860s and 1870s, he could also fight his enemy as a scout in the service of the United States Army.

The war ethic described here was of course an ideal to which Pawnee men aspired. The reality of war was sometimes different. There is no reason to assume that Pawnee men did not also experience fear, fatigue, and demoralization. Still, by the late 1700s, the war ethic of the Pawnees had helped to make them one of the great military powers on the Great Plains.

John Brown Dunbar, who grew up on the Pawnee reservation, where his father was a missionary, called the last decades of the eighteenth century the "heroic age" of the Pawnee tribe. Although Dunbar's assessment might be an overstatement, the Pawnees were undoubtedly at the height of their power at that time. South Band Pawnee war parties ventured deeply into Apache, Osage, Kiowa, and Comanche territory. To the north, meanwhile, the Skiri Pawnees had effectively checked the expansion of the Otoes, Omahas, and Poncas.

Unfortunately for the Pawnees, their supremacy would not last. By 1800, ominous signs of decline loomed ahead. Among the most devastating developments was the introduction of foreign diseases such as smallpox, influenza, measles, cholera, and whooping cough. These diseases spread quickly in the compact and densely populated towns of the Pawnees. Of all these maladies, smallpox was the most lethal. The disease struck the Pawnees in 1780–81, causing massive mortality. Tragically, the Pawnees had little time to recover from such devastating epidemics, which followed each other with remarkable frequency in the early 1800s. Recorded smallpox outbreaks caused many casualties in 1825, 1831, 1837–38, and 1852. The smallpox epidemics of 1831 and 1837–38 reportedly killed 3,000 and 2,000 Pawnees, respectively. The cholera epidemic of 1849 reportedly claimed the lives of 1,234 people, or one-fourth of the entire Pawnee population. In 1864, hundreds of Pawnees succumbed to measles and diphtheria.[74]

Around the same time that epidemic diseases began to take their toll among the Pawnees, the Sioux and Cheyennes began to expand into Pawnee territory. Though not immune to European-introduced germs, these tribes were more adaptable to them because their more flexible social organization allowed them to break up into smaller groups and thus escape infection. Their populations recovered faster and may indeed have been increasing even as those of the sedentary tribes (Mandans, Hidatsas, Arikaras, Omahas, Poncas, Otoes, Missourias, Wichitas, Kitsais, and Pawnees) were declining. As the Sioux and Cheyenne tribes grew more populous, they searched for new territories and hunting grounds. By the 1830s they had overpowered most of the sedentary tribes.[75]

The Pawnees kept up the most stubborn resistance against the nomadic tribes posed by any of the sedentary groups. Encounters between the Pawnees and their enemies were often extremely bloody. In 1819 a Skiri war party of ninety-three men was caught by surprise and nearly annihilated.[76] In 1829 the Skiris intercepted and massacred a Cheyenne war party. In 1830 the Cheyennes retaliated, but in the battle that followed they lost their famous "sacred medicine arrows."[77] In 1832, not long after the Pawnees had been weakened in a smallpox epidemic, some Sioux attacked a Skiri hunting camp and reportedly slaughtered one hundred people. In 1833 the Cheyennes and Arapahos surrounded a group of Pawnee hunters in southeastern Colorado and massacred them all.[78] Matters became even worse in 1840 when the Cheyennes, Sioux, and Arapahos formally established a military alliance against the Pawnees.[79] Several years later, in 1843, a large Sioux war party attacked a Pawnee town and killed around seventy people. This battle is still remembered among some Pawnees today as the "Battle of Burned Town."[80]

Pressure from the Sioux and Cheyennes forced the competing Skiri and Chawi bands finally to resolve their differences and assist each other against their common enemies. In the mid-1840s the four bands concentrated their towns in a small area near the Platte River in order to protect themselves better against enemy attacks. They continued to be vulnerable, however, while out on hunting expeditions. In 1847 a Sioux war party of about seven hundred warriors attacked a Pawnee camp of some two hundred people and killed eighty-three of them.[81] In the 1860s, warfare intensified as buffalo herds dwindled because of overhunting and the disruptive effect of Euro-American settlement and overland travel.

To the Pawnees, the appearance of the United States after 1804 was much less an immediate cause for alarm than the threat posed by the Sioux, Cheyennes, and Arapahos. Although the Pawnees had few illusions about the imperialist intentions of the United States, they were fully aware of its potential power as an enemy, an ally, or simply a supplier of badly needed guns and gunpowder. Rather than fight the United States, the Pawnees believed it was better to welcome its representatives.[82]

In 1816 and again in 1818, two Skiri chiefs attempted to abolish the sacrifice of enemy captives during the band's Morning Star ceremony, an action apparently meant to appease the United States and smooth the way for friendly diplomatic relations.[83] It appears that their strategy was successful, because in 1818 chiefs from all four bands traveled to St. Louis to sign a treaty of "perpetual peace and friendship" with the United States. The friendship between the Pawnees and the United States was further solidified in another treaty, signed in 1825.[84] In yet a third treaty, signed in 1833, the Pawnees agreed to cede their territories south of the Platte River in exchange for annuities, schools, and "twenty-five guns, with suitable ammunition, [to be placed] in the hands of the [government] farmers of each village, to be used in case of an attack from hostile bands."[85]

In their search for anything that might give them an advantage in the war against the Sioux and Cheyennes, the Pawnees even welcomed two Presbyterian missionaries into their towns in 1834. Although John Dunbar and Samuel Allis had been sent to preach peace and brotherhood under God, it is possible that the Pawnees hoped to obtain some form of additional supernatural power from them that would aid the tribe in its struggle against its enemies.[86]

Attempts by the United States to effect peace between the Pawnees and the Cheyennes and Arapahos met with little enthusiasm on either side. During peace talks in June 1835, the Cheyennes showed more interest in retrieving their sacred medicine arrows from the Pawnees than in establishing peace. Shortly after the talks ended, Walking Whirlwind of the Cheyennes organized another war party against the Pawnees. His warriors blundered straight into a large Pawnee camp one foggy morning and were all slain.[87] Another peace conference at Fort Kearny, Nebraska Territory, in October 1851 quickly broke down when one of the Cheyenne chiefs, Alight On The Clouds, refused to smoke the peace pipe. Ironically, Alight On The Clouds was killed in a skirmish with the Pawnees the next year when he was shot in the eye by a fifteen-year-old boy named Big Spotted Horse. Big Spotted Horse later enlisted as a U.S. Indian scout during the Red River war of 1874–75, against the Comanches, Kiowas, and Southern Cheyennes.[88]

While Sioux and Cheyenne raiders stole their horses, ambushed their hunting parties, and killed women on their way to the cornfields,[89] the Pawnees also faced pressures from Euro-American settlers and overland migrants, who, apart from spreading diseases, introduced liquor and destroyed valuable resources such as wood, fresh grass, and game. As a result of these combined pressures the Pawnees were reduced to poverty and stood in real danger of starvation. To avoid starving, some began to demand tribute from overland travelers while others simply took what they needed. Consequently, most migrants looked upon the Pawnees as beggars and thieves. Not infrequently, migrants and settlers filed false claims in order to receive Pawnee annuity money in compensation.[90]

To prevent confrontations with the growing number of settlers in the area and to provide desperately needed support for their people, the Pawnees agreed to a new treaty in 1857. In it they ceded more land in return for fixed reservation boundaries and new annuity payments.[91] Unfortunately, it offered them little protection against the Sioux. Around 1860 the Pawnees built a high sod wall to defend their now single, consolidated settlement on the west, south, and east against enemy attacks. Nevertheless, between April and September 1860, Sioux raiders struck the town no fewer than eight times.[92] The U.S. government, meanwhile, seemed more content with pacifying the resisting tribes such as the Sioux with gifts than with providing adequate protection for friendly tribes such as the Pawnees.[93]

Although military historians tend to reserve the concept of "total war" for conflicts between modern industrial nations, the term nevertheless most closely approaches the state of affairs between the Pawnees and the Sioux and Cheyennes. Both sides directed their actions not solely against warrior-combatants but against the people as a whole. Noncombatants were legitimate targets. Indeed, the taking of a scalp of a woman or child was considered honorable because it signified that the scalp taker had dared to enter the very heart of the enemy's territory. The war also had a distinct economic component, in that the Sioux and Cheyennes often targeted Pawnee women on their way to their gardens, plundered the storage pits in the towns, and attacked Pawnee hunting parties in search of buffalo. The relatively small scale of these conflicts should not obscure the fact that, to the Pawnees, the devastation wrought upon them by their enemies in the 1860s compares in magnitude to the burning of Atlanta several times over.

It is within this context that the military service of the Pawnee scouts must be viewed. Faced with the grim prospect of annihilation, the Pawnees seized the opportunity to fight their enemies as allies of the United States. When war broke out between the United States and the Sioux, Cheyennes, and Arapahos in the early 1860s, government officials in the War Department began to consider the potential value of a military alliance with the Pawnees. The United States needed help in locating and surprising the resisting tribes, and the Pawnees welcomed the opportunity to place their enemies on the defensive, take the war away from the Pawnee towns, and exact revenge for past losses. For the Pawnees, scout service was merely a continuation of a war that had begun a long time before.[94]

CHAPTER **2**

U.S. Military Tactics and the Recruitment of Pawnee Scouts

Neither the Wild Tribes, nor the Government Indian Scouts ever adopted any of the white soldiers' tactics. They thought their own much better.
—Captain Luther H. North, Pawnee scouts

The expansion of the Sioux and Cheyennes posed a problem not only for the Pawnees but for the United States as well. Although the Louisiana Purchase of 1803 had transferred the political title to the northern and central Great Plains from France to the United States, the military conquest of the region by the Americans was an entirely different matter. Contrary to popular imagination, the United States did not control the plains. The Sioux, Cheyennes, Kiowas, Comanches, and other tribes contested the United States' claim for control of the area. For much of the nineteenth century the U.S. Army was unable to impose its military hegemony over the powerful tribes of the West. It was this inability to subdue the tribes that prompted U.S. military commanders to seek the assistance of Indian nations who also suffered from the pressures of these tribes. The Pawnees did not approach the United States; rather, the United States approached them.[1]

Until the Mexican War of 1846–48, relations between the United States and the Indians of the Great Plains had been relatively peaceful. But the conclusion of the war marked a new phase of Anglo-American expansion into the West. The newly acquired territories in Oregon and the Southwest attracted thousands of settlers. Traffic along the Santa Fe

Trail increased, and new "highways," such as the Oregon and California Trails, sliced through the plains. The migrants were a source of irritation for the tribes living here. Their wagon trains disrupted hunting grounds and scared away buffalo and other game. They depleted the supply of timber along the trails, and their livestock consumed the grass that Indian horses depended on for forage. The Pawnees, arguably, suffered the most serious disruption, because the migrant trail ran through the heart of their territory, along the Platte River. The flow of settlers grew dramatically after the discovery of gold in California and Colorado in the 1840s and 1850s.[2]

As the volume of traffic along the trails increased, so did the number of confrontations between Indians and whites. Most tribes resented the disruption caused by the migrants, whom they regarded as trespassers. They deplored the disappearance of game and demanded gifts such as food and supplies as a form of compensation for allowing the migrants to travel through their territories. Others did not demand but simply took what they needed. They did not consider stealing a dishonorable occupation, especially if hunger was the alternative. The overland travelers, however, detested the presence of Indians along the trails.[3]

To prevent conflicts between Indian tribes and migrants and settlers, the United States government adopted several measures. It established a series of military posts along the main routes to guard the overland trails and to impress the Indian nations with the power of the United States.[4] In addition to building forts, government officials began to negotiate with the tribes living near the main migrant trails. In 1851 they concluded a treaty with a number of tribes of the northern plains at Fort Laramie. The Pawnees were not part of these negotiations. In this treaty the tribes agreed to leave the migrant trains alone, refrain from wars with the United States and each other, and permit the construction of forts and roads through their territories. In return, the United States promised to pay the Indians annuities and restitution for damages caused by travelers. Two years later, at Fort Atkinson, Kansas, a similar treaty was concluded with the tribes of the southern plains. Finally, during the 1850s, the United States adopted the reservation policy. This policy replaced the removal policy of the 1830s, which had become impractical after the

United States acquired the southwestern territories during the Mexican War. The reservation policy not only allowed the United States to contain tribes in relatively small areas but also enabled missionaries and other agents of "civilization" to begin their work of obliterating American Indian cultures.

These measures did little to appease the Indian tribes. Some tribes considered the presence of forts in the heart of their country humiliating. They also resented the sluggishness with which the United States implemented its treaty provisions. Annuities rarely arrived on time, and although the government was quick to punish Indians accused of committing depredations, it did little to prevent or punish violations against Indians. Most of all, the Sioux and Cheyennes resented attempts by the government to confine them on reservations. Forts, treaties, and reservations, then, were not a solution to Indian hostilities but frequently a cause of them.[5]

The U.S. government depended heavily on the army to maintain peace on the plains. The army's task was twofold: to protect travelers and settlers against hostile tribes and to protect friendly Indians from hostile and ignorant whites. Policy makers in Washington decided that the best way to keep these groups apart was to prevent the tribes from roaming the area by concentrating them on reservations, where they could be supervised by the army. But the army faced several problems that prevented it from achieving these goals.

One problem was the size of the regular army. Congress placed restrictions on the size of the army for budgetary as well as ideological reasons. Policy makers in Washington disagreed on the proper policy. Some, mostly western congressmen, advocated military conquest. Others, mostly eastern congressmen, favored "conquest by kindness." Washington never resolved this dilemma. As a result, the frontier army was always undermanned. Death, desertion, and discharge produced an average turnover rate of 28 percent per year. To make matters worse, the army was scattered over a large number of small, isolated military outposts in the West. Historian Robert M. Utley calculated that in 1853, each of the 54 stations in the West was manned by an average effective force of 124 men. The United States was unable to deploy enough troops to cover the entire territory west of the Mississippi River. This situation became even more acute between 1860 and 1876, when large numbers of troops were transferred east during the Civil War and Reconstruction years.[6]

The quality of the troops posed another problem. Although many of them were competent professionals, many others were not. All enlisted men were volunteers, but this did not mean that morale was high. According to Don Rickey, Jr., many recruits were recent immigrants who enlisted for five years in order to learn the English language and the ways of the new country. Most came from poor families. Many were illiterate. The average age of the recruits was twenty-three. The frontier army also attracted a large number of social outcasts such as vagabonds and criminals who enlisted to stay out of the hands of the law.

Until the 1880s, new recruits received little or no training. Recruitment depots merely served as temporary facilities for new recruits before they were sent to their respective regiments around the West. Ironically, many of the recruits assigned to cavalry regiments had never before been on horseback. Once they joined their regiments, the new soldiers usually learned military skills by observing the more experienced men in their company. Unfortunately for them, the army had not yet developed any formal doctrines or training techniques that taught soldiers how to fight Indian tribes. Indeed, many recruits saw action before their rudimentary military training was completed. As a result, most of the battle casualties in the Indian wars were inexperienced men.

Army life was unrewarding, monotonous, lonely, physically and mentally taxing, and occasionally dangerous. Pay was low and discipline was enforced strictly. Corporal punishment was common. Desertion remained a big problem. In his annual report for 1891, Secretary of War Stephen B. Elkins estimated that between 1867 and 1891, one-third of all the men recruited had deserted the army.[7]

In his memoirs, Captain J. Lee Humfreville, who met the Pawnee scouts on several occasions, described the hardships soldiers experienced during military campaigns against Indians. According to Humfreville, disease, fatigue, dirt, rancid or worm-filled rations, insufficient shelter, exposure to heat or cold, insects, and exhausting marches were more typical than battles and fire-fights. The soldier usually returned from such campaigns "half-dead," and his horse "would be much run down and weakened."

There was little romance or glory in Indian warfare. "This," Humfreville added bitterly, "is a true description of the actual trooper, in my time, as he usually engaged in battle with the Indians."[8]

During the Civil War, local volunteer and militia units replaced the regular troops, who were sent off to battlefields in the South. These volunteer units often consisted of rough frontiersmen who were quite prepared to deal with life in the field but who also harbored an intense hatred of Indians. Although most men serving in the regular army regarded their Indian enemies as brutal savages "who tortured, mutilated, and ravaged helpless enemies," this sentiment was perhaps even stronger among the western volunteers. These soldiers were even less inclined to show mercy toward Indians. Their brutal and exterminist attitude intensified the state of war between the United States and the Sioux and Cheyennes, particularly after the massacre of a peaceful Cheyenne camp near Sand Creek, Colorado, in November 1864.[9]

The quality of the officer corps, like that of the regular soldiers, ranged from the able and capable to the incompetent. Burdened by the experiences of the Civil War, the U.S. Military Academy at West Point, New York, continued to prepare officers for conventional warfare, not Indian warfare. Emphasis was placed on maneuvering large armies across battlefields in grand, Napoleonic-style warfare. Nothing prepared officers for service against Indian tribes. Furthermore, promotions depended on seniority rather than merit. The seniority system thus hampered the advancement of officers with experience in Indian fighting to top military positions. In an attempt to reward experience and ability, the army began to award officers brevet ranks in recognition of their performances in battle—although Indian battles did not qualify. A lieutenant or captain, for example, could claim a brevet rank of major or lieutenant colonel. In the late 1860s, more than half the colonels in the U.S. Army claimed brevets of brigadier or major general. Under certain circumstances, brevet ranks took effect in the field. This could lead to awkward situations. According to Robert Utley, a captain with no brevet might find himself serving under a lieutenant who had received a brevet of major during the Mexican War.[10]

Because of its conservatism, the army did not learn from past mistakes or successes in fighting Indians. Knowledge about Indian warfare was not systematically collected, debated, and shared. Consequently, the army never developed adequate policies and doctrines to deal more effectively with resisting Indian tribes. Summing up the army's military policy toward Indians, Robert Wooster concluded that "the strategy and tactics of the Indian wars were formulated in the same manner as the government's overall Indian Affairs were—as a haphazard, inconclusive response to the distinctive conditions of the western frontiers." In these circumstances, successes were largely the result of individual commanders using their personal experiences, creativity, and aggressiveness. Most often, success depended on sheer luck.[11]

Apart from the size and quality of the army, the peculiar environment of the plains posed great challenges. The climate ranged from extremely cold during the winter to intensely hot during the summer. The terrain was often inhospitable and hardly accessible for an army carrying heavy or light artillery. The lack of fuel, food, and fresh water made campaigning perilous. The army took provisions (usually large quantities of hardtack, coffee, flour, sugar, beans, salt, and bacon) on expeditions, but the wagons carrying the supplies slowed down the columns, limiting the army's effectiveness. The United States never quite managed to create an army that could live off the country as the Indians could. Instead, the army's Quartermaster Department established a logistical system that oversaw the delivery of supplies at certain rendezvous points during the campaigns. But even this system, because of the unpredictability of the Indians' movements, was inadequate. During the early phases of the Indian wars, the army's lack of knowledge of the region's geography also hindered campaigns.[12]

The greatest obstacles to military control of the plains, however, were the resisting Indian tribes themselves. Their style of warfare—sometimes called unconventional, guerilla, irregular, or "low-intensity" warfare—with its emphasis on ambushes and surprise attacks, made conventional warfare virtually impossible. Indian tribes generally avoided pitched battles in which the superior firepower of the U.S. Army would give the advantage to the Americans. Their mobility and ability to live off the country gave Indian tribes a great advantage over American troops.[13] To offset these disadvantages, the War Department developed a number of countermeasures. Among these were the deployment of "converging columns," in which commanders split their forces into separate columns to enhance the probability of contact. During the 1860s, the army had some success with so-called winter campaigns, which took full advantage of the winter conditions under which Indian mobility, too, was limited. During the campaigns of the 1870s, Brigadier General George Crook tried to improve the army's mobility by using pack mules to carry supplies. Finally, the army began to experiment with Indian auxiliaries who could track, locate, and attack enemy camps.[14]

The Pawnee scouts were not the first Native Americans to fight alongside Euro-Americans either as scouts or as auxiliary forces. American Indians had in fact been doing so since the colonial period. Without the assistance of the Hurons and other friendly tribes, the French presence in North America might have ended long before 1763. Without the Iroquois it is doubtful that the English would have been able to oust the French. The use of Indian allies and scouts continued during and after the American Revolution. Indian allies helped the United States defeat the Red Stick Creeks at Horseshoe Bend and the British at New Orleans. Indians also fought on both Union and Confederate sides during the Civil War. In all these instances, tribes and individuals always allied themselves with non-Indians for political and strategic considerations. Without the help of Indian allies, Europeans and Americans had a difficult time defeating hostile tribes and each other. Even George Washington commented in 1756 that "Indians are [the] only match for Indians; and without these, we shall ever fight upon unequal terms." Thus, the use of Indian allies and scouts was not unprecedented. But conservatism and perhaps also racist attitudes had prevented the army from enlisting Indian allies and scouts more systematically.[15]

The first Pawnees ever to serve as *raaripákusu'* (army scouts) for the U.S. Army joined Colonel Edwin Vose Sumner's campaign against the Cheyennes in 1857. Hostilities between the United States and the Sioux and Cheyennes had begun in 1854 when an overambitious young officer, Second Lieutenant John L. Grattan, rode with his company into a Sioux camp to investigate the theft of a cow belonging to a Mormon migrant. Grattan and his command were promptly annihilated. The following year, troops under Colonel William S. Harney retaliated by destroying a Sioux village under Little Thunder near Ash Hollow, Nebraska Territory. Many Indian noncombatants were killed in the battle, which angered the Sioux and their Cheyenne allies, who subsequently intensified their raids along the different migrant roads.

In October 1856, Secretary of War Jefferson Davis ordered his staff to devise plans for a military campaign against the Cheyennes. In April 1857 the plans were ready, and Winfield Scott, general in chief of the U.S. Army, instructed Colonel Edwin Vose Sumner, commander of the First Cavalry at Fort Leavenworth, to launch the expedition. The Cheyennes gathered that summer for their annual Sun Dance at a location between the Republican and Arkansas Rivers. To intercept them, Sumner received orders to mount two columns. The southern column, under the command of Major John Sedgwick, consisted of companies D, E, G, and H of the First Cavalry. Sedgwick followed the Santa Fe Trail in search of the Cheyennes and then moved north to rendezvous with Sumner's northern column near the South Platte River. Aiding Sedgwick's troops were five Delaware Indian scouts. His command left Fort Leavenworth on May 18.[16]

Sumner's column, which left Fort Leavenworth on May 20, 1857, took a northern route. The column consisted of companies A and B of the First Cavalry. Sumner followed the Oregon Trail and arrived at Fort Kearny, Nebraska, on June 4. There he enlisted the services of five Pawnees led by Ta ra da ka wa, reportedly a chief of the Pitahawiratas. The Pawnees had seen the Cheyenne camp near the Republican River a few weeks earlier and were hired to guide the troops to the site.[17]

After leaving Fort Kearny, Sumner proceeded to Fort Laramie, where he added three companies of the Sixth Infantry to his command. He then traveled to the meeting point on the South Platte, where he and Sedgwick combined their commands on July 6. The Pawnee scouts now directed the column over rough and broken landscape to the Republican River. The difficult terrain forced Sumner to pack his supplies on mules and send the wagons, except for an ambulance, back. The march in the scorching summer heat was hard on men and animals alike. On July 27 the Pawnee scouts discovered fresh Cheyenne horse tracks close to camp. Sumner's troops had been discovered. Fearing that the Cheyennes might try to escape, Sumner abandoned the infantry and ordered the cavalry to ride ahead to intercept the Indians.[18]

Sumner's fears were unfounded. The Cheyennes had no intention of moving. Their scouts had been following his command since it left the

South Platte River, and they had used the time to prepare for the upcoming battle. They believed that the medicine of White Bull and Grey Beard, two of their holy men, would sabotage the guns of the Americans. Certain of victory, the Cheyennes did not even prepare their village, located some fourteen miles from the battle site, for retreat.[19]

On July 29, 1857, the two armies met for battle at the South Fork of the Solomon River. The Cheyennes coolly awaited the arrival of the troops and then, in atypical fashion, lined up in battle formation. Sumner's troops, about three hundred men, also lined up. Fall Leaf, one of the Delaware scouts accompanying Sedgwick's command, rode out in front of the troops and fired his gun at the Cheyennes. The Cheyennes promptly returned the fire. According to Robert M. Peck, Sumner turned to First Lieutenant David S. Stanley and said, "Bear witness, Lieutenant Stanley, that an Indian fired the first shot!" Fall Leaf's action relieved Sumner from his instructions to negotiate with the Indians first. The colonel then issued his orders: "Gallop March! . . . Draw Sabres! . . . Charge!"[20]

When the Cheyennes saw the soldiers draw their sabers, their confidence crumbled. They had expected to fight troops armed with guns, as their medicine men had predicted. The sudden appearance of the sabers baffled them. In their confusion, they quickly discharged their arrows, then turned their horses and ran. A running fight ensued. The troopers chased the Cheyennes for seven miles until their horses gave out. Among the casualties on the American side were two troopers killed and nine wounded. The number of casualties on the Cheyenne side was difficult to determine. Private Robert Peck believed the troops had killed thirty Indians. Colonel Sumner estimated the enemy's losses at nine men killed and many wounded. The Cheyennes later admitted to George Bird Grinnell a loss of four men. The soldiers also captured one Cheyenne.

Ta ra da ka wa and the other Pawnees had been present at the battle, but not everyone appreciated their contribution. Private Peck was unimpressed with the conduct of the five Pawnees during the fight and claimed they stayed behind only to scalp the dead Cheyennes. They also gathered up sixty abandoned Indian ponies, which Sumner agreed to let them keep as "part pay for their services."[21] The Pawnees' behavior might be explained by the fact that they had been hired not to fight but merely to guide the troops. Furthermore, they probably recognized the danger of riding in among the troops, who might mistake them for hostiles. Finally, they did not understand the commands given in English or the tactics of the white troops. Under these circumstances, it was undoubtedly more prudent for them to stay behind the troops.

Peck, who was unfamiliar with Plains Indian warfare, was even more offended by the Pawnees' conduct after the fight. When the Pawnees learned that the soldiers had captured a Cheyenne, they immediately went to Colonel Sumner and offered to forgo their pay and return all the horses they had captured in exchange for the prisoner. Peck observed that the Pawnees wished "to have a grand scalp-dance over him, and put him to death by torture." They were angry and perhaps puzzled when Sumner refused to hand over the prisoner.[22]

The day after the battle, Sumner ordered Captain Rensselaer W. Foote and the men of his company to stay behind to look after the wounded until Sumner's return. While the Pawnees spent the day "stretching and drying the Cheyenne scalps they had taken," the troopers buried the two fallen soldiers. Captain Foote's men began constructing a small sod house stronghold they named "Fort Floyd," after Secretary of War John B. Floyd.[23]

Sumner's troops, including the Pawnee scouts, left Fort Floyd in pursuit of the Cheyennes on July 31. After traveling fourteen miles, they came upon the abandoned Indian camp. The Cheyennes had departed in a great hurry, leaving behind 170 of their lodges and most of their supplies. Among the items abandoned were thousands of pounds of dried buffalo meat, which the soldiers packed on their mules. Before turning south to continue the chase, Sumner ordered his men to burn the village. Three days later, on August 3, he sent the Pawnees back to Fort Floyd with new instructions for Captain Foote and dispatches to Fort Kearny. In his letter, Sumner ordered Foote to return to Fort Kearny as soon as the wounded men were able to travel. Sumner, meanwhile, continued the pursuit of the Cheyennes.[24]

Ta ra da ka wa and the other Pawnee scouts left Sumner's camp late that night. They took the horses they had captured with them. The journey to Fort Floyd was dangerous, for small parties of Cheyennes were still in the area. On August 5 a Cheyenne war party attacked the Pawnees as they approached Fort Floyd. Although the Pawnees killed one Cheyenne, they could not prevent the loss of their horses. They managed to escape with great difficulty and an hour or two later arrived at Fort Floyd. Their sudden appearance caused some alarm, for the men defending the fort believed they were hostile Indians. Fearing that they might be shot, the scouts yelled "Pawnee! Pawnee!" as they approached the soldiers.[25]

Upon receiving his letter of instructions from the Pawnees, Foote ordered his men to prepare for the journey to Fort Kearny. The soldiers constructed travois to transport the wounded men. Early on the morning of August 8 they left the tiny fort. The Pawnees led the way. On August 13 they crossed the Republican River. That night the Pawnees left the command secretly. According to First Lieutenant James E. B. Stuart, they decided to leave because Foote had been badgering them since their arrival at Fort Floyd. Without guides, the command had no idea in which direction to go. The troops were running out of supplies rapidly, so Stuart and a handful of men rode ahead in search of Fort Kearny. They got lost and did not find the fort until August 17, three days after the Pawnees had arrived there. A relief party, which included one of the Pawnees, was organized immediately to locate Captain Foote. While the relief party was out in search of the lost command, Foote and his men wandered into the fort on August 21, almost a week after chasing off the Pawnees.[26]

The Cheyenne campaign came officially to an end in September 1857. It had been a significant event. Not only was it the first confrontation between the United States and the Cheyennes, but it also involved some men who would become famous in the years following the battle of the Solomon. Eli Long, James ("Jeb") Stuart, and David Stanley, for example, rose to the rank of general. Among the Indians who were present at the battle were warriors such as Tall Bull, Roman Nose, Dull Knife, Little Wolf, and even a young Oglala Sioux warrior who would later become famous under the name Crazy Horse.[27]

For the five Pawnee scouts, who had been instrumental in locating the Cheyenne village, the campaign did not bring the rewards they had anticipated. Not only did they lose the horses they captured during the battle, but upon their return to Fort Kearny, they were dismissed without pay. A few weeks later, when a U.S. treaty commission under James W. Denver arrived at the Pawnee Agency to discuss further land cessions in exchange for military protection, Ta ra da ka wa and the other scouts demanded that their grievances be addressed. In one of the articles of the treaty, the commissioners agreed to reimburse the scouts for their service during the Cheyenne campaign:

> Ta-ra-da-ka-wa, head chief of the Tappahs [Pitahawirata] band, and four other Pawnees, having been out as guides for the United States troops, in their late expedition against the Cheyennes, and having to return by themselves, were overtaken and plundered of everything given them by the officers of the expedition, as well as their own property, barely escaping with their lives; and the value of their services being fully acknowledged, the United States agree to pay to each of them one hundred dollars, or, in lieu thereof, to give to each a horse worth one hundred dollars in value.[28]

The Pawnee scouts' service had not impressed the War Department. Officials in Washington were still reluctant to employ Indians as guides and scouts. The idea of mustering a whole battalion of Indian scouts was even more radical. Most officials believed that Indians, even friendly ones, were inherently untrustworthy. They considered Indians unreliable, treacherous, and undisciplined, and thus unfit for military service.[29]

J. L. Gillis, who was appointed Indian agent to the Pawnees in 1859, disagreed with the War Department that the Indians under his care had no discipline. Gillis organized a tribal police force of six men from each of the four Pawnee bands. He had colorful uniforms made for them, which gave them "a very respectable appearance." The police officers took great pride in their work and even assisted the agent in retrieving horses stolen by members of the tribe.[30] Agent Benjamin F. Lushbaugh, who assumed office in 1862, agreed with Gillis that the Pawnees, when given the opportunity, conducted themselves with great discipline. Lushbaugh revived Gillis's police system, recruiting some of the most prominent warriors and providing them with uniforms and other symbols of distinction. "This excites in them a spirit of martial pride and emulation which is productive of good results," Lushbaugh wrote in his report to Acting Commissioner of Indian Affairs Charles Mix. "They are very efficient in preserving order in the villages and reporting any depredations that may be committed."[31]

The success of the tribal police force encouraged Agent Lushbaugh to make another suggestion. In 1862 he traveled to Washington to request federal protection for the Pawnees against the Sioux. He also brought up the idea of forming a regiment of Pawnee scouts to aid the United States against its enemies. In a letter to the War Department, he proposed raising a fighting force of four hundred to five hundred Pawnees. They would be "of great service as scouts to one or two infantry regiments," Lushbaugh wrote, "and the effect of their being employed in Government service would be salutary."[32]

Lushbaugh's request was turned down on the advice of General-in-Chief H. W. Halleck. "The arming of the Pawnee Indians," Halleck wrote, "without further proof of their friendly character, would be of doubtful policy, if there were no other objections."[33] Halleck's rejection of Lushbaugh's plan seemed to put a definitive end to the idea of an Indian battalion. Two years later, however, circumstances on the plains had changed so dramatically that the idea of using the Pawnees as auxiliaries in the U.S. Army resurfaced.

Several events brought about a reconsideration of military policy. In 1862, a number of Eastern Sioux groups in Minnesota took up arms against the United States. They had been nearly starving to death on two untenable reservations and received virtually no supply of annuities from the government. They also opposed the increasing encroachment on their territory by white settlers. Fighting soon spilled over to the Western Sioux following the punitive campaigns under Brigadier Generals Henry H. Sibley and Alfred Sully in 1863 and 1864, respectively. Meanwhile, the discovery of gold in Montana Territory led to a gold rush into that region. The trail into Montana, blazed by John M. Bozeman in 1863–64, passed through the Powder River and Bighorn River country in Wyoming Territory and cut across Sioux, Cheyenne, and Arapaho hunting grounds. To protect miners, settlers, and other travelers against the angry Indian tribes, the army stationed garrisons and built supply stations and bridges at points along the trail.

Tensions between whites and Indians erupted into open warfare in the Territory of Colorado in 1864. There, newspapers and concerned citizens called for the removal, if not the extermination, of the Cheyennes and other Indian tribes living in the territory. Their appeals found a warm reception with the territorial governor, John Evans, who seized upon a few minor incidents to declare war on the Cheyennes in the spring of 1864. Evans ordered Colonel John M. Chivington of the military District of Colorado to pursue the "hostile" Indians. Chivington and his men of the First Colorado Cavalry began to harass Indians across the territory. Their actions provoked some Cheyenne warriors to retaliate. Although most Cheyennes and Arapahos remained peaceful, many citizens nevertheless believed that their fears of a general Indian uprising had come true. Small bands of Cheyenne warriors plundered settlements, attacked wagon trains, and carried off booty. Encouraged by the Cheyennes' successes, small groups of Sioux, Kiowa, Comanche, and Arapaho warriors also took to the warpath.[34]

When the troubles spread from Colorado to Kansas and Nebraska, the military commanders of the region began to prepare for war. Major General Samuel R. Curtis and Brigadier General Robert B. Mitchell organized expeditions in search of the hostiles and placed small units all along the North and South Platte Rivers to protect the migrant trails against Indian attacks.[35]

Most historians credit General Curtis with the order to enlist Pawnee scouts in the U.S. Army in the late summer of 1864. The historical evidence for this claim, however, is inconclusive.[36] According to Captain Eugene F. Ware of the Seventh Iowa Cavalry, which was stationed in Nebraska at the time, General Mitchell had already employed a large number of Pawnees earlier that summer. Unfortunately, the many discrepancies in Ware's account raise suspicions about its accuracy. Nevertheless, it is the only existing account of this episode.[37]

According to Ware, General Mitchell met with Spotted Tail of the Brulé Sioux in several councils near Cottonwood Springs on the Platte River to discuss the crisis on the plains. During the first meeting, in May 1864, he warned the Brulés to stay away from the emigrant road, avoid the Cheyennes, and stop their raids against the Pawnees. Spotted Tail replied that this was Brulé land, and the Brulés would travel it whenever they pleased. Although both men lost their tempers during the exchange, they agreed to meet for another council in July.[38]

When Mitchell arrived for the meeting on July 19, 1864, he was accompanied, according to Ware, by approximately eighty Pawnee scouts under Frank J. North, whose name would forever be linked to the Pawnee scout battalion.[39] It was Mitchell's intention to establish a peace between the Pawnees and the Brulés. But as soon as the Indians saw each other, they began exchanging insults. To prevent the outbreak of hostilities, Mitchell ordered that cavalry troops and a cannon loaded with shrapnel be situated between the two camps. Then he invited speakers from each side for a council. He addressed the Indians while seated on his horse, speaking slowly to allow the interpreters to translate his words for the Pawnees and Sioux.

In a short speech, Mitchell told the delegates that the Great Father in Washington had sent him to make peace between the Indians. Then he invited the Indians to respond to his proposal. After an awkward silence, a Sioux stepped forward. He announced that he did not think the Pawnees amounted to much, but he was willing to leave them alone if that was the president's desire. After another long wait, a Pawnee stepped forward to respond. Ware noticed that the Pawnee wore a pair of blue army trousers. The Indian said that "the Pawnees in olden times had owned all of the land south of the Platte, even the country they were then standing on, but that smallpox had scourged them and they were now settled on land which they liked, and which the white man conceded them, and that they preferred peace, and would be willing to live at peace with the Sioux and Cheyennes if the latter would be peaceful."[40]

Both sides made several more speeches. Most speakers boasted of their exploits against their enemies. The talks quickly broke down after one Sioux got up and said that he "did not see any particular reason for changing present conditions—that the Sioux nation was getting along all right." He then told Mitchell that if the Great Father could not stop his own white children from fighting each other (referring to the Civil War, which was raging back east), how could he expect to keep the Indians from fighting each other? The speeches that followed became increasingly hostile. Before Mitchell could restore order, the two sides were again taunting and threatening each other. A battle seemed imminent, but Mitchell intervened and ordered the Pawnees back. He then told the Sioux to pack up their camp and leave the Platte River valley immediately.[41]

After Mitchell's failure to establish peace between the Indians, his troops, including the Pawnee scouts, moved up the Platte toward Fort Laramie, Wyoming Territory.[42] During the trip Ware had a chance to observe the scouts in action. He was not impressed by what he saw. Before the command had set out from Fort Kearny to meet Spotted Tail's Brulés, the Pawnees had been issued army clothing consisting of a hat, a blouse, and a pair of trousers. By the time the party reached Julesburg, Colorado Territory, most of the scouts had lost their hats. Some had cut holes in the hats and placed them over their ponies' ears. Few were still wearing their blouses, and most had cut the seats out of their trousers, which they turned into leggings. Their unsoldierly appearance greatly irritated General Mitchell.

Although the Pawnees' captain, Frank North, was a "brave, industrious officer," Ware believed he was unable to maintain order in his ranks. Ever since the command had left Lodgepole Creek, Wyoming, on July 23, 1864, the Pawnees had ridden nervously about. Sensing the presence of hostile Indians nearby, they scattered out over the country in search of tracks and trails. Although Ware and the other men of the Seventh Iowa Cavalry were aware that Indians were near, they did not seem overconcerned. General Mitchell was not amused by the nervous spectacle the Pawnees created. Tired of the scouts' "antics," he ordered them to camp on the other side of the command for the night. The next day, when the troops continued the journey, the Pawnees continued to exhibit their peculiar behavior. They seemed greatly disturbed by smoke signals and other signs of the enemy in the distance. They dashed into camp, yelling and creating a "fuss" before dashing out again. According to John Smith, the white guide accompanying the command, they were just "showing off." Mitchell agreed but was unable to calm the scouts. That evening the general called in Frank North and his men and informed them that their services were no longer needed. He thanked them for their valorous service and ordered them to return to Fort Kearny the next morning. In private conversations with his officers, Mitchell disclosed that he was eager to get rid of the Pawnees.[43]

Neither Captain Ware nor General Mitchell was impressed with the performance of the Pawnee scouts during the expedition. Both doubted that Pawnees could be used effectively in combat. Ware believed that Indians were inherently inferior in physical strength, discipline, and heroism. "The Indian is not a soldier, and he cannot be made one," he wrote. "He lacks the right kind of endurance, pertinacity, mind, and courage."[44]

Ware's views of Indians were not untypical of his time. Many Americans, especially those living and operating in the West, held similar views. What Ware failed to recognize was the grave danger his command had been in as it traveled along Lodgepole Creek. General Mitchell, too, had failed to grasp the seriousness of the situation. The country around Julesburg and along Lodgepole Creek was infested with hostile Indians, as events later clearly revealed. For whatever reason, these Indians did not attack. But their presence, as the Pawnees already knew, was undeniable. One white officer later explained to Mitchell that the Pawnees understood that they were surrounded by hostiles who might have annihilated the entire command in an ambush.[45]

Despite Mitchell's negative evaluation of the scouts, it was not the end of the experiment. After Mitchell returned to Fort Kearny in August 1864, he received word that the Cheyennes had killed fifteen settlers along the Little Blue River. General Curtis immediately rushed up from Fort Leavenworth to organize the counteroffensive.[46] On his way to Fort Kearny, Curtis paused at the Pawnee Agency, where he requested the assistance of the Pawnees for the campaign.[47] The Pawnees responded with great enthusiasm, and Curtis enlisted seventy-seven men on the spot. More than two hundred other warriors also expressed a desire to go, but Agent Lushbaugh would not allow them to leave because they were needed for the defense of the reservation. Lushbaugh proposed, however, to give the general all the Indians he needed if he would station a company of cavalry on the reservation to protect the agency and its personnel. Curtis declined the offer.[48]

Curtis appointed Joseph McFadden and Frank North to lead the company. McFadden was a clerk in the trader's store at the Pawnee Agency and was married to a Pawnee woman. He had some military experience, having served under General Harney against the Sioux at Ash Hollow in 1855. Because of his previous military service, Curtis appointed him captain. Frank North had been hired at the agency in 1860, at the age of twenty. After mastering the Pawnee language, he became interpreter at the agency trading store. Because of his language skills, Curtis appointed him lieutenant over the Pawnees. The Pawnees furnished their own horses but would receive the same pay as regular enlisted men.[49]

At Fort Kearny, Curtis assembled his expeditionary force from detachments from different regiments. Apart from the Pawnee scouts, the troops consisted of companies of the First Nebraska Volunteers, the Seventh Iowa Cavalry, and the Sixteenth Kansas Cavalry. Artillery units supplemented the troops. General Mitchell accompanied the expedition, but General Curtis assumed overall command.[50] On Curtis's orders, the quartermaster issued each Pawnee scout with a blouse and a hat, to distinguish the Pawnees from the hostile Indians. "It gave them a distinctive and graphic appearance," Curtis wrote later, "which could not be mistaken."[51]

On September 1, 1864, Curtis issued his marching orders. The Pawnee scouts traveled in advance of the troops. Their task was to "seek after signs and report to the officer of the day or officer of the guard all intelligence received." The command first marched to Plum Creek, then turned southwest toward the Republican River. After crossing the Republican, the troops marched to the Solomon River. Because there were no signs of hostile Indians, Curtis decided to split his command. He ordered General Mitchell and the companies of the Seventh Iowa to follow the Solomon westward in search of hostile Indians. Captain McFadden and the majority of the Pawnee scouts joined Mitchell's command. Curtis, meanwhile, would follow the Solomon River in the other direction with the Kansas troops and the Nebraska volunteers. Lieutenant Frank North and a handful of scouts accompanied Curtis's command.[52]

Neither Curtis nor Mitchell discovered any Indian war parties. Although Mitchell found plenty of evidence of Indian depredations, he was unable to overtake the parties responsible for the devastations. By the time his command reached Cottonwood Springs on the Platte River, his horses were spent, and he had to abort the mission. Curtis, meanwhile, found no evidence of Indians at all. On September 15 he led his tired troops into Fort Riley, Kansas. There, he received word that Confederate forces under Major General Sterling Price were mounting a campaign into Missouri. Curtis immediately left Fort Riley with his Kansas troops to intercept the rebels. Before leaving Fort Riley, however, Curtis authorized Frank North to reorganize the Pawnee battalion.[53]

The Pawnees who accompanied Curtis and Mitchell in 1864 never received any compensation for their services. After discharging the scouts in October, Mitchell sent the muster rolls to the headquarters of the District of Nebraska to settle their accounts. But for reasons unknown, the Paymaster's Department neglected to pay the Pawnees.[54]

Both Curtis and Mitchell had been dissatisfied with McFadden's inability to lead the Pawnees. McFadden himself seemed uncomfortable with his responsibilities as commander of the scouts. He had lived with the Pawnees for years and had become fully integrated into their society. But his status in that society was that of a "commoner," not a warrior, and McFadden was fully aware of this fact. Although Curtis had appointed him to lead the Pawnees, he did not believe he had the authority to order the men in his company around. He lacked the confidence of his men to lead a war party, even if it was in the service of the U.S. Army. Furthermore, McFadden had married into one of the bands of the Pawnee tribe. As a result, the warriors belonging to the other bands did not accept his authority. In accordance with his social rank in Pawnee culture, McFadden would ask rather than order his men into action. Not surprisingly, few felt compelled to obey him.

Unlike McFadden, Frank North was unhindered by such cultural conventions. North was not closely identified with any particular band. Consequently, the Pawnees were more willing to obey his orders. As the campaign progressed, Curtis began to ignore his appointed captain and started issuing his orders directly to the twenty-four-year-old lieutenant.[55]

The Curtis-Mitchell campaign of 1864 ended without significant results. It did little to eliminate the Indian threat to the emigrant roads and to white settlements in Kansas and Nebraska. But the seriousness of the situation caused a few men, such as General Curtis, to reconsider the enlistment of Indian scouts to assist the troops. Many military commanders and officials in the War Department, however, remained skeptical about the usefulness of the Pawnee scouts. Despite the contributions of the Pawnees during the campaigns of 1857 and 1864, generals such as Sumner and Mitchell and officers such as Robert Morris Peck and Eugene F. Ware held the Pawnees in low esteem. They found the conduct of the scouts, particularly during battle, barbaric, offensive, and annoying. Their attitudes reflected Euro-American sentiments typical of the nineteenth century. According to this view, American Indians were undisciplined, cowardly, and uncivilized, and their social and cultural mores were inherently inferior to those of Anglo-American society.

Nevertheless, the year 1864 marked only the beginning of the Indian wars on the Great Plains. Soon the wars would escalate, and the United States would face stiffer opposition on the plains than ever before. When that happened, the Pawnee scouts received another chance to prove themselves in battle.

CHAPTER **3**

On the Powder River Campaign with Connor, 1865

The Pawnee scouts returned to their reservation in October 1864. While they were there, Frank North, following General Curtis's instructions, began to recruit a hundred Pawnees to serve as scouts for one year.[1] In less than an hour he enrolled one hundred warriors who were eager to go to war against the Sioux and Cheyennes. After informing General Mitchell that he had recruited a full company of scouts, North received orders to come to Omaha with a list of the Indians' names. Bureaucratic red tape in Omaha, however, delayed the enlistment. By the time North returned to the Pawnee Agency several weeks later, he found that the Pawnees had left for their annual winter hunt. North instructed his younger brother, Luther, to follow the tribe and persuade the enlisted men to return at once.[2]

Several attempts were made to reach the Pawnees, but with little success. Bad weather forced Luther North back. A second attempt by Frank North and Charles A. Small, Agent Lushbaugh's private secretary, fared little better. From his headquarters in Omaha, General Mitchell, who was no friend of the Pawnee battalion, wrote impatiently on December 1, 1864: "Unless your company is promptly filled and ready for muster the order for raising it will be rescinded."[3] North immediately returned to Omaha to ask for an extension to complete the enrollment of his men. Mitchell reluctantly granted him another twenty days.[4]

Upon his return to the Pawnee Agency, North learned that the Pawnees were returning from their hunt and were camping at different places along the Platte River. At Columbus, Nebraska, he recruited thirty-five men and appointed twenty-two-year-old Charles Small as first lieutenant of the new company. North then traveled to Fort Kearny and recruited another fifty men while his brother Luther recruited thirty-five more.[5] At Columbus, the acting assistant army surgeon, C. B. Stedman, conducted a physical examination of the recruits. Two Pawnees, thirty-year-old Ah roose ah too ta it ("Seeing The Horse") and twenty-nine-year-old Kit e ka rus oo kah wah ("First Man To War"), were rejected because of impaired vision. Five recruits, Kewuck ("Fox"), Ke wuck oo kit e butts ("Little Fox"), Ke wuck oo lar lih tah ("Comanche Fox"), La tah cots kit e butts ("Little Eagle"), and Koot tah we coots oo ter rar re ("Wandering Eagle"), left in the days before they were to be mustered in. They had learned from Baptiste Bayhylle (sometimes spelled Behale), the agency's interpreter, who was of mixed ancestry, and some white men that they were not going to fight the Sioux but would be sent south to "fight the negroes." Although the rumor was false, they would not return to the company.[6]

The remaining men were officially mustered into service as Company A, Pawnee Scouts, on January 13, 1865. Frank North received a commission as captain. Charles Small and James Murie were appointed, respectively, first and second lieutenant.[7] All three officers spoke Pawnee. Murie, who had been born in Scotland, had married a Pawnee woman with whom he had several children.[8] Twenty-one-year-old William N. Harvey was appointed first sergeant.[9]

After a brief stay at Columbus, the command traveled to Fort Kearny, arriving on February 11, 1865.[10] At Kearny the men received old Enfield and Springfield infantry muskets as well as a number of Colt Navy revolvers. Although they were issued guns, the scouts continued to carry their own weapons as well. They were also issued discarded infantry uniforms such as 1857-model infantry frock coats, 1854-model shakos, and 1858-model Hardee hats.[11] On February 15, Second Lieutenant Murie received orders to proceed with twenty scouts to Omaha "for the purpose of procuring horses" for the company.[12]

The scouts' appearance made a favorable impression on a newspaper correspondent for the Omaha *Nebraska Republican*. By exchanging their native garb for the uniform of the United States Army, the correspondent believed, the scouts had taken an important step on the road toward "civilization":

These men seem to be greatly improved since their transformation from the ill-clad, poorly fed, roving Pawnees, to the well-cared for position of a soldier. Their appearance generally has elicited some commendatory remarks. They are obedient and ever ready to do the duties required of them. It is certainly to be desired that all prejudice may be withdrawn from them, and a chance given them to show their ability and aptitude to become citizens in common with a more highly favored race.[13]

But looks are often deceiving, and they certainly were so in this instance. A change of clothes did not automatically entail a change in character. This became painfully clear during the early weeks at Fort Kearny, when the scouts received their first instruction in army discipline. Captain Lee P. Gillette, of the First Nebraska Volunteer Cavalry, commander of the post, insisted that the Pawnees be drilled in the manual of arms. Over the next ten days the Pawnees drilled for two hours a day, but with little effect. They could not understand English, and there were no words in their language that expressed the orders of the drill sergeants. Frank North complained to Captain Gillette that his men had been enlisted as scouts, spies, and trailers, not as regular infantrymen. He refused to drill them any longer, and Gillette relented.[14]

Perhaps Gillette wanted to punish the inexperienced captain for his "insubordination," or possibly he wished to see the experiment with the Pawnees fail. In any event, he ordered North to select twenty-five of his men to go on a scouting mission to the Niobrara River in the middle of winter. They received ten days' worth of rations but were forced to make the march on foot because no horses were yet available for them. North appointed First Lieutenant Small to command the troops. On February 24, 1865, the men started on their mission. They waded through the half-frozen Platte River. Despite the extreme temperatures, none of them uttered a complaint. On one of the forks of the Loup River, well below the Niobrara, a severe snowstorm forced them to remain in camp for a week. When their supplies ran out, Small turned his command back to Fort Kearny. During the march in the intense cold, several men had hands, feet, and ears frozen.[15]

Gillette also required the Pawnees to perform guard duty. This experiment was not very successful, either. Lacking English language skills, the

Pawnees occasionally held off soldiers who were returning to the fort. Usually Captain North had to come to their assistance. When Captain Gillette himself was held up in this way, he excused the Pawnees from guard duty.[16]

That spring, the Sioux and Cheyennes stepped up their raids along the Overland Trail. They sought to avenge the massacre of a large number of Cheyenne Indians under Black Kettle near Sand Creek, Colorado, on November 29, 1864, by troops under the command of Colonel John M. Chivington.[17] After the massacre, the Cheyennes sent out war pipes to the Sioux and the Arapahos. In December these tribes met in a large camp. Among the chiefs present were Tall Bull of the Cheyenne Dog Soldiers, Bad Wound and Pawnee Killer of the Oglalas, and Little Thunder and Spotted Tail of the Brulés. By accepting the pipe, they formally committed their bands to wage war against the United States.

They struck their first blow against the small, guarded settlement of Julesburg, Colorado, on January 7, 1865. A small decoy party lured a detachment of soldiers from nearby Fort Rankin (later renamed Fort Sedgwick) into an ambush. Fourteen soldiers and four civilians died in the skirmish. The Indians then looted and destroyed a store and a warehouse. In the weeks following the attack, their raiding parties spread along 150 miles of the South Platte River. They attacked and burned ranches, farms, and stage stations, ambushed trains, ran off cattle, and destroyed telegraph lines. On February 2 they again struck Julesburg. Soldiers and civilians watched helplessly from nearby Fort Rankin as the Indians burned the settlement. An expedition hastily organized by General Mitchell soon found itself snowed in at Fort Laramie. Unable to chase the Indians, Mitchell abandoned his plan and began dispersing troops all along the main roads.[18]

In March the Pawnees, now equipped with horses, received orders to ride to Fort Rankin to scout and defend the area against Sioux and Cheyenne war parties. Only eighty-five scouts left the fort on March 14, 1865. Seven scouts were left in the post hospital. The sick men were Lah low we hoo la shar (translated by the mustering officer as "The Buffalo Runner"), Corporal Ste tock tah hoo ra rick ("War Pipes"), Tah Kah ("White"), Te kit ta we lah we re ("The Great Spirit Sees Me"), Too re cha hoo ris ("Tracks On The Hill"), Wit te de root kah wah ("I Am The

Bravest"), and First Duty Sergeant Tuck oo wa ter roo ("The Man That Strikes The Enemy"). It is possible that these men had been on patrol with Lieutenant Small's platoon a few weeks earlier and were now suffering from frostbite and other maladies caused by exposure to cold. Nineteen-year-old bugler Samuel White was left with the sick to act as their interpreter. All the men eventually returned to duty except for Sergeant Tuck oo wa ter roo, who died in the hospital after a short illness.[19]

The march to Fort Rankin was uneventful but difficult. One hundred and fifty wagons carrying government supplies accompanied the command. The scouts reached the small army post at Plum Creek at one o'clock in the morning on March 15. They resumed their march later that morning. Several scouts lost weapons while crossing streams. Corporal Chuck kah ("Stars") and Privates Kah kah kit e butts ("Little Crow") and Ke wuck oo weete ("Sitting Fox") lost their Enfield rifles "due to carelessness" and were each charged $18 for the weapons. The money would be withheld from their salaries.[20]

Once they arrived at Fort Rankin they remained there through April, occupying themselves with ordinary post duties. In May, Lieutenant Small led a detachment of thirty scouts to obtain wood near Mud Creek. Otherwise, little of importance took place. Second Corporal Koot tah we coots oo lel la shar ("Hawk Chief") was promoted to first duty sergeant after North learned the news of Tuck oo wa ter roo's death. The only "loss" during this time was a Colt Navy revolver belonging to Private Tah we li hereis ("A Shield"), who lost the weapon while crossing the Platte River near Julesburg.[21]

On June 20 the scouts received orders to leave Fort Rankin, march to Fort Laramie, and await further orders there. Two scouts did not make the journey to Laramie. Thirty-year-old Ow it toost ("First To Run") died that day of consumption. Captain North forwarded an inventory of his possessions and earnings to the Adjutant General's Office in Washington.[22] Another scout, thirty-five-year-old Kah Deeks ("Man That Steals Horses"), deserted during the march, near Lodgepole Creek on June 25. His reasons for deserting are unknown.[23] Shortly thereafter, the remaining scouts arrived at Fort Laramie. Some time later, Captain North and thirty scouts made an uneventful, three-day, eighty-five-mile scout in search of government horses.[24]

Meanwhile, Ulysses S. Grant, general in chief of the U.S. Army, began a reorganization of the military command structure in the West. Grant was concerned over developments on the plains, and he removed Curtis and Mitchell and created a new military jurisdiction, the Division of the Missouri, under the command of Major General John Pope. This new jurisdiction, divided into several departments, covered most of the West. Major General Grenville M. Dodge was appointed to head the Department of the Missouri, which covered most of the plains region. Dodge and Pope believed that aggressive action against the hostile Indians there was a necessity. "In my opinion there is but one way to effectually terminate these Indian troubles," Dodge wrote to Pope: "to push our cavalry into the heart of their country from all directions, to punish them whenever and wherever we find them, and force them to respect our power and to sue for peace."[25] Pope agreed and instructed Dodge to plan a campaign against the Sioux and Cheyennes. To lead the campaign, the two generals favored Brigadier General Patrick Edward Connor. After some political wrangling, Connor was appointed to command the newly created District of the Plains, a subdivision of the Department of the Missouri, on March 28, 1865.[26]

Connor had achieved fame fighting Indians and Mormons in Utah. Born in Ireland in 1820, he had come to the United States around 1832. At the age of nineteen he enlisted in the army and fought the Seminoles in Florida. During the Mexican War he served under Zachary Taylor and Albert Sidney Johnston. After the war he joined the California gold rush. When the Civil War broke out, he was appointed colonel of the Third California Infantry. In October 1862 he assumed command of the Military District of Utah and constructed Fort Douglas, near Salt Lake City. His main assignment was to guard and protect the trails against hostile Indians. In 1863 he mounted a winter campaign against the Shoshones, who had committed depredations along the overland mail route. On January 27, 1863, his troops surprised a small Shoshone village under Bear Hunter, near Bear River, Utah. In the battle that followed, at least 224 Indians perished. The massacre and Connor's relentless pursuit of other hostile bands made him an instant favorite among western frontiersmen. Dodge and Pope believed that his experience, tenacity, and temperament made him the ideal man to lead a campaign against the Sioux and Cheyennes.[27]

On March 29, 1865, Major General Dodge sent his instructions to Connor. "The District of the Plains was formed to put under your control the entire overland route and to render effective the troops along it," he wrote. "With the force at your disposal you can make vigorous war upon the Indians and punish them so that they will be forced to keep the peace." Dodge ordered Connor to organize a three-pronged attack on the Sioux, Cheyennes, and Arapahos, who were now congregating in the Powder River area. Connor also received instructions to establish a military post on the Powder River from which future campaigns could be launched. Immediately after receiving his orders, Connor began to work out the details of the upcoming Indian campaign.[28]

The Powder River campaign would be carried out by three columns that would converge on the area from different directions. The right column, under the command of Colonel Nelson Cole, received orders to travel from Omaha to the east base of the Black Hills and from there to a rendezvous point on the Rosebud River. Cole's troops consisted of eight companies of his own Second Missouri Light Artillery (equipped as cavalry) and eight companies of the Twelfth Missouri Cavalry. The entire command numbered fourteen hundred men.[29] The center column of the expedition was under the command of Lieutenant Colonel Samuel Walker and consisted of six hundred men of the Sixteenth Kansas Cavalry. Walker received directions to march with his force from Fort Laramie to the Black Hills. From there he would move to the general rendezvous on the Rosebud River.[30]

Connor himself directed the left column, which consisted of 200 men of Colonel James H. Kidd's Sixth Michigan Cavalry, a company of the Seventh Iowa Cavalry, a company of the Eleventh Ohio Cavalry, 116 officers and men of the Second California Cavalry, 84 Omaha and Winnebago scouts under the leadership of Captain Edwin Nash and Chief Little Priest, and Captain North's company of Pawnee scouts. The entire command consisted of 675 men. It would travel from Fort Laramie to Horseshoe and then north to the Powder River. At Horseshoe, Captain Albert Brown, of the Second California Cavalry, and the Omaha and Winnebago scouts would be detached from the main body, travel to Platte Bridge, and follow a more westerly route before reuniting with Connor on the Powder River. At the Rosebud River, Connor, Cole, and Walker would combine their commands.[31]

The campaign was supposed to start in April or May, but it ran into logistical and organizational problems. Bad weather and administrative blunders delayed the arrival of supplies and fresh horses. Many soldiers, who had hoped to muster out when news arrived that the Civil War was over, became mutinous or deserted when they received orders to join the expedition. Few men were eager to go on an Indian campaign. As a result of these problems, Cole's command did not leave its headquarters at Omaha until the first of July. Walker did not leave Fort Laramie until later that month. Neither man had a thorough knowledge of the territory or much experience fighting Indians. Connor advised Cole to hire a number of guides and scouts at the Pawnee Agency.[32]

Connor's ruthless temperament surfaced in his instructions. On July 4, 1865, he wrote to Cole: "You will not receive overtures of peace or submission from Indians, but will attack and kill every male Indian over twelve years of age." Walker received the same order on July 28.[33] When a copy of Connor's instructions reached the desk of General Pope on August 11, Pope immediately commanded General Dodge to repeal the order. "These instructions are atrocious, and are in direct violation of my repeated orders. You will please take immediate steps to countermand such orders. If any such orders as General Connor's are carried out it will be disgraceful to the government, and will cost him his commission, if not worse. Have it rectified without delay."[34]

Pope's furious response did not reach Connor until August 20. By this time the expedition was well under way. Connor's column, including the Pawnee scouts, had left Fort Laramie on July 30.[35] Small parties of Pawnees rode in advance and on the flanks of the column to scout the land in search of enemy trails. Apart from these scouting missions, they supplemented the command's provisions by hunting buffalo. They also carried Connor's dispatches, informing General Dodge of the progress of the expedition, to distant stations and military posts.[36]

On August 1 Connor's troops crossed the North Platte River. Three days later he split his command. Captain Brown's two companies of the

Second California Cavalry and Captain Nash's Omaha and Winnebago scouts continued up the Platte while the main column turned north. The Pawnee scouts remained with Connor.[37]

After an uneventful journey, Connor's column reached the Powder River on August 11. While the men set up camp, some Pawnees went out to hunt buffalo. Captain B. F. Rockafellow noted that the Pawnees used their bows and arrows for the hunt, possibly in an effort to avoid alerting nearby hostile Indians of their presence or to be able to distinguish the hunters who killed the animals and so could claim their meat and hides. The scouts cornered a large bull that turned on them often, pawing and shaking its head in rage. They filled the animal with many arrows before it was finally brought down.[38]

A few days after the column's arrival at the Powder River, Connor selected a site at which to construct a fort. His selection could not have been better. According to George Bent, a Cheyenne mixed-blood who lived among his Indian relatives for most of his life, Connor constructed his fort on the point where the Indians usually crossed the Powder River. It was also a favorite wintering ground for the Cheyennes.[39]

Signs of Indians appeared everywhere. On Sunday, August 13, a scouting party under Captain Roberts found the hastily made grave of an Indian woman. The body was covered with beads, indicating that she belonged to a rich family. According to the Pawnees, the Indians must have been in a great hurry, because they had been unable to give her a proper burial. That same day General Connor ordered ten Pawnees to take some dispatches to Platte Bridge Station. This was a dangerous mission, for Sioux, Cheyenne, and Arapaho bands were scouring the country between Connor's camp and the station. Nevertheless, after a hazardous journey, the Pawnees arrived at Platte Bridge during the third week of August.[40]

Construction of Fort Connor began on August 14. While the soldiers cut the timber for the fort, the Pawnees scouted the country for enemy Indians. On August 16 a handful of Cheyennes appeared on the bluffs near the fort. Connor ordered Captain North's scouts in pursuit. A few white officers joined the scouts but decided to return when darkness fell. The scouts, however, pushed on all night, covering some sixty miles. At daybreak they discovered the enemy camp and prepared to attack it.[41]

There are several different accounts of the fight that followed. According to guide Fincelius ("Finn") Burnett, Captain North had wanted to camp for the night and continue the pursuit the following morning, but the Pawnees insisted on moving on in the dark. They reasoned that the Cheyennes believed that white troops were following them and would never expect white soldiers to continue their pursuit during the night.[42] When the scouts discovered the Cheyenne camp, they formed a column in order to make the Cheyennes believe they were indeed white troops. As the Cheyennes prepared for battle, some Pawnee warriors advised North to paint himself like an Indian, possibly to make himself a less conspicuous target when the fight began. North wrapped a red scarf around his head and painted his face with war paint. When the column came within two hundred yards of the Cheyennes, the Pawnees shouted their war whoops and began the charge. When the Cheyennes realized that the "soldiers" were in fact Pawnees, they panicked and scattered in different directions, making it easy for the scouts to chase and kill them separately. The Pawnees killed all twenty-four Cheyennes, including one woman. One of the Cheyennes took no part in the fight because he had been seriously wounded in another battle. During the battle with the Pawnees he tried to hide in a small ravine, but a Pawnee sergeant, armed with a saber, followed and killed him. During the battle the Pawnees lost only four horses.[43]

The fight with the Cheyennes is believed to have taken place near the present-day town of Sussex, some thirty miles east of Kaycee, Wyoming. The scouts not only captured sixteen horses and twelve mules but also found quantities of coffee, sugar, dried apples, and tobacco, a number of calico dresses and other white women's and children's clothing, and letters belonging to members of the Seventh Michigan Regiment, then stationed along the Overland Trail.[44]

After the battle the Pawnees returned to Connor's camp, arriving around three o'clock the next afternoon. In typical Pawnee fashion they announced the success of their war party by storming into the fort, shouting and displaying the scalps of the slain enemies.[45] Connor and the entire garrison turned out to receive them. The American soldiers "formed a double line through which the Pawnees marched, singing their war songs and flourishing in the air their scalp-poles, to which the [Cheyenne] scalps were attached."[46] Connor was pleased with the results of the fight. Among the spoils the Pawnees brought in were twenty-nine animals, including four government mules and six government and Overland Stage Line horses. All evidence indicated that these Cheyennes had been present at a fight several months earlier in which Captain William D. Fouts and four soldiers of the Seventh Iowa Cavalry had been killed.[17]

Although the Pawnees had been in the saddle for more than thirty hours without food, they did not seem tired. With Connor's permission they prepared for a great feast. That evening, many curious officers and soldiers witnessed the festivities. The Pawnees built a large fire and danced a scalp dance. Among the spoils and trophies of the battle were scalps, buffalo robes, blankets, and a woman's belt ornamented with silver brooches and brass buttons. Some of the dancers carried the captured scalps, which they had tanned and stretched, on small hoops attached to scalp poles. During the dance the Indians sang about their exploits.[48] Not everybody approved of the display, however. Captain Henry E. Palmer called it "the most savage scene" he had ever witnessed. After midnight General Connor ordered North to stop the noise. It took North considerable effort to end the festivities.[49]

Connor authorized North to distribute the spoils of the battle among his men. Some of the regular soldiers tried to buy trophies from the Indians. During the celebrations that night, the Pawnees held name-giving ceremonies for the men who had fought in the battle. Among those who received new honorary titles was Frank North, whose Indian name hitherto had been Skiri Tah Kah ("White Wolf"). Rather than select a new name himself, North asked some Pawnees to select a name for him. They bestowed on him the name Pani Leshar ("Pawnee Chief"), and North returned the honor by presenting one of the captured horses to the men who had given him the new name.[50]

The celebrations were overshadowed by a distressing accident the next day. On August 18, an accidental discharge from a gun ended the life of twenty-five-year-old Kah Hah Liens ("Little Ears"), a Chawi Pawnee, who served as Frank North's orderly at the time. The bullet struck him in the forehead. Not all the Pawnees believed the shooting was accidental. The bullet came from the pistol of a Skiri, who claimed the gun had gone off while he was describing the recent battle to Little Ears. The incident threatened to cause a fight between the two bands. Frank North investigated the matter and concluded that the incident was indeed an accident. Little Ears was buried with full military honors. After the funeral, the leaders among the Pawnees calmed their men by declaring that the accident was the Great Spirit's punishment for their excessive glorification over the recent fight. Apparently this explanation satisfied the rest of the Pawnees.[51]

On August 19 North's scouts discovered several small parties of Indians. During one pursuit near Crazy Woman's Fork, North's mount outran the rest of the troops, and North soon found himself in a tight spot when the Indians turned on him. According to George Bird Grinnell, the arrival of Lieutenant Small relieved North from his precarious situation. Finn Burnett claimed that North was saved by a Pawnee scout named Bob White, who, instead of going back to get reinforcements, stayed with North until help arrived. After North returned to the rest of his troops, he discovered that the scouts had surrounded a lone Indian, later identified as Red Bull, an old Cheyenne chief. The chief signaled to the scouts that he had killed many white people and "was proud to die on the warpath," and he at once began shooting at the scouts. The Pawnees reportedly "amused" themselves by shooting at him, wounding him in many places. According to Grinnell's account, North ended the torture and ordered his men to kill the man at once. According to a Pawnee version recorded by ethnologist Gene Weltfish in 1938, North told his men to leave the Cheyenne chief alone, but the scouts ignored the order. One of the scouts, Ki wa ku ta hi ra sa, told North that the man had "killed Pawnees and white people;" thus the Pawnees killed him. The Pawnees captured six horses in this fight.[52]

On the afternoon of August 20, guards at the fort spotted a number of Indians, probably Cheyennes, on a hill. Captain North and some of his scouts gave chase and later returned to camp with three scalps, several ponies and mules, and some other goods. On the body of one of the Indians the scouts found some letters that belonged to a Private Baker, of Company B of the Seventh Michigan Cavalry, as well as a book belonging to another soldier of the same regiment.[53]

While chasing the Indians, the scouts discovered a train of one thousand Cheyennes. North sent a dispatch to Connor, who ordered Colonel Kidd's Sixth Michigan Cavalry to assist the Pawnees. About half a mile from the fort, Kidd met North, who was returning with the three scalps. The captain explained that his horses were exhausted and he had been forced to give up the chase. But he ordered Lieutenant Murie to accompany the colonel with a few of his men whose mounts were still fresh. When Kidd's command neared the place where the Cheyennes had last been seen, the colonel sent Murie and his scouts in advance to determine the exact location of the Indians. Murie did as ordered and found the Cheyenne camp. But when he returned to inform Kidd, he found that the troops had left. According to Grinnell, Kidd's mutinous troops were not eager for a fight with the Indians and had returned to camp. Colonel Kidd reported to Connor that there were only thirty Cheyennes and that he had been unable to chase them. Later that evening North and Murie reported what had transpired, and the following morning Connor reprimanded Kidd for abandoning Murie's scouts in front of the other officers of the command.[54]

According to Finn Burnett, the scouts brought in scalps every day. Burnett recalled that the Pawnees used a white horse to try to lure the Sioux and Cheyennes into an ambush, although he did not say whether the tactic was successful or not.[55] Luther North never mentioned this trick in any of his writings. Other companies also skirmished with small parties of Sioux, Cheyennes, and Arapahos. Usually, individual Pawnees accompanied these troops. On August 21 a few Pawnees who had accompanied Captain Marshall and forty men of the Eleventh Ohio Cavalry returned from a patrol with two more scalps.[56] Despite these small successes, a "decisive" battle still eluded Connor. On August 22 he assembled his troops and began the journey to the Tongue River and the rendezvous point at the Rosebud. He ordered Colonel Kidd and the Sixth Michigan Cavalry to stay behind and garrison Fort Connor.[57] On the same day Connor ordered a number of Pawnee scouts under Sergeant William N. Harvey and Corporal Se gule kah wah de ("Wandering Sun") back with instructions to Fort Laramie.[58]

On August 23, while the command was marching toward the Tongue River, a scout strolled into some bushes to pick chokecherries. He almost immediately reappeared, chased by a large female grizzly bear. After a short sprint the bear overtook the scout on the edge of a steep canyon and swatted at the man's face with a claw. "She caught the Indian on the side of his head and took his ear off as clean as you could cut it with a knife," Luther North later remembered. Both grizzly and scout tumbled into the canyon. By the time North and several other scouts reached the canyon, they saw the grizzly trying to make its escape on the opposite side. They killed the bear with their guns. Meanwhile, the unfortunate scout lay unconscious on the bottom, badly wounded. His muscles had been torn away from one of his arms. According to North, he eventually recovered, "minus one ear" and with a "badly crippled arm." The scouts soon discovered why the grizzly had attacked without provocation: they found two bear cubs nearby. Just as they had killed the mother, the scouts dispatched the cubs and took their skins and claws.[59]

After a four-day march, Connor's troops reached Peno Creek, today called Prairie Dog Creek. As they gazed down the Tongue River valley, Jim Bridger, the famous mountain man and one of the white scouts in the command, spotted a column of smoke in the distance. General Connor ordered Captain North and some of his scouts to investigate the matter.[60] On August 27 the scouts discovered the Indian camp. In order to determine its size, North sent two men ahead to count the number of lodges. The two men stripped themselves of their clothes, according to Pawnee custom before a possible fight. They approached the camp and hid underneath the bank of a creek. They came so near to a woman that they could have touched her by reaching over the bank. When they returned, they reported that it was a large camp, and North immediately sent two other men back to Connor to report the discovery. The messengers reached Connor's camp on August 28. Connor hurried his troops to finish their supper. Among the troops were Captain Brown's Second California Cavalry and the Omaha and Winnebago scouts, who had reached the command a few days earlier. Connor immediately put together a force to attack the Indian camp. He selected only troopers with the best horses. The exact composition of the force is not entirely clear, but historian John McDermott wrote that it consisted of about 310 men, including some 30 Pawnee scouts under the command of Captain North and Lieutenant Charles A. Small, 40 Omaha and Winnebago scouts, and two cannons. Around eight o'clock that evening, after finishing supper, Connor led the column toward the camp.[61]

The Indian camp belonged to a band of Arapahos under Chiefs Black Bear and Medicine Man. It consisted of 250 lodges and numbered around 1,500 men, women, and children, among them perhaps as many as 500 warriors. A few Cheyennes were also present. Although a Cheyenne named Little Horse had alerted the villagers to the soldiers' approach, the Arapahos ignored his warning. Connor's troops marched all night but still arrived almost too late. The Arapahos were preparing to move, and the women had already taken down and packed most of the lodges. It is unclear whether or not they broke camp because they thought the soldiers were near, but from what occurred next, it appears that they were unaware of the impending attack. Still, the warriors had gathered most of the ponies, and half the villagers were already mounted when Connor's troops finally arrived on the scene.[62]

At nine o'clock on the morning of August 29, Connor launched his assault. According to Henry E. Palmer, who witnessed the charge, more than "a thousand dogs commenced barking, and more than seven hundred [Arapaho] Indians made the hills ring with their fearful yelling." When the soldiers came in sight, the Arapahos dropped their supplies and fled up a small stream. The Pawnee scouts dashed ahead into the camp, followed by the soldiers and the Omaha and Winnebago scouts. In the chaos of the fight, the soldiers and their Indian allies took little time to direct their aim. According to Palmer, "squaws and children, as well as warriors, fell among the dead and wounded." Connor instructed North to take some of his scouts and gather as many of the Arapahos' horses as possible. Then the general stormed after the fleeing Indians, whose valiant defense allowed many of the women and children to escape.[63]

Connor pursued the Arapahos for almost ten miles when suddenly he found himself with only three officers and ten men left. The horses had become so fatigued that most of the soldiers had turned back. Some troopers, including a number of Pawnee scouts, returned to loot the camp. When the Arapahos noticed that the troops had aborted the chase, they regrouped and turned around for a counterattack. Now Connor found himself in dire straits.[64] As he fell back, around eleven o'clock, he picked up more soldiers along the way, but now it was the Arapahos' turn to chase the troops. When Connor reached the Indian camp around 12:30

that afternoon, he ordered his men to destroy the property the Arapahos had left behind. The men collected buffalo robes, blankets, tepee covers, and dried buffalo meat and threw them on top of the pile of burning lodge poles. They burned all 250 lodges as well as an enormous amount of supplies.[65]

At 2:30 Connor ordered his men to retreat from the village. The Arapahos continued the pursuit, hoping to retrieve the horses that had been rounded up by the Pawnee scouts. They made desperate attempts to stampede the herd and probably would have succeeded had it not been for the scouts. According to Palmer, the fighting continued until midnight, when the Arapahos finally gave up the chase. At two o'clock in the morning on August 30, the exhausted command returned to the army's main camp on the Tongue River.[66]

Apart from destroying 250 lodges and a great quantity of supplies, the soldiers captured seven women and eleven children. The captives were released a few days later and sent back to their camp with instructions to persuade Black Bear to come to Fort Laramie for a peace council. The sources disagree on the exact number of horses captured during the fight. According to Burnett, the Pawnees captured more than 2,000 horses. Palmer estimated the number at 1,100, and Grinnell put the estimate at 750. In his official report, Connor reported the capture of 500 horses and mules. The accounts also vary on the number of enemy casualties. According to Grinnell, 162 Arapahos died in the battle. Palmer and Burnett seem to agree that between 60 and 70 Indians were killed, including Black Bear's son. According to Connor, 35 warriors were killed, but his report makes no mention of any women and children who died in the battle. The general probably thought it wiser not to mention the deaths of noncombatants after General Pope's blistering reprimand for his previous order to kill all males over the age of twelve. Seven soldiers were wounded in the battle. Little Bird, a twenty-two-year-old Omaha scout, was the only man killed among Connor's troops.[67]

Despite the victory, Connor was incensed at the conduct of some of his troopers during the fight. He was especially angry at the soldiers and Indian scouts who had abandoned the chase in order to plunder the Arapaho village. The day after the fight he ordered the troops to pile their plunder in front of their respective company quarters. Among the trophies taken were a large number of scalps. Then Connor ordered some of his officers to burn the piles. The general made a few exceptions for the handful of men who had performed well during the battle.[68]

Connor's decision to burn the spoils must have puzzled the Pawnee scouts. Taking plunder had always been an important aspect of Indian warfare. Destroying the spoils was a great waste. Furthermore, many Pawnees probably believed that Connor's decision to pursue the Arapahos for ten miles after chasing them from the village had been foolish. Indeed, by doing so Connor had violated one of the oldest military principles, posed first by the Roman tactician Vegetius, that he "who rashly pursues a flying enemy with troops in disorder, seems inclined to resign that victory which he had before obtained."[69] By chasing the enemy over a long distance, Connor increased the risk of becoming isolated from the rest of his command. Furthermore, many of the horses were already exhausted, and to continue the chase was not only useless but reckless. Connor's wild pursuit nearly cost him his life. Punishing the Pawnees for going after the spoils rather than risking an ill-advised and hopeless chase bewildered them. One must also keep in mind that during the previous campaign, under Generals Curtis and Mitchell, the Pawnees had been promised pay, which they never received. Perhaps they thought it prudent to take what they could as "reimbursement" for that service.

The battle at the Tongue River did not end the Powder River campaign. Connor was eager for another fight. But first he had to join with Cole's and Walker's commands farther east. "I should have pursued the enemy farther after resting my horses," Connor wrote Dodge, "were it not that the right column of my expedition is out of supplies, and are [a]waiting me near the Yellowstone." By this time the weather had taken a turn for the worse. Rainstorms and falling temperatures made travel extremely uncomfortable. On September 1 Connor directed Captain North and twenty Pawnees to join Captain Marshall and thirty men of the Eleventh Ohio Cavalry and travel to the rendezvous point to meet Cole and Walker. The remainder of the troops followed in the same direction. Five days later North's advance party returned. They had found no sign of Cole.[70]

One party, however, made contact with the enemy. On September 2, a patrol consisting of some soldiers accompanied by a few scouts surprised a lone Cheyenne named Brave Wolf. Although the troops wounded his horse, Brave Wolf was able to escape. He recorded the event in a ledger book drawing that was discovered at the Summit Springs battlefield four years later.[71]

Connor was unaware that Cole's and Walker's commands had bogged down farther east. On September 8 he again sent North and some scouts in search of the lost command. When they reached the Powder River, the Pawnees spotted a large Indian camp in the distance. Pushing on, they stumbled upon a scene of tremendous carnage. Before them lay the remains of hundreds of dead cavalry horses, undoubtedly belonging to Cole's command. Most of them had been shot in the head. North immediately turned his men around and returned to Connor's camp on September 11. Upon receiving North's alarming report, Connor dispatched Sergeant Charles L. Thomas and two Pawnees to find Cole and Walker and direct them to Fort Connor, where they would find supplies for their troops. This was a dangerous mission, and the general instructed the Pawnees to "travel only by night and to run the gauntlet at all hazards, otherwise Cole and his men might perish within close proximity to the fort where there was an abundance of supplies, food, and ammunition."[72]

Both Cole and Walker had run into major problems on their expeditions. One of the main problems was the lack of knowledgeable guides. In early June, Colonel Cole had stopped at the Pawnee Agency and enlisted the services of George Sandas, a white man, as well as a few Pawnee Indians. Unfortunately, Sandas proved to be wholly incompetent, and the Pawnee guides left the command a few weeks into the march, possibly in disgust over Cole's ineptitude in handling his unruly troops.[73] Walker's command, too, lacked adequate guides. The rough, broken character of the country made travel difficult, and the lack of fresh water and grass weakened the horses. Scurvy and exhaustion took their toll among the men, who grew increasingly insubordinate. Although the two columns met on the Belle Fourche River, north of the Black Hills, Cole and Walker, who disliked each other immensely, preferred to march in separated columns. On September 1, while Cole's men camped on the Powder River, a large party of Cheyennes and Sioux under Roman Nose attacked their horse herd. Over the next ten days the Indians continued their attacks. Apart from the Indians, the soldiers battled starvation and deteriorating weather. During an ice storm Cole lost more than four hundred horses. According to one account, the hungry soldiers stripped the flesh from the dead mounts and devoured the meat raw.[74]

On September 13 Sergeant Thomas and the two Pawnee scouts rode into Cole and Walker's camp.[75] Along the way they had found a lone soldier who had been separated from his command. For carrying Connor's message through hostile territory, Sergeant Thomas was eventually awarded a Congressional Medal of Honor. The two Pawnee scouts who escorted him received no such honors. Indeed, Thomas, in his application letter for the medal in 1894, failed to credit them for their role in the mission.[76]

The arrival of Sergeant Thomas and the scouts was a great relief for Cole and Walker. According to Connor's instructions, they were to move to Fort Connor, but their soldiers were in no condition to travel. Fortunately for them, some additional relief came a few days later. On September 14 Connor ordered Captain North and some of his scouts and some of Marshall's soldiers to leave with supplies to aid Cole and Walker. When North and the Pawnees found the starving troops, they distributed not only Connor's supplies but also their own rations. On September 20 the Pawnee scouts guided Cole and Walker's tired troops into Fort Connor. That night the Pawnees and the Omaha and Winnebago scouts staged a war dance. Four days later the general himself arrived at the fort. With him were the remaining Pawnee scouts, who drove the horses captured from Black Bear's village into the fort.[77]

With Connor's return to the fort, the Powder River campaign came to an end. Major General John Pope, fed up with Connor's "mishandling" of the campaign, had issued an order on August 22 relieving the general of his command. Brigadier General Frank Wheaton replaced Connor as commander of the District of the Plains. Connor received these instructions two days before his arrival at the fort. He had intended to reorganize his troops and continue to scout the territory and was greatly disappointed with the order. General Dodge, Connor's immediate superior, and western newspaper editors were also furious at Pope's decision to end the campaign. They feared that the Indians would soon return to the trails and disrupt the traffic there.[78]

On September 26 Connor left the fort bearing his name. Captain North and the Pawnee scouts accompanied him, driving the captured Arapaho horses toward Fort Laramie. By this time only six hundred horses were left. Some had died as a result of bad weather on the trail from the Tongue River. Others had simply escaped. At Fort Laramie, General Wheaton officially assumed command of the District of the Plains from Connor, who journeyed to Salt Lake City to assume command of the District of Utah. Wheaton gave North the option to muster his men out or travel back to Nebraska to relieve a company of the Seventh Cavalry at the Pawnee Agency. North accepted the latter proposition, "as the Pawnees would thus be at home with their people and yet would draw pay and rations."[79]

The Powder River campaign of 1865 was not the success its planners had hoped for. The War Department had pumped millions of dollars into a campaign that had rendered few positive results. Cole's and Walker's commands had nearly perished in the harsh environment of the northern plains, and many historians have questioned Cole's claim that his troops killed hundreds of Indians. Connor's own victory at the battle of the Tongue River had been followed by a long and hard-fought retreat.

Still, the campaign had not been a complete loss. According to Robert M. Utley, it focused public attention on the Bozeman Trail and allowed the military to gain better knowledge of the territory. The establishment of Connor's fort, soon rechristened Fort Reno, ensured that the Bozeman Trail would attract increasing numbers of travelers. Utley might have added that the employment of the Pawnee battalion had been a great success. The Pawnees had been instrumental in locating and tracking hostile Indians. They had taken nearly a hundred enemy scalps and corralled a great number of horses at Black Bear's camp. Finally, they had saved Cole's and Walker's commands from death by starvation. If the Powder River campaign did anything, it established the reputation of the Pawnee scouts.[80]

While the Pawnee scouts were marching toward Fort Laramie, new regiments began arriving from the east to garrison the stations along the Platte River trails. Among these was the Sixth West Virginia Veteran Cavalry, under the command of Lieutenant Colonel Rufus E. Fleming. In September 1865 Fleming was on his way to Julesburg from Fort Kearny, accompanied by several Pawnee scouts, possibly the men who had been sent down from Fort Connor under Corporal Se gule kah wah de on August 22. While marching through the country, Fleming took a small party of men, including four of his Pawnees, on a hunt. After riding several miles they found a small wagon train that had been attacked by unidentified

Indians. These Indians had killed several teamsters and driven off 125 mules. Fleming and his small detachment of troops and scouts immediately went in pursuit. They soon spotted a large party of Indians, who appeared to flee when the soldiers came in sight. Fleming pursued them until they reached a narrow canyon. Sensing an ambush, he halted his men. When the Indians turned on the soldiers, he ordered the retreat. According to Fleming, his men rushed toward the Platte River with "tingling scalplocks." Fleming, a survivor of several Civil War battles, wrote later that this was "the only time in my war experience that despair entered my mind." Fortunately for them, Fleming and his little detachment reached the river, where they were able to fend off the Indians. It was an instructive experience in Plains Indian warfare for the accomplished Civil War veteran.[81]

Another member of the Sixth West Virginia Veteran Cavalry, George H. Holliday of Company G, later met twenty-five Pawnee scouts at Deer Creek Station, west of Fort Laramie, Wyoming. The scouts, who were accompanied by a white officer, were carrying mail between the various posts. They freely associated with the white soldiers at the station. Holliday witnessed a poker game between two scouts and a lieutenant and a private of the Eleventh Ohio Volunteer Cavalry. The lieutenant cheated the Pawnees out off their money and also won a horse that one of the scouts had wagered. The scout would have had to continue his service on foot if the lieutenant had not returned the horse and the money he had unfairly won the next morning. He also showed the scouts the trick he had used to cheat them during the card game.[82]

In the fall of 1865 the scouts returned home and settled down comfortably at the Pawnee Agency. Occasionally they went out on patrols. In January 1866 Frank North received orders to send a company of his scouts to Fort Kearny to join scouting missions along the Republican River. North sent Lieutenant James Murie and fifty men. Luther North received permission from his brother to join the scouts as an observer. The complete scouting party consisted of two regular troops of cavalry, some supply wagons, and the Pawnees.[83]

The mission was largely uneventful except for one encounter between the scouts and some Cheyennes. A squad of ten Pawnees ran into a party of 150 Cheyennes near present-day Frenchman Creek. Luther North, who accompanied the scouts on this occasion, wrote that although the

Cheyennes outnumbered the Pawnees, the Pawnees carried superior arms. The Cheyennes carried mostly bows and arrows, whereas the army had issued seven-shot Spencer carbines to the Pawnees. Despite their superior arms, Luther North advised the men to retreat. When they were near the creek, North's horse slipped on some ice and fell. North was thrown from the saddle, struck the ice with his head, and lost consciousness. When he came to, a Pawnee had his head in his lap and was rubbing snow in his face while the rest of the men had formed a defensive circle around him. Instead of fleeing, they had remained to save North's life. During the fight, the Cheyennes wounded three horses with arrows but were unable to break through the defensive perimeter. At daybreak they gave up their siege, and North's party was able to return to camp around midnight. The next morning, when the command was ready to start in pursuit of the Cheyennes, a dispatch arrived ordering all troops to return to Fort Kearny. When they arrived at the fort, the campaign ended, and the Pawnees returned to their agency.[84]

In April 1866, Captain G. M. Bailey, of the Commissary Department, received orders to muster the Pawnees out of service. As had happened after the Curtis campaigns of 1864, the Pawnees nearly missed another payment when Bailey's ambulance carrying their pay was attacked by a band of desperadoes. Fortunately, Bailey's men were able to keep the bandits at a distance, and after some delay the shipment arrived safely at Columbus. After mustering the Pawnees out and paying them, Bailey and his men witnessed their "novel war dance and other Indian ceremonies."[85]

Although the Pawnee battalion had disbanded for the time being, it appears that individual Pawnees continued to act as scouts and guides throughout 1866. Among them was Bob White. Although it is impossible to trace his whereabouts during all of this time, in August 1866 White was laid up in an army post hospital, having been admitted on August 8 with "intermittent fever" and "Bubo [infected lymph gland] following chancroid." His treatment included dressings with poultices of flaxseed on the affected places and several other medications. A week later, on August 14, his condition had improved, and he was discharged from the hospital.[86]

A few months earlier, one Pawnee scout, possibly Bob White again, had accompanied a cattle train from Fort Kearny, Nebraska, to Fort C. F. Smith, Montana. It is unclear when or where this scout joined the cattle transport, but the train had set out from Fort Kearny in April 1866, about the same time the scouts were mustered out there. Perhaps the scout joined the transport there. At Fort Laramie the cattle drivers were joined by a horse and mule train. They also received a shipment of new Henry repeating rifles, which were to be delivered to gun dealers in Virginia City, Montana. Unluckily for them, the presence of the horses and mules attracted the attention of a Sioux war party. A day's march above Fort Laramie, a Sioux warrior stole a horse belonging to one of the men with the train in broad daylight. The owner of the horse wanted to pursue the thief but was prevented from doing so by the Pawnee scout, who expected a trap behind the next hill. Some time later, after crossing the divide between the Cheyenne and Powder Rivers, the Pawnee discovered a Sioux war party in a small valley. He raced back to alert the men in the train, who immediately prepared to defend themselves. They placed the wagons in a circle, moved the animals inside it, and armed themselves with the Henry repeating rifles. When the Indians launched their attack, their muzzle-loading guns were no match for the repeating rifles. While the Henry rifles kept the Sioux at a distance, the Pawnee scout taunted the enemy. According to an eyewitness, he stood on top of a wagon "making all manner of insulting gestures to let them know that there was a Pawnee on the job." The Sioux soon abandoned the fight, and less than an hour later the train resumed its journey.[87]

Unfortunately, it is difficult to trace the movements of such individual Pawnee scouts. Indeed, it is not easy to determine whether there were many such freelancers at all, especially if they joined as hired hands rather than as government scouts. In any event, whether they served individually or as members of the Pawnee battalion, these men proved to be of great value to their American allies, and their role in breaking the military power of their enemies in the American West should not be underestimated.

CHAPTER 4

Guarding the Union Pacific Railroad, 1867–1868

> ... we all went northwestward and finally saw what we thought was a herd of buffalos in the distance but this turned out to be hostile Cheyennes and perhaps other Indians and they swooped down on us and we had a fight. I found Major North and another white officer hiding under a cliff and Major North told me that I had saved them when I came upon them.
> —Ruling His Sun, Pawnee scout, April 11, 1928

In 1867 the Union Pacific Railroad (UPRR) Company requested military assistance to protect its surveying and construction crews, who were building the first transcontinental railroad in the United States. The assignment fell to a new battalion of Pawnee scouts, again recruited by Frank North. For the next two years the Pawnees served as guards along the railroad.

The idea of a transcontinental railroad originated in the 1830s with New York merchant and China trader Asa Whitney. In 1845 Whitney "proposed to Congress that the federal government grant a strip of land sixty miles wide, from Lake Superior to the Oregon country to a firm willing to construct a railway to the Pacific Ocean." Although Congress failed to act, politicians such as Missouri's Senator Thomas Hart Benton kept Whitney's dream alive. In the 1850s the idea for a transcontinental railroad received greater political support, but considerable sectional debate arose over the best route. Northern congressmen pushed for a northern route while southern congressmen, such as Jefferson Davis, favored a southern route. Senator Stephen A. Douglas suggested the construction of three transcontinental roads: one from the North, one from the South, and one from

Douglas's own state of Illinois through the central Great Plains. After the secession of the Confederate states, Congress passed the Pacific Railroad Act in 1862. The act provided loans and land grants to the Central Pacific Railroad, which would start construction from San Francisco eastward, and the newly incorporated Union Pacific Railroad, whose construction crews would move westward from Omaha, Nebraska.[1]

Among the principal characters of the Union Pacific Railroad was Major General Grenville M. Dodge. After the Powder River campaign, Dodge became frustrated with the inconsistent course of the army's Indian policy. In May 1866 he resigned his post as commander of the Department of the Missouri and accepted a position as chief engineer for the UPRR, at a salary of $1,000 a month. Dodge had acquired ample experience as an industrial engineer. Born in Danvers (present-day Peabody), Massachusetts, in 1831, he attended Partridge's School of Practical Engineering in Massachusetts. After receiving a degree in military and industrial engineering, Dodge moved to Council Bluffs, Iowa, in 1853. While surveying the town of Columbus, Nebraska, in 1854, he met the Pawnees. For a short period he lived near the Pawnee Agency. Because of his work as a surveyor, the Pawnees reportedly named him "Sharp Eye," "Long Eye," and "Hawk Eye."[2] When the Civil War broke out, Governor Samuel J. Kirkwood of Iowa commissioned Dodge a colonel in the Fourth Iowa Volunteer Infantry. During the war his command captured fifty-five Confederate locomotives and hundreds of wagons, and in 1863 Ulysses S. Grant promoted him to major general. During Sherman's epic "March to the Sea," which included the burning of Atlanta, Dodge's engineering crew constructed a double-track trestle bridge near Roswell, Georgia, in only three days. The completion of the bridge and this strategic railroad proved essential for Sherman's campaign. In 1864 General Grant appointed Dodge commander of the Department of the Missouri. The following year Dodge planned the Powder River campaign, before resigning his post in 1866.[3]

Because of capital shortages and the disruption of the Civil War, construction of the UPRR did not begin in earnest until 1864. In the late fall of that year the road reached the Pawnee Agency, where the company hired a number of Pawnees to work as laborers on the railway. Agent Lushbaugh proudly reported to his superiors in Washington that the Pawnees did a wonderful job. They received regular pay and completed four miles of track before the work had to be suspended because of bad weather.[4] The Pawnees took full advantage of the railroad and caught free rides to Omaha and back on the *cáhiks-rararaaha* ("passenger trains"). The company allowed this practice in order to maintain friendly relations with the Pawnees. The only condition was that the Indians had to travel on top of boxcars so that they would not bother the white passengers.

In October 1866, Dodge and Thomas C. Durant, the vice president of the Union Pacific, invited a number of distinguished guests for a trip to the one-hundredth meridian aboard one of their trains. Among the visitors were Senators Benjamin Wade and J. W. Patterson, future president Rutherford B. Hayes, palace car baron George M. Pullman, and numerous governors, generals, journalists, railroad officials, doctors, judges, and other notables. The company of visitors stopped at the Pawnee Agency, where the Pawnees, hired by Dodge and Durant, performed a war dance. Many of the Pawnees remembered Dodge from ten years earlier, and others had recently served under him during the Powder River campaign. At Dodge's direction, the Pawnees staged a sham Indian raid to wake up the excursionists the following day. The performance caused some of the unsuspecting campers nearly to flee in terror. Near the bridge across the Loup River, the Pawnees performed a mock battle with some members of their tribe dressed as Sioux warriors.[5]

So far, railroad construction had progressed with little interference and few problems. Beyond the hundredth meridian, however, surveying and construction crews entered Sioux and Cheyenne territory. The Sioux and Cheyennes objected to the construction of the railroad through their hunting grounds. Red Cloud's Oglala warriors were also incensed at Patrick Connor's audacity in having constructed a fort in the heart of the Powder River country and swore revenge. The Indian war that had begun in 1864 and climaxed with the Sand Creek Massacre lingered on. Cheyenne and Sioux war parties scoured the area in search of horses and scalps. The surveying and construction crews were easy prey.

To deal with the Sioux and Cheyennes, chief engineer Dodge ordered that each surveying crew be composed of at least eighteen men. Apart from an experienced engineer and his assistants, the crews consisted of rodmen, flagmen, chainmen, axmen, teamsters, and herders. Hunters were added to provide the workers and surveyors with beef. All men in the party were to be armed. Crews operating in hostile Indian country also received some military training. Dodge gave the crews specific instructions never to run when attacked by Indians. His military experience had taught him that it was better for units to fight until relief arrived than to attempt to outrun Indian war parties.[6]

Fortunately for the railroad crews, they did not have to face the Indians alone. Dodge could rely on the support of some of his old friends in the War Department. Among the strongest proponents of the transcontinental railroad was General William T. Sherman, Dodge's commander during the Civil War. In 1865 Sherman had assumed command of the Military Division of the Missouri, which included the northern and central plains. He immediately grasped the strategic importance of the railroad for military operations against the hostile Plains Indian tribes. The railroad, Sherman reasoned, would make the string of expensive and difficult-to-supply military posts nearly obsolete. Troops could travel to conflict areas quickly from a few strategically located posts along the railroad. "I regard this Road of yours," Sherman wrote Dodge, "as the solution of 'our Indian affairs' . . . and therefore, [will] give you all the aid I possibly can." Sherman also emphasized the importance of the railroad to his superior, General Grant. "The great advantage of the railroad," Sherman wrote Grant in 1868, "is that it give[s] us rapid communication and cannot be stolen like the horses and mules of trains of old."[7]

Sherman reassured Dodge that he would do all he could to protect the surveying parties who examined the country for the best possible route and the construction crews who were laying the tracks. The railroads were so important to the army that in the spring of 1866 it created a new military jurisdiction called the Department of the Platte. Brigadier General Philip St. George Cooke became its first commander, but he was soon replaced by Colonel Christopher Columbus Augur. The headquarters of the new department were at Omaha, Nebraska. The department's main purpose was to protect construction crews along the rail route. The department also furnished military escorts to crews operating in hostile territory.[8]

An act of Congress in 1866 greatly facilitated Sherman's plan to protect the Union Pacific Railroad. On July 28 that year, President Andrew Johnson signed into law an "Act to increase and fix the Military Peace

Establishment of the United States." It was a sweeping reorganization of the army. Its purpose was to increase the size of the army and make it more professional. The number of cavalry regiments increased from six to ten, and the number of infantry regiments, from nineteen to forty-five. Among the newly created units were two black cavalry and four black infantry regiments. Each regiment consisted of twelve companies and stood under the command of one colonel, one lieutenant colonel, and three majors. Each company was under the command of a captain, who was assisted by a first and a second lieutenant. The act also reorganized the administrative structure of the War Department by creating ten different bureaus. The most important of these bureaus were the Adjutant General's Office, which sent orders and kept archives of records, and the Quartermaster Department, which coordinated the distribution of men and supplies.[9]

The act of 1866 was designed also to deal with the Indian "problem" in the West. For that purpose, section six of the act authorized the president "to enlist and employ in the territories and Indian country a force of Indians, not to exceed one thousand, to act as scouts, who shall receive the pay and allowances of cavalry soldiers, and be discharged whenever the necessity for their further employment is abated, or at the discretion of the department commander." With the expansion of the army and the authorization to hire Indian scouts, Sherman received the manpower to guard the transcontinental railroad more effectively.[10]

On February 27, 1867, Colonel Augur telegraphed the commissioner of Indian affairs and requested the services of Frank North to assist in organizing the new Pawnee battalion. A few months earlier, in October 1866, President Johnson had appointed North trader at the Pawnee Agency. Augur asked that the Indian Office grant North a leave of absence to aid in the protection of the UPRR.[11] North accepted Augur's proposition to organize the Pawnee scouts on the condition that he be granted the rank of major in the United States Army. Augur consented, and in March North enlisted nearly two hundred Pawnees for service.[12]

North created four companies and appointed white men as officers. Each company consisted of members of one of the bands of the Pawnee tribe. Captain Edward W. Arnold and First Lieutenant Isaac Davis commanded Company A, which was composed of Chawis. Captain James

Murie and First Lieutenant Fred Matthews commanded Company B, which encompassed Pitahawiratas. Captain Charles E. Morse and First Lieutenant William Harvey commanded Company C, consisting of Skiris. Finally, Luther North was appointed captain of Company D, which was composed of Kitkahahkis. Gustavus G. Becher assisted North as first lieutenant in this company. Captain Lewis Merrill officially mustered the Pawnees into service on March 15, 1867. Four days later the scouts arrived at Fort Kearny.[13]

At Fort Kearny the scouts waited until April before their horses arrived. They also received muzzle-loading Springfield rifles and Colt revolvers with paper cartridge ammunition. After receiving the horses and arms, the battalion traveled to the end of the railroad tracks, near present-day Ogallala, Nebraska. While Captain Morse's company of Skiris and Luther North's company of Kitkahahkis acted as guards for the track layers, Murie's Pitahawiratas and Arnold's Chawis traveled to Fort Sedgwick to exchange their old Springfield rifles for new Spencer carbines.

While scouting the area for hostiles around Ogallala, some scouts discovered a party of Sioux who had stolen fifty or sixty mules from a grading camp a few days earlier. There is some disagreement between Frank North's and Luther North's recollections about whether these Indians belonged to Red Cloud's band of Oglalas or Spotted Tail's Brulés, whose village was located nearby. Perhaps the war party consisted of warriors of both bands. In either case, Frank North gathered some scouts and followed in pursuit. Luther North and Captain Charles Morse accompanied him. The scouts overtook the Indians near the North Platte River and had a running fight for several miles, during which they recaptured the mules.[14]

One of the Pawnee scouts in Morse's company, the mixed-race former interpreter Baptiste Bayhylle, killed one of the Sioux. Bayhylle ran up to within a few hundred feet of the Sioux and shot him in the right side with an arrow. The Sioux stopped, grasped the arrow, pulled it through his body, fitted it to his own bow, and shot it back at Bayhylle. The shot missed, and after taking a few more steps, the Sioux fell dead. As soon as he fell, Bayhylle rode toward him and leaned over to count coup on him. But Bayhylle's horse shied off, and another Pawnee, named Fox, rushed up to take the honor. That night in camp Bayhylle claimed first honor, arguing that he would have touched the Sioux first if his horse had not shied. A council that debated the matter, however, decided unanimously to bestow the honor on Fox, who, on the basis of his brave act, changed his name to Luk tuts oo ri ee Coots ("Brave Shield").[15]

The dead Sioux turned out to be a brother of the Brulé chief Spotted Tail.[16] As was their custom, the scouts held a big dance in celebration of their victory. A few days later Colonel Augur asked the scouts to repeat their dance for some UPRR dignitaries. A correspondent for the *New York Times* witnessed the event but was unimpressed. The reporter was disappointed when the scouts appeared in their military uniforms, "a style of dress so ludicrously at variance with the character assumed that it knocked the romance of the thing into 'smithereens.'" One of the spectators obtained the scalp the Pawnees had taken in the fight. Still attached to it was one of the ears of the dead Sioux. The spectator also obtained the arrow that had mortally wounded the Sioux and that he had shot back at the scout before dying.[17]

After Captains Murie and Arnold returned with their new Spencer carbines, it was the turn of the other two companies to travel to Fort Sedgwick to exchange their guns. On the second day, when they were about ten miles from Fort Sedgwick but still on the north bank of the South Platte River, North's and Morse's scouts discovered an enemy war party consisting of a hundred warriors chasing some U.S. troops on the other side of the river. They desperately tried to cross the Platte to assist the troops, but the river was too high, and the attempt failed. Three horses drowned, and all the ammunition got wet. The Pawnees watched helplessly as the Indians killed the soldiers. The next day the Pawnees finally made it to the fort, where they received their new rifles.[18]

That evening Major Frank North, General Sherman, and Colonel Augur arrived at Fort Sedgwick. Sherman and Augur were on an inspection tour of some western forts. Captain Luther North's Company D and Captain Morse's Company C escorted the generals first to Fort Morgan, Colorado, and then to Fort Laramie, Wyoming Territory. According to Luther North, many of the regular troops accompanying the party were deserting while they camped at Fort Morgan. One night, one of Sherman's personal guards deserted, taking a horse belonging to an officer with him. Sherman then ordered Frank North to furnish the guard for his headquarters. The irony of Indians guarding the head of the U.S. Army did not escape Luther North. No more horses were stolen.[19]

On June 20, while escorting General Sherman to Fort Laramie, Luther North and an advance party of scouts stumbled on a party of twenty Arapaho warriors near Lodgepole Creek. The Arapahos were driving a herd of horses and mules. As they approached the Arapahos, the Pawnees gave their war whoop, which, according to North, sounded like "Ki-de-de-de!" Then the Pawnees scattered, and each man fought individually, chasing the Arapahos as fast as his horse could run. After a running fight covering ten miles, the scouts killed several Arapahos and captured one, along with fifty-five horses and mules. The attack earned them praise from General Sherman. After the fight the Pawnees honored Luther North by giving him an Indian name, Le shar kit e butts ("Little Chief"). Captain Charles Morse, who had killed one of the Arapahos, also received a Pawnee name, La shar oo led ee hoo ("Big Chief").[20]

Over the next few weeks, the Pawnee scouts were deployed all along the western portions of the Union Pacific railway.[21] They became a common sight along the railroad line. Occasionally they became friends with men on the working crews. They frequently bivouacked near the camps of the construction crews and invited the laborers to attend their ceremonies. An Irish hand named Thomas O'Donnell became friends with Baptiste Bayhylle. At Bayhylle's invitation O'Donnell attended a Pawnee dance, where O'Donnell noticed a scalp pole upon which many scalps were fastened. The dancers "marched in circles three deep with the braves in the center fighting an imaginary foe all fully armed." Occasionally, O'Donnell reported, "some brave would rush at me with uplifted tomahawk and knife as [if] to strike the fatal blow and on several occasions I stepped back to avoid it." At the end of the dance a chief made a speech "telling how the Sioux killed the Pawnees and their wives and children, stole their horses and drove them from their hunting ground. Then they vowed war with the Sioux till death."[22]

Another railroad worker who saw the Pawnee scouts in action was E. T. Scovill, a surveyor for the UPRR. While working between Julesburg and what would become the town of Cheyenne, Wyoming, Scovill frequently met Frank North and the scouts. "The Pawnees were never disciplined in a military sense," Scovill wrote later. Instead of dragging their supplies along, the scouts would devour as much as possible on the first day and hunt for game when they got hungry again. When Scovill asked North if "that was the way his command always transported their supplies," North replied that "he had given up all attempt to control such matters." North also confessed to Scovill that the scouts were impossible to control during battle. "They obeyed orders and suggestions preliminary to a combat, but in a charge or sudden attack they reverted to their own methods and were whirlwinds in a fight," Scovill recalled. While chasing a Sioux war party near Wood River, Nebraska, the scouts first fired at the Sioux with their carbines. When these were empty, they cast them aside and used revolvers until those, too, were empty and discarded. At the end of the chase the scouts were armed only with bows and arrows. After the chase, they would return to gather their discarded weapons. One day Scovill saw the scouts as they passed through Julesburg on their return from a successful engagement. They carried a number of scalps, all decorated and attached to hoops and sticks. The next night Scovill attended their scalp dance and found it the most thrilling rite he had ever seen.[23]

Although the Pawnees had been sent to protect the workers, occasionally their sudden and unexpected appearance caused alarm among construction crews. Thomas O'Donnell recalled that the Pawnees left his crew to get supplies at Fort McPherson. While they were gone, rumors spread that Red Cloud's Oglala warriors were heading in the direction of the railroad camp. When the Pawnees returned several weeks later, their horses got mired in a swamp near the laborers' camp. The Pawnees raised a fierce war whoop, which the workers mistook for a Sioux attack. They were relieved to discover that the yell had been raised by the Pawnees to help pull their horses from the swamp.[24]

Early in the summer of 1867 a surveying party under Jacob Blickensderfer Jr. set out from Julesburg to examine the country along the eastern base of the Rocky Mountains. The party included, among others, General Dodge; T. J. Carter, one of the government directors of the railroad; John R. Duff, son of the vice president of the Union Pacific; civil engineer Silas Seymour, who left an account of the trip; and Brigadier General John A. Rawlins, then Grant's chief of staff. On July 3 the surveyors arrived at

Crow Creek, in present-day Wyoming, where they began to lay out the town of Cheyenne. There they met General Augur, who was in the country accompanied by one or two companies of U.S. Cavalry and a large detachment of Pawnee scouts under the command of Frank North. After a merry Fourth of July celebration, engineer Seymour set out to examine a section of the country west of Crow Creek. Division engineer Marshall F. Hurd, a teamster, and a cook joined him, and General Augur ordered Lieutenant Fred Matthews with a detachment of twenty Pawnee scouts to escort the party.[25]

Seymour's party left camp on the morning of July 11, 1867. Seymour and Hurd, armed with carbines and revolvers, rode in advance. Lieutenant Matthews and some of his men followed at a short distance. Then came the government wagon that carried the camp equipage and supplies. The remaining scouts followed the wagon as a rear guard. After a few hours the party reached Granite Canyon. While Seymour was examining the area, he suddenly saw the wagon escort dash up a hill and at the same instant heard a "most unnatural and uncertain sound from a bugle, blown by one of my braves," from the top of a high bluff in the same direction. The Pawnees had discovered a party of Sioux. It soon turned out that these were the same Indians who had stolen some mules from another outfit a few days earlier. The scouts immediately dismounted and, without waiting for instructions, "commenced unsaddling their ponies, and divesting themselves of their military caps, coats, pantaloons, boots and other superfluous appendages." They then remounted and dashed after the Indians, ignoring Seymour's "orders and protestations to the contrary." Lieutenant Matthews and Hurd joined the chase. Hurd, unable to keep pace with the scouts, returned to the outfit a little while later. With his entire escort gone, Seymour decided to return to camp headquarters as fast as possible. The nervous engineers believed they saw the heads of several Sioux peeping over the ridge, but upon their approach, these turned out to be nothing more than "rocks, bushes, or large tufts of grass." The party made it back to camp late that evening.[26]

The following day Lieutenant Matthews returned with his warriors. They had recaptured the mules and taken a number of scalps. Although Matthews's scouts expected praise for their quick action, Seymour severely chastised the lieutenant for abandoning his party. Matthews apologized but explained that had he not followed his warriors in pursuit of the Sioux, he probably would never have seen them again. Seymour noticed that the Pawnees had adorned the ears and tails of the mules they had recaptured with feathers, ribbons, and "grotesque appendages" such as enemy scalps. General Dodge also reprimanded Matthews for deserting the party. Dodge later wrote that the Pawnees were "utterly disgusted" with the reprimand. He also noted that the scouts "made the nights hideous for a week with their war dances over their fights and scalps."[27]

Enemy parties kept the Pawnees busy that July. As soon as an enemy was sighted, they rushed to their horses to mount a pursuit. Recognizing that quick action was the best guarantee of success, they wasted little time preparing for the chase. Laborer Thomas O'Donnell recalled how the Pawnees were bathing in Lodgepole Creek one hot July morning when the alarm "Sioux" came. The Pawnees immediately jumped on their horses, some half dressed, others completely naked, and set out in pursuit. Although the Sioux escaped, the Pawnees returned that night with ninety freighters' horses that had been stolen from supply trains earlier.[28]

Perhaps one of the most gripping accounts of an encounter between the scouts and an enemy war party during this time was recorded by William F. Hynes, a private in Company E, Second U.S. Cavalry. In the summer of 1867, while camped on Crow Creek, near present-day Cheyenne, Wyoming, Hynes's company received orders from Fort Laramie to join the search for a band of Sioux that had been raiding in the area. A contingent of Pawnee scouts accompanied the soldiers. The scouts carried Colt Navy pistols and breech-loading Spencer carbines. Hynes marveled at the "Indian costume" and noticed that the scouts made necklaces from used metallic cartridge shells, which they strung on a cord and hung around their ponies' necks. When the animal moved, the necklace made "a soft tinkling sound like sleigh bells." Although the scouts made "a most unusual and attractive cavalry force," Hynes had no doubt that they were also a "fighting corps."[29]

For several days, scouts and soldiers moved northeast in the direction of the Black Hills, where the Sioux were believed to be headed. When in camp, the scouts and soldiers fraternized around the campfires, although communication between the two groups was difficult. Near Chimney Rock, Nebraska, the command caught up with the Sioux. The scouts in advance discovered a camp of some three hundred warriors and reported their presence to the main column. The scouts immediately prepared for the attack. When they came in sight of the Sioux, the Pawnees broke into a wild charge—"a reckless race for the enemy," as Hynes later recalled. The whoops and yells of the scouts "mingled with the sound of the stringed, empty cartridge shells" hanging from the horses' necks. Although the scouts rode in apparent "violent disorder," Hynes believed that "order was there, which would appear and respond when the command was given." The Sioux, spooked by the sudden appearance of the scouts, immediately broke in panic, running in different directions. Many of them plunged into the North Platte River in order to escape.[30]

At this time Hynes and a fellow soldier were covering the left flank together with a Pawnee scout whose name, unfortunately, is unknown. They joined the chase and tried to head off a small group of six to eight Sioux warriors who were racing for the broken country near Scotts Bluff to the left. While dashing across the prairie, the Sioux discarded clothes and other items to make themselves lighter. Nevertheless, several fell back and were captured. Despite cautions by Hynes to stay together, the Pawnee scout dashed ahead in pursuit of one warrior. This warrior carried no gun but brandished a knife in either hand. When the Pawnee scout caught up, he hit the Sioux across the face with his riding whip. The Sioux lunged at the scout with his knife and inflicted a "ghastly opening" in the scout's thigh, all the way to his kneecap. The scout then snatched his carbine, but the Sioux, sensing the danger, also grabbed the weapon, and a "short, wicked struggle took place for its possession." During this struggle, on horseback at breakneck speed, the scout tried to grasp the enemy by the throat but accidentally stuck his finger between the teeth of the Sioux, who "promptly snapped off some of it like a pair of nippers, and spat it in his face."[31]

The Sioux had now won the struggle for the carbine, but being unable to use it, he threw it away. At the same time he reached for his knives, lunged forward, and caught the Pawnee just above the forehead, cutting a gaping wound from which blood streamed down the scout's face, almost blinding him. Despite bleeding heavily from face, thigh, and hand, the scout pressed on. He finally drew his Colt Navy pistol to end the fight, but the percussion cap failed to set off the charge.[32]

Unable to shake off the Pawnee, the Sioux warrior made one last desperate attempt to escape. While holding onto his horse with his right hand, he leaned down, reached under the belly of the Pawnee's horse, and disemboweled it "in one lightning stroke." At the same time, the scout grabbed his Colt Navy pistol by the barrel and landed a "frightful blow" on the Sioux's head, which was crushed "like an egg-shell." Both riders and their mounts then tumbled to the ground in a terrible crash.[33]

When Hynes and his companion reached the two men, they found the Sioux "quite dead" and the scout "living but unconscious." Although the soldiers carried no medical supplies (troops at this time did not carry first aid kits), they treated the scout as best as they could, using only some water and a few pieces of cloth torn from their clothing.[34]

Hynes was puzzled by the fact that the scout had not immediately killed his adversary with his guns but had instead insisted on a hand-to-hand fight with the Sioux. The scout later explained that there was no honor in shooting a man from a distance. In camp that evening, several soldiers expressed their sympathy to the scout for his injuries. The scout responded by stating that he felt "sick" where he was wounded but, placing his hand over his heart, that he was "no sick here."[35]

According to Hynes, the scouts held a scalp dance that night in which some of them took the part of the Pawnee women back home and opened the ceremony with a song of triumph for the victorious men. The soldiers joined in the dance. They were "as wild as the Indians, and perhaps more so, because the latter's observance was somewhat regulated by a set purpose; their attitude was the dignified performance of a rite; in fact, was semi-religious, while the [soldiers] saw only an opportunity offering unlimited freedom to what they considered a frolic without curb or restraint."[36]

A valuable advantage of the Pawnee scouts was their familiarity with the tactics of their enemies. Major Richard Irving Dodge, for example, recalled an incident in which he was attacked by a Sioux war party during a hunting trip. Fortunately for Dodge, a Pawnee scout named Li heris oo la shar (also known as Frank White) was with him. The two men took cover and were able to hold off the attackers. When the Sioux retreated,

Dodge wanted to mount his horse and return to camp, but the scout told him to wait. After waiting for nearly an hour, the Sioux appeared again and made another attempt to overtake them. Again the Sioux were unsuccessful. Finally, they gave up, turned their horses, and disappeared. Dodge and Li heris oo la shar reached their camp later that night. Dodge would never forget that he owed his life to a Pawnee scout, and they remained friends for life.[37]

William Henry Jackson, whose camera chronicled much of the history of the post–Civil War West, observed some of the scouts on his return to Omaha from the mining fields of Montana. In his diary for Monday, July 29, 1867, Jackson recorded that he met groups of uniformed Pawnees. "Some of them appear like good soldiers," Jackson wrote, noting that some still carried their tomahawks among their weapons. Jackson had a long "talk" with one scout, chiefly by signs. The scout told him how many scalps he had taken from the Sioux and the Cheyennes.[38] Jackson also noted that the Pawnees "wore the regulation uniform, with carbine and pistol—the Indian trait appearing occasionally in blankets wrapped around their waists, trousers converted into leggings and tomahawks tucked under their belts." There was no white officer with the scouts. Jackson observed that "an Indian sergeant [was] commanding that particular detachment."[39] Over the years, Jackson photographed many Pawnee Indians, including a number of scouts, in his Omaha studio as well as on the Pawnee reservation.[40]

Another description of the appearance of the Pawnee scouts comes from E. T. Scovill, surveyor for the UPRR. "A Pawnee stripped for action and in war paint was a striking object," Scovill recalled later. The scouts wore the typical roach hairstyle, which extended "from the forehead to the crown where it ended in a scalp-lock." They had painted large black circles around each eye, while "the rest of the face and portions of the body were streaked with vermillion and yellow." It is possible that this design was typical of one of the Pawnees' society colors. Perhaps it was also intended to strike fear into an enemy. In any event, Scovill believed that at "a short distance their faces resembled decorated skulls."[41]

One of the hostile Indian parties that was operating in the area near the UPRR was Turkey Leg's band of Northern Cheyennes. Although the Northern Cheyennes usually camped on the Powder River with Red Cloud's

Sioux, Turkey Leg frequently traveled south with his followers to visit the Southern Cheyennes. In the summer of 1867 Turkey Leg joined the Cheyenne Dog Soldiers and some Brulé Sioux under Chief Pawnee Killer on the Republican River. In June he attended some peace councils between Pawnee Killer and George Armstrong Custer. Sensing Pawnee Killer's desire for war, Turkey Leg decided to move his camp north in order to stay out of the way of the soldiers. In August, however, he returned and set up camp near Plum Creek on the Platte River. On August 6 a party of his warriors, under the leadership of Spotted Wolf, cut a telegraph line near Plum Creek Station. When a working crew came to investigate the matter, the Indians attacked and massacred the men.[42] One of the workers, William Thompson, was scalped but survived the ordeal by playing dead.[43]

Besides cutting the telegraph line, the Cheyennes sabotaged the railroad itself, detaching one of the rails. As they did so, two trains approached. On board the first train were engineer Brookes Bowers, fireman George Henshaw, and four others. The train derailed, and the Cheyennes shot and scalped Bowers and Henshaw. The other men on board rushed back and warned the second train, which quickly reversed its gears and backed up eastward. Before the Indians burned the derailed train, they plundered the boxcars of everything that might prove of some value or that attracted their fancy. They made a bonfire of the plundered boxes. In the light of the fire they decorated their bodies, tying colored pieces of ribbon to their scalplocks and hanging pieces of velvet over their shoulders. They decorated their ponies with pieces of muslin and tied ribbons to their ponies' tails. They also discovered a barrel of old bourbon whisky, which they quickly consumed and "which set their brain on fire and rendered them delirious." They celebrated their victory with a "violent war-song," and at daybreak they set fire to the wreck, taking burning coal from the furnace and throwing it in the boxcars. The bodies of the railroad crew were thrown into the fire. When they saw their work fully accomplished, they left. After they were gone, Thompson managed to crawl away. He found refuge near Willow Island Station, where a search party discovered him. Thompson later returned to Omaha, where a doctor made an unsuccessful attempt to reattach his scalp. Despite the failed surgery, Thompson lived to tell the tale of the massacre.[44]

After the attack on the train near Plum Creek, officials of the Department of the Platte at Omaha deployed several companies of infantry along strategic points on the railroad. At the time of Spotted Wolf's attack, Major North and the Pawnees had been guarding the rail lines two hundred miles farther west. Upon receiving news of the massacre, North and some of the Pawnee companies boarded a train and traveled to Plum Creek Station. On the morning of Saturday, August 17, North received a telegram from headquarters at Omaha informing him that Indians had again destroyed the telegraph line, a few miles from Plum Creek Station. North immediately sent Lieutenant Davis and twenty scouts of Company A with instructions to investigate the matter and, if the enemy was still nearby, to "attack and endeavor to whip them sufficiently to rid that station of further trouble from that band of Indians."[45]

When Davis arrived at Plum Creek he found 154 Cheyennes belonging to Turkey Leg's band. Turkey Leg had taken his people to the site of the train wreck in search of more spoils. Not expecting danger, he had even taken women and children along to help collect the plunder.[46] Finding himself outnumbered, Davis immediately notified Frank North of the situation and called for reinforcements. North at once ordered Captain Murie and thirty men of Company B to Plum Creek.

By the time Murie's scouts arrived, the Cheyennes had formed a skirmish line. Most of the warriors had concealed themselves on the east side of the stage road bridge that crossed Plum Creek. Eight or ten others had posted themselves in full view near the stage station. When these warriors saw the approaching scouts, clad in their blue uniforms, they quickly retreated across the bridge, hoping to lure the soldiers into following them. Fearing an ambush, the scouts devised a plan of their own. They dismounted in the dry bed of the river and, concealed by the tall grass, prepared for battle. They took off all their clothes except for their uniform hats and overcoats. Each man buttoned only the top button of his coat. Then they remounted and headed for the bridge in formation. To the Cheyennes they looked like regular troops. Overconfident, the Cheyennes awaited the opportunity to spring the trap. As soon as the front scouts reached the end of the bridge, however, they veered to the left, allowing the scouts in the rear to move up rapidly.

Nearly half the scouts had crossed the bridge when the Cheyennes began their charge. The Cheyennes cried out furiously and waved buffalo robes to throw the troops into disarray by spooking their horses. But when the Cheyennes had approached within fifty yards, the scouts suddenly threw off their hats and overcoats. With their chilling war cry they charged the stunned Cheyennes. This unexpected turn of events caused a panic among the Cheyennes, who quickly turned their horses and fled. In a matter of minutes the scouts had routed the Cheyennes. Although the Pawnees' superior armaments contributed to the outcome of the battle, the coolness with which they executed their maneuver was crucial during the fight. The Pawnees killed between fifteen and twenty Cheyennes and captured thirty horses. They also took three prisoners—a middle-aged woman, a thirteen-year-old boy, and a ten-year-old girl.[47]

Major Richard Irving Dodge, who had witnessed the battle from afar, called the Plum Creek battle "one of the prettiest and most successful fights that I have ever known among Indians." Henry M. Stanley, a newspaper correspondent for the *Missouri Democrat* who covered the incident, wrote that Captain Murie and Lieutenant Davis "did their utmost to prevent the mutilating of the dead, but it was impossible, for when the Indian blood is heated, they seldom listen to orders of that nature."[48]

While the scout company crossed the Platte River that evening, the captured girl escaped and reportedly found her way back to Turkey Leg's band. Murie's troops returned to camp later that night with fifteen scalps, the horses, a large number of blankets, and the two remaining prisoners.[49]

Later that summer, Turkey Leg and some other prominent Indian leaders met with an American peace commission under General Sherman. Turkey Leg took advantage of the occasion to exchange some white captives for the two remaining Cheyenne prisoners captured by the Pawnee scouts at Plum Creek. He explained that the little boy was his nephew. In exchange for the prisoners, Turkey Leg surrendered six white captives.[50]

The Plum Creek fight was significant for several reasons. It was a serious blow to the Cheyennes and effectively ended their major hostile operations against the railroad in 1867. It further showed that the tactics employed by the Pawnees, based on their understanding of the Cheyennes, were crucial to the successful guarding of the rail line. The Cheyennes were less intimidated by white soldiers than by their Pawnee enemies, and the scouts used this knowledge to their advantage. They devised a plan and executed it with skill and discipline. The result was a complete rout of the Cheyennes. Although they were unfamiliar with the maxims of the ancient Chinese military theorist Sun Tzu, that all "warfare is deception" and that to win a battle one must "know the enemy and know yourself," the scouts applied these principles to perfection in this fight. Their tactical knowledge came from centuries of collective experience in warfare, distilled and preserved in the Pawnee warrior societies.[51]

The battle was widely reported in newspapers around the country, but perhaps because it involved only Indian scouts, it has been treated merely as a footnote in most history books. It was, however, a major engagement. Although it was relatively small in scale, more enemy Indians were killed in this battle than in many widely publicized, large-scale engagements between U.S. troops and Indian tribes. The fight was also a morale booster for Frank North, who reportedly told an Omaha newspaper that "he could with his braves alone conquer the Cheyennes, but he can't fight all the Indians on the plains at once while guarding the railroad."[52] Because it was one of the few major military successes of that year, Colonel Augur reported that "Capt. Murie, Lieut. Davis and their brave Pawnees are entitled to great credit for this most decided success."[53]

The Plum Creek fight in one way symbolizes the true character of Pawnee scout service. Although they wore the uniform of the U.S. Cavalry with pride, underneath it they remained Pawnee. When the time came to do battle, they threw off their coats, shirts, and hats and fought the enemy as Pawnees.

After the Plum Creek fight, North received orders to gather his battalion at Cheyenne, Wyoming, to accompany the U.S. paymaster on a trip into the Powder River region. But ranchmen in the vicinity of Laramie and along the Platte River feared that the presence of the Pawnees might incite another war, and so North received orders to return to Fort Kearny.[54] On their way back, the Pawnees met a band of 300 to 400 Sioux, including 150 warriors, near Pine Bluffs, Wyoming. As the Pawnees prepared for battle, Nick Janise (LaJeunesse), who was in charge of the Sioux, rode up and explained that they were on their way to Fort Laramie for a peace council. Janise demanded that the Pawnees clear the road so the Sioux could pass. Frank North insisted that the Sioux should get out of the way, unless they were willing to fight. Janise left, and shortly thereafter the Sioux moved to the side of the road. The Pawnees passed them at a distance of about fifty yards. "I guess that was the first time that the Pawnees and Sioux ever got so close together without exchanging shots," Luther North later wrote. It appears that the presence of women and children prevented the Sioux from making an attack on the scouts.[55]

While at Fort Kearny, Frank North and a company of his scouts (possibly Luther North's Company D) escorted a hunting party composed of some of the directors of the Union Pacific Railroad Company, including Vice President Thomas C. Durant, Oliver Ames, Sidney Dillon, Charles Bushnell, and George Francis Train. None was a good horseman. The Pawnees spotted a small herd of buffalo, and the chase was on. One of the Pawnees, Co rux ah kah wah de ("Traveling Bear"), shot a buffalo with two arrows, one of which went clear through the animal's body. After the excitement of the chase, George Bird Grinnell wrote, the sophisticated easterners "expressed a wish to see some hostile Sioux and if possible, to witness a fight with them."[56]

Apart from the buffalo chase, there was little to do around Fort Kearny. The Pawnees went on a few more scouts, but they found no hostile Indians. By the end of October most of the scouts were eager to return to their relatives at the Pawnee Agency. Inactivity and boredom caused dissent among the scouts. When Frank North attempted to discipline one of his men, a number of scouts decided to go home without the formality of discharge. The exact circumstances of this incident are unclear, but in 1935 Gene Weltfish learned that a scout named Takuwutiru had once "cut rope against the Major's wishes and let down the fellows who were tied by their thumbs." Perhaps this was the event that prompted the "mutiny." It is significant because it reveals the scouts' attitude toward discipline and punishment. There is no doubt that the scouts were willing to submit to authority and accept punishment if it was deserved. Pawnee society, indeed, operated on a similar basis. But the Pawnees also believed that punishment should be fitting. In this case the scouts apparently thought North had overstepped his authority, and they would have none of it.[57]

According to the muster rolls, twenty-six scouts "mutinied and left camp without leave" on October 31, 1867. One of the "deserters" was Co rux ("Bear," later called High Eagle), who afterward declared that the trouble "had started over a Pethawerat [Pitahawirata] but all became involved in the mutiny." Although he did not serve at the time, a Pawnee named Ruling His Sun stated to an official of the Veterans Administration pension office in 1928 that most of the men who left were Chawis and Pitahawiratas. Co rux and his fellow "deserters" were probably unaware that their departure violated military law. They simply believed they had done their work and were free to go home. Fortunately, Colonel Augur proved understanding and decided not to pursue the matter legally. Instead, he gave Major North a number of blank discharge forms on which to fill in the names of the missing scouts and instructed the paymaster to pay the Pawnees. Although the incident did not affect future enlistment of the Pawnee battalion, neither Frank nor Luther North ever mentioned a "mutiny" among his men in any of his writings. Two weeks later, on November 14, the 168 remaining scouts were officially mustered out. During the eight months they had been in service, none of the Pawnees were killed. Only one scout did not return home: twenty-eight-year-old Pe ah tah wuck oo died of consumption near the Laramie Hills, in present-day Wyoming, on September 21, 1867.[58]

Augur and Sherman were pleased with the performance of the scouts. "I have never seen more obedient or better behaved troops; they have done most excellent service," Augur wrote. He added, "They are peculiarly qualified for service on the Plains; unequalled as riders, know the country thoroughly, are hardly ever sick, never desert and are careful of their horses." To assuage possible concerns of the Office of Indian Affairs, Augur pointed out that he had "never seen [a scout] under the influence of liquor, though they have had every opportunity of getting it." He hoped to reenlist the Pawnees in the spring to guard the Union Pacific and asked permission to organize several Indian battalions of four hundred men each from the friendly tribes in his department. Sherman passed Augur's request on and asked for a total of two thousand Indian troops. Both generals were aware of the objections of the Office of Indian Affairs to the enlistment of Indians as scouts and argued that military service would have an educational and civilizing effect on the Indians. It would launch them on "useful careers," make them more "tractable," and instill in them "regular habits and discipline" that would stay with them after they were discharged.[59]

Despite the opposition of some of the officials in the Indian Office, Sherman and Augur prevailed. But Augur did not win approval of the battalions he requested. Instead, he received permission to enlist only one hundred Pawnees. Once again, at the request of the Union Pacific, their main assignment was to guard and patrol the railroad.

In February 1868 Frank North enlisted two companies of fifty men each. Captain Charles E. Morse and First Lieutenant William Harvey were placed in charge of Company A. Fred Matthews, now promoted to captain, commanded Company B. Gustavus Becher assisted Matthews as his first lieutenant. Luther North did not join the battalion that year but remained behind to help his brother James E. North, who had taken over as Indian trader at the Pawnee Agency.[60] Captain Lewis Merrill officially mustered the Pawnees in at their agency in May 1868.[61]

One of the scouts who was mustered in was Ke wuck oo lah la shar ("Fox Chief"), later known as Ruling His Sun. Ke wuck oo lah la shar and the other Kitkahahki scouts first received their supplies. "I had a bluish army suit and a black hat," he later recalled. "My hat had a couple of short swords across the front of it [but] I had no stripes on my pants or on my arms." The men also received army tents. Ke wuck oo lah la shar shared his tent with five others: La sah root e cha ris ("Brave Chief" or "Mean Chief"), Luck tah choo ("Shield"), Cah we hoo roo ("Wandering Around"), Tah he rus ke tah ("Leader" or "Leader Of Scouts"), and Bob White.[62]

The scouts received orders to patrol one hundred miles of the railroad from Wood River Station to Willow Island and as far as Julesburg. Apparently their service the previous year had made an impression. The scouts found little enemy activity along the railroad. According to Luther North, the scouts were organized into "squads of twenty men" who were dispersed at different points along the railroad. George Bird Grinnell, however, said that Major North sent out a patrol every week along the hundred miles of track to look for hostile Indians. During one of these patrols, a squad of scouts skirmished with an Indian war party near Ogallala, Nebraska. The hostile Indians had piled some ties on the track and attacked a train carrying a carload of workmen. North's platoon arrived just in time to prevent a massacre. After chasing the Indians to the North Platte near Ash Hollow, the scouts killed three enemies, captured thirty horses, and destroyed the Indians' camp equipage. Unfortunately, Luther North did not mention when this fight took place.[63]

Little else happened while the scouts patrolled the railroad. On June 6, however, Private Co roox ah kah was killed accidentally by gunshot. The exact circumstances of his death, as well as the location where he was buried, are unknown.[64]

Perhaps the absence of hostile war parties along the railroad prompted Frank North and his scouts to agree to escort four white excursionists on a hunting trip near the Republican River in July.[65] Among them was John J. Aldrich, who published a detailed account of the trip in the *Omaha Weekly Herald* several weeks later. Also present was Francis Wayland Dunn, editor of the newspaper the *Chicago Christian Freeman*, who kept a detailed diary of the excursion. The other two tenderfoot excursionists were Henry Wells Magee, a Chicago merchant, and Sumner Oaks, a citizen of Omaha. In late July this party boarded the Union Pacific train at Omaha and traveled to Wood River Station, where North and a detachment of forty or fifty scouts awaited them. Captains Morse and Matthews and two teamsters also accompanied the party. Lieutenants Becher and Harvey remained behind to guard the railroad.[66]

The party set out for the Republican River that afternoon. After crossing the Platte River, the men made camp. Their wagon train formed a half circle, and the excursionists and officers pitched their tents in the center. They had "sow-belly and Indian bread" and other "fixings" usually eaten for supper by soldiers on the march. While in camp, Major North discovered a Pawnee who had deserted the battalion some time before. North took the man's government-issued arms but did not arrest him.[67] Aldrich spent an uncomfortable night in his tent, which he shared with thousands of bloodthirsty mosquitoes. The next day the party halted at Fort Kearny, where Major North "made a raid on the Quartermaster" for supplies. Then, on July 24, they spotted a large Pawnee camp on some bluffs overlooking the Blue River. The Pawnees were on their way to the Republican River for their annual buffalo hunt.[68]

On July 25 Major North's command joined the tribe on its march to the hunting grounds. The "soldiers" and priests of the tribe rode in advance of the camp. Despite the heat, the priests wore beautifully painted but heavy buffalo robes. They brought with them a long staff "fancifully painted" and decorated with goose down and a pair of buffalo horns. No person was allowed to pass ahead of the staff, and the soldiers were present to punish those who did. Soon a number of "soldiers" returned to the main group with news that they had found a buffalo herd nearby. Immediately the men mounted their horses and gave chase.[69] Aldrich observed how the Indians, "as if by magic, had [their] horses unpacked of their goods and chattels and divesting themselves of what wearing apparel they had on (which was but little,) were to be seen mounted bare-backed, with rifles, revolvers, bows and arrows in hand ready for the prey." Soon the hunters were dashing across the plains chasing buffalo. By the end of the day they had killed between 750 and 1,000 of the animals. That night, in camp, the excursionists joined the scouts and the tribe in a feast. The scouts stood guard around the camp.[70]

The next morning, one of the scouts, "Johnny White," who "never slept at night," woke up Aldrich's party. The visitors joined the Pawnee hunters and returned to the ground to clear up what meat had not yet been secured. That afternoon the alarm was raised. A Sioux war party was believed to have been spotted. While the Pawnee women continued to jerk the meat and scrape hides, their men painted their faces with white clay and rode out to meet them. Fortunately, the alarm turned out to be false.[71]

Several days later, after crossing the Republican River, the Pawnees and their white companions reached Mud Creek. So far everything had gone well, although one Indian died when he was struck by lightning on July 29. Near Mud Creek on July 30 the "soldiers" discovered another herd of buffalo, and another exciting chase followed. The Pawnee scouts, who traveled along the right flank of the tribe, joined in the fun, as did Major North. Captain Morse and some of the better mounted scouts soon took the lead. The hunters scattered across the plains, chasing small groups of buffalo. Aldrich, Dunn, and the other tenderfeet also joined in the chase.[72]

Suddenly a scout rode up to Major North and cried out that his group of hunters was surrounded by Sioux. North at first did not believe him, but soon he saw nearly 150 Sioux warriors appear on the hills. He had only six scouts with him, but Morse and two more scouts joined them a few minutes later. Among the scouts were White Eagle, Billy Osborne, and

Noted Fox. North and the scouts sought cover behind the carcasses of some of the buffalo they had killed. Although outnumbered, they were better armed and thus able to hold off the Sioux. Nevertheless, North sent one of his scouts, "Man That Left His Enemy Lying In The Water," to the main camp for help. This scout miraculously broke through the Sioux ranks and made it back to the main camp. According to Luther North, this was an act of tremendous bravery.[73]

Meanwhile, another Sioux force of several hundred warriors attacked the Pawnee camp. It was a chaotic fight in which charges and counter-charges followed each other in rapid succession. Newspaperman Francis Dunn, who witnessed the battle from a hill, thought it was "the most mixed up affair" he had ever seen. "A squad of the Pawnees would charge out on the Sioux and the Sioux would run," he later wrote. "Then the Sioux would charge [and] the whole lot of Pawnee would run."[74]

Then a rumor spread that the Sioux had killed Major North and a number of his scouts. According to Aldrich, the rumor of the major's death "left [the Pawnees] frantic, and it would be a waste of time to attempt to describe the fearful screams, yelling, and other manifestations of grief and sorrow that rent the air." Unwilling to believe North was dead, Aldrich and five scouts gathered nearly a thousand rounds of ammunition and rode in the direction of the major's position. After a dangerous ride they reached North and his handful of men. A large Pawnee force finally came to the rescue of North and his small contingent of scouts. The Pawnees drove the Sioux off and briefly pursued them. They reportedly killed twenty Indians before their horses gave out and they had to return to their camp. The whole affair had lasted three hours.[75] When North and his scouts returned, they were welcomed by many relieved Indians. "The rejoicings at the gallant Major's appearance in camp went to show how much the Pawnee tribe love and cherish him," Aldrich wrote later. "His troops were crazy with joy to catch his tired and worn [out] horse by the bridle.[76]

Sixty years later, in 1928, Ruling His Sun gave his account of the battle. Although short, it is perhaps the only Pawnee version of the battle and for this reason is worth reproducing here in full:

> We left the fort and went up the Platt River and camped for a long time in the fork of the Platt River. When we were camping there we were ordered to march westward and when near the Forks we were

joined by a band of Pawnees and we all went northwestward and finally saw what we thought was a herd of buffaloes in the distance but this turned out to be hostile Cheyennes and perhaps other Indians and they swooped down on us and we had a fight. I found Major North and another white officer hiding under a cliff and Major North told me that I had saved them when I came upon them. This other white officer appeared to have been wounded or his nose skinned. Major North had instructed me and some other Indians to guard the wagons and when the battle started we all started to get into the fight. I recall one of the Petahawerat band that lost his life but I do not know his name. There was also a Skeede lost his life but he was not a soldier. That [happened] somewhere in the Western Part of Nebraska but I cannot designate the place. That was in the summer time.[77]

According to Aldrich, two scouts were killed in the battle, as well as four Pawnee warriors. The official muster rolls, however, support Ruling His Sun's statement that only one scout died in the engagement. The lifeless body of Koot tah we coots oo hadde was found not far from the place where he had killed two Sioux. The Sioux had scalped him, cut off his hands and feet, and nearly severed his head from his body. His entire body was pierced with arrows.[78] Several other scouts had received severe wounds during the battle. One of them, Ke wuck oo la shar ("Fox Chief"), died shortly thereafter from his injuries.[79] The Pawnees were devastated by the deaths. They considered the loss of a scalp a great stain on their nation. According to Aldrich, the fact that they had secured no scalps themselves made the humiliation even greater.[80]

That night and the following day the Pawnees mourned the loss of their men. The women cut long gashes in their arms and legs. The dead were buried in gulches, according to Dunn, "so that the Sioux can not find their graves." For three days and nights people mourned at the graves of their loved ones. Then, on August 2, they broke camp again and moved on.[81]

Despite the attack, the Pawnees continued their hunting expedition. Over the next few days they shot nearly fifteen hundred buffalo. While the women prepared the meat, the men smoked and gambled. Frank North joined the chiefs in several councils. Although North's opinion carried much weight among the chiefs, Aldrich's statement that North's word was "law" among the Pawnees was certainly an exaggeration. According to Aldrich, Frank North "had the full confidence of the nation . . . and were he to order them to charge through a river of fire, I believe they would do it, and I don't know but if there was a little brimstone in it, they would go, such is their love and fear of 'Pawnee Laschell.'" When North announced that he and his men would leave the tribe soon, the chiefs, to no avail, pleaded with him to stay. When North's command left on August 6, the Pawnee people cheered their scouts. Several days later the command crossed the Blue River and reached Wood River Station on the Union Pacific Railroad.[82]

At Wood River Station, North's scouts were reunited with the companies under Lieutenants Becher and Harvey. Harvey's platoon, too, had seen some hard fighting with the Sioux, on July 28. That day a party of Sioux had stolen some stock near Wood River, and Harvey and eighteen scouts had set out to intercept them. Among the scouts was Bob White. According to Luther North, Harvey's scouts caught up with the Sioux after a forty-mile ride. Another account, reportedly coming from Harvey himself, says that the Sioux were resting on top of a sand hill only three miles away when the Pawnees came upon them. When Harvey spotted the Sioux with his field glass, he discovered that they were Yanktons. This discovery posed a dilemma, because the Yanktons were supposedly at peace with the United States. To attack them might jeopardize the peace.

Harvey's scouts, however, would not be dissuaded. If Harvey did not wish to attack them out of fear that he might be punished by his superiors, they said, then they would attack without him. One scout told Harvey that he could go back to camp while they attacked the Yanktons not as government scouts but as Pawnee Indians in the defense of their people. Perhaps because he was afraid to lose face in front of his men, Harvey decided to go forward with the attack.

Although outnumbered three to one, the scouts prepared for battle. When they were discovered by the Yanktons, a shouting match ensued, followed by a heated exchange of gunfire. After half an hour a rush by the Pawnees threw the Yanktons into confusion, and they fled from the field, hotly pursued by the scouts. According to one account, eight Yanktons were killed in the pursuit, but Luther North's statement that only two were killed may be more accurate. The scouts recovered the stolen stock. But they, too, had suffered casualties. Several men were wounded, and one scout, Loo law we luck oo la it, died of his wounds shortly afterward.[83]

Reports of the battles of July 28 and 30 soon filtered back to Omaha, where they received unexpected criticism in the local newspaper. On August 21 the *Omaha Weekly Herald* printed an editorial blaming Major North for provoking an Indian war. Since the battle, the editorial pointed out, the Sioux and Cheyennes had retaliated by attacking several stations along the Kansas Pacific Railroad. The editors feared that North's presence along the Republican had ended a fragile peace on the frontier. The report sparked a response from Francis Dunn, the Chicago journalist who had been present during the battle at Mud Creek. In a letter to the *Herald* Dunn pointed out that the Indians had been responsible for depredations several weeks before the battle. He claimed that talk about an Indian peace was "moonshine." The depredations "are not retaliations but robberies," Dunn wrote, and "the Indians that commit them will continue to do so in spite of treaties, their chiefs or anything short of cold lead."

General Augur, of the Department of the Platte, agreed with Dunn that the Cheyennes had seized upon Major North's presence during the buffalo hunt as a pretext for their massacre of whites in Kansas and Nebraska.[84] Nevertheless, when the Pawnees were once again hired to guard the Union Pacific Railroad two years later, in September 1870, North's instructions stated explicitly that "the Pawnees must make no scout at any great distance from the line of rail road. They will confine their operations to the line of said road and to a distance North or South of it, not exceeding twenty five (25) miles." Apparently, the ambush on North's company while it escorted the Pawnee tribe on its annual buffalo hunt in 1868 prompted these instructions.[85]

In August 1868, after rejoining Lieutenant Becher's scouts on the Union Pacific Railroad, Major North's scouts went back to guarding the rail line. On August 28 Captain Charles Morse's A Company skirmished with enemy Indians, and the hostiles fled south. After receiving reinforcements from Captain Matthews's Company B, Morse's scouts went in pursuit. They caught up with the hostiles near the Republican River on August 30. It appears that the two sides disengaged without major casualties. Neither Luther North nor Grinnell mentions any of these engagements in his account, possibly because no scalps were taken.[86]

According to one source, little of interest occurred until the middle of October. That month a party of Indians reportedly stole some horses from ranchmen near Sidney, Nebraska. According to Grinnell, General Augur telegraphed North with instructions to send a company of his scouts to Potter Station, where they were to join Major Wells of the Second Cavalry in search of the hostiles. The scouts discovered the Indians near Court House Rock, on the opposite bank of the North Platte River. Major North immediately ordered Lieutenant Becher and some of his men in pursuit across the ice-cold river. In the fight that followed, Becher's scouts killed two Indians and recaptured all the stolen horses, as well as a number of Indian ponies.[87]

Later in October, Frank North and nineteen of his Pawnees went on a short trip south of Elm Creek, between present-day Lexington and Kearney, Nebraska, in search of buffalo. Accompanying North and the scouts were several white visitors, including a Presbyterian minister known only by his initials, "F.M.D." The scouts and their guests killed about a dozen buffalo on this brief excursion. In camp that night, F.M.D. described how the scouts roasted some meat over a fire of buffalo chips. The scouts seemed to have enjoyed the meal, for when the minister woke up the next morning he noticed, to his amazement, that they were still eating. Later that day the scouts carried the meat, or what was left of it, back to the main camp in a six-mule wagon.[88]

That same month, fifty Pawnees went on another scout of the Republican River. Its purpose was to locate hostile Sioux and Cheyenne bands. The scouts accompanied General Augur and several officers as well as a detachment of 150 men of the Second Cavalry.[89] Also present were British officers C. P. Kendall and F. Trench Townshend, the latter of whom published a detailed account of the expedition. Twelve wagons carried supplies. The command left Plum Creek Station on October 18, and the scouts guided it safely across the Platte River. When the party camped that evening, the wagons were arranged in a half circle, and the horses were left to graze while the men pitched their A-tents.[90]

Townshend commented on the scouts' horses and Indian-style saddles, each made of a wooden frame covered by rawhide. Although not quite comfortable, the saddles were very light. The Pawnees' horses were "wonderfully tough little beasts, and on the hardest fare will do an amount of work that would kill most horses." The horses were not afraid to run alongside the biggest buffalo bulls and even tried to "seize" these animals with their teeth.[91]

The scouts themselves were armed with Spencer carbines. As usual, they scouted the territory in front and on the flanks of the column. Townshend was impressed with their skill at "following at full gallop a trail, of which we could not make out the faintest sign."[92]

The appearance of the scouts amused Townshend. They had painted their faces in red and yellow. Although they received clothing from the army, many wore only a simple blanket. Townshend attributed their sparse outfits to the fact that they were avid gamblers who had gambled their clothes away. The scouts who wore uniforms, according to Townshend, looked "ludicrous." Still, they had "great natural dignity of manner, and a calm gravity of countenance."[93]

On the twentieth the scouts discovered an Indian trail. The next day a detachment of Pawnees was sent out to investigate it. They followed the trail for forty miles but did not make contact with the enemy. They returned that evening, bringing in the meat of three buffalo they had killed along the way. After reaching camp, they made a fire and bent some green wood across it, over which they hung the meat to roast. Occasionally they cut off strips of meat, which they "devoured" with great relish.[94]

When the expedition found no hostile Indians in the area, the scouts, soldiers, and their officers entertained themselves by hunting buffalo and other game. On October 22 Townshend and his companions persuaded the Pawnees to stage a dance. At first the scouts were reluctant, saying that they had taken no scalps to warrant a dance. But after a few scouts began to sing and dance, the "whole party rose up" and joined in. According to Townshend, they soon worked themselves into a "state of the most violent excitement."[95]

On the twenty-third the command departed the Republican River and turned northwest. The next day Townshend shared a ride in the ambulance with a scout named "Bob," almost certainly Bob White. Townshend had been wounded by a buffalo during a hunt, and Bob was suffering from a severe cut on his hand that had become infected and was causing him great pain. Townshend described him as "one of the best-looking and most intelligent of the Pawnees." Bob spoke some English and told Townshend that he had been to Washington and New York. He believed the people in New York had great mysterious power, "because they had picked his pocket without his discovering the thief."[96]

On October 27 the command arrived at Fort McPherson. The men had found no hostile Indians, but this apparently did not bother General Augur. He had enjoyed the ten-day excursion, during which the party had killed sixty-five buffalo and a number of smaller game animals.[97] At Fort McPherson Townshend bade farewell to the Pawnee scouts, who returned eastward to Fort Kearny.

With the onset of winter, enemy activity stopped almost entirely. This did not mean that the scouts were free of danger, for the cold winter weather posed challenges of its own. According to Ruling His Sun, a Kitkahahki scout by the name of Le tah kuts kee le pah kee ("Young Eagle") froze his feet and legs up to the knees. The exact circumstances of this accident are unclear, but it illustrates the fact that the scouts were battling not only hostile Indians but also the harsh elements of nature.[98]

On December 7, 1868, the Pawnees received their discharge papers at Fort Kearny, Nebraska. Major North remained in service throughout the winter. He was placed in charge of the horses at Fort Kearny and ordered to keep them in condition. They were to be ready for the Pawnees the next spring.[99]

On May 10, 1869, the Union Pacific and Central Pacific Railroads met at Promontory, Utah. The railroad connected the East to the West. It linked markets from New York to San Francisco and beyond. It also opened up large segments of the Great Plains for white settlement. Farmers could now ship their produce to urban centers on both sides of the United States. The role of the Pawnees in the construction of the road should not be understated. During 1867 and 1868 the Pawnees held off enemy war parties along the railroad in Nebraska and Wyoming. The Union Pacific Railroad Company valued their contributions and in the fall of 1870 once again hired them for service along the road. In 1869, however, the scouts embarked on another mission. This time they joined General Eugene Asa Carr in his pursuit of a band of Cheyenne Dog Soldiers who had committed depredations against homesteads and settlements in Kansas.

CHAPTER 5

The Republican River Expedition and the Battle of Summit Springs, 1869

> We went into what is now called Colorado, and we were close [to] the mountain Pikes Peak and we could look at the mountain and the Pawnee [word] for the mountain is Mountain That Reaches The Sky.... We were scouting after the hostile Indians but I do not now remember what Indians they were the first [fight] but the second time we were after Chief High Bison, a Cheyenne, and his band. We killed High Bison in a fight ... on this side of the mountains and after we killed High Bison most of the men and women surrendered but some escaped and were not captured.
>
> —John Box, Pawnee scout, September 4, 1923

After the Pawnees were discharged in December 1868, Frank North spent the next two months caring for the horses and mules at Fort Kearny. He frequently traveled back to Columbus, Nebraska, to be with his wife, Mary Louise Smith. In the evenings he attended dances and theater performances and visited friends and relatives.[1] The Pawnees returned to their towns. They, too, spent their days visiting with friends and relatives and talking about their exploits while serving as scouts during the past year. Like Frank North, they attended dances and theatrical performances, albeit those of the Medicine Lodge ceremony of the Pawnee doctor societies.

Meanwhile, Sioux and Cheyenne war parties continued to threaten isolated settlements along the frontier. In January 1869, small raiding parties attacked mail couriers near Fort Dodge, Kansas. Another war party ambushed a stagecoach near Big Timbers Station, also in Kansas, and later killed two stage company employees near Lake Station, Colorado.² The appearance of these war parties alarmed settlers in western Kansas. In typical nineteenth-century fashion, most settlers branded all Indians as treacherous, thievish, murderous villains. They did not distinguish between friendly and "hostile" Indians, so settlers often accused friendly Indians of causing trouble and subjected them to harassment. Kansas newspapers called for a resolution of the "Indian problem." Some favored the removal of all tribes to Indian Territory. Others favored more draconian measures and called for the extermination of resisting tribes such as the Cheyennes. In this volatile atmosphere, charged with racial bigotry, fear, and greed, any Indian in the area was looked upon as a threat.³

The Pawnees frequently passed through western Kansas on their hunting expeditions, much to the consternation of farmers and ranchers, who complained that they destroyed crops and stole cattle. Pawnee war parties that traveled through the region on their way to raid Kiowas and Comanches for horses further fueled the settlers' anxiety. Although no conclusive evidence ever linked the Pawnees to depredations in Kansas, many settlers were convinced that the Pawnees could not be trusted. Tensions between Pawnee travelers and Kansas settlers climaxed on January 29, 1869, with the killing of perhaps nine Pitahawirata Pawnees near Mulberry Creek, Kansas. All the Pawnees had been scouts for the United States and had recently been discharged from service.⁴

Reports of the events of that day conflict with each other. According to the report of Captain Edward Byrne, Tenth Cavalry (the famous "Buffalo Soldiers"), settlers discovered an Indian war party on January 28. The alarmed settlers rode into Byrne's camp "in a great state of excitement" and reported that a group of about thirty Indians had appeared in the area and tried to break into a house on the Saline River. Byrne and twenty-five men of Company C started in pursuit of the Indians the next morning. After losing their trail, Byrne divided his command into four squads, one of which discovered some Pawnees on the farm of Charles Martin near Mulberry Creek, Ellsworth County, Kansas. According to Martin's testimony, the Pawnees had come to his farm, identified themselves as Sioux, and demanded flour, coffee, and money. They also took some whiskey and bacon. While the Indians were at the house, two soldiers arrived. They placed the Indians under arrest, but the Pawnees refused to go to the soldiers' camp. One of the soldiers then left and notified Captain Byrne, who arrived shortly thereafter.

In the meantime, the Pawnees had fled into a canyon nearby. Byrne ordered them to lay down their arms and surrender. Instead of obeying, the Pawnees began to fire at the captain, who was less than fifty yards away and clearly visible in his army uniform. The Pawnees had stripped themselves for the fight. The soldiers immediately returned fire. They also gathered some hay, set it on fire, and threw it into the canyon to smoke out the Indians. When the Pawnees retreated to the open prairie, the soldiers shot and killed six of them and took a wounded man prisoner. A few others escaped. One soldier was wounded in the fight. After the battle was over, the soldiers discovered that the Pawnees had many horsehair lariats with them, indicating that they were on a horse-stealing expedition. Some settlers later killed another Pawnee who had escaped from the battlefield.[5]

The Pawnee version of the incident is much different. According to the Pawnees, a party of fourteen men, all of whom had served as scouts and had recently been honorably discharged from the army, set out on foot from their reservation to trade with members of the southern tribes at the Kiowa, Comanche, and Wichita Agency in Indian Territory and to visit their Wichita relatives. They traveled light, carrying only "bows and arrows, light rifles, extra moccasins, lariats, and packs containing dried meat." Along the way they stopped at Martin's farm and asked for some flour and potatoes. While they were there, two soldiers arrived and examined the scouts' discharge papers. The soldiers left but soon returned with more men, who immediately opened fire on the Pawnees. According to the Pawnees, nine warriors died in the fight that afternoon. Only five escaped. The survivors later returned to the place of the carnage and buried their friends before turning back to the Pawnee Agency.[6]

Ironically, while the survivors of the Mulberry Creek attack were on their way home, Frank North was busy enlisting a new company of Pawnee scouts for military service. On Wednesday, February 10, 1869, while at Columbus, North received orders to organize a company of scouts to assist Captain Henry E. Noyes on an expedition to the Republican River. On February 11 North enlisted fifty men. He appointed his brother Luther captain and

Fred Matthews first lieutenant of the company. After receiving clothing, horses, and equipment at Fort Kearny, the Pawnees boarded a train the same day and traveled to Fort McPherson, or "Crow Valley," as the Pawnees called the area. There, Captain Alfred E. Bates mustered them in as "Company A, Pawnee Scouts."[7] They received additional supplies before going into camp. That night a torrential rain swept over the camp. "All got wet and nearly froze during the night," Frank North wrote in his diary. A few days later North returned to Columbus and left his brother in charge of the scouts.[8]

Captain North, Lieutenant Matthews, and the Pawnee scouts departed from Fort McPherson a few days later. Two wagons accompanied the little command. Near the Republican River they met Captain Noyes and his four companies of the Second Cavalry. The weather had become increasingly severe. Rain turned into snow, and temperatures dropped well below freezing. Luther North recalled that his hands were so frostbitten that he lost some of his fingernails. After several days on the trail, Noyes's troops, whose horses were in better condition, rode in advance of the Pawnee scouts. Noyes informed North that they would rendezvous with North's company and camp on Frenchman Creek, a tributary of the Republican River.

During the march the weather grew worse. Rather than trying to catch up with Captain Noyes, North decided to establish camp and seek shelter from the cold. One of his sergeants, Co rux ah kah wah de ("Traveling Bear") discovered a small canyon with plenty of wood and grass. Co rux ah kah wah de and some other men cut some poles and used the covers of two wagons to build a tipi. Then he ordered some of the other Pawnees to cut grass with their butcher knives to make beds for the men and build a fire in the center of the tipi. "We spread our robes and blankets," Luther North wrote later, "and in an hour we were perfectly warm and dry." While the men rested, Co rux ah kah wah de attended to a teamster whose foot had frozen stiff after he stepped into a creek earlier that day. Traveling Bear filled a kettle with snow and stuck the man's foot in it. From his medicine bag he took some powdered roots and chewed on them for some time. Then he spat the medicine into his hand and began rubbing it over the patient's foot and ankle. He repeated this treatment several times over the course of the night. Luther North watched Traveling Bear as he attended the man. "Of course I don't know whether it was his treatment or not," North wrote later, "but this man only lost the nail off one toe, yet I felt sure, when I first saw it, that he would lose his foot."9

Many of Captain Noyes's men were unluckier than the teamster in North's command. When the Pawnees resumed their journey the next morning, they found the troops in camp in the open prairie. More than fifty horses and mules had frozen to death during the night. Although the soldiers had burned some of their wagons in order to stay warm, many of the men were badly frozen. A number lost their feet, hands, or fingers and toes after their return to Fort McPherson. After a difficult three-day march, the Pawnees guided the troops safely back to the fort.10

In the meantime, while Luther North's company was scouting the area along the Republican River with Major Noyes, the survivors of the Mulberry Creek attack arrived at the Pawnee Agency. During their march they had suffered tremendously, nearly perishing of hunger and cold. Three died of exposure shortly after arriving at the reservation. On March 22 the chiefs called a council with Agent Charles H. Whaley to address the incident. Frank North was also present. The chiefs expressed their outrage at the slaughter and said that "they had not done, and did not intend to do any wrong to any white men, and have not, since the occurrence, done any wrong to any white people by way of revenge." They demanded an investigation and an interview with the Great Father in Washington. Agent Whaley, who kept minutes of the council, also reported that "Major North had recently enlisted one company from the tribe for service against the Sioux Indians this spring, and was about to enlist two more companies for this purpose, but the chiefs now refuse to have any more of their men enlisted until they hear what reply is made to their requests."11

Superintendent H. B. Denman passed the chiefs' request for an investigation on to the commissioner of Indian affairs. "If this course is not pursued and justice done," Denman wrote, "I have reason to believe from the known character of the 'Pawnee Indian' that they will seek redress for the outrage done to their people, and it may result in acts of retaliation upon innocent whites."12

Despite Denman's fears, the Pawnees did not retaliate. Although they did not receive the protection from the government promised in the treaty of 1857, they were unwilling to jeopardize their relations with the United States. Furthermore, retaliation might have given surrounding settlers an excuse to wage war against them in order to expel them from the territory. Trusting that their requests would receive a sympathetic ear in Washington, the chiefs allowed Frank North to enlist another company of scouts from the tribe a month later.

The chiefs might not have allowed their warriors to enlist if they had known what happened to the remains of the men killed at Mulberry Creek. Shortly after the fight, army surgeon B. E. Fryer disinterred the bodies of six Pawnees. Acting on orders from the Surgeon General's Office in Washington, D.C., Fryer removed their heads for scientific research. After boiling the heads and preparing them for study, Fryer sent the skulls to the Army Medical Museum for further analysis. Fryer and other surgeons similarly collected thousands of Indian skulls between 1868 and 1872. Not until 1995 were the skulls returned to the Pawnee tribe and buried with full military honors at Genoa City Cemetery in Nebraska. In April 1869 the chiefs were unaware of the desecration of the bodies of their kinsmen and thus allowed North to select more warriors from the tribe.[13]

On April 23 North shipped two train cars full of men to Fort Kearny. The next day the Pawnees received tents and teams and were officially mustered in as Company B of the Pawnee scouts. The company consisted of fifty men. North appointed his brother-in-law, Sylvanus E. Cushing, captain of the new company. On Sunday, April 25, the recruits received arms and horse equipment, and the next morning they were issued clothing and bayonets to use as pickets for tethering their horses. The scouts never used bayonets in battle.[14]

After traveling to Fort McPherson, Major North and his scouts joined Luther North and the scouts of Company A. Over the next few weeks the scouts went on several short missions. Usually the two companies split up into smaller detachments to cover a wider area.[15] Occasionally the scouts made contact with the enemy. It was perhaps during one of these encounters that Co rux ("Bear") was injured. During a skirmish with some Sioux on the North Platte River, Co rux's horse tripped and fell, and Co rux was kicked in the face. The blow fractured his nasal bones, causing facial deformity. The fall may have also cracked some ribs, because years later, when his name was High Eagle (a name given to him by Buffalo Bill), he sought an invalid's pension from the government for lung trouble, which he ascribed to this accident.[16]

While scouting near the North Platte in May, the Pawnees spied two horsemen in the distance. Major North ordered three of his men to see who they were, and he gave one of the scouts one of his own horses. When the Pawnees approached the horsemen, they discovered that they were Sioux warriors. A high-speed chase followed. The two Sioux went in different directions, and their pursuers also separated. The Pawnees who followed one of the Sioux quickly overtook and killed him. The scout on North's horse, Loo ree wah ka we rah rick soo, who chased the other Indian, was less fortunate. He pursued the Indian over a sand hill. As he rode along the hill, he saw his enemy coming back up the hill on the other side, holding a knife in his hand. The Pawnee jumped off his horse to shoot the Sioux, but the cartridge was defective. Before he could load another cartridge, the Sioux grabbed the gun and struck at the Pawnee with his knife. The Pawnee was able to pin the Sioux to the ground, where he held him until the other two scouts came to his aid. One of the Pawnees put his gun against the Indian's side and pulled the trigger. The gun went off, but the bullet hit only the ground. Seeing that he had missed, the Pawnee immediately ran for his horse, shouting to his comrades that the bullet had bounced off the Sioux's body and the man was a "medicine man" who could not be killed. Upon hearing this, Loo ree wah ka we rah rick soo, who was holding the Sioux to the ground, let him go and was promptly slashed by the knife. The Sioux then grabbed the Pawnee's gun and Major North's horse and rode away.

The incident reveals the role of belief in the supernatural in Pawnee warfare. But what happened next is also significant. When the three Pawnees reported the incident, North chastised them severely for their "superstition." He then mounted another horse and started in pursuit of the Indian himself. After a brief chase, North killed the Indian with two shots from his rifle. He announced to his men that the Sioux's "medicine" had been merely luck, and their foolishness had allowed the man to escape. North believed he had effectively dispelled his men's superstition, but certain ideas die hard. It seems more likely that the Pawnees saw in North's act confirmation that the major himself was protected by some higher power.[17]

In 1928, Ruling His Sun gave a slightly different account of this event in his deposition in support of his pension application:

> Now while I was a soldier a foreign Indian, a Sioux or a Cheyenne was found scouting around camp and one of our soldiers started after him on Major North's horse and finally the foreign Indian got the horse and [raced] off and other Pawnees shot his horse from under him and killed the Indian. This foreign Indian had already stabbed our Indian that started after him. The one that got stabbed was in my company and he was Loo ree wah ka we rah rick soo (Whatever he says is the Truth—translated). After they caught this hostile Indian there was one of our men helped and we called him Co rux rah roo coo (Acts Like a Bear).[18]

Ruling His Sun's account poses a slight problem of chronology. As far as the records tell us, Ruling His Sun served as a scout in 1868, not in 1869, when, according to Luther North, this incident took place. Although Ruling His Sun gave his account sixty years after the event occurred, it might have been Luther North who was mistaken. One piece of evidence in support of this event's having taken place in 1868 rather than 1869 is that Frank North never mentioned it in his 1869 diary. Regrettably, in old age Luther frequently confused dates, people, and events.

In 1935, Pawnee historian Mark Evarts gave ethnographer Gene Weltfish yet a third account of the incident involving Frank North's horse. According to Evarts, the men involved were a Chawi named Karituhuiwu and a Kitkahaki named Pakixtsaks ("Shot-Throat"). Both men were considered among the bravest in the tribe. They had a friendly competition going in which they occasionally took turns whipping each other, in order to show that they could take the beatings like men and not get angry at each other. Both were serving as scouts when the event with Major North's horse took place, and Shot-Throat was one of the scouts who went in pursuit of the Sioux. The scouts were unable to overtake the Sioux, except for the scout who was riding North's horse. After a short wrestling match, the Pawnee was able to pin the knife-carrying Sioux to the ground. Unable to let go without being stabbed, the Pawnee waited for help. During the duel the Sioux bit the scout's finger, and the scout bit the Sioux's head to make him drop the knife.

After a while the Pawnee, who was the smaller of the two, began to tire. At this point Shot-Throat appeared. Surprisingly, he did not help the other scout but simply went away again. Finally, the Pawnee who had pinned the Sioux had to release his grip and was summarily stabbed in the thigh. The Sioux escaped on North's horse. A few scouts eventually managed to kill him after shooting North's horse first. North was not upset, saying that it was a government horse and not his own that had been killed. Shot-Throat's inexplicable behavior, however, did not go unpunished. After hearing what had transpired, Karituhuiwu blamed Shot-Throat for what had happened to the third scout. Karituhuiwu told Shot-Throat that although Shot-Throat might whip him, his friend and competitor, bravely enough, "when it comes to a Sioux you do nothing." Karituhuiwu later beat Shot-Throat severely on several occasions, until one of the chiefs thought he would kill him. The chief called both men to his lodge, invited them to a feast, and told them to stop fighting. The two men agreed and never fought each other again.[19]

On May 19 the men of Company B received their pay. Two days later, on May 21, the paymaster arrived at Fort McPherson, and the next morning the remaining Pawnees received their pay. Frank North and the captains of the different companies oversaw the payment. The men were pleased and spent the rest of the day enjoying themselves. "After dinner we pitched horse shoes," North wrote in his diary, "and raised ned Generaly."[20]

So far, little of interest had happened, but trouble was brewing on the western plains. Some Cheyenne bands were ready to resume their war against the United States. In 1868 they had attacked settlements all along the western frontier. During the battle of Beecher's Island, for example, they had besieged a company of U.S. soldiers under Major (Brevet Colonel) George A. Forsyth for several days.[21] Among the Indians present at the Beecher's Island fight was Tall Bull's band of Dog Soldiers. The Dog Soldiers (or Hotamitaniu) were a band of ferocious fighters, best known for their reckless bravery during battle.[22]

In retaliation for the attack on Forsyth's troops at Beecher's Island and other depredations, Major General Philip H. Sheridan, commander of the Military Division of the Missouri, ordered Lieutenant Colonel George

Armstrong Custer on a winter campaign against the Cheyennes.[23] In November 1868 Custer's troops surprised the Cheyennes at their camp on the Washita River in present-day Oklahoma. During the battle the soldiers killed a large number of Indians, including Chief Black Kettle. Custer's winter campaign, which ended in April 1869, was only partially successful, however.[24] The Cheyennes under Black Kettle's successor, Little Robe, favored peace and wished to settle with Little Raven's Arapahos near Camp Supply, Oklahoma.[25] The Dog Soldiers, under Tall Bull (Hotu'a e hka'ash tait) and White Horse, refused to make peace. They vowed revenge for Custer's attack on the Cheyenne camp at the Washita and planned to travel north to join the Northern Cheyennes and Red Cloud's Sioux. While in camp near the Republican River in Kansas, they were joined by Sioux under Pawnee Killer, Little Wound, and Whistler. Soon the camp numbered around five hundred warriors.[26]

Before the Dog Soldiers could make their big strike, they ran into the Fifth Cavalry, under the command of Major (Brevet Major General) Eugene Asa Carr, on May 13, 1869.[27] Carr's troops were on their way from Fort Lyon, Colorado, to Fort McPherson, Nebraska, when they discovered Tall Bull's village near Beaver Creek. In the battle that followed, four soldiers died and three were wounded. Carr estimated the Indian losses at twenty-five dead and fifty wounded. Three days later Carr's troops fought another skirmish with the Dog Soldiers. He attempted to follow the Cheyennes, but when they scattered in all directions over the prairie, he was forced to abandon the pursuit.[28] The battle at Beaver Creek only infuriated the Dog Soldiers and their allies even more. In revenge, they attacked white settlements in western Kansas. On May 21 they killed four Scandinavian farmers at White Rock Creek. In the following days they also killed ten hunters before striking farms in the area. On May 28 a party of thirty Cheyennes attacked seven railroad workers near Fossil Creek Station and derailed two trains. Two days later Cheyenne war parties raided a number of German and Scandinavian homesteads on Spillman Creek. They killed nine settlers and took several captives. One of the captives, Maria Weichell, watched helplessly while the Dog Soldiers took her husband's scalp and fingers. The other captives were Susanna Alderice and her baby.[29]

The attacks caused panic among the western settlements in Kansas and Nebraska, but there was some confusion about the identity of the tribe responsible for the attacks. According to some reports, the raiders had been Pawnees. Once again the bad reputation of the Pawnees made them suspects for raids committed by others. Fortunately for the Pawnees, the identity of the actual perpetrators was soon established.

Newspapers in Kansas and Nebraska demanded action against the hostiles. Governor Harvey of Kansas quickly organized the state militia and traveled to Fort Leavenworth to request the assistance of Major General John M. Schofield. Schofield, who had recently succeeded Philip Sheridan as commander of the Department of the Missouri, immediately ordered Lieutenant Colonel Custer and his Seventh Cavalry into the field. But Custer had little success locating the Indians.[30] Governor David Butler of Nebraska, meanwhile, contacted General Augur of the Department of the Platte in Omaha, requesting troops or, if these were unavailable, ammunition, subsistence, and transportation for one hundred men.[31]

Brigadier General Augur did more than send a company of soldiers. On June 7 he ordered Carr to lead an expedition to the Republican River to intercept the Dog Soldiers. Carr received orders to leave Fort McPherson on the morning of June 9 with eight companies of the Fifth Cavalry. Accompanying the troops would be two companies of Pawnee scouts, totaling one hundred men. Two other companies of the Fifth Cavalry would rendezvous with his command twenty days later at Thickwood Creek. The objective of the mission was to "clear the Republican Territory of Indians." "All Indians found in that country," the order continued, "will be treated as hostile, unless they submit themselves as ready and willing to go to the proper reservation. In that event, you will disarm them, and require such hostages and guarantees of their good faith as you deem fully satisfactory."[32]

Carr was not thrilled with the assignment. He complained of shortages of men, horses, equipment, and supplies. His companies were only half full, and because he had never commanded Indians before, he was skeptical of the usefulness of the Pawnee scouts. But he could rely on some experienced officers, such as Major William Bedford Royall and Major Eugene W. Crittenden. Carr also insisted that William Frederick Cody, better known as Buffalo Bill, be retained as chief of scouts of the command.[33] Several frontiersmen, such as James E. Welch, also joined the command as volunteers.[34]

On June 8 General Augur and some of his staff members arrived at Fort McPherson to witness a full-dress parade by Carr's troops, including the Pawnees. The companies of the Fifth Cavalry, dressed in crisp blue and yellow uniforms, went through the drill with great precision and discipline. The Pawnees had been issued cavalry uniforms for the occasion, but when they appeared in front of the distinguished audience, they turned out in all sorts of styles. Some wore their overcoats; others did not. Although they had been issued army pantaloons, many wore only breechcloths. A few had turned their pantaloons into leggings by cutting out the seats. To the people attending the parade, their ranks presented a sad lack of uniformity in dress.[35]

Still, the Pawnees performed well during the drill. "They were well mounted," William Cody recalled, "and felt proud of the fact that they were regular United States soldiers." Later that evening they held a dance in preparation for the upcoming campaign. Many of the officers' wives attended the dance. The scouts put on quite a show. Cody, too, was impressed. Of all the Indians he had ever seen, the Pawnees were "the most accomplished dancers."[36]

The parade must have made a good impression on General Augur and the other officers in attendance, because Frank North received instructions to recruit a third company of scouts at the Pawnee Agency that same day. North placed his brother in charge of companies A and B and traveled to Columbus with Lieutenant Fred Matthews. They arrived early in the morning the next day. That afternoon, at the Pawnee Agency, they enlisted Company C. The men in this company were primarily Skiris. North appointed Captain James Murie as company commander. The next day the new recruits were mustered into service. After obtaining horses, North and his troops boarded a train for Fort Kearny, where they drew clothing, tents, guns, and other supplies. On the morning of June 15 they left Fort Kearny and proceeded south to join Major Carr's command.[37]

Carr's troops had left Fort McPherson on the morning of Wednesday, June 9. While the troops rode out of the fort, the regimental band played. The song "The Girl I Left Behind Me" was traditionally played on such occasions. The two companies of Pawnee scouts rode in advance of the cavalry troops. Fifty-four wagons, manned by civilian teamsters and wagoners, formed the supply train.[38] From the start the expedition was plagued by problems. The weather was unpredictable. Some days were intensely hot, and on others, torrential rainstorms hampered the troops' progress. After a few days on the trail, the mules were already exhausted. Many teamsters were drunk, and one of the officers, Captain Jeremiah C. Denney, whose wife had died recently, suffered a complete mental breakdown and had to be sent back to the fort, where he eventually committed suicide.[39] The heat and the strains of the march also took their toll on the scouts' horses. Two scouts lost their mounts while crossing the Platte River, and another lost his horse somewhere else. These men were now dismounted and may have had to follow the expedition on foot.[40]

Scouting operations began on June 12. Small units of Pawnees accompanied cavalry detachments in search of hostiles or went out on scouts of their own. One scouting party, under Second Lieutenant William J. Volkmar, discovered a small group of about twenty Cheyenne hunters on the first day, but they disappeared before the troops could attack. After news of the discovery reached his camp, Carr ordered one of his companies and a group of Pawnees in pursuit. In their eagerness to overtake the Cheyennes, two scouts ran their horses to death. By the time the scouts arrived, the enemy had scattered in different directions.[41]

On June 15 the command set up camp at the Republican River near Prairie Dog Creek. The Pawnees, under Captains North and Cushing, built their camp half a mile below that of the cavalry. The wagon train was situated between the Pawnees and the cavalry camp. The wagon boss sent the mules to a green pasture across the river to graze, and two teamsters guarded the herd. While the Pawnees were eating their supper, they suddenly heard a war whoop across the river. A party of seven Cheyennes attacked the two teamsters guarding the mule herd. One of them was killed instantly; the other was shot through the body with an arrow and died later that night. Before the soldiers realized what was happening, the Pawnees had shed their uniforms and rushed to their horses in pursuit of the Cheyennes. In the running fight that ensued, the Pawnees killed two Cheyennes and recaptured the mule herd. The other Cheyennes were able to escape under the cover of darkness.[42]

The following day, Luther North reported to Major Carr. North expected praise for the prompt action of his men, who had saved the mule herd and thereby prevented a premature end to the campaign. Instead, Carr reprimanded him in front of all the other officers. The major believed he had good reasons to criticize the actions of the young captain. By rushing after the Cheyennes, he had exposed himself to a possible enemy ambush, and he had left the wagon camp exposed to a hostile attack. Although the North brothers generally had their scouts under control, when under attack or when the enemy was near it became increasingly difficult to restrain them.[43]

North did not appreciate the general's reprimand and responded that when Indians attacked his camp he intended to go for them and would not wait for orders from the general "or any other man." After speaking his mind, North spurred his pony and returned to his company. Faced with this insubordination, Carr promptly placed Captain Cushing in command of the Pawnees.[44]

Cushing did not command the two companies of scouts for long. On Thursday, June 17, Frank North and the Skiris of Company C joined Carr's troops after a long and difficult march.[45] North brought with him some instructions from Colonel George D. Ruggles, assistant adjutant general of the Department of the Platte. Ruggles ordered Carr to detach Captain Robert Sweatman's Company B, which was to proceed to the Little Blue River to cover and protect settlements there. Carr was not pleased with the order. "It is very disheartening to me for my command to be reduced," he wrote in his day report. "It was already too small (companies not half full) and there are a good many men whose terms will soon expire." Carr was not happy to see these troops replaced by Pawnees. Not only were the Pawnees miserably mounted, but Carr also found his scouts "rather lazy and shiftless." He reported that their knowledge of the country was "vague and general" and that he would like to exchange all but "thirty of them for good cavalry soldiers."[46]

On June 18 Carr moved camp one mile and then sent out scouting parties. The events of June 15, when the Pawnees had recklessly "endangered" themselves and the command, prompted him to make sure that "each scouting party was made up of both a group of Pawnees and one or two companies of cavalry." Clearly, the major had little confidence in the Pawnees.[47] Over the next few days the Pawnees went on several scouts of the area but found no sign of the enemy. Occasionally, the scouts and the rest of the troops entertained themselves by hunting or riding bucking horses.[48] On June 23 the Pawnees demonstrated their hunting skills when they surrounded and slaughtered a small herd of buffalo. Not to be outdone, William Cody mounted his horse and joined the hunt. In less than a half-mile run he dropped thirty-six buffalo. The Pawnees were impressed. "They called me 'Big Chief,'" Cody wrote later, "and thereafter I had a high place in their esteem."[49]

After the hunt Major North scribbled in his diary that the men had "killed lots of buffalo [and] had lots of ribs." During the chase Luther North had lost his pocketbook, with $95 in it, when his horse tried to buck him. He searched the area where he believed it happened, but had to give up. One of the scouts, however, remembered where the horse had tried to throw the captain. After dinner the scout guided Major North and his brother to the place, and within minutes the money was found. "How he could have remembered just where it was I do not know," Luther North later wrote, "for I had ridden back and forth over the hill for half an hour before I had gone to camp and couldn't find the place."[50]

So far the expedition had proceeded without major incident. But on Thursday, June 24, one of the scouts of Company B accidentally shot himself in the leg. The next day another scout accidentally shot himself in the hand. According to Luther North, the bullet entered the man's wrist, breaking the bones, then went up his arm and exited near the elbow. The army surgeon, Dr. Louis S. Tesson, attended him, but when the wound got worse, the doctor said he would have to amputate the arm. The scout adamantly refused to have his arm taken off. On June 30 Major North sent the two wounded men home with a wagon train from Fort McPherson. The wound of the scout who had been shot in the arm was in serious condition—according to Luther North, "badly swollen and full of maggots." The scout returned to the Pawnee reservation, where a medicine man attended to him. When North returned to the agency later that fall, he was surprised to learn that the arm had healed except for a slight stiffness of the wrist.[51]

The weather and the hardship of the march caused much sickness among the men on the expedition. In his report of June 30 to Colonel George Ruggles, Carr complained that "at one time our two ambulances overflowed so that a sick Officer could not find a place. We should have three Ambulances with the command and one with the train escort."[52]

Among the sick were some of the noncommissioned officers of the Pawnee battalion. In his diary, Major North recorded that Second Sergeant George Lehman and Captain James Murie were quite ill.[53]

The wagon train that arrived from Fort McPherson on June 29 brought some relief in the form of fresh food supplies. "[We] will live high again for a while," Major North wrote in his diary. Carr took advantage of the occasion to muster and inspect the troops and write his report to Colonel Ruggles.[54] In the report, Carr observed, "I think the Pawnees are improving somewhat in discipline and general usefulness; and [I] hope to get good service out of them."[55] Still, problems with discipline occasionally arose. On July 6 Major North punished two of his men for "disobeying the q. m. [quartermaster]." Both men were ordered to march on foot for ten miles. The identity of these two men cannot be determined with certainty, but perhaps one of them was First Sergeant Sam Wallace, and the other might have been Barton Hunt, a teamster. Both men belonged to Company B of the scouts.[56]

On Saturday morning, July 3, Major North sent out ten Pawnees under Sergeant Wallace on a scout. When the party returned later that day, the men reported that they had found a fresh trail.[57] They estimated that the Cheyenne camp consisted of about 160 to 200 tepees, or about 400 warriors.[58] This was the most promising news since the start of the campaign. The following morning, Major Carr ordered Major William B. Royall and three companies to pursue the lead. Lieutenant Gus Becher, Lieutenant George D. Barclay, and fifty scouts accompanied the troops. Royall's orders were simple: "to surprise [the enemy], kill as many warriors as possible and capture their families and animals." On July 5 the Pawnees in Royall's party spotted twelve Cheyennes carrying a wounded warrior on a stretcher. The wounded Cheyenne was Howling Magpie, who reportedly had been shot through both thighs. The Pawnees did not wait for orders from Royall but immediately gave chase. In the fight that followed, they took three scalps and captured eight horses. One of the Cheyennes killed was Howling Magpie. His two cousins, Shave Head and Little Man, refused to abandon him and were also killed. Sergeant Co rux te chod ish ("Mad Bear") killed two of the Cheyennes.[59]

Upon their return from the scout on July 7, Becher's scouts rushed into camp announcing their victory and displaying the scalps they had taken in the fight. In typical Pawnee fashion, the scouts discharged their guns in celebration. Their sudden appearance and the sound of screaming Indians and discharging guns caused a stir among the sentries on duty, who subsequently called the alarm. Fortunately, the Pawnees were recognized, and the scare ended in cheers.[60] Major North was pleased. He gave six of the captured horses to the scouts and returned two horses with cavalry brands on them to the army. "I am in hopes we can find the small village in a few days," North wrote in his diary. That night the scouts celebrated with a victory dance.[61]

Major Carr was less pleased. He was certain that the surviving Cheyennes would alert the other Indians. Nevertheless, he decided to push on. "I had little hope of overtaking the Indians," he wrote later, "but thought I could at least hunt them out of the country."[62]

The next day, July 8, the column marched back up the North Fork of the Republican River. One small platoon, under the command of Corporal John Kyle of Company M, was searching for some stray horses when it was attacked by a party of Indians. The men escaped unharmed but lost one horse in the skirmish.[63] The rest of the command went into camp after a fifteen-mile march. At eleven o'clock that night, gunfire awoke the sleeping men of the command. Five Cheyenne warriors charged into the camp, whooping and shouting and shooting their guns in an attempt to stampede the horse herd.[64] One of the Pawnee scouts, Sergeant Co rux te chod ish, ran out after a Cheyenne who had been thrown from his horse. As Co rux te chod ish was about to overtake and count coup on the Indian, he was accidentally wounded by a bullet fired by one of the soldiers. Luckily, his injury was not serious. Major Carr wrote in his final report that Co rux te chod ish deserved special mention for his action that night "and also for killing two of those killed by [Major] Royalls [sic] command."[65]

Although the raid made it clear that the Cheyennes were aware of the troops' presence, it was also clear that the trail was getting warmer. Carr now pushed his men even harder in a desperate attempt to overtake the Dog Soldiers. On July 9 he directed his men northward and back to the place where Major Royall had battled the Cheyennes two days earlier. It was his last chance to make contact with the Cheyenne camp. "Marched 30 miles without water and oh how hot and dry," wrote Major North; "we have poor water nothing but standing rain water." The next day the men broke camp at six in the morning and traveled thirty-five miles. They were gaining rapidly on the Indians. Along the trail they discovered prints of a woman's shoe, which confirmed that the trail belonged to the Indians of Tall Bull's Dog Soldier camp. Before the soldiers could rest their weary bodies, Carr assembled his command and gave his orders for the next day. "I took all available men, that is, all those, whose horses were fit for service," he wrote later, "and they amounted to two hundred and forty-four (244) officers and soldiers, and fifty (50) Pawnees out of seven companies 5th Cavalry and one hundred and fifty Pawnees."[66]

While Carr's command moved north, Tall Bull moved his camp to the South Platte River, stopping at a place called Summit Springs in Colorado Territory. When the Dog Soldier band reached the river, the water was so high that they were compelled to lie in camp waiting for the flood to subside. As a precautionary measure, Tall Bull sent scouts south to locate the soldiers. He also sent Two Crows and five other Cheyennes up the Platte to find a place where the river could be forded safely. Two Crows and his men returned later that evening, having found a place where they could cross the river and marked it with sticks. A Sioux war party also came in that night and reported that the troops were following the trail. Upon hearing this news, the Sioux under Pawnee Killer, Whistler, and Two Strikes decided to cross the river immediately. Tall Bull, however, believed the Dog Soldier camp was safe for the moment and decided to stay there. The reason Tall Bull thought the band was safe is unclear. According to First Lieutenant George F. Price of the Fifth Cavalry, the Dog Soldiers remained in camp at the suggestion of a medicine man. According to one historian, Tall Bull trusted that Carr's cavalry would follow the trail of a decoy party he had sent out. Luther North believed the Cheyennes had seen the soldiers turn toward Fort McPherson and assumed that they were heading back to the fort. Whatever the reason, subsequent generations of Cheyennes, wrote George Bent later, "say it was poor judgment for Tall Bull to insist in going into camp instead of crossing the South Platte that evening."[67]

Around 5:30 in the morning on July 11, Carr set out from his camp with his command, including 150 Pawnee scouts under Major North, and three days' worth of rations. The wagon train followed as fast as it could, escorted by Company M and a handful of scouts.[68] During the morning there were two reports of Indians ahead. Carr ordered the gallop, but when they reached the "hostiles," they turned out to be only wild horses. When the troops reached Platte Bluffs, the Pawnees reported seeing two horsemen. On their advice, Carr led the entire command through a ravine to escape detection. There the trail of the hostile camp divided into two. A heavy trail went left, and a lighter trail turned right, toward the South Platte River. Carr believed the heavy trail was designed to mislead the troops and decided to follow the lighter trail toward the river, in the belief that the Indians needed water just as badly as his own command.[69]

As the command struggled through heavy sand, two scouting parties came in. One reported the presence of mounted Indians to the left. The other reported having seen a herd of animals in a valley near the stream to the right. Carr detached three companies under Major Royall and William Cody to move toward the herd while he took the remaining troops, including the Pawnees, along the main trail.[70] Shortly thereafter, some scouts reported that they had seen some tepees apparently belonging to the Cheyenne village. Carr immediately dispatched a messenger to Royall with orders to send a company to reinforce his command. Then he ordered the gallop. The horses struggled through the loose sand for an hour. They had had no water since morning and were becoming exhausted. Carr doubted he would ever overtake the Cheyenne village. Around two o'clock that afternoon the members of a Pawnee advance party beckoned Carr to follow them, pointing to a herd of animals about four miles away. Carr, who had received several false reports earlier that day, thought the herd was probably buffalo, but he determined to see for himself anyway. The Pawnees began to strip themselves for the fight. They unsaddled their horses and took off as much of their clothing "as could be dispensed with and still leave something to distinguish them from the hostiles." According to volunteer James Welch, the scouts also daubed their faces with paint.[71]

While Carr's command prepared for battle, Major Royall returned with his troops. He had traveled twenty miles but found no Indians. Royall's men joined Carr's command and rapidly proceeded in the direction of the village at Summit Springs, taking advantage of depressions, ravines, and sand hills to remain undetected. When they came within a mile of the village, Carr halted his troops and ordered the battle formation. According to Lieutenant George H. Price, the regimental historian, who was present during the battle, Carr placed Captain Leicester Walker's Company H on the left column and Price's own Company A on the right column. It was their task to attack the flanks of the Cheyenne village and cut off its escape routes. The center column, meanwhile, consisted of Company D, under the command of Captain Samuel S. Sumner, Company C, under Captain Thomas E. Maley, and the Pawnee scouts, under Major North, who occupied the left flank of the center column. Carr and Royall, meanwhile, followed the advance columns with companies E and G, which were held in reserve to reinforce the troops ahead if necessary. Carr placed Major Eugene Crittenden in command of the front line and then sounded the charge.[72]

It was now around three o'clock in the afternoon on July 11, 1869. The companies on the front line charged toward the Cheyenne village at full speed.[73] Carr's line, with the tired ponies of companies E and G, followed at gallop pace. The lines were stretched longer as tired horses fell behind. The attack was made from the northwest and came as a complete surprise to the Dog Soldiers. Most of the Cheyennes were eating their midday meal when Carr's troops appeared on the horizon. From that point soldiers had to cover almost a mile before they reached the village. Little Hawk, one of the Cheyennes, who was riding some distance from the camp, first discovered the troops. He tried to reach the village to warn his friends, but his horse was too slow and the Pawnees reached the village before he did. Little Hawk survived the battle, however, and escaped with a number of other Cheyennes. A Cheyenne boy who was tending horses tried to drive the herd back to the village to warn the Indians and provide their escape, but he died in a volley of gunfire from the charging troops. "No braver man ever lived," Captain Luther North wrote later, "than that fifteen-year-old boy."[74]

The Pawnees reached the village ahead of the troops. Among them were some of the men who many years later described their role in the fight when they applied for pensions, such as John Box (Red Fox), Eli Shotwell (Flying Hawk Whistling), High Eagle (Bear), Billy Osborne (Brave Hawk), Robert Taylor (Riding Stolen Horse), Peter Wood, and Dog Chief.[75] Like the other scouts, they had stripped for the fight, and although they could not see the village, they charged ahead at full speed in the direction of the Cheyenne horse herd. When they reached the next ridge, they spotted the village to their left and in front of them and let out their war cry.[76]

The sudden appearance of the Pawnees and the troops caused a panic among the Cheyennes. As soon as they heard the shots, they ran from their lodges to catch their horses before they stampeded. Lieutenant Price's company, which approached the village from the left, succeeded in killing seven warriors and capturing three hundred horses. Captain Walker's right-flank advance to the village, however, was blocked by a ravine, which delayed his progress and allowed a number of Indians to escape.[77] Those Cheyenne men who had horses quickly mounted the women and children and, as they tried to escape, stayed behind to hold off the soldiers and the Pawnees. They put up a brave fight. Two Crows, one of the Cheyenne Dog Soldiers, saw his friend Lone Bear charge again and again into a party of Pawnees who were chasing the fleeing Indians. Lone Bear went down "fighting like a wild animal."[78] James Welch, one of the white volunteers, chased a mounted Indian and shot him through the head. The Indian's name was "Pretty Bear"—a Cheyenne chief, according to Welch. "The Pawnees knew him," Welch later recalled, "and were anxious to secure his scalp, which I was glad to give them as I soon as became disgusted with the ghastly trophy."[79]

Tall Bull, seeing that all was lost, put one of his wives and a daughter on a horse. The woman begged him to escape with her, but Tall Bull "shut his ears" and then killed his own horse, choosing to die in the fight.[80] He led some of his men and his two other wives into a small ravine with sharp, high banks, from where they held off the Pawnees and the troops. Among the Indians in the ravine with the Dog Soldier leader were Powder Chief, his Sioux wife, and his son, Black Moon. Big Gip and his wife also followed Tall Bull into the ravine. A young Dog Soldier named Wolf With Plenty Of Hair staked himself out with a "dog rope" at the head of the ravine, signaling that he would fight there to the death. All of them were killed.[81]

A great deal of controversy has existed over who killed Tall Bull. Luther North claimed that his brother, Major Frank North, killed the chief with a shot to the head.[82] William Cody also claimed the dubious honor and for many years reenacted the scene in his Wild West Show.[83] According to James Welch, Tall Bull was killed by Lieutenant George Mason, "who rode up to him and shot him through the heart with a derringer."[84] In 1901 Major Carr claimed that Sergeant Daniel McGrath had killed the chief.[85]

Strangely, none of these accounts took into consideration the possibility that a Pawnee might have killed the chief of the Dog Soldiers. Although no Pawnee stepped forward to claim credit for the killing, the fact remains that the Pawnees were the first to reach the village, and according to the Cheyennes, they "did most of the killing [and] captured the greater part of the pony herd."[86] Furthermore, in a letter written to William F. Cody in 1906, Carr mentioned that one of Tall Bull's wives had told him that the Pawnees killed her husband in the fight. Unfortunately, Carr's testimony cannot be relied upon, because on other occasions he credited Cody and Sergeant McGrath, respectively, with the deed.[87]

There seems to be less disagreement over what happened to Tall Bull after he was struck by the fatal bullet. According to one account, High Eagle, one of the Pawnee scouts, took Tall Bull's scalp during the fight. After the removal of the Pawnee tribe to Indian Territory in the mid-1870s, High Eagle sold the scalp to Gordon W. Lillie ("Pawnee Bill") for his museum in the town of Pawnee, Oklahoma.[88]

The Pawnees played an important role in the battle of Summit Springs. Only volunteer James Welch was unimpressed with their fighting qualities. "The Pawnees," he wrote later, "did not fight well. They skulked and killed the women and children."[89] Several daring feats by Pawnees, however, clearly refute Welch's view of their conduct during the fight. Sergeant Co rux ah kah wah de—Traveling Bear—for example, charged into the canyon where Tall Bull and his warriors had made their last stand. A few moments later he returned with four scalps.[90] Carr, who had previously called the Pawnees "lazy and shiftless," reevaluated his impression of them after the fight. "The Pawnees under Major Frank North," he wrote in his official report of the expedition, "were of the greatest service to us in the campaign. This is the first time since coming west that we have been supplied with Indian scouts—and the result has shown their value."[91]

The victory seemed complete. According to Carr's report, the soldiers had killed 52 Indians, destroyed 84 lodges, and captured 17 women and children, as well as 274 horses and 144 mules. Furthermore, they captured an enormous quantity of supplies from the Cheyennes, including 56 rifles, 22 revolvers, 50 pounds of gunpowder, 20 pounds of bullets, 8 lead bars, 14 bullet molds, 12,000 percussion caps, 17 sabers, 9 lances, and 20 tomahawks. "The above material," wrote Carr, "will materially reduce their means of killing white people."[92]

Apart from guns and ammunition, Carr's command captured 9,300 pounds of dried meat, clothes (moccasins, women's dresses, 690 buffalo robes, etc.), 75 lodge skins, 361 saddles, and 319 raw hides, as well as $1,500 in cash and many other things. Besides the articles captured, Carr concluded that "at least ten (10) tons of various Indian property, such as clothing, flour, coffee, corn meal, saddle equipments, fancy articles, etc. [were] destroyed by the command before leaving the camp, by burning." He noted that 160 fires were burning to destroy the Indians' property. The troops also found silverware, photographs, and other goods stolen by the Indians during their raids in Kansas, as well as numerous scalps and a necklace of human fingers.[93]

Two white captives were discovered in the camp. Major North, as he stopped for a drink during the battle, discovered Maria Weichell crawling from a tipi, bleeding from a bullet wound through her breast. A short while later some men found the other captive, Susanna Alderice, who had been shot and struck in the head with a tomahawk by one of Tall Bull's wives. Both women had been mistreated during their captivity. Both were pregnant after having been raped repeatedly. They had been abused by Tall Bull's wives, who were jealous because he had kept both of them in his lodges. The Cheyennes had killed Susanna's baby three days after her capture. Its continued crying reportedly "annoyed them so much that they wrung its head off and threw the several parts of its body into a stream beside which they were camped."

Susanna Alderice did not survive her injuries; she died shortly after the soldiers found her. The day after the battle, on July 12, a funeral service was held for her. The soldiers wrapped her body in lodge skins and buffalo robes and buried her at the site of the battlefield. They left at the grave a wooden headboard with an inscription stating what was known of her. After the battle, the soldiers, including the Pawnees, donated most of the money they had retrieved from the Cheyenne camp ($845.35 and four twenty-dollar gold pieces) to Maria Weichell, who recovered from her injuries.[94]

The American losses were negligible. One soldier received a slight wound from an arrow. The Pawnee scouts, who had led the charge and had been in the thick of the fight, had a few wounded men. Billy Osborne, who had enlisted under the name Koot tah we coots oo la ri e coots ("Brave Hawk"), was injured on his right side and chest when his horse fell on him.[95] La tah cots too ri ha ("Good Eagle") injured his hip in the battle. Although the injury was not serious enough to keep him from enlisting again in 1870, it would cause him to limp later in life.[96] High Eagle suffered a serious injury on one of his legs just above the knee.[97] Undoubtedly there were more scouts who, in addition to the usual nicks and bruises, suffered more serious injuries. But because they preferred to be treated by their own Indian doctors, no formal records of their injuries exist in the army's medical files.

The battle had been hard on the horses. Although the Cheyennes had killed only one cavalry horse, twelve others had died of exhaustion during the charge. The other horses belonging to the command were in such poor condition that Carr decided to march the men to Fort Sedgwick, the nearest military post. On Monday, July 12, he set out for the fort. After a brief march, the command made camp at the South Platte River some sixty-five miles from Fort Sedgwick. Carr sent Second Sergeant George Lehman and ten men to the fort with dispatches recounting the recent victory. Three days later, on Thursday, July 15, the exhausted troops finally reached the fort.[98]

At Sedgwick, Carr wrote his final report on the expedition. "It is a source of extreme gratification to the 5th Cavalry that, after all our hardships and exposures for ten months in the field, we have at last met with an undisputed success. . . . I have, as usual, to express my obligations to the officers and soldiers of my command for their energy, activity and cheerful endurance of hardships."[99] Among the men who received honorable mention in his report was Sergeant Co rux te chod ish ("Mad Bear"), for his prompt action during the Cheyenne night raid on July 8. On Carr's recommendation, Congress awarded Mad Bear the Medal of Honor on August 24, 1869. The official citation read, "Ran out from command in pursuit of a dismounted Indian; was shot down and badly wounded by a bullet from his own command."[100] According to Luther North, Carr accidentally awarded the medal to the wrong man. In his letters and memoirs, the captain insisted that Carr had intended to award the medal to Sergeant Co rux ah kah wah de, or Traveling Bear, for his brave action during the battle at Summit Springs, when he entered the ravine in pursuit of four Cheyennes, whom he subsequently killed and scalped. According to Captain North, his brother corrected the "error" by presenting the medal to Traveling Bear after all. If this was the case, the medal did go to the wrong man, although Sergeant Traveling Bear was certainly deserving of the honor.[101] However, Jeff Broome, author of a book about the Summit Springs battle, discovered a letter from the Pawnee Agency, dated September 29, that bears Co rux te chod ish's mark acknowledging receipt of the medal.[102]

At Fort Sedgwick, Major North divided the spoils of the battle among his men. On July 16 he awarded some of the captured horses to scouts who had distinguished themselves in the fight. At Sedgwick the scouts also received their pay. Over the next few days the Pawnees entertained themselves with horse races and other games. The races were intended to select the best and fastest horses. Avid gamblers, the Pawnees raised $300 to run one of their horses against William Cody's best horse. Unfortunately for the Pawnees, their horse lost.[103]

The campaign against the Sioux and Cheyennes did not end with the arrival of the troops at Fort Sedgwick. Carr planned to continue his search for the Indians as soon as his men and horses had recovered from the long march. Some of the escaped Cheyennes apparently had gone north, and the major intended another expedition to the Platte to flush them out. Furthermore, although Carr might not have been aware of it at the time, Pawnee Killer and Whistler's band of Sioux were still roaming the area. But Carr would not lead the follow-up campaign. A personal tragedy intervened. On July 25 he received a telegram from his wife with the news that his five-month-old son, George Oscar, had died suddenly. After turning over his command to Major Royall, the grief-stricken Carr boarded a train for St. Louis. Responsibility for the follow-up expedition rested now on the shoulders of Major Royall.[104]

Royall received orders "to find the trail of the refugees of the Battle of Summit Springs, if possible, and to kill any hostiles encountered." His command consisted of companies C, D, F, G, H, I, and L of the Fifth Cavalry, as well as the Pawnee battalion. William F. Cody again accompanied the expedition as guide. The command left the fort on August 2 in the direction of the Republican River.[105] Frank North was not present when Royall's command left Fort Sedgwick. A few days earlier he had traveled to Columbus to assist in the investigation of the murder of a white man named Edward McMurtry, whose bloated body had been found in a pond on an island in the Platte River on June 20, 1869. As in the incidents earlier that year, settlers pointed to the Pawnees as perpetrators of the crime. The case was of special interest to Major North because one of the accused was a former Pawnee scout named Blue Hawk, who had served with North in 1867. The investigation and subsequent trial would drag on for years, until the charges were eventually dropped. North soon returned to join his command during Royall's follow-up operations in Kansas and Nebraska.[106]

After traveling ten miles on August 2, some Pawnee scouts reported that they had discovered a small party of Indians five miles to the south. Royall ordered Captain Leicester Walker's Company H and fifty Pawnee scouts to investigate. Walker discovered a large Indian party and immediately dispatched a Pawnee scout to the army's camp requesting reinforcements. Royall sent Captain Samuel Sumner's Company D and the remaining Pawnee scouts to support Walker. The Indians belonged to a group of Oglalas under Pawnee Killer, augmented by refugees from Tall Bull's Dog Soldier camp. A skirmish between the troops and the small party of Sioux and Cheyennes followed. But this group was a decoy party. As soon as the Indians in the large camp received word that the soldiers and Pawnee scouts were near, they burned their lodges and fled in all directions. The decoy party lured the troops away and secured the villagers' safe escape. There were no casualties. The troops returned to camp later that night.[107]

The next day, August 3, Royall continued the pursuit of the escaping Indians. The trail led toward the head of Frenchman Creek. The Pawnee scouts found many dropped skins and green lodge poles, indicating that some of the fleeing Indians had indeed belonged to Tall Bull's camp; they had been making new lodges to replace those destroyed at Summit Springs. The Indians traveled lightly and fast. After crossing Frenchman Creek, they turned north again in an attempt to outdistance Royall's troops, who were slowed down by their supply wagons. Royall decided to leave the supply train behind with a rear guard in order to keep up with the Indians. He pursued them across the South Platte River about five miles west of Ogallala Station on the Union Pacific Railroad. There, on August 6, Major North rejoined the command.[108]

On August 8 Royall's command camped on a little slough where the Indians had bivouacked a few days earlier. "The trail here is very plain," Major North wrote in his diary, "and I have some hopes of overtaking the Red devils." But North's hopes were soon dashed. Despite some hard traveling, Royall was unable to overtake the Indians, who managed, with tremendous effort, to stay ahead of the troops. The hot weather and lack of water exhausted the troops; horses and mules collapsed. On August 12, near the Niobrara River, Royall gave up the chase. The horses were no longer able to continue the pursuit, and the men were spent. Just how exhausted both men and horses were became clear over the following days. On August 14 the troops lost ten horses. Major North scribbled in his diary that they simply "gave out" and had to be shot. The next day, one of the Pawnee scouts belonging to Lieutenant Fred Kislingsberry's Company A, nineteen-year-old Co rux tah kah tah, died. He had been sick for several weeks, and the difficult march had aggravated his condition. The scouts buried him the same day. Although North wrote in his diary that he did not know the cause of death, the muster roll stated that Co rux tah kah tah "died in the field August 15th 1869 of Disease of the Heart."[109]

While camping near the Niobrara River, the Pawnee scouts found some very large fossilized bones. The army surgeon declared that one of the bones was a giant human thigh bone. The Pawnees explained that the bone belonged to a race of giants who, according to Pawnee mythology, were exterminated by a flood after they insulted Tiiraawaahat. After destroying the giants, Tiiraawaahat created a race of smaller human beings.[110]

On August 21 the command reached Fort McPherson. Royall had been unable to engage the Indians. All he could show for his efforts were two mules and forty horses that the fleeing Indians had lost or abandoned. These mounts were given to the Pawnees for their faithful service during the campaign. The horses, unfit for military service, were presented to the Pawnees on the condition that they would be transported to the Pawnee Agency without expense to the government. Major North loaded the horses on a train bound for the agency on August 25. While at Fort McPherson the scouts spent their time doing drills, racing horses, and dancing.[111]

At Fort McPherson Royall turned his command over to Lieutenant Colonel (Brevet Brigadier General) Thomas Duncan. Duncan continued the expedition with companies B, C, F, L, and M of the Fifth Cavalry and companies B, C, and M of the Second Cavalry. Major North, the Pawnee scouts, and William F. Cody complemented the troops. On September 15 the command left Fort McPherson. Companies A and I of the Fifth Cavalry were held in reserve to accompany the supply train, which was to meet Duncan's troops in twenty days.[112]

After moving into camp that night, Major North received instructions to detach one company of Pawnee scouts for duty at the Pawnee Agency. Lieutenant Colonel Duncan had received news that some Sioux were threatening the reservation, and the scouts were needed to protect the agency. The following day North sent Lieutenant Kislingsberry's company.[113]

During the first week of the expedition, little of interest occurred. The Pawnees went on scouts in search of Indian trails or hunted buffalo and other game to supply the camp. They also guarded the camp at night. Guard duty led to some amusing incidents after Lieutenant Colonel Duncan issued new orders for the sentinels, insisting that they should call the hours throughout the night. Few of the Pawnee scouts understood English, and fewer still spoke it. North advised the scout guards to listen carefully and then repeat the call as closely as they could. The resulting calls made little sense to either the American soldiers or the Pawnees. According to Cody, the scouts' efforts to repeat the calls were so ridiculous that Duncan "finally gave it up and countermanded the order."[114]

On Sunday, September 26, Major North and William Cody were out hunting in advance of the command when they were attacked by a party of six Sioux warriors. Fortunately for them, two small advance detachments under Lieutenants William Jefferson Volkmar and George Frederick Price were nearby, as were a number of Pawnee scouts. The troops and scouts charged the Sioux, who were soon joined by other warriors. After a chase over five miles, the soldiers spotted a Sioux camp in the distance. It belonged to Pawnee Killer and Whistler's group of Oglalas and consisted of fifty-six lodges. When the soldiers appeared, the Oglalas abandoned their village in haste. During the chase, the scouts killed one Indian and wounded several others. In his diary, North reported that they also captured two ponies, a mule, and "lots of trash." The scouts pursued the fleeing Indians until dark. When they returned to the main camp, they found Lieutenant Colonel Duncan there; he had been unaware of the presence of the village. One party of scouts was left in charge of the abandoned village.[115]

The following day, September 27, Duncan ordered his men to destroy the village. The soldiers burned lodges, robes, saddles, meat, and everything else the Oglalas had left behind. Among the goods were some instruments belonging to a surveying party under William E. Daugherty, which had been attacked a few weeks earlier. Duncan also ordered Companies F and M, under Captain William H. Brown, and some Pawnee scouts under George Lehman and Fred Kislingsberry to locate the fleeing Oglalas. They did not find the Indians but brought back three abandoned horses and a mule.[116]

On September 28 North ordered Second Sergeant Elias Stowe and six scouts to escort companies F and M, Second Cavalry, under Captain Mix, with seventy-five captured mules, to Sheridan, Kansas. The mules had been captured at Summit Springs and belonged to a Morris Mitchell of Sheridan. The next day Duncan again sent Captain Brown out with two companies and twelve scouts under Lieutenant George D. Barclay. Four days later, on October 2, Duncan's command captured an old Oglala woman who had strayed from the village and was unable to catch up. She was near starvation, and the soldiers fed her. She had been on her way to Spotted Tail's Brulé village when she was captured. A Ponca Indian serving with the Pawnee scouts interpreted her words. She told Lieutenant Colonel Duncan that she had no knowledge of the Indians' plans and claimed there were no longer any hostiles in the upper Republican River country. Later, after the troops had taken her to Fort McPherson, she admitted that the pursued band belonged to Pawnee Killer, her son, and Whistler.[117]

On October 9 Duncan sent two companies of the Fifth Cavalry under Captain Philip Dwyer and fifteen scouts under Lieutenant Kislingsberry in search of the Indians. The next day Sergeants Elias Stowe (Company A) and James Deyo (Company C) and fifteen scouts joined two cavalry companies under First Lieutenant James N. Wheelan for a scout on the South Fork of the Republican River. Meanwhile, Duncan ordered companies A and F, Fifth Cavalry, under Major Irwin, to scout the North Fork of the Republican. Lieutenants Barclay and Hunt and fifteen Pawnees joined this party. None of the parties encountered any hostile Indians, which confirmed the statement by the old Oglala woman that the Oglalas had abandoned the area.[118]

Duncan's troops stayed in the field several more days. Apart from going on an occasional scout, the men relaxed and entertained themselves with card games and other forms of recreation. On October 23 Duncan received orders to return to Fort McPherson and disband the expedition. Five days later the command reached the fort, and Major North received orders to send his men back to the Pawnee reservation. The order came as a relief to the men of the expedition, and in his diary North recorded that "we are all on tip toe to get home." Before leaving the fort, Lieutenant Colonel Duncan praised the Pawnee scouts for their valuable service and Major North for his good discipline. With Duncan's speech, the Republican River campaign officially came to an end. On October 30 Major North and the men of the Pawnee battalion boarded a train and traveled back to the Pawnee Agency, arriving the next morning.[119] The Pawnees remained in service until November 10, 1869, when they were mustered out at the Pawnee Agency.[120]

From the army's standpoint, the Republican River expedition of 1869 had been a great success. The Cheyenne Dog Soldiers had received a stunning blow at Summit Springs, from which they never completely recovered, and the follow-up expeditions by Royall and Duncan, though less spectacular, had driven the Sioux and Cheyennes from the area. The significance of the campaign, particularly of the Summit Springs battle, was not lost on the legislatures of Colorado and Nebraska. On January 25, 1870, the Colorado legislature adopted a formal resolution expressing "the thanks of the people of Colorado . . . to Brevet Major General Eugene A. Carr, of the United States Army, and the brave officers and soldiers of his command for their victory thus achieved."[121]

A month later, on February 28, 1870, the State of Nebraska adopted a similar resolution, which more specifically addressed the performance of the Pawnee scouts. The first clause thanked Carr and his officers and soldiers. The second thanked Major North and the Pawnees: "RESOLVED, That the thanks of this body and of the people of the state of Nebraska, are hereby also tendered to Major Frank J. North and the officers and soldiers under his command of the 'Pawnee scouts' for the manner in which they have assisted in driving hostile Indians from our frontier settlements."[122]

Although the battle of Summit Springs did not receive the attention it deserved at the time, historians now agree that it was a major event in the history of U.S.-Indian relations. It was the last major engagement with Plains Indians in Colorado, and it facilitated the opening of the territory to a new wave of settlers. Perhaps the battle would have faded from memory entirely if not for Buffalo Bill Cody, who, according to one historian, "recognized the theatrical qualities of the fight at Summit Springs." Featuring himself in the center of events, Cody incorporated the reenactment of the battle in his Wild West Show and performed it as late as 1907.[123]

As Royall and Duncan drove the last resisting Indians out of Kansas, calm returned to the Kansas frontier. The only trouble during the closing months of 1869 was caused by some militia troops, who, as historian Lonnie J. White pointed out, "did some stealing and plundering of their own, which was what the state paid them each $1.40 a day to prevent the Indians from doing." Although raids took place occasionally in the years following the Republican River expedition, they would never "equal those of 1869 in either number or destruction."[124]

La ta cuts la shar ("Eagle Chief"), a member of the Skiri band. According to the photographer, William Henry Jackson, he was "the oldest, and consequently the head chief of the tribe." Although Eagle Chief was probably not the head chief, it is noticeable that he is wearing a military coat, possibly a sign of status or a symbol of friendship with the United States. Elders such as Eagle Chief may have been influential in deciding whether or not to let Pawnee men serve as scouts. Nebraska State Historical Society, RG2065.PH:7-1.

Te low a lut la sha ("Sky Chief") in an army long coat. Photographer William Henry Jackson described him as follows: "A chief, and a brave leader of his band, taking the first place in war or peace. Was killed by the Sioux in the massacre of the Pawnees in 1873, while hunting buffalo in the valley of the Republican [River]." National Anthropological Archives, Smithsonian Institution, neg. 01293.

Standing, Coo towy goots oo ter a oos ("Blue Hawk"); *sitting*, Tuc ca rix te ta ru pe row ("Coming Around With The Herd"). Both were members of the Pitahawirata band. Photograph by William Henry Jackson. National Anthropological Archives, Smithsonian Institution, neg. 01308A1.

Major Frank North (1840–85), photographed in 1867. Nebraska State Historical Society, RG2320.PH:0-39.

Luther North (1846–1935), photographed at Plum Creek, Nebraska, in 1867. Nebraska State Historical Society, RG2320.PH:9.

Loots tow oots ("Rattlesnake") wearing a cavalry coat with corporal's chevrons. The saber may be a model 1840 dragoon saber. It is possibly a studio prop, although sometimes Indian scouts kept such sabers as personal items. Photograph by William Henry Jackson. Nebraska State Historical Society, RG2065.PH:5-3.

Four Kitkahahki Pawnees and Baptiste Bayhylle, Pawnee interpreter. *Left to right:* La roo rutk a haw la shar ("Night Chief"), La roo ra shar roo cosh ("A Man That Left His Enemy Lying In The Water"), Baptiste Bayhylle, also known as La shara se re ter rek ("One Whom The Great Spirit Smiles Upon"), Tec ta sha cod dic ("One Who Strikes The Chiefs First"), and Te low a lut la sha ("Sky Chief"). Photograph by William Henry Jackson. Nebraska State Historical Society, RG2065.PH:3 5.

Tuh cod ix te cah wah ("One Who Brings Herds"). Photograph by William Henry Jackson. Nebraska State Historical Society, RG2065.PH:1-15.

Ke wuk o we terah rook ("Like A Fox" or "Acting As A Fox") wearing a cavalry coat and what appears to be a Hudson's Bay blanket. He holds a cap-and-ball revolver. Like A Fox served as a scout in 1870. He was about twenty-six years old at the time and a member of the Skiri band. Photograph by William Henry Jackson. Nebraska State Historical Society, RG2065.PH:5-1.

Ta caw deex taw see ux ("Driving A Herd"). Although this name does not appear on the muster rolls, he might have served as a scout under a different name. It was not unusual for a Pawnee man to change his name several times during his life. Photograph by William Henry Jackson. Nebraska State Historical Society, RG2065.PH:5-2.

As sau taw ka ("White Horse"), a member of the Pitahawirata band. According to the army's rolls, two Pawnees with that name served as scouts, in 1867 and 1868. Photograph by William Henry Jackson. Nebraska State Historical Society, RG2065.PH:5 6.

Echo Hawk (circa 1854–1924) enlisted in 1876 under the name Tah wee he say ("Leader of the Group"). He was a private in the Pawnee scout battalion and served in the Powder River campaign against the Northern Cheyennes and the Sioux during the "Great Sioux War." Photograph courtesy of Walter R. Echo-Hawk.

Pawnee men posing for the camera during the hundredth meridian excursion organized by the Union Pacific Railroad Company in 1866. Photograph by John C. Carbutt. J. C. Carbutt Collection, no. 204 10/1866, Union Pacific Historical Collection, Omaha, Nebraska.

Left to right: Eagle Chief, Knife Chief, Brave Chief, and Young Chief, about 1890. These former scouts joined other American Indians and William ("Buffalo Bill") Cody as performers at the Pan-American Exposition in Buffalo, New York, in 1901. Nebraska State Historical Society, RG2065.PH:13-2.

Ki ri ki ri see ra ki wa ri ("Roaming Scout") was born around 1845 and served as a U.S. Army scout. He later became one of the most prominent Skiri Pawnee religious leaders. He died in 1916. Photograph by De Lancey W. Gill, 1907. National Anthropological Archives, Smithsonian Institution, neg. 01218.

Some surviving scouts and interpreter James R. Murie, 1911. *Back row:* John Buffalo, John Box, High Eagle, Seeing Eagle. *Front row:* Captain Jim, James R. Murie (son of Pawnee scout Captain James Murie), and Billy Osborne. Nebraska State Historical Society, RG2065.PH:10-10.

Rush Roberts enlisted in the army under the name Ahrekarard ("Antlers") in 1876. He was later renamed Ray tah cots tey sah ru ("Fancy Eagle"). He was the last surviving scout, passing away in 1958. Photograph by Thomas William Smillie, 1905. National Anthropological Archives, Smithsonian Institution, neg. 01214.

CHAPTER **6**

Freelance Scouting Operations, 1870–1874

While the Pawnee scouts were scouring the country with the Fifth Cavalry in search of Sioux and Cheyennes, changes were taking place at the Pawnee Agency. After assuming the presidency in 1869, Ulysses S. Grant set out to reform Indian policy. Shortly after his inauguration he launched his so-called Peace Policy. The idea was to transfer control of Indian agencies from civil appointees to religious denominations, who would attempt to resocialize the American Indians and integrate them into American society by peaceful means. The underlying assumption was that religious denominations were less motivated by greed and self-interest and were less corrupt than agents of the old system. The new policy was also dubbed the "Quaker Policy," because Quakers had been the principal advocates of the program. During the experimental phase of the new policy, Quakers filled most of the positions as Indian agents on the Great Plains, including that position at the Pawnee Agency.[1]

By 1869 the Society of Friends, as the Quakers were known officially, was split into two separate but nearly identical branches. Grant placed the Orthodox branch of the society in charge of the Central Superintendency, which oversaw Indian agencies in Kansas and Indian Territory. The Hicksite branch, so called after its leader, Elias Hicks, was placed in charge of the Northern Superintendency, which consisted of the Indian agencies in Nebraska.

The appointment of Quakers as agents and superintendents to the Indians in Nebraska had far-reaching consequences for the Pawnee tribe as a whole and for the Pawnee scouts in particular. Despite some dogmatic differences, the two branches of the Society of Friends shared certain principles and attitudes toward Indians. Both sought to transform the Indian from "savage" to "civilized" subject. Quakers believed Indians should give up hunting and their (semi-)nomadic ways, abolish their tribal governments, surrender their ideas of communal property ownership, and instead adopt agriculture and allotment of their land to individual ownership as prerequisites for civilization. Of more immediate concern for the continuation of the Pawnee battalion was the Quakers' adherence to pacifism, a fundamental element of their spiritual and religious philosophy. These ideas were at odds not only with Pawnee cultural norms and values but also with social and political realities on the plains. Although it was the Quakers' intention to "uplift" and assist the Indians under their care, many of their policies in fact contributed to the decline of the Pawnee tribe.

In June 1869, sixty-eight-year-old Samuel M. Janney, of the Hicksite branch of the Society of Friends, assumed control of the Northern Superintendency in Omaha, and forty-one-year-old Jacob M. Troth arrived in Columbus, Nebraska, to take over as agent at the Pawnee Agency. Both men faced enormous challenges. The Pawnees were hungry, impoverished, and demoralized as a result of diseases, the overhunting of buffalo, the destruction of their crops by grasshoppers, and constant pressure from the Sioux and hostile white settlers. Janney and Troth quickly identified the Sioux threat as one of the greatest obstacles to Pawnee advancement. Armed with good intentions, they outlined a three-step program to "save" the Indians under their care. They hoped to establish peace on the plains by ending Pawnee horse raids, dismantling the Pawnee scouts, and commencing peace negotiations with the Oglala and Brulé Sioux.[2]

The first test for the new policy came in January 1870 when a Pawnee war party under Uh sah wuck oo led ee hoor ("Big Spotted Horse") returned to the Pawnee Agency from a horse raid in Indian Territory.[3] On January 4 the party had attacked a camp of Southern Cheyennes and Arapahos under Little Robe and Yellow Bear and captured more than a hundred horses.[4] When news of the Pawnee raid reached the headquarters of the Military Division of the Missouri in Chicago, General Philip Sheridan ordered General C. C. Augur to recover the stolen horses, arrest the thieves, "and confine them with ball and chain attached to their leg, at the nearest military Post, until further orders from these Headquarters."[5]

Whereas Superintendent Janney and Agent Troth supported Sheridan's order wholeheartedly, General Augur was much less eager to arrest the Pawnees and return the stolen horses to the Cheyennes. In a letter to Sheridan on March 17, Augur reported that the Pawnees were confined at Omaha Barracks and that he had confiscated the horses. But he also pleaded for leniency toward the prisoners. "[All] the Indians engaged in this raid," Augur wrote, "have been faithful soldiers of ours in the past two or three summers, and have been of great service to us against the very Indians, from whom the horses were stolen, and I do not believe they were aware of any friendly relations having been established between the whites [and] those southern Indians." Harsh punishment of these men, Augur explained, might have undesirable consequences for the recruitment of scouts in the future. "These Pawnees as I have stated before, have made us faithful [and] efficient soldiers, and hereafter may be very necessary to us, and the Chiefs are confident of their ability hereafter, to prevent any recurrence of such raids."[6]

On April 21 Augur released the six prisoners from Omaha Barracks. Agent Troth, meanwhile, made arrangements with Luther North and several Pawnees to escort the stolen horses to Fort Harker, Kansas, from where they would be returned to their rightful owners. The Pawnees claimed that many of the horses had died of "mysterious" ailments or had been stolen by Sioux during the winter. When they delivered the horses to be returned to Fort Harker, only thirty-five sickly animals were left. Luther North and nine Pawnees, eight of whom had served as scouts in his company the previous year, drove the motley herd to the fort later that month. Among the former scouts in North's party were Sa gule ah la shar ("Sun Chief"), Nick Koots ("Bird"), and Pe isk ee la shar ("Boy Chief," also known as Peter Headman). A chief named Co rux ta puk ("Fighting Bear") also joined the escort. During the trip they met several white parties who regarded the Pawnees with great suspicion. Near Belleville, Kansas, they found themselves surrounded by a group of alarmed citizens who threatened to hang the Pawnees. After some strong language by Captain North, who showed them General Augur's letter of instructions, they allowed the Pawnees to continue their march. A few days later one of the Pawnees, while out riding alone, was arrested by some soldiers, but North resolved this incident, too. Clearly, Kansas was a dangerous place for a small group of Indians, even if those Indians were allies of the United States.[7]

After delivering the horses to Fort Harker, the men returned to the Pawnee Agency. Most of the Indians traveled home on foot. One night they saw ten men lurking around their camp, probably intent on killing the entire party. Captain North moved his men out unseen and avoided unnecessary bloodshed. The following day, Sun Chief and Boy Chief challenged each other to a foot race back to the agency. They left camp at dawn and rested for only short periods during the race. Sun Chief made the mistake of drinking too much water during one stop and thus lost the race to Boy Chief, who covered the distance of eighty-five miles to the agency in twelve hours, including a two-hour stop on the Blue River. The race serves as an excellent example of the remarkable endurance and physical condition of the Pawnees who served as scouts, even if Sun Chief made a tactical error during the run.[8]

Although the Pawnees had returned some of the stolen horses, their actions were not reciprocated when their enemies stole horses from them. Several Sioux raiding parties visited the Pawnees that spring and stole ponies on several occasions. During a raid on May 19 they killed a woman and shot a man in the leg. The next day Agent Troth held a council with the chiefs, who were angry over the government's inability to protect their people from the Sioux and for failing to have the Sioux return the stolen horses. They told Troth they intended to avenge themselves on the Sioux and recover their horses one way or another. Troth forbade them to raid the Sioux and promised to arrange a peace council with the Sioux chiefs in Washington to resolve all problems between the two nations. On June 22 Superintendent Janney met the Oglala head chief, Red Cloud, in Omaha. Red Cloud rejected Janney's suggestion to meet with the Pawnees. He replied that the Pawnees "had once been one people with them, but had turned against them while they were contending for their rights [and] that they had joined the white soldiers [and] had killed many of the best men among the Sioux." Janney contacted other Sioux chiefs in the area, including Spotted Tail of the Brulés, but none of them expressed any serious interest in peace talks.[9]

Imprisoning the Pawnees for stealing horses from their arch-enemies and forcing them to return the horses was humiliating enough for the Pawnees. But the Quakers in charge of the tribe also insisted that the Pawnee scout battalion be discontinued. In February 1870 Frank North had approached Agent Troth with a request to reorganize the scouts. Although Troth passed the request on to Janney, he added that in his opinion, military service was harmful to the cause of bringing peace and civilization to the tribe. Janney agreed. In a letter to Commissioner of Indian Affairs Ely S. Parker, Janney listed his objections to Pawnee military service. It made young men "less tractable" than those who did not serve, and the scouts "associate with bad white men" and "learn to drink [and] gamble, which unfits them for useful occupation and has an unfavorable effect on others." Furthermore, their service only fueled hostilities with the Sioux, a matter of concern not only to the agent and his staff but also to white settlers in the area. Janney saved his greatest objection for last: military service retarded the civilization program that the Indian Office was trying to implement. To support his case, Janney reported that the Pawnee chiefs themselves objected to the enlistment of their young men. The chiefs, he wrote, "say they wish them to stay at home [and] go to work as tillers of the soil." It seems more likely, however, that the chiefs wanted their young warriors to stay home to defend their towns against Sioux war parties.[10]

Janney's case against scout service was rather far-fetched. Although Sioux war parties had ridden out to avenge the Pawnee scouts' attacks against Pawnee Killer's band at Summit Springs and on the Republican River, it is doubtful that the Sioux would have given up their raids against the Pawnees even if North's battalion had been permanently disbanded.[11] And although it is true that the scouts were avid gamblers, one must bear in mind that gambling had always been a favorite pastime among the Pawnee people in general. Military service did not compromise Pawnee morals and lead to gambling. Nor does it appear to have caused alcoholism. On the contrary, during the thirteen years in which the Pawnee battalion was in existence, the records show no incidences of alcohol abuse by scouts while in the service of the army.

In one respect, however, the Quakers were correct. Military service did not speed up the process of acculturation as Generals Augur and Sherman, in 1867, had proclaimed it would do. In fact their service reinforced the

Pawnees' martial values and gave them a sense of ethnic pride and self-esteem. Janney's observation that service made them "less tractable" was not completely imaginary. Many of the men joining the battalion were recent graduates of the agency school. Their exposure to white values in the classroom caused their alienation from the tribe, whereas service as a Pawnee scout allowed them to gain status as warriors and be reintegrated into the tribe. In 1869 Elvira Platt, a teacher at the Pawnee Agency school, observed that many students faced great difficulties after leaving school. They felt they had no home, and the whites would not accept them. A few boys solved the problem by enlisting as scouts in the Pawnee battalion, thus "reinstating themselves with their own people by becoming good warriors."[12]

Commissioner Parker of the Indian Office adopted Janney's recommendations and informed the secretary of war of his decision. When General Augur asked permission to enlist Pawnee scouts for service, the War Department denied his request. Augur complained about this decision to General John Pope, who also hoped to enlist scouts for operations along the Republican River. In a telegram to General Sherman on June 2, 1870, Pope wrote, "I need eight or ten very much as they are the only guides who know the country thoroughly, along the Upper Republican and Head waters of Saline and Solomon. Can I employ that number as guides for Woods and Custer who are moving on the Republican after Indians, the first with five the last with six troops of cavalry." Adjutant General E. D. Townsend in Washington, however, informed Pope that because the "Indian Department has expressed the wish not to have Pawnees employed because of bad effects upon them [the] Secretary of War thinks it best not to use them as guides."[13]

Pope and Augur were not the only ones who wanted to employ Pawnee scouts. O. G. Hammond, superintendent of the Union Pacific Railroad, also wished to hire Pawnees, to guard the railroad against Sioux and Cheyenne war parties, which had already piled ties on the track and fired upon their trains once. Hammond wrote to House Representative Oakes Ames, a strong supporter of the railroad, asking him to use his influence in the government to overturn the Indian Office's decision to disband the Pawnee battalion.

Hammond offered several arguments in support of the Pawnee scouts. "These scouts have been enlisted and served in this work for two summers," he wrote, "and are and have been so efficient as scouts that the military authorities think them indispensable." According to Hammond, the scouts "will go further in the same time than white soldiers, will go where white soldiers cannot, and have so much experience that they can trace the most intricate movements of the enemy and give notice of hostile parties, always in advance of any information otherwise obtained." Hammond dismissed arguments put forward by the Quakers that military service made the Pawnees less controllable and that their service only angered the Sioux.[14] "The truth is just the reverse," Hammond wrote: "It is believed that the refusal of the Government to employ these scouts has emboldened [the Sioux]." He added that enlisting the Pawnees was a cost-effective means of controlling four hundred miles of railroad.[15]

Hammond's letter to Ames appears to have had the desired effect. But the wheels of the bureaucracy in Washington, then as now, turned slowly. The Pawnee battalion would not be reorganized until September, and it was limited to two companies. In the meantime, a few individual Pawnees served as "freelance" scouts and guides, though only for nonmilitary purposes. In June 1870 Frank North and two Pawnee scouts joined Professor Othniel Charles Marsh's scientific expedition to the western plains.

O. C. Marsh (1831–1899) had received his degree from Yale University. An adherent of Darwin's theory of evolution, he was fascinated with extinct animal species, whose fossilized remains he collected. He pioneered the field of paleontology, and in 1866 his uncle, millionaire George Peabody, founded the Peabody Museum of Natural History at Yale with a gift of $150,000. That same year Marsh was appointed professor of paleontology at Yale. In August 1868 he traveled to Chicago to attend a meeting of the American Association for the Advancement of Science. At the close of the meeting he joined an excursion to Omaha at the western end of the Union Pacific Railroad. During the trip he became interested in the geological features of the Great Plains and obtained some fossilized animal bones. He determined to return to continue the search for extinct animal species.

After Peabody's death in 1869, Marsh received a substantial inheritance that would allow him to put his ideas into practice. In 1870 he announced plans for a scientific expedition to the western plains and Rocky Mountains. The expedition would consist of Marsh and a team of students. Among the first to join the team was a young student named George Bird Grinnell, whose experiences during the trip would spark his life-long interest in Indian cultures. During the expedition Grinnell would also meet Major Frank North and some Pawnee scouts, which would lay the foundation for his history of the Pawnee battalion. Apart from Marsh and Grinnell, the members of the expedition consisted of Charles T. Ballard, Harry Degen Ziegler, Alexander Hamilton Ewing, John Wool Griswold, John Reed Nicholson, Charles McCormick Reeve, James Matson Russell, Henry Bradford Sargent, James Wolcott Wadsworth (who would later serve two terms in Congress as representative of the Sate of New York), Eli Whitney (grandson of the inventor of the cotton gin), and Charles Wyllys Betts, who published an account of the expedition in the October 1871 edition of *Harper's New Monthly Magazine*.[16]

General William Sherman wrote a letter of introduction granting Marsh access to all military posts, and General Philip Sheridan promised to provide the expedition with military escorts while it was in the field. Officials of the Union Pacific Railroad were also interested in Marsh's undertaking and drastically reduced train fares for the members of the expedition. On June 30, 1870, they left New Haven. In Omaha they received some arms and instructions in how to use their Henry rifles, for the expedition would take them into hostile Indian territory. A few days later they traveled by train to North Platte Station and from there marched to Fort McPherson. Shortly after their arrival at the fort, they were reminded of the dangerous character of their mission: a party of hunters had just come in after a skirmish with several hostile Indians. One of the men had received an arrow through the arm.[17]

Major Eugene Asa Carr welcomed Marsh and his students at the fort and began preparations for the expedition. Carr ordered some troops of Company I, Fifth Cavalry, under the command of First Lieutenant Bernard Reilly Jr. and Second Lieutenant Earl D. Thomas, to accompany the scientists. A day or two later Major Frank North and two Pawnee scouts arrived at the post. Carr assigned them to guide the expedition into Loup River territory. Marsh and his students were taken to a corral, where they selected their horses from the herd that had been captured from Tall Bull's camp the previous summer. According to Grinnell, there were some "amusing scenes when these young men, many of whom had never mounted a horse, attempted to ride." Fortunately, most of the horses were gentle and did not try to throw their riders.[18]

On July 15 the expedition left Fort McPherson. Major North and the two scouts led the command, the scouts riding about a mile in advance of the column. According to expedition member Charles Betts, the scouts, "with movements characteristic of their wary race, crept up each high bluff, and from behind a bunch of grass peered over the top for signs of hostile savages." Following the scouts were Lieutenants Reilly and Thomas and the Yale party. Although they were in hostile country, some of the students were disposed to wander off from the group, much to the alarm of Professor Marsh, who "was obliged to use strong language, and to summon to his aid Major North before he could keep the party together and with the escort." Buffalo Bill also joined the expedition on the first day. At the rear of the column, a small detachment of troops escorted six army wagons loaded with provisions, forage, tents, and ammunition.[19]

Grinnell was fascinated by the two Indian scouts. The name of the older scout was Tucky tee Ious. Major North explained that the name meant "The Duellist" or "When He Being Alone Meets A Sioux Alone And They Both Shoot." Tucky tee Ious was a celebrated warrior. The name of the younger scout was La hoor a sac, or "Best One Of All." He was best known for his skill as a hunter.[20] Grinnell described the appearance of the two Indians:

> When we first saw them they were clothed simply with moccasins, breech clouts and a blanket apiece, but before starting they were fitted out with a full suit of cavalry clothes, and although they were very proud and went around pointing to themselves and saying "heap o' good," it was easy to see that they were very uncomfortable. As soon as we got away from the fort, they took off everything but their shirts and pantaloons and packed them carefully away and did not take them out again until we got back. . . . Just before reaching the fort, they dressed up again [and] came in, in all their finery.
>
> They wore their hair long and had their scalp locks neatly braided, and sometimes they would decorate them with a piece of bright colored cloth or a feather.[21]

While thirst and heat plagued the young scientists, Professor Marsh lectured on the strange geological formations along the trail. Marsh's discourse puzzled the soldiers accompanying the expedition and prompted Buffalo Bill to say that the "professor told the boys some mighty tough yarns to-day." On July 17 the scouts guided the expedition across the Dismal River and on to the Middle Loup River. There they stumbled upon several Sioux burial sites. The bodies of the dead Indians had been wrapped in robes and blankets and placed on scaffolds. The corpses were adorned in beads, bracelets, and face paint. One scalpless warrior clutched a rusty shotgun and a pack of cards in his crumbling hands. At the foot of the scaffold lay the remains of a pony, killed during the funeral service to accompany the dead on their journey to the afterworld. Professor Marsh brought the awestruck students back to reality when he announced, "Well, boys, perhaps they died of small-pox; but we can't study the origin of the Indian race unless we have those skulls!"

Unfortunately, the sources do not reveal whether Marsh took the skulls back to Connecticut with him or replaced them on the scaffolds after examining them. Nor do they reveal how the Pawnees reacted to the desecration of the graves. They were probably bewildered by the professor's peculiar interest in the skulls of their enemies, but it is unlikely that they voiced any complaint.[22] In January 1871 Frank North received a letter from Marsh asking if it was possible to send him the two Indian skulls the expedition had found the previous summer. North answered that "had I known two weeks ago that you wanted them I should have got them with pleasure," but he had disbanded the Pawnee battalion a few days earlier, and it would be impossible for him to gather the skulls now. However, North promised to send Marsh some skulls from "some of [the] other tribes if I have an opportunity."[23]

A few days later the Pawnee scouts guided the expedition to a rocky canyon littered with fossilized bones. Lieutenant Reilly posted guards around the site, and the scientists began to unearth the remains of extinct animals. The soldiers not only guarded the men against hostile Indians, who appeared to be lurking around, but also assisted in the hard work of collecting specimens. The Pawnees initially refused to assist. They claimed that the petrified bones belonged to an extinct race of giants who had been destroyed in a great flood because they insulted Tiiraawaahat, the Great Spirit. But after Marsh picked up a fossilized jaw of a horse and showed them how it corresponded to the mouths of their own horses, the Pawnees joined the hunt for bones. Betts reported that "they rarely returned to camp without bringing fossils for the 'Bone Medicine-man.'"[24]

After securing a large number of fossils, the expeditionaries resumed their journey. Every day Major North took one of the students with him to hunt for fresh meat. There was plenty of game around, but none of the inexperienced scientists killed anything, because they knew nothing of hunting or rifle shooting. One day they spotted a herd of antelope. Although they "unloaded" their guns at the animals, they managed to kill only one fawn. Fortunately for them, Major North and the Pawnee scouts were around to keep the expedition supplied with fresh meat.[25]

On July 21 clouds of smoke appeared in the sky, and a prairie fire inched its way toward the expedition. It appeared that the fire had been set by Indians intent on stealing the expedition's horses and hoping the fire would disorient the troops and scare the ponies away. For a short time the situation looked serious, but a sudden thunderstorm and changing winds brought relief. Despite the obvious signs that Indians were near, the scientific party was left unmolested for the remainder of the trip. Only once did the members of the expedition see an Indian in the distance. Grinnell, who at this time still shared the prejudices against Indians so characteristic of his age, wrote to his parents with some disappointment that "only one Indian was seen [in range] and no one was able to get a shot at him."[26]

The expeditionaries spent most evenings around the campfire. Professor Marsh lectured on a variety of subjects, and occasionally the Pawnees entertained the scientists with one of their dances. Grinnell recalled the scene in his memoirs:

> They were jolly fellows, both of them, and they would sing and dance for us frequently. There were not enough to have a war dance, but La-hoo-a-sac gave us the buffalo dance one night while Tucky-tee-lous sang.
>
> The last night in camp we had a good deal of fun. We all put on our blankets and marched in single file to the Indian tent, where we sat in a circle and smoked the pipe of peace. Then the major made a speech in Pawnee, La-hoor-a-sac answered him, and then

Reeve, one of our fellows, made a stump speech to the Indians which, as they did not understand English, delighted them. . . . They sang the buffalo song, . . . we sang some college songs, and then the council broke up.[27]

On July 26 the party started the return trip to Fort McPherson across desertlike country. The men obtained water by digging in the dry bed of an alkaline lake. After two days of travel in scorching temperatures, they finally reached the North Platte River. On reaching the Platte, the Pawnees led the command across the treacherous quicksands and announced their arrival at the town of North Platte with a typical Pawnee whoop. Charles Betts recalled that the townspeople "mistook us for a party of Sioux, and rose in arms to repel the invaders." On July 29 the expedition arrived at Fort McPherson.[28]

Professor Marsh and his students soon boarded a train west, where they went on two more scientific excursions that resulted in several other spectacular discoveries, including the complete skeleton of a dinosaur. Major North and the two Pawnee scouts did not join them. Most likely they returned to the Pawnee Agency. Although the Marsh expedition did not involve the entire Pawnee battalion or result in any clashes with hostile Indians, it was a significant event, the first of its kind in the West. Marsh returned to Yale with a great number of fossils of then unidentified extinct species. The expedition greatly advanced the science of paleontology, and two Pawnee scouts played an important part in this chapter of American scientific development.

While Major North, Tucky tee lous, and La hoor a sac were with Marsh's expedition, lobbyists for the Union Pacific Railroad in Washington obtained clearance to employ the Pawnee battalion. Instead of the desired four companies, however, the Indian Office allowed only two companies to enlist. On September 4, 1870, Frank North and a Captain Litchfield mustered in the two companies at Columbus. Luther North commanded Company A, assisted by First Lieutenants James F. Smith and Jay E. White and Company Sergeant Ira Mullen. Several Pawnees also held noncommissioned ranks. Among them was Chatiks tah kah lah shar ("White Man Chief"). According to Weltfish's informants in 1938, North appointed him sergeant because he had a white ancestor. Apparently the "politics of blood" did matter to North, who appointed only white people (especially if they were in any way related to him) as officers. Company A totaled about fifty men and officers. Captain Sylvanus E. Cushing, Frank North's brother-in-law, commanded "Company B, Pawnee Scouts."[29]

After drawing their arms and uniforms at Fort McPherson, the scouts received their marching orders on September 8. Their assignment was once again to guard the Union Pacific Railroad. Luther North's Company A received orders to relieve Company F of the Fifth Cavalry at Plum Creek. Captain Cushing's B Company, meanwhile, was to march to O'Fallon's Station, where it would relieve Company M, Fifth Cavalry. Major Frank North was ordered to establish his headquarters at O'Fallon's Station. He received instructions to "visit and inspect all portions of his Command once every two weeks and make a written report" to the district headquarters at Fort McPherson.[30]

Despite the alarming reports by O. G. Hammond and other railroad officials earlier that year, the scouts' service along the UPRR in 1870 was uneventful. Detachments of Pawnee scouts patrolled the area north and south of the tracks but found no hostiles. In October Major Carr ordered Luther North and Company A to Fort McPherson to join an army expedition into the Republican River country. Several gentlemen from Syracuse, New York, and a few Englishmen, along with Carr, accompanied the expedition. Although the purpose was to search for hostile Indians, Carr and his guests entertained themselves primarily with hunting buffalo and other game.[31]

In December, Frank North took twenty-five men from Captain Cushing's company to escort a hunting party composed of several railroad officials, a few army officers, and other distinguished gentlemen. Among the guests was James Wadsworth, who had been a member of O. C. Marsh's expedition earlier that year. Wadsworth would later serve two consecutive terms in the U.S. House of Representatives, and his son eventually became a U.S. senator from the state of New York. Luther North also joined the party. Despite the cold weather, the Pawnee scouts guided the group to the buffalo grounds. They frequently carried their distinguished guests across icy rivers. Luther North recalled that his brother, as a prank, ordered one of his scouts, in Pawnee, to "fall down" and drop the man he was carrying on his back in the cold water. The order was promptly obeyed. During one hunt, William Cody impressed everyone by shooting sixteen buffalo with sixteen shots while mounted on an untrained horse. This feat earned him the admiration of Luther North and the Pawnees. The gentlemen in the party also shot their share of buffalo, usually after the Pawnees drove the animals in the direction of the inexperienced hunters.[32] Later that month the Pawnee battalion gathered at Fort McPherson, where it was disbanded on December 31.[33]

Although the scouts' service during 1870 had been brief and had resulted in no clashes with hostile Indians, Agent Jacob M. Troth believed their enlistment had nevertheless provoked and angered the Sioux. In February 1871 he wrote to Superintendent Janney that the Sioux raids on the Pawnee reservation the previous year had begun only after Major North organized the scouts. In order to prevent future Sioux retaliations against the Pawnees, Troth suggested that the Indian Office not authorize the reorganization of the battalion. Janney endorsed Troth's recommendation in his report to Commissioner Parker.[34]

The Pawnee battalion would not be reorganized in 1871. In April General Augur informed the Office of Indian Affairs that he would not enlist the Pawnees for service that year. His decision probably had more to do with the fact that the Indians had been quiet during the previous year than with the Quakers' objections to enlisting the Pawnees. Nevertheless, Augur's decision greatly pleased Janney and Troth. They believed the employment of the scouts was an obstacle to their efforts to effect a peace between the Pawnees and the Sioux. Since December 1870 they had tried to arrange a meeting between the two tribes. They received the full support and cooperation of the Pawnee chiefs for their plan, but the Brulés and Oglalas appeared much less interested in a cessation of hostilities between the two tribes. They effectively stalled all attempts by the Quakers to arrange for a meeting. Although Spotted Tail of the Brulés time and again expressed his desire and commitment to peace, he did little to prevent his young warriors from organizing war parties into Pawnee territory.

Still, prospects for peace seemed favorable in the spring of 1871. The Pawnees agreed to meet with Spotted Tail at the Santee Agency in northeastern Nebraska. But as they prepared to meet the Brulé chief, they received news that Spotted Tail had called the meeting off. Spotted Tail explained that a peace with the Pawnees might upset the other Sioux bands.[35] Spotted Tail proved to be a masterful diplomat. Not only did he stall the peace process with the Pawnees without appearing openly hostile, but by doing so, he also prevented the reorganization of the Pawnee battalion. That summer the Sioux killed three women and two boys during raids on the Pawnee Agency. The boys were students at the Pawnee manual labor school. Rather than questioning the effectiveness of his policy of reconciliation, Agent Troth rested comfortably in the thought that "we have the satisfaction of believing they [the students] were prepared for the sad change."[36]

In the fall of 1871, Superintendent Janney retired and was replaced by Barclay White. White, who was also a member of the Hicksite branch of the Society of Friends, adopted his predecessor's policy of discouraging the employment of Pawnees as army scouts. Anticipating a request from the War Department to enlist the scouts, he wrote a letter to newly appointed Commissioner of Indian Affairs F. A. Walker. White referred to Janney's report of February 17, 1870, in which Janney listed his objections to the service of the scouts. It represented, White said, "the subject and situations accurately as it is at the present time, contains my views, and is as definate as anything I could write." In other words, like Janney, White believed that military service would have a demoralizing effect on the Pawnees and obstruct the peace process with the Sioux. As a result of White's position, the Pawnee battalion would not be reorganized for 1872.[37]

White also refused to allow the Pawnees to join exhibitions and "Wild West shows." The scouts' reputation as fierce Indian fighters for Uncle Sam had spread around the country. Some enterprising individuals hoped to capitalize on their accomplishments and display some of them at public exhibits. In June 1872 White received a request from a Sidney Barnett of Niagara Falls, Canada, to send him some Pawnee Indians for a buffalo hunt exhibition. Earlier that month Barnett had traveled to Nebraska, where he had captured some bison. While there, he had also made arrangements with Major Frank North and Captain Fred Matthews to have five Pawnees take part in the hunt. Barnett arranged for the transport of the Indians and their horses and had begun advertising the event when he received notice from Agent Troth that the Pawnees would under no circumstances be allowed to leave the reservation to perform in his exhibition. Barnett appealed to the commissioner of Indian affairs and even to President Grant, but all his pleas were rejected. "I never knew that any law of the

United States prevented the Indians leaving their homes to travel into civilized countries," a desperate Barnett wrote to Grant on July 18, 1872. "I was always under the impression that such travel under proper persons [and] restrictions must be beneficial to the Indians tending to enlighten [and] civilize them." Barnett complained that "[had] I been aware of any law or regulation preventing them from leaving their homes I should not have incurred the large expenditures I have." But neither the commissioner nor the president would budge.[38]

Several months later White received a similar request from several eastern businessmen and William F. Cody. Cody and his partners wished to take six Pawnees on a five-week tour of Philadelphia, New York, and Chicago. Although the consortium offered to pay for the Indians' expenses, the Office of Indian Affairs again refused permission. Superintendent White, following Quaker doctrine, explained that he disapproved of exhibitions that "encourage the Indians to continue or practice any of their savage customs, or of placing them under the care of any persons, who will not be to them Christian examples in every respect."[39]

The Quaker administrators had successfully blocked the reorganization of the Pawnee battalion. Keeping Pawnee war parties from raiding the southern tribes for horses and preventing the tribe from going on its semiannual buffalo hunts proved to be different matters altogether. The Quakers objected to the tribal hunts because they thwarted their efforts at turning the Indians into sedentary farmers. Furthermore, during their long absences from the agency while chasing buffalo near the Republican River, the Indians would be "free from agency control and free to live in the old way without interference." Finally, the Quakers feared the Pawnees might clash with the Sioux on the open plains and negate whatever advancements had been made in the peace process. Nevertheless, the chiefs insisted on going on their summer and winter hunts, for their food stores were low and the survival of their people depended on them.[40]

In 1872, at the insistence of the chiefs, Agent Troth allowed the tribe to go on its annual summer hunt. He hired John Burwell Omohundro, also known as "Texas Jack," to act as trail agent for the Indians. It was Omohundro's task to prevent confrontations between the Indians and the white settlers who had been moving into the Republican River area. To avoid being mistaken for hostile Indians by the U.S. Army, the Pawnees carried four white flags, each measuring three by four feet, with a large "P" in the center to identify the group. Shortly after the Pawnees left the agency, Luther North and George Bird Grinnell joined them. The expedition was a great success. The hunters killed several thousand buffalo and did not encounter any Sioux. After several months on the trail, the Pawnees returned to the reservation. Later that year the tribe went on its winter hunt, but this time the Sioux were nearby. A large war party of Brulés and Oglalas attacked the Pawnee hunting camp and stole a great number of their horses. The Pawnees were forced to abort the hunt and abandon most of the meat and skins they had collected.[11]

In 1873, a number of Pawnees again expressed their desire to go on the summer hunt. Agent William Burgess, who had replaced Jacob Troth, reluctantly gave his permission, because he thought it was a necessary step to prevent starvation. As trail agent, Burgess appointed twenty-three-year-old John W. Williamson, the agency farmer. Williamson received orders "to use all precaution to guard [the Pawnees against] any predatory raids [and] incursions by their enemies." On July 3, 1873, between 350 and 400 Pawnees under Ti ra wa hut Re sa ru ("Sky Chief"), a former Pawnee scout, left the agency to go on the hunt. Among the Indians were several other former scouts, including Traveling Bear, hero of the Summit Springs battle.[12] After several successful hunts along the Republican River, the Pawnees turned north and began the journey home. Although a number of white hunters warned that they had seen Sioux Indians lurking in the area, Sky Chief ignored their warnings and decided to push on. His men had found no sign indicating that hostile Indians were near. According to one account, the military authorities also assured the Pawnees that there was no danger. But the Sioux were indeed nearby. A large band of Brulés, supplemented by a group of Oglalas, had been trailing the hunters for several days and were intent on attacking the Pawnees.

On August 5, while their trail agent stood passively by, the Sioux attacked the Pawnee camp. The surprise was complete. Although greatly outnumbered, the Pawnee warriors put up a brave stand. After several hours of relentless fighting, at least sixty-nine Pawnees lay dead. Agent Burgess later determined that twenty men, thirty-nine women, and ten children had died. According to unofficial sources, the death toll was much higher. When soldiers from Fort McPherson visited the site shortly after the battle, they found mutilated corpses everywhere. "It was a horrible sight," wrote one of them. "Dead braves with bows still tightly grasped in dead and stiffened fingers; sucking infants pinned to their mothers' breasts with arrows; bowels protruding from openings made by fiendish knives; heads scalped with the red blood glazed upon them—a stinking mass, many already fly-blown and scorched with heat."[43]

According to one account, Sky Chief killed his own infant son rather than have him killed and mutilated by the Sioux. Sky Chief himself died while defending his people. Another former scout, Nick Coots ("Bird"), also died in the massacre. Traveling Bear survived the battle despite severe injuries. The Sioux killed his family and left him for dead at the canyon. When a Sioux returned to take his scalp, Traveling Bear wrested the knife away from him and killed him. After a long and difficult march, he eventually reached the Pawnee Agency, where he died a few months later. According to some sources he died of grief.[44]

Some scholars have suggested that the tragedy at what came to be known as Massacre Canyon was a major turning point in the history of the Pawnee tribe.[45] Undoubtedly, the event was an important factor in the decision of some Pawnees to leave Nebraska and move to Indian Territory to live with their kin, the Wichitas. But the tragedy at Massacre Canyon was only one episode in a long line of disastrous events that had devastated the Pawnee tribe since the 1830s. Apart from the Sioux threat, diseases continued to weaken the tribe. Overhunting depleted the buffalo herds. Drought and grasshoppers destroyed crops and, in the absence of adequate rations or buffalo meat, caused hunger and poverty. As the keepers of the medicine bundles died at alarming rates, knowledge of the sacred rites passed away with them. Without the knowledge to revitalize the tribe, the Pawnees experienced a spiritual demoralization. Settlers pillaged the Pawnee reserve of valuable timber and scared off game. Quaker policies undermined the authority of the Pawnee chiefs, resulting in a crisis of authority. And through it all, the United States government proved wholly incapable of providing the tribe with adequate aid and protection.[46]

As a result of these pressures, some Pawnees began to consider moving to Indian Territory. In March 1873, even before the events at Massacre Canyon, a Pawnee tribal faction visited Kicking Bird's Kiowa camp in Indian Territory to make peace with these former enemies in the event that the Pawnees should come to live near their Wichita relatives. At the end of the successful council, the Kiowas presented their guests with horses, and the Pawnees reciprocated by putting blankets and shawls on the shoulders of their hosts. The peace agreement eliminated one obstacle to Pawnee removal. Although at this point most Pawnees still objected to moving to Indian Territory, it appears that the catastrophe at Massacre Canyon wore down some of their resolve.[47]

In October 1873, Uh sah wuck oo led ee hoor ("Big Spotted Horse") asked Agent Burgess for permission to be taken off the tribal roll, travel to Indian Territory, and be placed on the Wichita tribal roll. Lone Chief and Frank White joined him in asking permission to leave. Burgess reluctantly agreed. Big Spotted Horse, Lone Chief, and White were all prominent tribal soldiers and had served as scouts under Frank North. Perhaps the agent considered them a dangerous and disruptive element in the tribe. He undoubtedly recalled Big Spotted Horse's role in the horse raid against the Cheyennes early in 1870.[48]

Although Big Spotted Horse, Lone Chief, and White were not chiefs, nearly three hundred Pawnees chose to follow them. They left the reservation around the middle of October. Few Indians in the party had permission to leave. Burgess immediately contacted Chief Pitalesharo, whom he considered head chief of the tribe, and demanded that the Indians be brought back.[49] Pitalesharo sent out runners, and Big Spotted Horse returned with his followers. A confrontation between the chiefs and Big Spotted Horse's supporters followed. This time there was no reconciliation. By the end of October, Big Spotted Horse and twenty-seven lodges, numbering about 250 followers, had left the agency for good. In January 1874 they arrived at the Wichita Agency, where they set up camp.[50]

Big Spotted Horse's move to Indian Territory was an important event in the history of the Pawnee scouts. It indirectly brought about a change in the Quaker policy toward the enlistment of Pawnees in the American army. Big Spotted Horse's departure was a major embarrassment for the Hicksites in charge of the Pawnee Agency. Other Pawnees threatened to follow Big Spotted Horse's example. Over the following months, small parties of Indians clandestinely left the agency to join the Wichitas on the Washita River in Indian Territory, where they lived under the supervision of the rival Orthodox branch of the Society of Friends. As Sioux raids continued in 1874, most of the Pawnees remaining at the agency began to express their desire to follow Big Spotted Horse's example and move to Indian Territory as well.[51] Superintendent White and Agent Burgess tried to stem the tide. White once again tried to induce the Sioux to reach a peace agreement with the Pawnees. When this failed, he compromised his opposition to the Pawnee scouts. White still objected "to the use of Pawnee scouts in the military operations of the United States against the Sioux tribe of Indians on account of its causing retaliation by the Sioux upon the inhabitants of the Pawnee villages." But he informed the War Department, "I can see no objection to the use of Pawnee scouts for aiding the U.S. troops in searching out straggling bands of outlaw Indians, who, away from their reservations are engaged in deeds of violence and theft."[52]

In August 1874 Brigadier General Edward O. C. Ord requested permission to enlist four Pawnee Indians as scouts for a military expedition against the Sioux, who had committed depredations around the settlements of Steele, Rawlins, and Seminole, Wyoming Territory. According to intelligence reports, they were hiding out in the Bighorn Mountains near old Fort Reno. Ord placed Captain Anson Mills in command of the expeditionary force, which consisted of several companies of the Second and Third Cavalries and two companies of infantry. Besides the four Pawnee scouts, William Cody and Tom Sun joined as guides. A caravan of seventy pack mules and twenty-eight wagons completed Mills's command.[53]

The identities of the four Pawnee scouts are unknown. In his report of the expedition, Mills listed the name of one of the scouts as "White." Possibly this was Bob White, Frank White's brother, who had served with the North brothers in 1869. White and the three other scouts joined Mills's troops at Fort McPherson and boarded a Union Pacific train to Rawlins' Station, Wyoming Territory. They arrived on August 15. Mills spent the first two weeks gathering his troops and waiting for supplies. He used the time to send out detachments on scouting missions in search of fresh Indian trails. The scouting reports were not encouraging. It appeared that the Indians had been alarmed and left the area. Nevertheless, Mills decided to march to the Powder River area in the hope of surprising some parties that had remained behind.[54]

The command left Rawlins' Station under cover of darkness on the night of August 31. The next day a severe snowstorm compelled the troops to stay in camp. The storm raged for thirty-six hours and tortured the horses and mules. On September 3 the weather cleared, and Mills resumed the march. The troopers' progress was slow because they traveled over broken landscape and the animals had been weakened by the storm and the lack of fresh grass. One of the Pawnees shot a buffalo, and the meat was a welcome addition to the usual rations of hardtack and coffee. The party found plenty of wildlife but few Indians. On September 7, Mills, while riding ahead with Cody and the Pawnees, came upon a bear and her cubs. They "despatched" the animals in less than two minutes. Undoubtedly, the Pawnees claimed the valuable bear claws as trophies.

On September 9 the command reached the north fork of the Powder River, where the men found signs of a large Indian camp that had been abandoned in great haste some six weeks earlier. Mills dispatched his scouts and guides in search of other villages, but they soon returned and reported that all the villages had been broken up six weeks before. It appeared that the Indians had all left before the storm and were headed for their reservations. Upon receiving this news, Mills decided to return to his base camp. He still believed there were some hostile Indians in the area and was determined to organize another expedition to the Tongue River, where he suspected they were hiding out. But on September 25 he received orders from General Ord to return with his command to Rawlins' Station, where the expedition would be dissolved. On September 26 Mills's troops began the march back. Nothing eventful happened along the way except that one of the soldiers, Private Miller, was seized by a bear and "horribly mangled." Soldiers quickly came to his rescue and killed the animal, but Miller died from his wounds soon after the command's arrival at Fort McPherson. The records do not reveal when the Pawnees received their discharge papers.[55]

Apart from improving existing maps of the hitherto rarely explored Bighorn territory, Mills's expedition was relatively unimportant. The same could not be said for another campaign in 1874 in which Pawnee Indians participated as scouts. After moving to Indian Territory, Big Spotted Horse and several other Pawnees enlisted in the U.S. Army during what would be called the Red River war. Unlike Mills's expedition, the Red River war was a crucial event in U.S.-Indian relations because it marked the final military subjugation of the Kiowas, Comanches, and Southern Cheyennes on the southern plains. Although only a handful of Pawnees joined the army against the hostiles in 1874, their service deserves attention.

The cause of the Red River war was the destruction of the buffalo herds on the southern and central plains. In 1870, Josiah Wright Mooar, a young entrepreneur from Vermont, began the buffalo hide bonanza in Kansas. Soon others followed in what would be an unprecedented slaughter of the bison. Between 1872 and 1874, according to some estimates, buffalo hunters killed between 4.5 million and 5.5 million animals solely for their skins. After hunters rapidly depleted the buffalo herds along the railroad lines in Kansas and Nebraska, they began to shift their operations to the southern plains. In violation of the Treaty of Medicine Lodge, signed between the United States and the southern Plains tribes in 1867, in which the tribes agreed to a smaller territory in return for annuities and support, hunters established a trading post near "Adobe Walls" in the Texas Panhandle. As the prospect of starvation became more imminent, the Kiowas, Comanches, and Southern Cheyennes protested the slaughter of the buffalo, but they received little sympathy from official quarters. Their Quaker agents seized upon the bison slaughter to promulgate farming, and the government did little to enforce the Treaty of Medicine Lodge. Annuity payments were habitually late and insufficient. Occasional harassment by soldiers and the activities of whiskey peddlers, gun traders (the so-called *comancheros*), and Mexican horse thieves added to the Indians' grievances.[56]

In May 1874 the Comanches held their first ever Sun Dance at the suggestion of Isa-tai, a prophet belonging to the Quahadi band of Comanches. A large number of Cheyennes, Arapahos, and Kiowas also attended the ceremony. The dance was intended to stir up passions against the whites, who were destroying their way of life. Isa-tai's message of war received strong support among most of the Comanches and Cheyennes and some of the Kiowas. War parties swarmed out to attack posts and settlements in Texas and Kansas. Among the main leaders of the Indian war factions were Lone Wolf, Satanta, Big Tree, Maman-ti, White Wolf, and Woman's Heart of the Kiowas; Quanah Parker and Big Red Meat of the Comanches; and Medicine Water, Iron Shirt, and Stone Calf of the Cheyennes. On

June 27, 1874, a large party of Kiowa, Comanche, and Cheyenne warriors launched an unsuccessful assault on the trading post at Adobe Walls. Several weeks later a party of Kiowas under Lone Wolf ambushed a company of Texas Rangers under Major John B. Jones at Lost Valley, Texas.[57]

Shortly after the fight at Adobe Walls, General Philip Sheridan of the Division of the Missouri began planning a campaign to disarm the Indians and drive them back to their reservations. First, he ordered agencies to enroll all friendly Indians. Indians who were found outside reservation boundaries after the deadline for enrollment had passed would be considered hostile. During the second phase of the campaign, the army would round up the hostiles in a series of military maneuvers. The Indians were hiding out on the Llano Estacado—the "Staked Plains"—a rough and inhospitable area in west Texas and southeastern New Mexico. Sheridan's plan involved a five-column attack. Lieutenant Colonel Nelson A. Miles would march south from Fort Dodge, Kansas, with companies from the Sixth Cavalry and the Fifth Infantry. Major William Redwood Price's Eighth Cavalry would move eastward from Fort Bascom, New Mexico. The Fourth Cavalry, under Lieutenant Colonel Ranald S. Mackenzie, meanwhile, would march north from Fort Concho, Texas. The last two columns consisted of two regiments of black troops, also known as "buffalo soldiers." Lieutenant Colonel George P. Buell's troops of the Eleventh Cavalry would march from Fort Griffin, Texas, and follow a northwestern course. Lieutenant Colonel John W. "Black Jack" Davidson's Tenth Cavalry, finally, would march westward from its main base at Fort Sill, Indian Territory. Among Davidson's troops was a company of Indian scouts, including Big Spotted Horse and some other Pawnees.[58]

Before starting west to drive the hostiles into the trap set by Miles and Mackenzie, Davidson marched to the Wichita Agency at Anadarko, Indian Territory. He had received some alarming dispatches from agency clerk John Connell reporting that Lone Wolf's Kiowas and Big Red Meat's Nokoni Comanches were camping near the agency. Davidson immediately left Fort Sill to disarm the Indians. On August 22, 1874, he arrived at Anadarko and ordered the Indians to surrender their arms. A firefight broke out in which four troopers were wounded and possibly fourteen Indians killed. After the battle, the hostiles fled the scene.[59]

The Anadarko fight slowed down Davidson's preparations for the campaign. He had to postpone his march for nearly three weeks. While

Davidson was busy organizing his troops, General C. C. Augur, now in charge of the Department of Texas, visited the Wichita Agency. Augur granted Davidson permission to recruit a company of friendly Indians to act as scouts for the upcoming expedition. Davidson placed Lieutenant Richard Henry Pratt in charge of the new company. Among the forty-four volunteers whom Pratt enlisted were a number of Pawnees. One of them was thirty-five-year-old Big Spotted Horse, who, because of his previous military experience, received the rank of sergeant. On September 1 the Indian scouts were officially mustered in by Lieutenant Woodward at Fort Sill.[60]

Table 6.1 gives the names of the Pawnee scouts who served in the Red River war as they appear in the sources. It is possible that more Pawnees served in this campaign, but their identities are difficult to determine from the names in the muster rolls. In addition, many Pawnee-sounding names are actually Wichita. These names are not included in the table.

Although the historical records are silent about the reasons these Pawnees enlisted, it is not difficult to imagine their motivations. First, the Pawnees were no friends of the Kiowas and Comanches, with whom they had been at war for most of the nineteenth century. Pawnee war parties frequently traveled into Kiowa and Comanche territory in search of horses. Some of the younger warriors undoubtedly seized the opportunity to gain recognition and earn war honors. Another incentive was to leave the confines of the Wichita Agency, which was becoming increasingly crowded with Pawnee refugees as well as other Indians wishing to enroll before Sheridan's deadline. The arrival of these Indians placed a tremendous drain on the available food supply. It is also possible that Big Spotted Horse believed his service was in accord with the long-standing military alliance between the Pawnee tribe and the Americans. Although the United States often failed to honor its obligations, Big Spotted Horse might have hoped his service would ensure the future goodwill of the Americans, especially because many of his fellow Pawnees had left their agency in Nebraska illegally.

General Augur had reasons of his own for allowing the Indians to enlist as scouts. Not only would they provide a valuable service to the army, but he also believed it would be a good gesture toward the friendly tribes. "The friendly tribes appear anxious to have the wild Indians punished," Augur

TABLE 6.1
Pawnee Scouts in the Red River War,
August–September 1874 to December 1874

Pawnee Name	English Name	Also Known as
—	Little Bear*	Charley White
—	Pawnee Tom*	—
Ah loo sa te tah oht*	He Stole A Horse	Robert Taylor
As sa kah lah**	Proud Horse	Robert Hopkins
Coo lah we coots cho tar kar*	White Hawk	Captain Jim
Coo rux*	Bear	High Eagle
Esauah Kedadeho†	Big Spotted Horse	—
Kew o ko et touk†	Fox —	"Charlie"
Kit Tokes†	Beaver	"Dollar"/Alex Hand
Koot tah we coots oo tah kah*†	White Hawk	Peter Headman, Sergeant Peter, Pe isk ee la shar ("Boy Chief")
Kuttowa kuts sow kurrah†	Lone Hawk	Lone Bird
Lah roo wah le roo hat*	His Mountain Range	Jackson Coosah
Ne he de sou arde†	One Going In The Lead	Leading Man
Ne saw de teeck ar ish†	Brave Chief	—
Nuh he da so sick†	One Stopped In The Lead	Leader
Sou kou oot†	—	"Lincoln"
Tee tah wee wah lee‡	—	William Riding In
Us sa ke os saits†	— Horse	"Davidson"/Walking Sun

SOURCES: Name translations by William R. Anderson, American Indian Studies Research Institute, Indiana University, Bloomington, personal communication, February 16, 2008.

*Rev. A. G. Murray to D. J. Flynn, April 24, 1900, in High Eagle Pension File, National Archives and Records Administration, Records of the Veterans Administration, Record Group 15.7.4, "Pension and Bounty Land Warrant Application Files" ("VA Records, Pension Application Files").

** Robert Hopkins Pension File, VA Records, Pension Application Files. In his pension application Hopkins gave the year of his enlistment as 1868. From the other information in the application, however, it becomes clear that he served in 1874.

† National Archives and Records Administration, Records Relating to Military Service, Record Group 94, "Register of Enlistments in the United States Army, 1798–1914," Microfilm Publications M233, Roll 70, vol. 151, "1866–1873, Indian Scouts."

‡ William Riding In Pension File, VA Records, Pension Application Files. See also Bruce, *Pawnee Naming Ceremonial*, 5.

wrote to Sheridan on September 13. "They all wish to be represented however among the scouts, and I thought it best to have them all committed against the hostile bands to that extent."[61]

Apart from the Pawnees, the Wichitas, Caddos, Tawakonis, Wacos, Kitsais, Delawares, and some other tribes were also represented in Pratt's company. They received their equipment and training at Fort Sill, where Pratt drilled them in preparation for the expedition. Pratt's Indian scouts were part of Davidson's Fort Sill column. In addition to the scouts, the column consisted of companies B, C, H, K, L, and M of the Tenth Cavalry, companies D, E, and I of the Eleventh Infantry, and a detachment of mountain howitzers. A supply train of forty-six wagons carrying three weeks' worth of supplies formed the rear of the command. On September 10, 1874, Davidson set out. It was his intention to move up the Washita River and catch any Indians between himself and Miles's column, then turn south along the eastern base of the Staked Plains to drive Indians in that part of the country toward Mackenzie's forces or catch those that Mackenzie was driving toward him.[62]

Pratt's scouts, including the Pawnees, carefully scanned a forty-mile area along the Washita and the north fork of the Red River in search of hostiles. On September 17 the scouts captured a "Kiowa Mexican" belonging to Lone Wolf's band, with three head of stock. The man was arrested and placed in iron shackles. On September 22 Davidson met Miles. Two days later he resumed his march, this time in the direction of Mackenzie's column. "General Davidson is more than pleased with his scouts," Pratt wrote to his wife. "They cover his march from five to twenty miles on each side and in front, saving his cavalry, which is now in [as] good condition as when leaving [Fort] Sill."[63]

On September 25 Lieutenant Pratt's scouts discovered a buffalo herd near McClellan Creek and killed enough animals to supply Davidson's command with fresh meat. After the hunt the scouts discovered a lone Cheyenne, who was quickly overtaken and captured. On October 2 Davidson received word that a few Indians had been seen. He ordered a detachment of troops and Pratt's scouts to pursue them. After twenty miles the troops gave up the chase, but the scouts continued for another ten miles. They captured eight horses but were unable to overtake the Indians, who had the advantage of changing onto the fresh horses they had been driving. Two days later, on October 4, Davidson ordered the scouts to follow the trail of a Noconi war party. Unfortunately for Pratt, his scouts lost the trail in a rainstorm on the second day of the pursuit. On October 10 Davidson's command returned at Fort Sill. So far the expedition had yielded little success. Although his troops had captured two hostiles and a handful of horses, they had also lost fifty-eight horses and mules to exhaustion during the arduous march.[64]

That month General Philip Sheridan personally visited Fort Sill to oversee the military operations. On his second evening at the post, Pratt's scouts performed a war dance in Sheridan's honor. Sheridan, never a firm supporter of Indian scouts, nevertheless authorized Davidson to recruit sixty more of them from the Wichita Agency. On October 15 Lieutenant Pratt mustered these additional scouts in at Fort Sill.[65]

After drawing supplies at Fort Sill, Davidson was ready to resume operations. When his command left Fort Sill on October 21, fifteen Pawnee scouts rode out with him. Among them were Big Spotted Horse, William Riding In, and twenty-six-year-old Pe isk ee la shar ("Boy Chief"), better known to whites as Peter Headman. There were too few winter uniforms available to clothe the new recruits, so when the troops left the fort, many scouts wore the "meager garb" they wore in their camps.[66] Watching the troops as they left Fort Sill was General Sheridan. The scouts, riding in column by twos, sang their war songs and shook their gourd rattles. Sheridan applauded the scouts and commended Captain Pratt on his management of them.[67]

Shortly after leaving the fort, Pratt's Indian scouts discovered a small Kiowa mule herd beyond the authorized grazing grounds. The scouts captured twenty-four mules, which they added to the train. Over the next few weeks Pratt sent small groups of his scouts on missions with detachments of regular troops. Unfortunately, his reports do not specify which scouts joined which operations, so it is impossible to determine the exact role the Pawnees played during this expedition. As usual, they rode in advance of the troops in search of trails. Despite the cold and deteriorating weather, they also served as couriers, carrying dispatches between the advance parties and Davidson's main command.[68] It is also likely that they saw action in some of the skirmishes that Davidson's troops fought with hostile Indians. On October 22, for example, Pratt sent fifteen scouts with

Major George W. Schofield's detachment. On the twenty-fourth Schofield successfully routed a Noconi Comanche camp, capturing 69 warriors, 250 women and children, and approximately 2,000 horses. Among the captives were several prominent chiefs, including Big Red Meat, the instigator of the Anadarko fight. Fifteen other scouts were with Captain Louis H. Carpenter's troops when they discovered a Kiowa village near Pond Creek. In the attack that followed, Carpenter captured 20 warriors, 50 women and children, and 200 horses. The remaining Kiowas escaped but shortly thereafter surrendered at Fort Sill.[69]

Pratt himself was present in several skirmishes. While on patrol with twenty-two scouts and eight soldiers, he stumbled upon a hastily deserted Cheyenne camp on Mule Creek. The troops burned several hundred lodge poles and other property. Several days later Pratt joined Captain Charles D. Viele's command with thirty of his scouts. The scouts soon discovered a party of Cheyennes, and Viele ordered the pursuit. Although the troopers chased the Cheyennes for five days, they were unable to overtake them. The Cheyennes, however, lost fifty horses and mules during the retreat. Many of the mules carried supplies.

Cold weather began to plague the troops in the field. A severe ice storm, which lasted for four days, killed more than ninety of Davidson's horses and incapacitated twenty-six of his men with frostbite. But the same cold that plagued the troops also tormented the hostile Indians.[70]

By the time Davidson, Pratt, and the Pawnee scouts returned to Fort Sill on November 29, they had captured more than 450 prisoners (including 113 warriors) and several thousand horses and mules. Although their successes were less spectacular than Colonel Mackenzie's victory over the hostiles at Palo Duro Canyon, where the soldiers captured some thousand horses and destroyed large quantities of supplies belonging to the Kiowas, Comanches, and Cheyennes, Davidson's troops had kept the resisting Indians on the run. They not only destroyed most of the Indians' supplies but also prevented them from hunting buffalo to replenish their supplies. Faced with cold and starvation, most resisters surrendered over the following weeks and months. On December 1, 1874, Pratt's Indian scouts, including the Pawnees, were mustered out.[71]

In his final report on the expedition, Pratt praised the performance of his scouts. Among the few Indians he mentioned by name was Big Spotted

Horse, who deserved a "special commendation for services." Pratt was particularly impressed by Big Spotted Horse's performance under difficult circumstances. On one occasion, while his command was snowbound, Colonel Davidson ordered Pratt to send some couriers to one of his commands in the field. None of the white scouts was willing to go, because of the weather and the weak condition of their horses. Pratt approached Big Spotted Horse instead. Big Spotted Horse, whom Pratt described as "a tall fine specimen of a man who relished perilous service," selected another Pawnee scout to accompany him. The two left camp while a winter storm was raging and returned four days later with an answer. Pratt took the two scouts to Davidson, who was very pleased with them. When Davidson offered Big Spotted Horse and his companion some whiskey, the scouts refused, "saying that they did not drink whiskey."[72]

Big Spotted Horse's refusal to share a drink with a high-ranking officer in the United States Army belies the charge made by the Quaker administrators that military service had an inevitable demoralizing effect on the Indians. Although it is true that their service exposed them to the ills of white society, it is also true that traditional Pawnee culture continued to exert a powerful hold on these men. Temperance was one aspect of this culture, as was the martial tradition. Thus, even though they wore on occasion the uniform of the U.S. Army, the scouts never ceased to be Pawnees. They were soldiers as well as warriors.

Apart from ending Grant's Peace Policy, the Red River war was significant for the future of the Pawnee battalion. Although Quakers and other religious denominations remained in charge of Indian agencies, they could no longer prevent the enlistment of Pawnees into the army. The Office of Indian Affairs formally had the last word on the employment of Indian scouts, but in reality the military establishment always received permission to enlist Indians for military service, especially in emergency situations.

CHAPTER 7

The Powder River Campaign with Crook and Mackenzie, 1876–1877

Between 1874 and 1875, the Pawnees remaining at the original Pawnee Agency in Nebraska followed in Big Spotted Horse's footsteps and moved to Indian Territory. They eventually settled on a 283,026-acre reservation on Black Bear Creek in present-day north-central Oklahoma. There they began the difficult and desperate struggle for survival in a new environment. Although the Pawnees were now far removed from any Sioux threat, the climatic and social circumstances of Indian Territory proved equally devastating to the tribe. Strange ailments such as malaria and influenza sent population numbers spiraling downward for the next two decades. The Pawnees were no longer free to roam the prairies in search of buffalo, and government agents ordered the men to take up farming for subsistence. When not working in the fields, the Pawnees passed the time with dances and visiting their Wichita relatives or other friendly tribes. Mostly, however, they were restricted from leaving their reservation. The trauma of removal and high mortality, combined with boredom and poverty, demoralized many on the new reservation. A once proud people seemed to have lost its sense of self-esteem.[1]

Although individual Pawnees had, on occasion, continued to serve as scouts for the United States Army, the Pawnee battalion had not been reactivated since 1870. But in 1876, as the Pawnees struggled for survival on their new reservation, events elsewhere set in motion the wheels that would lead to the battalion's resurrection. That year the Western Sioux and Northern Cheyennes took up arms against the United States and nearly brought the western army to its knees. In the war that followed, the Pawnee scouts once again played an important role.

The causes of the "Great Sioux War" (the term is inaccurate, because the Northern Cheyennes were also involved) dated back to the early 1870s. The Panic of 1873 had plunged the United States into a severe economic depression. A large number of banks collapsed, unemployment rose, railroad construction halted, and paper money declined in value. The nation faced a deep financial crisis. The rumor of enormous gold deposits in the Black Hills of South Dakota sparked the interest of the national government. In 1874 General William T. Sherman ordered Lieutenant Colonel George Armstrong Custer to organize a reconnaissance expedition into the Black Hills to establish the accuracy of the rumors. Custer had achieved great popularity with the general public for his daring campaigns during the Civil War and his attack on the Southern Cheyennes at the battle of the Washita in 1868. He was a brave but unimaginative officer (he finished last in his class at West Point in 1861) who preferred to charge the enemy head-on. Despite his crude and reckless tactics, he enjoyed an incredible amount of luck (widely known as "Custer's Luck") and achieved great success on the field of battle. Custer's Black Hills expedition consisted of his beloved Seventh Cavalry and a large group of scientists, including George Bird Grinnell, who invited Luther North along as an assistant.[2] Despite the peaceful nature of the trip, Custer's expedition violated the spirit, if not the terms, of the Fort Laramie Treaty of 1868, which included the Black Hills as part of the Great Sioux Reservation.[3]

Although Custer found little of the precious metal, he returned from the expedition with the news that gold had indeed been found. The report sparked a genuine gold rush into the Black Hills. Miners and prospectors invaded the area from all sides. Rather than preventing intruders from trespassing on Indian land, as it was obliged to do under to the stipulations of the Fort Laramie Treaty, the federal government did little to prevent the miners from going in. It also arranged for negotiations with the Sioux to obtain possession of the land itself. In 1875 President Ulysses S. Grant offered to pay the Indians $6 million for the Black Hills and the land around the Little Bighorn River. The Sioux under Sitting Bull and Crazy Horse, and the Northern Cheyennes under Dull Knife and Little Wolf, rejected the government's offer. Although Red Cloud of the Oglalas and Spotted Tail of the Brulés did not reject the sale of the land, their demands were unacceptable to the administration.

Instead of continuing negotiations, the United States began to prepare for war. Secretary of the Interior Zachariah Chandler and Commissioner of Indian Affairs Edward P. Smith ordered all Indians in the area to return to their reservations by January 31, 1876. Any Indian found off reservation land would be considered hostile. The ultimatum ignored the fact that the Indians had a legal right to reside on unceded land. Over the next few months, opponents of the sale of the Black Hills gathered near the Bighorn Mountains.

Back at his headquarters in Chicago, General Philip Sheridan, commander of the Division of the Missouri, began to plan a massive military campaign against those Indians who chose to ignore the order to return to their reservations. On February 7, 1876, Sheridan instructed Brigadier Generals George Crook and Alfred Howe Terry to mount expeditions into the Little Bighorn and Powder River areas in order to disarm the Indians and drive them back to their agencies.[4] Crook's column would march against the Indians from the south while Terry's force, which was divided into two columns—one under the command of Colonel John R. Gibbon and the other under Lieutenant Colonel George A. Custer—would move against the Indians from the west and east, respectively. In many ways the plan resembled the successful strategy Sheridan had employed during the Red River war two years earlier. About forty Arikara scouts, close relatives and friends of the Pawnees, accompanied Custer's command. Like the Pawnees, the Arikaras had suffered for many decades from Sioux harassment and welcomed the opportunity to serve as scouts against their enemies.

Sheridan's plan suffered setbacks from the start. Poor weather delayed Terry from marching ahead. Fortune spared one of Crook's advance parties, under the command of Colonel Joseph Reynolds, from annihilation in a battle with Cheyennes on March 17. As a result of the Reynolds fight, more Indians joined Sitting Bull and Crazy Horse against the army. Two months later, on June 17, 1876, Crook himself suffered an embarrassing defeat at the battle of the Rosebud. Although he lost only nine dead and twenty-one wounded, his forces took a severe thrashing and had to withdraw from the area. Eight days later, on June 25, 1876, Lieutenant Colonel Custer finally ran out of luck when he attacked a large Indian camp near the Little Bighorn River. Among the Indians at the Little Bighorn were Sitting Bull's Hunkpapa Sioux, Crazy Horse's Oglala Sioux, and Dull Knife's Northern Cheyennes. Instead of running away as Custer expected, the Indians made a determined stand. In the ensuing battle, Custer, who once boasted that the Seventh Cavalry could handle the Indians of the plains alone, died with about 250 men in his command. According to Indian sources, Custer never made a "stand." Most of his panic-stricken soldiers died while running for their lives.[5]

The annihilation of Custer's battalion stunned a nation on the eve of its centennial anniversary celebrations. But as historian Charles M. Robinson observed, "Custer was performing greater service dead than he had ever done alive." His death prompted Congress to overturn its post–Civil War policy of downsizing the army. On the day before the Custer battle, Congress had adopted an army appropriations bill that, among other things, limited the number of Indian scouts the army could employ to three hundred. But as soon news of the defeat of Custer's command trickled back to Washington, Congress decided to support the military with all necessary and available resources. Seizing the moment, General Sheridan immediately demanded an increase in the size of the army, authority to construct two forts in the heart of enemy territory along the Yellowstone, and direct military control over the Indian agencies. Congress swiftly granted all his wishes.[6]

Among the measures Congress adopted was an "Act Concerning the Employment of Indian Scouts." The bill, which went into effect on August 12, 1876, repealed the previous act (of July 24) and authorized the employment of one thousand Indian scouts. It also stipulated that scouts who furnished their own horses and horse equipment were entitled to forty cents a day extra "for their use and risk so long as thus employed."[7]

Although never a warm supporter of Indian scouts, General Sheridan used the act to recruit several companies of scouts to assist in the upcoming campaigns against the Sioux and Cheyennes.[8] Among the Indians he wished to enlist for service were the Pawnees. On August 15, 1876, Frank

North departed for Chicago at Sheridan's orders.[9] Sheridan, under the mistaken assumption that the Pawnees still resided at the Wichita Agency, instructed North to travel there to enlist one hundred scouts. According to Sheridan's instructions, the "Pawnees enlisted must be able bodied, active Indians." They would be armed, clothed, and rationed by the government but should furnish their own horses, for which they would receive a "per diem allowance of forty cents for each horse." The Pawnees were to be taken to Sidney Barracks, Nebraska, where they would receive their training and await further orders. In case the Pawnees could not furnish their own horses, Sheridan authorized North to buy horses for them.[10]

Several days later Major North and his brother traveled to Fort Sill, Indian Territory. When they learned that the Pawnees no longer lived at the Wichita Agency, they boarded a train north to Coffeyville, Kansas, and from there proceeded south again to the Pawnee reservation by wagon. After a difficult three-day journey across rough terrain, they reached the agency around midnight on September 2. The trip had been demanding on North's health; he is known to have suffered from asthma and respiratory problems throughout his life. When the brothers woke up the next morning, they found the entire tribe outside waiting to meet them. According to Luther North, when the Pawnees saw his brother, "a great shout went up from them, ah-ti-us Pawnee Lashar (Father, the Pawnee Chief), and they fairly climbed over each other trying to get to him."[11]

The scene of devastation and poverty on the Pawnee reservation shocked Luther North. "The tribe was in very bad shape," he wrote in his memoir. "They were miserably poor, nearly all of them had ague, and many of them were dying. They were very much discouraged and many of them were longing to get back to Nebraska."[12]

After explaining the purpose of his visit in a council with the chiefs, Major North opened a recruiting office in the Pawnee council house. He was forced to vacate the office when hundreds of young men tried to get in and sign up for the new battalion all at once. North set up a desk outside the house and within an hour had penned the names of one hundred men.[13]

The Pawnees were eager to enlist. Some scholars have observed that the main incentive to join the expedition was economic.[14] Frank North himself seemed to believe that the Pawnees wished to go on the warpath against the Sioux in order to "draw from the government abundant rations, good uniforms, and fair pay."[15] But there were other, more personal motives as well. Many men signed up to escape the confines of the reservation. As Grinnell pointed out, "each man, at any cost, sought to get away from the suffering of his present life; from the fever that made him quake, the chill that caused him to shiver, and above all from the deadly monotony of the reservation life."[16] One man implored North to take his fifteen-year-old son with him on the expedition. He told North that the boy needed no pay and could serve as a personal servant to the major. North eventually gave in. Why the father wanted his son to go on the campaign is unclear, but the young man had his own reasons. Ah re Kah rard ("Antlers," later known by his English name, Rush Roberts) was a survivor of Massacre Canyon and joined the campaign in search of revenge. The "Sioux and Cheyennes were our enemies," Roberts remembered later, "and I had this chance to operate against them."[17]

Although economic destitution, revenge, and escaping boredom and disease were the most important incentives for young Pawnees to enlist, it is easy to imagine that many also signed up in the hope of earning war honors. Poverty and government policies were slowly eroding the old social structures, which emphasized rank, hierarchy, and social position. Military service allowed men to gain social recognition on the field of battle. Furthermore, old habits die slowly, and some may not die at all.

In a letter to Robert Bruce in 1931, Rush Roberts remarked that being selected to serve in the 1876 campaign was a great honor in itself. "I well remember the day the men were selected," Roberts wrote. "Every ablebodied man and boy [was] eager to engage in warfare with our old enemies, the Sioux and Cheyennes." According to Roberts, those selected "were easily recognized by the broad smiles with which they greeted everyone." He added that it was "a great honor."[18]

Many more Pawnees were eager to enlist than North could take along. Among those lining up to enlist were a young Wichita Blaine and his uncle, "He Who Reveres Goals." When North walked up, Blaine's uncle said, "This is my nephew. We are ready to go." North looked at the old man and replied, "You cannot go, but your nephew can go." Blaine's uncle pleaded with North to let him come along. His nephew was still young, he said. "Let me go. . . . If anyone is to die, let me die." But North refused. "No," he told the old man, "you are wise; stay here and teach the young people what you know."[19] Wichita Blaine was enlisted under his Indian name, Tah Kah ("White"). Because there were three scouts by that name, Blaine received the designation "#2" to distinguish him from the others.[20]

Among the men joining the Norths were Li Heris oo la shar ("Leading Chief," also known by his English name, Frank White) and Ralph J. Weeks, an educated Indian who spoke fluent English.[21] Both were appointed to the rank of sergeant in the battalion. John G. Bourke, aide-de-camp to General Crook, later wrote that Frank White had a "good face, prominent cheek bones, aquiline nose, large mouth and frank, open eyes." Although White appeared judicious and deliberate, Bourke continued, "he was no lamb, as the outlines of his countenance plainly showed that, if aroused, he would be a bad enemy."[22]

The recruits included veterans such as Walking Sun (Us sa kouht, or "Horse With Downy Feathers"), who had served two previous enlistments, including one with Captain Pratt on the southern plains in 1874. Simond Adams (Us sah kip pe di la shah, or "Dog Chief"), son of the fabled Pawnee warrior Crooked Hand, had served in 1870. Many others were first-time enlistees. Of these fresh recruits, Wichita Blaine, Rush Roberts, and Red Hawk (later known as "Roam Chief"), were only in their mid-teens. Much depended on the experience of the veterans as they assisted these newcomers in Indian warfare.

Other young scouts included twenty-two-year-old Tow we his ee ("Leader of The Group," later known as Echo Hawk), and Abraham Lincoln. Like so many other Pawnees, Tow we his ee had lost relatives at Massacre Canyon. He followed in the footsteps of his father and his uncle, who had served as scouts in 1864 and 1865, respectively. Abraham Lincoln was a Kitkahahki, born around 1851 or 1852. He had received his English name while a student at the Pawnee manual labor school in Nebraska.[23]

Those fortunate to go gathered their clothes and, most important, their personal medicine bundles. Wichita Blaine packed the little bird bundle that his uncle had given him. Many years earlier his uncle had received a vision in which he saw a warrior and received instructions to prepare the bird bundle and two sacred songs to accompany it. When his nephew came of age, he gave him the bundle and instructed him in its use. His uncle told Blaine that if he wore the little bag in his hair when he went to battle, he would never be killed.[24]

Before they set out for Coffeyville, Kansas, Eagle Chief and Curly Chief made short speeches to the departing scouts. Ruling His Sun also spoke. According to Luther North, he warned the younger men that they must obey their officers or they would be punished like white soldiers. He also told Frank North that "if he had to punish any of them he shouldn't tie them to wagon wheels."[25] The comment amused North, but Ruling His Sun was undoubtedly referring to an incident in 1867 when some Pawnees mutinied after North tried to impose a severe punishment on a scout.

The men left the Pawnee Agency and traveled to Coffeyville on foot. A large group of Pawnees who had been rejected for service followed them as far as possible, begging Major North to be allowed to go. At Coffeyville, North and his men boarded a train. Some of the men following the group desperately tried to climb aboard the train, much to North's dismay. According to one account:

> One old man bothered North, begging him to be allowed to go, and kept crawling onto the train. North finally strapped him across the back. The old man said, "You have shamed me." North replied, "No, you have shamed me. Here you are an old man and I have to strike you, an old man, so you will know you cannot go." Many other men standing there said, "Grandfather, let us ride with you a little way." It was hard for North to refuse them, but he had to. So many wanted to go because life was hard on the reservation, they were hungry, and they wanted to be warriors and feel successful again.[26]

From Coffeyville the scouts rode the train to Kansas City, where they changed cars and traveled to Omaha, Nebraska. Their excitement grew as they recognized more and more sites along the road. Their morale seemed to improve with each mile as they came closer to their old home. They spent the nights talking about the old days in Nebraska, singing, and dancing.[27] One evening, while visiting an old, abandoned Pawnee town site, some of the scouts "heard voices and village sounds as if the people were still alive."[28] When they arrived at Columbus, Nebraska, they picked up Sylvanus E. Cushing, who would accompany the Pawnee scouts once again as a captain. Cushing, Luther North, and the scouts continued their journey to Sidney Barracks. Frank North, still not fully recovered from his bout of poor health, stayed in Columbus to visit a doctor.

On September 18 the Pawnees were mustered in at Sidney Barracks. The white officer entered September 3, the day Major North had recruited the men at the Pawnee Agency, as the official day of muster. After receiving their arms, ammunition, clothing, and camp equipment, the Pawnees went into camp on Lodgepole Creek, one mile below the town. A few days later Frank North joined them. Luther North traveled to Julesburg to buy horses for the men. At Sidney Barracks the men also received their first training. The drills were designed not to instill discipline but to bring the men into shape again. Captain North also ordered them to ride up and down the roads to get them accustomed to their ponies. Some of the younger scouts had learned to play baseball and competed against a team of soldiers from the fort. Although the soldiers won most of the games, North commented that it "kept the men in good condition, and took their minds off their wait for marching orders." The scouts also treated the people of Sidney to a war dance one evening. According to the local newspaper, hundreds of citizens attended, "and all seemed to be well satisfied with their performance." Several weeks later the scouts also performed a "Dog Tail War Dance" for the people of Sidney.[29]

Although the Pawnees' health and strength steadily improved, several scouts died of ailments previously contracted in Indian Territory. Ke wuck oo kah lah died on Monday, September 25, of typhoid fever. He was buried the following Tuesday in the graveyard at Sidney, with full military honors.[30] A week later, on October 3, Stu le kit tah we ait died of "congestion of lungs" (pneumonia). Ke wuck oo hod de succumbed to "typhoid malarial fever" at Sidney Barracks on October 12.[31]

While the Pawnees received their arms, horses, and training at Sidney Barracks, preparations for the upcoming campaigns were in full swing. After the Custer battle, the resisting Indians had dispersed into small bands. Dull Knife had taken his Northern Cheyennes deeper into the Bighorn Mountains. Crazy Horse's Oglalas were rumored to be in the Powder River area, and Sitting Bull's Hunkpapas, Miniconjous, and Sans

Arcs were encamped in Montana Territory. The army hoped to round up these Indians through a series of expeditions. The situation was urgent, because hundreds of Indians, attracted by the spectacular victories over Custer and Crook, drifted away from their reservations to join the resisting Sioux and Cheyennes. Among them were many young warriors from the Red Cloud Agency in northwestern Nebraska.

General Sheridan, in charge of the operations on the plains, unfolded his three-part plan to end the war. First, he ordered Colonel Nelson A. Miles and his Fifth Infantry into the Yellowstone area to contain the hostile Sioux from the north and prevent them from escaping into Canada. Part two of Sheridan's plan called for the military takeover of the Sioux agencies in Dakota Territory and western Nebraska, in order to prevent warriors from leaving their reservations to join the hostile Indians. To make certain these Indians would not take up arms against the United States, Sheridan wished to disarm and dismount them in a number of swift and decisive actions. Finally, he proposed that General Crook mount another campaign into the Powder River area in order to drive the Sioux and Cheyennes back to their reservations. To assist Crook's winter campaign, Sheridan ordered Colonel Ranald S. Mackenzie and the Fourth Cavalry to Camp Robinson, Nebraska. Sheridan intended for the Pawnees to assist Crook and Mackenzie in the winter campaign.[32]

Despite his humiliating encounter with the Sioux and Cheyennes at the battle of the Rosebud, General George Crook was one of the most distinguished and successful military commanders in the West. In large part his success depended on his understanding of Indian warfare. Rejecting orthodox military tactics as taught at West Point, Crook developed his own ideas about campaigning against Indians. He did not like to use slow-moving wagon trains but preferred pack mules and a minimum of supplies to keep up with fast-traveling Indians. He admired Indians for their superior skills as scouts and warriors and advocated the use of Indians as scouts and auxiliaries of the frontier army. In an interview in the *Army and Navy Journal* of October 21, 1876, Crook said he always tried to get Indian scouts, "because scouting is with them the business of their lives." Experience had also taught him that Indian scouts were reliable. If "you can make it to the Indian's interest to tell the truth," he said, "you get correct information."

In the same interview, Crook gave his view on using Indians against Indians. He believed that the presence of Indian scouts had a demoralizing effect on the enemy, particularly when those scouts belonged to the same tribe as the hostile Indians. He believed that Indians were unafraid of American soldiers, whom they considered cowardly and inferior in man-to-man combat. But they feared Indian warriors like themselves. "Some people say it is wrong to use the people of a tribe against itself," Crook said, "but pshaw! if I can kill one rattlesnake by making another bite him, I shall do it."[33]

Crook's humane treatment of his Indian scouts often provoked the scorn and disgust of his American troops. During the Powder River campaign, Lieutenant Colonel Richard Irving Dodge complained that the Indian scouts were treated better than the regular soldiers. "He scarcely treats McKenzie [sic] and I decently," Dodge wrote in his diary, "but he will spend hours chatting pleasantly with an Indian or a dirty scout."[34]

Colonel Ranald Slidell Mackenzie commanded the Fourth Cavalry, a regiment that, under his leadership, had been turned into a crack fighting unit. Mackenzie had graduated first in his class from West Point in 1862 and made a reputation for himself as a brave and able commander during the Shenandoah and Appomattox campaigns in the Civil War. His performance greatly impressed General U. S. Grant, who called him "the most promising young officer in the army." During the Civil War he also received a severe injury to his right hand, which would earn him the nickname "Bad Hand" among the Indian tribes of the West. Among his greatest successes in the Indian campaigns after the Civil War was his victory over the Kiowas and Comanches at Palo Duro Canyon during the Red River war in 1874. But in 1875 he received a severe head injury, which may have contributed to strange psychotic episodes that, years later, developed into full-blown insanity.[35]

In the late summer, Mackenzie arrived at Camp Robinson, Nebraska, with six companies of the Fourth Cavalry. Camp Robinson, at this time only a small military post, had been established on March 8, 1874, to maintain order among the Sioux warriors settled there.[36] Most of these Indians belonged to Red Cloud's band of Oglalas. Shortly after his arrival, Mackenzie undertook a census of the Indians at the Red Cloud Agency.

According to previous reports, 12,873 Sioux and about 1,200 Northern Cheyennes were enrolled at Red Cloud. Mackenzie's census indicated that presently there were only about 4,760 Sioux and between 600 and 700 Cheyennes at the agency. A similar census at the Spotted Tail Agency showed similar results. Of the 9,170 Indians enrolled there, only 4,775 remained. Although the official numbers furnished by the agents had been grossly inflated in order to provide more rations for the Indians, it was clear that many Indians had joined the resisters under Crazy Horse and Sitting Bull. Mackenzie immediately sent an alarming report to his superiors.[37] General Crook endorsed Mackenzie's report: "These Agencies are and have been the head and front of all the trouble and hostilities which have been in progress," Crook wrote to Sheridan. "They are and have been regular depots of recruits and supplies."[38]

On September 21 Sheridan met with Crook and Mackenzie at Fort Laramie to discuss the upcoming winter campaign and the disarmament of the Indians at the Red Cloud and Spotted Tail Agencies. The situation became urgent in October when the Oglalas under Red Cloud and a group of Brulés under Red Leaf and Swift Bear broke away from their agencies in protest of government proposals to remove the Sioux to Indian Territory. They settled in two camps on Chadron Creek, Nebraska. Mackenzie ordered the Indians to return to Camp Robinson, but Red Cloud and Red Leaf refused and demanded that their rations be sent to their new camps on Chadron Creek. Although Mackenzie withheld their rations altogether, they would not budge. On October 22, as the situation became more critical, Mackenzie sent First Lieutenant Oscar Elting to Major North asking for assistance. He then gathered his troops—six companies of the Fourth Cavalry and two detached companies of the Fifth Cavalry under Major George A. Gordon—and rode in the direction of Chadron Creek. They started at night and circumvented the Red Cloud Agency in order not to draw the attention of possible Indian spies.[39]

While Mackenzie's men prepared themselves to move against Red Cloud and Red Leaf, North and the Pawnee scouts were in camp on the Niobrara River, a hundred miles north of Sidney. They were eating dinner when Lieutenant Elting arrived from Camp Robinson. He carried a dispatch from Mackenzie ordering the scouts to join the troops at once to assist in the surrounding of the Indian camps on Chadron Creek. Major North took his brother and forty-two scouts and pressed forward in an all-night ride to overtake Mackenzie. Lieutenant Cushing, meanwhile, proceeded with the remaining scouts to Camp Robinson, where they arrived at three o'clock in the morning on Sunday, October 23.[40]

North's Pawnees rode seventy miles that night to link up with Mackenzie's forces. They rode at a steady pace for five hours until coming in sight of the troops. Their sudden appearance briefly caused some alarm among the soldiers. After a few minutes rest, the combined force continued the march. When they came within twenty miles of the two Indian camps, Mackenzie divided his command into two equal battalions. He placed Major Gordon in charge of surrounding Red Leaf's camp. Luther North and half the scouts (twenty-one men) joined Gordon. Mackenzie himself took charge of the remaining troops, including Frank North and the remaining Pawnees, to surround Red Cloud's camp. When the trail they followed separated, the two commands parted ways.[41]

After traveling for a while in complete silence, Mackenzie's battalion reached Red Cloud's camp. To his surprise, he found Gordon's troops already there. Gordon's guide had directed him mistakenly to the wrong camp. Mackenzie ordered Gordon to the other camp at once and then began to prepare his men for the dawn attack. By five o'clock that morning his troops had surrounded the camp. On Mackenzie's orders, one of his interpreters called out in Lakota that the camp was surrounded. Some of the women and children emerged from their tepees and sought cover in the nearby brush. On Major North's order, the Pawnee scouts rushed into the camp and rounded up all the horses. Then Captain Clarence Mauck entered the camp. The Indians had been taken by complete surprise and surrendered without firing a shot. They were quickly disarmed. Mackenzie ordered the women to break down the camp and select a few ponies from the captured herd on which to mount their baggage. When the women hesitated, Mackenzie's men torched a few tepees, whereupon they complied.[42]

Meanwhile, Major Gordon's troops surrounded Red Leaf's camp. Gordon ordered Luther North's scouts to dash through the camp to round up all horses. The men received orders not to fire unless the Indians fired first. The Pawnee scouts gave their war whoop as they dashed through the camp, but none of the Indians came outside their lodges. Many of the horses were scattered around the camp, and most of them were tied down. It took the scouts almost an hour to gather the entire herd. After the scouts had collected the horses, the Indians came out and surrendered. They were taking down their lodges when Mackenzie arrived. Mackenzie allowed the Indians to take enough horses to pack their camp and for the old and feeble people to ride on, but he made the young warriors walk.[43]

The surrounds had been a complete success, in no mean part because of the presence of the Pawnee scouts. Many years later, while attending a banquet at Fort Robinson, Luther North chuckled when an old Sioux pointed at him and said that "if it wasn't for his Pawnees protecting the soldiers they never would have gotten our horses." North thought the "idea of our 40 Pawnees protecting about 600 soldiers was funny."[44]

The Pawnees drove the captured horse herd, some 722 animals, toward Camp Robinson. They were followed by Mackenzie's troops, who escorted the defeated Indians. They arrived at Camp Robinson early in the morning of October 24. After the soldiers searched the Indians' baggage for ammunition, they were sent to the Red Cloud Agency, where they set up camp again. That same day General Crook dismissed Red Cloud from his position as "principal" chief of the Lakotas and replaced him with Spotted Tail. Crook argued that Spotted Tail's Indians were the true friends of the whites and, contrary to Sheridan's orders, refused to disarm and dismount all of them. Indeed, he hoped to enlist the "loyal" Sioux for the upcoming winter campaign against Crazy Horse and the other hostiles.[45] Several days later Crook sent three of his white scouts, William Garnett, Baptiste ("Big Bat") Pourier, and Frank Grouard, to the Spotted Tail Agency to recruit Indians to serve as scouts for the impending expedition.[46]

Rumors that some of the Indians might attempt to recapture their horses prompted General Crook to order Major North to take some of his scouts and drive the herd to Fort Laramie, Wyoming Territory. Although they had been in the saddle for nearly three days, with little or no sleep since the twenty-second, North and forty or fifty scouts left Camp Robinson on October 24. That night they ran into a wagon train of soldiers carrying supplies for Camp Robinson. The nervous soldiers, alarmed at the sudden appearance of the Pawnees, nearly fired at them in the darkness. Fortunately, the Indians' true identity was established just in time, and the Pawnees arrived safely at Fort Laramie the next day.[47]

North turned the herd over to the quartermaster at Fort Laramie on October 25. Luther North, Lieutenant Cushing, and the remaining scouts arrived at Fort Laramie on October 28. A few days later General Crook told Major North to bring the men who had taken part in the capture of Red Cloud's and Red Leaf's camps to select a horse apiece from the captured herd. Then he authorized North to take seventy more horses as a reserve to replace any horses that might die or give out during the winter campaign he was planning. After North and the Pawnees had made their selections, Crook himself chose several hundred animals to serve as extra saddle horses for the other scouts in the upcoming campaign.[48] The remainder of the Sioux horses, some 450 animals, were sold at auctions at Fort Laramie, Cheyenne Depot, and Sidney Barracks. With the proceeds of the auction, supplies were bought for the Indians at the Red Cloud Agency.[49]

At Fort Laramie, Crook began to gather troops and supplies for the Powder River expedition. His goal was to capture Crazy Horse's band. Over the next few days, units from various regiments trickled into Fort Laramie and reported to Crook for duty. The expedition consisted of three components. The cavalry was composed of companies B, D, E, F, I, and M of the Fourth Cavalry, H and L of the Fifth Cavalry, K of the Second Cavalry, and K of the Third Cavalry. The cavalry would take the field under the command of Colonel Mackenzie. Crook placed Lieutenant Colonel Richard I. Dodge in charge of the infantry. Dodge had at his disposal companies A, B, D, I, F, and K of the Ninth Infantry, D and G of the Fourteenth Infantry, and C, G, and I of his own Twenty-third Infantry. Four companies of the Fourth Artillery formed the final component of the command. They, too, were placed under Dodge's command.[50]

In addition to the regular troops, Crook had a large number of Indian and white scouts at his disposal. Many of the white scouts were in fact of mixed ancestry, among them Frank Grouard and Baptiste Pourier. The Indian scouts consisted of "loyal" Indians. The Arapahos included Sharp Nose, Black Coal, Old Eagle, Six Feathers, Little Fork, White Horse, and interpreter William Friday. Among the Sioux were Three Bears, Fast

Thunder, Charging Bear, Pretty Voiced Bull, Yellow Shirt, Singing Bear, Tall Wild Cat, and Black Mouse. A handful of Cheyennes, including Thunder Cloud, Bird, Blown Away, Old Crow, Fisher, and Hard Robe, were also present. Three of the Cheyennes were brothers-in-law of William Rowland, a white man who had married into the tribe and who also accompanied the expedition. First Lieutenant William Philo Clark and Second Lieutenant Hayden Delaney were in charge of the Sioux, Arapaho, and Cheyenne scouts. "Captain" Tom Cosgrove and First Lieutenant Walter S. Schuyler's battalion of Shoshone scouts joined the command on November 17, when the expedition was well under way.[51] Seventy-six Crow scouts under the command of a Major Randall were supposed to join the troops, but bad weather hampered their progress and they did not reach Crook's camp until December.[52] Civilian and medical personnel completed the expedition. The entire command consisted of 61 officers, 1,436 enlisted men, 367 Indian scouts, 400 pack mules attended to by 65 packers, 168 wagons, and 7 ambulances.[53]

At Laramie the Pawnees received supplies for the upcoming expedition, including heavy underclothing, fur caps, gloves, leggings, arctic overshoes, blankets, and "A"-tents.[54] While Crook was gathering troops and supplies for the Powder River expedition, the scouts entertained themselves with horse races. Although the races were mainly intended to test the endurance and speed of the captured horses, the Pawnees' display of their captured trophies was a major source of frustration among the Sioux and Arapaho scouts.[55]

Major North expected great discipline from his men, and he took some strict measures whenever his men disobeyed orders. When two scouts failed to show up for a mounted inspection on October 31, North had one of them tied up and the other carry a log in front of his tent for an hour as an example to the other men in the battalion.[56] Carrying a log around was a common punishment for soldiers who were intoxicated.

At Laramie the Pawnee scouts mingled freely with the regular troops. Occasionally, Indians and white soldiers made new friendships, and some old ones were rekindled. Lieutenant Colonel Dodge, for example, was pleased to see Pawnee Sergeant Frank White (Li Heris oo la shar) again. Dodge and White had first met in 1867 while stationed along the Union Pacific line in Nebraska. Together they had fought off a Sioux war party that cornered them during a hunting expedition. John G. Bourke recalled that the scouts honored First Lieutenant Charles Rockwell with an Indian name, "Six Feathers," as a token of friendship. Bourke believed, however, that this special honor might have been induced by the fact that Rockwell, as commissary, controlled large quantities of bacon, sugar, and coffee.[57] Lieutenant William P. Clark, called "White Hat" by the Indian scouts, was particularly fascinated by the scouts' ability to communicate with members of other tribes through sign language. He began to study the Indian sign language and eventually published a book about it.[58]

Some of the regularly enlisted men and officers, however, held their Indian allies in low regard. Second Lieutenant Henry H. Bellas, Fourth Cavalry, for example, believed that all Indians were treacherous and unreliable. Unable to understand the complexities of Indian social relations, he noted that "any Indian will betray even those of his own tribe, including all his wife's relations, provided the reward offered be sufficiently tempting."[59] Of course such a view did not take into consideration social and political divisions within tribes or intratribal disagreements over proper courses of action. Only little more than a decade earlier, the Civil War had split white families and pitched brothers against brothers on the field of battle. For the Pawnee scouts, however, such considerations played no role. They were fighting their old enemies and were eager to settle past scores.

The Pawnees could trust neither the Sioux nor the regular soldiers. After placing the horses captured at Chadron Creek in the care of the quartermaster of the command, the Pawnees noticed that some of the horses began to disappear mysteriously during the night. To prevent the further theft of the horses, Major North ordered his men to guard the animals at all times and kill anyone who tried to take them away. After this order was issued, no more thefts were reported.[60]

General Crook left Fort Laramie on November 5 and set out for Fort Fetterman, Wyoming Territory, where he arrived two days later. He left without properly notifying Major North of the move. Crook's sudden departure surprised even Mackenzie, who quickly gathered his troops to follow the general. Mackenzie arrived at Fetterman on November 9. Major North's scouts arrived the next day, together with Dodge's infantry. Crook's vague instructions and seemingly erratic marching orders soon became a source of frustration for Major North.[61]

North was also outraged by rumors that he would be placed under the command of Lieutenant William Clark, who had suggested combining all the Indian scouts under his command. North rejected the proposal, saying that he would take orders only from Crook or Mackenzie. He argued that the Pawnees and Sioux had been mortal enemies, and combining them into one command would only create chaos. Crook agreed, and the Pawnee battalion remained under North's command.[62]

From Fort Fetterman the expedition marched northwest. As usual, the Pawnees' main task was to search the area for hostile Indians and guide the troops. According to Bourke, the scouts "covered the country for thirty to forty miles on each side of the column, letting nothing escape their scrutiny, but keeping their own movements well concealed."[63] On November 18 the expedition passed the remains of Fort Reno (old Fort Connor), which had been abandoned in 1868. Shortly thereafter they arrived at Cantonment Reno, on the north bank of the Powder River at the foot of the Bighorn Mountains. The camp had been constructed on Crook's orders on October 12, 1876, in preparation for the expedition. Its purpose was to serve as a supply station for the troops. There the command also met Tom Cosgrove and his battalion of one hundred Shoshone scouts. The entire command now numbered more that two thousand men.[64]

At Reno the scouts also received their pay. On November 18 Major North reported that his scouts were "making the money fly." Undoubtedly, some of the money was gambled away, but most of the scouts sent their pay home.[65] Ah re Kah rard (Rush Roberts), the youngest scout in the campaign, recalled that he sent his pay to his mother and brother-in-law back at the Pawnee reservation.[66] In his diary, Major North kept track of the accounts of Indians who borrowed money from him or other officers and enlisted men, as well as all transactions among his scouts.[67]

Apart from keeping accounts, preventing Sioux and Pawnee scouts from attacking each other kept North occupied. Tensions between the two groups frequently ran high. One day while the Pawnees were marching along the road, a Sioux scout rode up and struck one of the Pawnees with his "coup-stick." Lieutenant Colonel Dodge, who witnessed the event, later recalled that instantly a half-dozen revolvers were drawn. The "Sioux would have paid for his temerity then and there but that the Pawnee discipline was so excellent that a word from the officer restrained them," Dodge wrote. Later that night, the Pawnee who had been struck by the Sioux begged for North's permission to kill the assailant. North refused the request but called on General Crook to prevent future incidents.[68]

Another incident occurred shortly after the Pawnees arrived at Reno. During a council with the Sioux, Cheyenne, and Arapaho scouts on November 7, General Crook had promised them some of the horses herded by the Pawnees. But Crook failed to inform Major North of his decision. A few days later, Lieutenant Clark, commanding officer of the Sioux scouts, and Three Bears, a Sioux sergeant, rode into the Pawnee camp to collect the horses. The Pawnee guards immediately notified North, who arrived on the scene just as Three Bears was leading North's own horse from the herd. North ordered Clark back and threatened to kill Three Bears if he did not let the horse go. Faced with this "insult," Three Bears returned to the Sioux camp and began to rally his men for an attack on the Pawnee scouts. Upon receiving the news that the Sioux were preparing an attack to "clean out the Pawnees," North ordered his men to get ready to repel them. Then he and his brother mounted their horses to inform General Crook. On their way to Crook's headquarters, they passed by the Sioux camp. The angry Sioux watched them approach. Instead of stopping, Major North began to sing a Pawnee war song. Luther North joined him, and they paraded their horses past the Sioux. The Sioux, however, refrained from attacking the major and his scouts.[69]

Crook himself later resolved the dispute over the horses in favor of North. But to avoid such events in the future, Crook held a series of councils with his Indian scouts. On November 19 he approached North and informed him that the Sioux and Cheyenne scouts had complained that the Pawnees remained distant and cool, but that they wished to be friends with them. Crook suggested holding a council to establish peace between the two camps. Frank North discussed the matter with his scouts, who were unimpressed with their old enemies' complaints. According to the Pawnees, the Sioux merely pretended that they wanted to become friends "so that they could have a better opportunity of getting their captured horses back from the Pawnees, among whom a large number of the horses had been distributed." Nevertheless, wishing to abide by Crook's orders, they agreed to go to the council. Sergeants Li Heris oo la shar (Frank White) and Us sak kish oo kah lah joined Major North as representatives of the Pawnee battalion.[70]

The prospects for peace seemed poor when some of the Sioux delegates appeared at the council in full war regalia. North called Crook's attention to this fact and urged the general to bar these Indians from the council, but Crook paid little attention to the matter.[71] He opened the council with a long speech in which he called on the Indians to change their ways. In the speech, recorded by his aide-de-camp John Bourke, Crook added that the Indians needed to adopt the "white man's road." They should to learn to keep cattle, farm, and live in houses like white people. According to Crook, Indians should "live like the white man and [be] at peace with him, or be wiped off the face of the earth." He then urged the tribes to "bury their hatchets" and "reconcile [their] petty differences." Tup si paw and O ho a tay spoke next for the Bannocks and Shoshones. They were followed by Three Bears, a Sioux sergeant, and Sharp Nose, principal man among the Arapaho scouts. They, too, professed their loyalty to Crook and asked for fair treatment of their relatives at the agencies.[72] The irony of Crook's call for them to become farmers must not have escaped the Indians present at the council. After all, it was Crook himself who had enlisted them to fight in this war.

Li Heris oo la shar (Frank White) spoke for the Pawnees. For the occasion he wore a suit that had been given to him by officials at the Interior Department during a visit to Washington. Although he did not look like an Indian in the suit, his hair and face paint revealed that he was still a Pawnee. His eyelids, ears, and the "median line of forehead and chin" were blushed with vermillion. His cheekbones were "stained a dark brown, and the lower half of the face a dirty lemon." His hair was divided into two pigtails wrapped in yellow tape and hanging over the ears.[73]

Li Heris oo la shar's appearance revealed both the soldier and the warrior that the Pawnee scouts seemed to embody. When he spoke, he tried to make the most of the occasion. His words were intended to impress Crook with the Pawnees' unconditional loyalty to the white man and their desire to travel the "white man's road."

> I am talking to friends. This our head chief [General Crook] talking to us and asking us to be brothers. I hope the Great Spirit will smile

on us. Brothers. We are all Indians and have the same kind of skin. The Pawnees have lived with the white men a long time and know how strong they are. We are afraid of them, because they are so strong. Brothers. I don't think there is one of you can come out here today and say you ever heard of the Pawnee killing a white man. Brothers. We are all of the same color and we are all Indians. Today, this Big Chief has called us together to have a Council and I am glad of it and glad to meet you all. Father [turning to General Crook], I suppose you know the Pawnees are civilized. We plough, farm and work the ground like white people. Father, it is so what the Arapahoes said. We have all gone on this Expedition to help and hope it may be a successful one.

Father, I'm glad you have said you would listen to what we had to say. If we have any wrongs, we'll come to tell you about them. I suppose you have heard it is a good many years since we [Pawnees] have been to war. We have given it up long ago. When I was at home, I did what our Agent wanted us to do: farmed and worked the land. When they said at Washington, they wanted us for this trip, we threw everything aside but when we go back, we'll take to farming again. Father, it is good what you have said to us. I hope these people understand it too and that we shall all be good friends. This is all I have to say. I am glad you have told us what you did about the captured stock. The horses taken will help us to work our land."[74]

At the conclusion of the council, the representatives agreed to be on friendly terms from then on. To formalize the agreement, Three Bears presented Frank White with a horse. White accepted the horse and thus the friendship of the Sioux. The Pawnees then responded by giving away some of their own horses.[75]

It seemed that Crook's attempt to reconcile his scouts had been successful. *New York Herald* correspondent Jerry Roche, who covered the expedition, wrote that "no apprehensions are now felt of disturbances between our Sioux and Pawnee soldiers." According to Roche, the Indians "have stopped calling each other taunting names, as was their habit for a little time after our departure from Fort Laramie."[76] In the days following the council, Bourke observed that the Indian scouts continued "a delightful series of peace-talks, smokes and dances, in which there was mutual serenading, plenty in quantity, wretched in quality, some present-giving and protestations innumerable of the most affectionate friendship."[77]

On November 21 a Sioux-Arapaho scouting party returned with a Cheyenne prisoner named Beaver Dam or Many Beaver Dams. Under interrogation, Beaver Dam revealed the location of some of the hostile camps. Dull Knife, the Northern Cheyenne chief, had moved his camp into the Bighorn Mountains, a few days' march south of Cantonment Reno. Crazy Horse's camp was on the Rosebud, farther north, not far from the place where Crook's troops had engaged the Sioux earlier that year. Crook at once ordered his men to prepare to move against Crazy Horse. The next day the command left Reno at 6:20 in the morning and traveled twenty-five miles over rough, broken terrain. The next morning, November 23, as the men broke camp, Crook received news that his troops had been spotted by some Indians, who were now on their way to warn Crazy Horse of their approach. Recognizing that a surprise attack was now impossible, Crook decided to attack the Cheyenne village instead. He ordered Mackenzie to take the cavalry and the Indian scouts and proceed in the direction of the Cheyenne village, to the south.[78] Several parties of scouts were sent out that day to locate the Cheyenne camp. Major North sent five scouts under a Pawnee sergeant. The Sioux and Arapahos also sent out scouting parties.[79]

Mackenzie's column, which consisted of some eleven hundred officers and men, of whom about one-third were Indian scouts, left camp at noon on November 23 and traveled southward along the foot of the Bighorn Mountains.[80] They marched twelve miles before setting up camp. The weather had become increasingly cold, and the men spent an uncomfortable night in the open air, having left their tents behind with Crook's column. On the twenty-fourth they continued the journey. After they had marched ten miles, the Arapaho scouting party appeared in the distance. As the scouts neared the soldiers' camp, they circled their ponies at full gallop "in a wild and excited manner" to signal their discovery of the village. When the other scouts saw this signal, they began to yell in excitement. Their sudden cries alarmed the soldiers in the camp, who believed an Indian attack was imminent. The soldiers soon learned that the scouts merely yelled in "triumph at the return of the others."[81]

The scouts reported that the village was about fifteen miles to the south. Mackenzie immediately halted the column, wanting to wait until dark before moving toward the village. While his troops rested, Second Lieutenant Homer W. Wheeler saw some of the Indian scouts race their horses as fast as they could go. Frank Grouard, one of the white scouts with the command, explained that it was an old custom to do this before going into a fight, "as it gave the ponies their second wind."[82]

Mackenzie forbade the men to make fires or smoke cigarettes. Few of the soldiers enjoyed a good rest. Many were anxious about the upcoming fight, particularly the young recruits who had never been in an Indian battle before. A young soldier caused quite an uproar when he rushed into camp and woke everyone up by exclaiming that the Indians were coming. When it turned out that the Indians were U.S. Indian scouts, the panic subsided.[83]

Around four o'clock that afternoon, Mackenzie ordered his men to mount their horses. To avoid detection, they were not allowed to light fires, smoke, or talk loudly, and they were instructed to fasten personal items securely to their saddles. To protect themselves against the cold, the soldiers wore heavy overcoats, sealskin caps, gauntlets, overshoes, thick scarves, and heavy underwear. The troops and scouts were armed with Springfield 1873-model carbines, Colt .45 revolvers, hunting knives, and the 1858-model light saber.[84] Each soldier and scouts also carried his own weapons of choice if he had these available.

Luther North recalled that the following march was the hardest the Pawnee scouts had ever made. As the hours passed, the temperature dropped. The steep, snow-covered trail was extremely difficult. When the column passed through a narrow canyon, Major North ordered Luther North to let the men pass by and try to count them to make certain none had fallen behind.[85] As he counted his men, Luther noticed that many of the regular soldiers as well as a few of his scouts were "sick at the stomach." Luther blamed their condition on the high altitude and the cold.[86]

Just before daylight on November 25, the troops heard the faint thump of Indian drums in the distance. They were now near the village. The settlement belonged to a band of Northern Cheyennes under Dull Knife (whose actual name was more properly "Morning Star"), Wild Hog, and Little Wolf. Black Hairy Dog, keeper of the medicine arrows, and Coal Bear, keeper of the sacred hat, were also in the village. Altogether there were approximately twelve hundred people in the camp, including three hundred warriors. Many of these Indians had been present at the Little Bighorn at the time of Custer's attack. After the Custer battle, Dull Knife had taken his people deep into the Bighorn Mountains and out of reach of the army.[87]

When the troopers were within a mile of the village, Mackenzie halted them to issue orders to his officers. The Indian scouts would spearhead the attack. Mackenzie ordered Major North and the Pawnees to charge the village on the left-hand side of the creek that ran through the valley. The Shoshone scouts would follow closely behind them. The soldiers, meanwhile, would charge the village on the right-hand side of the creek. It was too late to surround the camp silently, and the shape of the valley made it impossible for the troops to take their positions without being detected. The plan was to encircle the village in a sweeping charge and cut off the Cheyennes' escape routes.

Mackenzie gave his Indian scouts time to move ahead of the command and prepare for battle. The Pawnees filed by the troops through a narrow canyon and unsaddled their horses as they always did before making a charge.[88] They were armed with Springfield carbines and revolvers. They wore their trousers, but despite the arctic temperatures, they discarded their heavy winter coats and jackets and went into the fight in their shirt-sleeves.[89] According to Luther North, all the scouts wore handkerchiefs on their heads to distinguish themselves from the hostiles.[90] The scouts also took out their personal medicine bundles and other charms they carried with them. Wichita Blaine tied his grandfather's little bird bundle to his hair for protection and good fortune.[91]

Just before the attack, Mackenzie gave his instructions to Lieutenant Lawton, who led Private William Earl Smith's company. Smith recalled that Mackenzie "sed we were to late to surround the camp and we would have to make a dash for it. He says we will keep the Indins [the scouts] right a hed of us and make them go in first and if there is any trap, they will catch it first and then we can open on them from the rear."[92] Mackenzie's order showed little regard for his Indian allies.

The attack on the village began at dawn. When the bugler sounded the signal for the attack, the Pawnees raced ahead of the other Indian scouts, who were in turn followed by the white troops.[93] As they approached the village, the scouts raised their war cry. Some of the white soldiers noticed that some of the scouts used whistles, which added a strange and uncanny effect to the attack. Colonel Mackenzie, who observed the attack from a distance, reported that his men had not gone far "when our Indians commenced howling and blowing on hideous voiced wind instruments."[94] His aide-de-camp, John Bourke, later remembered the "clatter and clangor of arms, the ear-piercing shrieks and yells of savage allies, their blood-curdling war songs, and the weird croon of the sacred flageolets of the Pawnee medicine men who, like the Celtic bands of old, rode boldly at the head of their people."[95] The purpose of the terrible noise was to send the villagers into a panic and spook their horses. Second Lieutenant Henry H. Bellas, who charged the village behind the scouts, recalled a Pawnee scout "who sounded a wild humming tune on a pipe that rose above all other sounds and somewhat resembled the prolonged shriek of a steam whistle."[96]

The attack caught the Cheyennes by surprise. Oddly enough, there is ample evidence that the Cheyennes had been forewarned that the soldiers were near. According to some Cheyenne accounts, the chiefs had sent out several scouts in the days before the attack to investigate reports that soldiers were in the field nearby. When the scouts discovered Crook's camp, they reported the information to the chiefs. Some, such as Black Hairy Dog, wanted to break camp and leave immediately. But Last Bull of the Fox Soldier society, who was in charge of the defense of the camp, disagreed. When Crow Split Nose ordered his followers to go, Last Bull's Fox Soldiers even prevented them from leaving the camp. Perhaps Last Bull believed the Cheyennes could defeat the soldiers again, as they had at the Little Bighorn. It is possible that the Cheyennes believed American troops would not force a march over rough terrain in near-arctic temperatures. Furthermore, as historian Jerome A. Greene pointed out, the Cheyennes did not know that Many Beaver Dams had given away the location of the village. They believed Crook was still looking for Crazy Horse. This would explain why they felt relatively safe despite the reports that soldiers had been seen.[97]

The Pawnee and Shoshone scouts entered the valley on the south side of the creek but soon discovered that the terrain in front of them could not be passed. The Shoshone scouts took a sharp turn to the left and rode up into the mountains, where they took a position on top of some cliffs. From there they kept up rifle fire on the Cheyennes, who were trying to escape from the back of the village. Luther North, however, thought they did little damage, because they were almost half a mile away from the

Indians.[98] Major North, meanwhile, led his men across the creek to join the troops. Because the creek was muddy and difficult to cross, they lost considerable time, allowing many Cheyenne women and children to escape.[99]

After crossing the creek, the Pawnees charged alongside the troops. Despite the professions of friendship by the Sioux and Arapaho scouts, the Pawnee scouts ran great risk of being shot from their horses by their Indian "allies." The Cheyennes fired at the Pawnees from the ridges in front, while the Sioux scouts rode up right behind them. According to Luther North, the Sioux were "not very particular whether they shot at us or the Cheyennes."[100] Perhaps for this reason, the Pawnees recrossed the creek in order to attack the lower end of the village.

When the Pawnees charged the village, many of the surprised Cheyennes had no time to gather their clothes. The Cheyennes suffered their heaviest losses "as the Pawnees poured deadly volleys into teepees, killing without discretion all whom they contacted."[101] When Luther North rode into the village, a Cheyenne boy jumped in front of his horse and raised an old muzzle-loading gun. North killed the boy with a gunshot. The boy later proved to be one of Dull Knife's sons. The Pawnees counted coup on his body as they passed by.[102] Luther later went back to look at the boy he had killed and had one of his men take the boy's scalp.[103]

Occasionally the Pawnees were caught in crossfire between the troops and the Cheyennes. When Second Lieutenant Homer Wheeler discovered an Indian lying in a little depression in the ground about two hundred yards in front of him, he ordered his men to open fire. Immediately, a Pawnee scout who happened to be with them cried out, "Pawnee! Pawnee!" and the firing ceased. "It seems the Indian was recognized from the way he wore his hair," Wheeler wrote in his memoir. "He had been unhorsed and was lying low between the two fires. He must have borne a charmed life."[104]

The Pawnees found many of the tepees already deserted. They dismounted and climbed a small hill, from which they began to shoot across the valley at the Cheyennes, who were covering the retreat of the women and children from a number of rocky ridges.[105] A group of soldiers under First Lieutenant John A. McKinney charged the village on the right flank. Ralph Weeks, who had been educated at the Pawnee Agency school and who spoke English well, joined McKinney's troops with some of the other Pawnees. When they neared the village, they suddenly came under fire from some Cheyennes who had taken position in a ravine north of the village. McKinney was shot and killed almost instantly. Shortly afterward, his first sergeant fell as well, leaving the troops without a commander. When the soldiers began to retreat, Ralph Weeks rode up to them and yelled, "Get off your horses and come ahead on foot. There are only seven of them. We will kill them all." The soldiers followed Weeks into the ravine and killed the Indians who had shot Lieutenant McKinney.[106]

McKinney was not the only casualty. Several other soldiers were killed, and a fair number received serious injuries. The wounded men were taken off the battlefield and placed behind a hill, which was later aptly named "hospital hill." There they were attended by medical personnel. But soon Cheyenne sharpshooters fired on the men from some rocks up on the mountainside. Mackenzie immediately asked North if his scouts could drive the Cheyenne sharpshooters away. According to Second Lieutenant Wheeler, North blew on an Indian whistle, and in a short time six Pawnees and a noncommissioned officer appeared. After receiving their instructions from North, they stripped down to their breechclouts and replaced their boots with moccasins. They tied handkerchiefs around their heads in order not to be mistaken for hostiles. Then they quickly disappeared up the mountainside. "The firing soon ceased," Wheeler reported. "I was later informed that the scouts killed one or two of the hostiles and scalped them."[107]

The fighting was fierce. Iron Teeth, a Cheyenne woman who was in the village at the time of the attack, recalled that the scouts and soldiers killed men, women, and children with their rifles. Those who could do so ran away. Iron Teeth's husband died in the fight. She watched from the hilltops as the scouts and soldiers burned the village.[108]

The Cheyennes scalped Private John Sullivan of Company B, Fourth Cavalry. The Pawnees joined in the bloodbath and showed their opponents no mercy. When *New York Herald* correspondent Jerry Roche entered the village, he found the body of an old Cheyenne woman who had just been scalped by a Pawnee scout. A soldier of the Second Cavalry had told the scouts not to harm her, but when Pawnees and Cheyennes met in battle they rarely took prisoners.[109] Among those who took a scalp during the battle was Corporal Co rux kit e butts ("Little Bear"), who was later described as a great admirer of General Crook.[110]

The scouts counted many coups that day. When First Sergeant James S. McClellan shot a Cheyenne warrior, he ran up to him and shot him a few times more. As he was taking the fallen warrior's gun and carbine, a Pawnee came by and took the coup.[111]

The fighting lasted all day. Slowly, the Cheyennes were forced to abandon their village, but the troops did not succeed in driving them out of range. The Cheyennes had taken a position in the hills and kept up an unrelenting fire on the troops. Underneath the cliff from which they made their stand was a small herd of ninety or one hundred horses. Several attempts were made to secure these ponies. Four or five Arapaho scouts made a dash for them but were driven back. Shortly afterward, a handful of Shoshone scouts attempted to run off the horses, but they, too, failed. During the attempt, one of the Shoshones, a young warrior named Ahusan or Anzi, was shot through the body. Then Three Bears and three of his Sioux scouts tried to take the horses, but enemy fire drove them back as well. Finally, Luther North received permission from his brother to give it a try. North selected Pe isk le shar ("Boy Chief," or Peter Headman) to help him. Each man carried a blanket and a revolver and was able to ride in close to the herd. Then the two dashed into the herd, waving their blankets and shouting loudly to stampede the horses. Despite heavy enemy fire, they were able to lead the ponies away successfully. A few days after the battle, Colonel Mackenzie distributed the horses among the Pawnees as a reward for their valorous service.[112]

At two o'clock that afternoon Mackenzie ordered Major North to take his Pawnees and destroy the village. The scouts pulled down the Cheyenne tepees and used the lodge poles as fuelwood. On top of the burning poles they threw clothing, weapons, dried meat, buffalo robes, and other supplies. The Cheyennes watched helplessly from the hills as their village went up in flames.[113]

That evening the Pawnees camped in the burning village. The fighting now had subsided. Occasionally, Cheyenne sharpshooters fired some rounds into the camp. While his men were having supper, Major North and his brother rested around a fire. They were sitting on a log drinking coffee when a bullet whizzed over their heads and killed a mule on the other side of the fire from them. They built a breastwork of dried buffalo meat from the Indian camp and took cover behind it.[114] As night fell,

Major North pulled out his pocket diary and summarized the events of the day in a short paragraph:

> Saturda[y] 25th
> Had a hard nights march and at 7 a.m. struck Little Wolf's village of Cheyennes [illegible] 173 Lodges and had a hard fight which lasted all day and part of the night. we are camped in the village tonight and bullets are dropping all around us. we have burned all the lodges. 18 dead Indians are lying all around us. one lieut. and four men are killed on our side and 17 soldiers and one snake [Shoshone] Indian wounded[.] a stray bullet just [hit] a mule within 30 paces of Lute + I.[115]

While the Pawnees were camped in the village, the Cheyennes spent the night in the cold hills. "We wallowed through the mountain snows for several days," recalled Iron Teeth, one of the refugees. Most of the Cheyennes were afoot. They had no lodges and carried only a few blankets and a little dry meat for food. "Men died of wounds," Iron Teeth remembered, "women and children froze to death."[116] Luther North later commented that the thermometer never got higher than twenty-five degrees below zero. "Those poor Cheyennes were out in that weather with nothing to eat, no shelter, we had burned their village, and hardly had any clothing," he wrote. Many children died from cold and exposure. "It makes me sort of sick to think about it," North said.[117] The Cheyennes sought refuge with Crazy Horse's people, but the Oglalas were unable to help, because they were running low on supplies as well. Hence, several weeks later Dull Knife and his followers surrendered at Camp Robinson, Nebraska.[118]

During the battle, after the Cheyennes had abandoned their village, soldiers and scouts began looting the camp. The Pawnees joined the search for plunder. According to newspaper correspondent Roche, a number of Pawnees were "systematically going through the village and securing large quantities of plunder." Private William Earl Smith hurried to join the hunt for trophies, for the "Pawneys were [already] plundering the camp."[119] John Bourke added that "seven hundred head of stock fell into our hands, not quite [one] hundred of [that] number being loaded by our Pawnees with such plunder as appealed to their fancy."[120] Many items that had originally belonged to Custer's troops were found, including letters, photographs, watches, money, and uniforms. The victors also discovered three necklaces made of human fingers and a buckskin bag containing the right hands of twelve Shoshone babies—probably identifiable by other, clearly recognizable Shoshone plunder. The discovery of these ghastly trophies caused great distress among the Shoshone scouts, whose cries of mourning could be heard in the days and nights following the battle.[121]

Bourke wrote that the Pawnees and Shoshones took sixteen scalps in the battle but that the other scouts took none, out of respect for "the wishes and prejudices of the white soldiers about them."[122] Although it might be true that the Sioux, Arapahos, and friendly Cheyennes took no scalps, it is more likely that they refrained from doing so out of respect for their former allies than from an expressed desire to please the white officers in the command. According to Luther North, the "Sioux, Arapahos, and [the] few Cheyennes with us were more or less friendly with the hostile Cheyennes we were attacking—which is sufficient reason why they did not scalp the latter; but there was no such feeling on the part of the Pawnees or Shoshones."[123]

The attack had been a great success, but the battle had been hard fought. Several weeks afterward, Luther North wrote to a friend that the Cheyennes were "the bravest people I ever saw." Although the troops had taken possession of the village and destroyed everything in it, North also acknowledged that "we didn't get much the best of them in fighting. . . . I don't think there were more than three hundred warriors in the village, and we had about one thousand men, and were fighting them all day, yet did not succeed in driving them more than half a mile from the village."[124]

Mackenzie estimated the number of Cheyennes killed at thirty. Among them were three of Dull Knife's sons. The troops had destroyed 173 lodges and a large quantity of supplies. Furthermore, they had captured nearly the entire horse herd of the Cheyennes, forcing these people to travel through the snow and cold on foot.[125] Six cavalrymen were killed during the attack: Lieutenant John McKinney, Corporal Patrick F. Ryan, and Privates Joseph Mengis, Alexander Keller, John Sullivan, and a man whose surname was Beard. Private Alexander McFarland died of injuries several days later. Twenty-two men were wounded.[126] Second Lieutenant Homer Wheeler was placed in charge of their transportation to Cantonment Reno.

Although the Indian scouts had been among the first to enter the village during the charge, only one of them, a Shoshone, was severely wounded.

The Pawnees suffered only minor bruises and injuries. First Sergeant High Eagle, for example, received a nasty gash on one of his hands. He later proudly displayed the scar he had obtained in the battle to visitors. Newspaperman Roche explained that the small number of casualties among the scouts was "traceable to their familiarity with the manner of fighting of their own people and to the shrewdness with which they evaded fire on the field while fighting at times quite as well as our regulars." Historian Jerome Greene has further pointed out that many of the enlisted men were inexperienced troops, the so-called Custer's Avengers, which might account for the higher casualty rate among them. In any event, the presence of the scouts severely demoralized the enemy. They were instrumental in capturing the Cheyenne horse herd. They had proved to be highly useful despite (or perhaps because of) the fact that, as Roche put it, they "cannot be disciplined to fight like white soldiers."[127]

The *Army and Navy Journal* of December 2, 1876, reported that the "Indian allies behaved well at the start, but stopped to plunder, and were but of little use thereafter." This description seems to have applied more to the Sioux, Cheyenne, and Arapahoe scouts than to the Pawnees, because the same article also stated that the "Pawnees are a very orderly, well drilled and disciplined lot of soldiers, many of whom can speak and write English." The article further said that so far "the Sioux and Arapahoes have been difficult to handle, but they are gradually being instructed and will soon present a tolerably good appearance."[128]

Mackenzie was pleased with the Pawnees' performance during the fight. Two days after the attack on the village, Mackenzie distributed the captured ponies among his Indian scouts. The Sioux scouts were allowed to keep the handful of horses they had captured, but when they tried to distribute the horses among themselves, an ugly fistfight broke out in their ranks. The Pawnees received sixty ponies, and Major North saw to it that the horses were distributed fairly. For example, Pe isk le shar (Peter Headman), who had secured the Cheyenne herd with Luther North, received an extra horse because he had lost one during the battle.[129]

On November 26, the day after the battle, Mackenzie gave the order to return to Crook's column. When they went into camp later that day, the small Pawnee scouting party that Major North had sent out on the twenty-second rode into the camp. The men had been scouting farther to the northwest than the Arapaho scouts who discovered the Cheyenne village. They had found a fresh trail and followed it until they came in sight of five or six Cheyennes driving a herd of horses. When the Pawnees gave chase, the Cheyennes abandoned their horses and ran away. Unable to overtake the Cheyennes, the Pawnees gave up the chase and began driving the captured horses, some eighty animals, toward Mackenzie's camp. This was on the day of the attack on Dull Knife's village. The next day, as they were coming toward the camp, they ran into the retreating Cheyennes and were forced to abandon the captured horses and run for safety. The Cheyennes briefly gave chase. Later that evening the Pawnees arrived at Mackenzie's camp.[130]

They arrived just in time to join the other Pawnees in celebrating the victory over the Cheyennes with feasts and name-giving ceremonies. John Bourke observed that the Shoshone scouts were so grief stricken after discovering that the Cheyennes had recently attacked one of their villages and taken trophies from the bodies of friends and relatives that they neglected to "assume the new battle-names which the Pawnees alongside of them adopted, according to the usage of the Plains' tribes, with much smoking and other ceremonial."[131] Among the Pawnees honored with new names was Tow we his ee ("Leader of the Group"), who adopted the name Echo Hawk.[132]

The Pawnees celebrated their victory with a scalp dance. Private William Earl Smith witnessed the dance at Rock Creek the day after the battle. He recorded in his diary that "our Indins had a skelp dance and I went over to see it. They had a good meny [scalps] and they made the valey ring with there shouts."[133] After the dance, the scouts prepared the scalps and cut them into small pieces to decorate their clothing, saddles, bags, and other objects. Sergeant Frank White (Li Heris oo la shar) honored Frank North and Richard Irving Dodge with a piece of the scalp of one of Dull Knife's sons. "This makes us almost brothers in the Indian idea, & is the greatest compliment he can pay North & I," Dodge recorded in his diary. "I dont want the thing at all, but it would be an insult not to accept it."[134]

The small Pawnee scouting party that returned on the twenty-sixth reported to Mackenzie the presence of the large party of hostile Indians some six miles away. Mackenzie decided not to pursue them; he had reached the point of diminishing returns. He decided to let "General

Winter" do the rest.[135] The rumors of a hostile Indian party nearby, however, alarmed many of the soldiers, especially the new recruits. When a small herd of buffalo accidentally strolled into a camp of scouts and the Indians fired a volley into them, the shots caused a panic among the soldiers, who believed they were under attack. They soon learned what had occurred. The next day the Indians shared the buffalo meat with the hungry soldiers.[136]

On November 29 Mackenzie's cavalry caught up with Crook's column. The scouts carried the captured scalps on sticks in front of their saddles and sang their victory songs as they entered the camp.[137] The next day a funeral was held for the enlisted men killed in the fight.[138] That same day Luther North went on a scout with four of his men. His party soon bogged down in heavy snow and nearly froze to death at night. They returned without locating the hostiles.[139]

In the days and weeks following the Dull Knife fight, Crook's expedition seems to have lost its sense of purpose and direction. After returning to Cantonment Reno on December 2, the soldiers and scouts marched to Buffalo Springs, on what is recorded as the "Dry Fork" of the Powder River, where they made camp. The horses and pack mules were worn out from the long march over difficult terrain. The weather also took a turn for the worse. Snowstorms swept in over the country and tormented men and animals even more. Horse feed was scarce, and supplies from Fort Fetterman came in irregularly. For the next few weeks Crook continued to send his men out on scouts along the Belle Fourche and Powder Rivers, but they encountered no enemies, and the effect of these operations was merely the exhaustion of men and animals. Meanwhile, Crook's seemingly indecisive action and "erratic" orders taxed the patience of his officers and staff.[140]

As a result of the extreme cold, the troops lost many horses during the scouts in the Belle Fourche River country. Snowstorms made scouting expeditions virtually impossible. To escape the freezing temperatures and the blistering wind, Luther North moved his men to a deep canyon three miles below the main camp. They found some good grass for the horses there and discovered a large number of deer and elk. They killed more than half the animals and took enough meat to last them two or three days. They gave the rest to the soldiers.[141]

As the weather deteriorated, the Pawnees were forced to stay in camp. They entertained themselves with visits, dances, and games. Among the games they played was a race between a horse and an Indian runner, forty yards and back. Major North noted that his Indians came out ahead every time.[112]

On December 22 Crook's expedition began the march back to Fort Fetterman. The frigid temperatures made travel extremely difficult. On December 24, thermometers froze when the temperature dropped to minus forty-two degrees. Major North suffered terribly from asthma, and Lieutenant Cushing suffered several frozen fingers and a toe. The other men and horses were suffering as well. In his diary that evening, Major North scribbled, "Tonight is Christmas eve and oh what a christmas eve it is with us nearly freezing and so far from home and loved ones."[143]

The troops arrived at Fort Fetterman on the twenty-ninth. There they went into camp and received new rations. In the evenings, Indian scouts from the different camps visited each other to exchange gifts. Their dances lasted until the early hours of the morning, and the sounds of the drum and the high-pitched voices of the singers kept many of the regular soldiers awake at night. Lieutenant Colonel Dodge witnessed what he called a "begging dance" that the Sioux performed for the Pawnees. The purpose of the dance, according to Dodge, was to swindle the Pawnee hosts out of gifts. When the Sioux honored the Pawnees with a dance, Plains Indian custom obligated the Pawnees to reciprocate with gifts such as horses and clothes. In his diary, Dodge noted that the "wily Sioux" had fleeced the Pawnees out of "50 or 60 horses & a great many other valuable things."[144] According to Luther North, however, the Pawnees gave away only about twenty-five horses, most of which they won back in friendly gambles with the Sioux. At the end of the night, according to North, the Sioux and Pawnees "parted pretty good friends."[145]

According to Bourke, the Indians feasted and danced almost every night. After the Sioux had "serenaded" the Pawnees, the latter returned the honor by dancing for the Sioux the next night. The Arapahos and Cheyennes also joined the round of dances. "Nobody growled about that," Bourke wrote; "we were assured it was a ceremonial observance among our aboriginal friends and having been paid to cheerfully suffer all such little privations, we made the best face we could over the matter and smiled through our tears."[146]

On December 31 the Pawnees drew their pay at Fort Fetterman and returned the guns that had been issued to them before the expedition. Most of the guns were in poor shape because of the wear and abuse they had received during the battle and the hard marches afterward. Fortunately, Lieutenant Robinson, the mustering officer, did not inspect the arms closely. The next day the Pawnees departed for Fort Laramie, where they arrived on January 6. They stayed there for a few days before setting out for Sidney Barracks on January 11.[147]

The Pawnees returned to Sidney Barracks in triumph. According to Major North's diary entry for January 20, 1877, the Pawnees made "quite a display of scalps" when they rode into the post.[148] "The whole town was out to watch the Pawnee Scouts return," Luther North later reminisced. "The boys were carrying the scalps they had taken fastened on the ends of poles, which were held upright over their heads, and as we marched down the main street they sang their war songs."[149] The next day Major North wrote letters at the request of his men to their loved ones at home. "I have been writing all day for the men," he wrote in his diary later that evening, "telling their people all about the fight and all the news we could think of. wrote 27 pages of letter paper and am tired out."[150]

At Sidney the Pawnee scouts participated in their last "battle" on April 10, 1877. It was a friendly confrontation between the Pawnees and Company H of the Third Cavalry to settle an argument between Major North and Second Lieutenant Charles L. Hammond. North believed his men could run off Hammond's horses. Although both sides used blank ammunition, several Pawnees suffered powder burns, and some horses received saber cuts. One white trooper nearly lost an eye when he was shot in the face at close range with a blank charge.[151] The scouts lost the contest. Sergeant James S. McClellan, who witnessed the fight, explained that the horses were probably too exhausted from the recent expedition to be chased away from their comfortable shelters. Several scouts who were trying to lead the horses away were pulled from the backs of their ponies by the unwilling animals.[152]

The Pawnees stayed at Sidney for nearly three months. During this time they were frequently visited by curious townspeople. "There are many visitors at the Pawnee camp these days," reported the *Sidney Telegraph*. "Their beadwork is really marvelous [and] Major North has his command in excellent shape and is ably assisted by his lieutenants."[153] A reporter for the *Omaha Daily Republican* also visited the scouts and in his newspaper commended them for their service. He was particularly impressed with Ralph J. Weeks, who had been promoted to orderly sergeant of the company after the Dull Knife battle:

> He took a Sioux scalp in the Dull Knife Fight, which earned to a great extent his promotion. He talks English well, and writes a handsome hand. Ralph has many friends already in Sidney, and will have many more before the company breaks camp which will be in about six weeks, as is now predicted. He is the first Pawnee subscriber to the republican, and probably the first man in his nation to subscribe to any newspaper.[154]

The scouts' "war dances" attracted the attention of many local people, a few of whom were eager to buy trophies captured on the Dull Knife battlefield. "The Pawnees have captured a good many handsome things at the burning of the [Cheyenne] village," wrote the wife of an army surgeon stationed at the post, "but they won't part with them for love or money."[155]

While at Sidney, a scout by the name of Big Hawk Chief demonstrated his ability as a sprinter. Luther North asked him to run a mile in order to settle a bet he had made with a local gambler. Big Hawk Chief rose to the challenge and ran the one-mile "track" in three minutes and fifty-eight seconds. Not even North could believe his eyes, and he had the track measured again with a steel tape. The four-minute mark was not broken officially until 1954, when Englishman Roger Bannister established the world record with a time of 3:59:4. A doctor who examined Big Hawk Chief after his race commented that he was "the most perfect specimen of man" he had ever seen.[156]

Meanwhile, Captain Samuel S. Sumner, commander at Sidney Barracks, was impressed with the self-imposed discipline displayed by the Pawnee scouts. His guardhouse was full of soldiers who had slipped away from camp to make trouble in town. Not one of the Pawnees was ever sent to the guardhouse for disobeying orders.[157]

On April 19 General Crook wrote to Frank North, informing him that General Sheridan had ordered the mustering out of the Pawnee scouts.

Crook regretted that he was no longer able to retain the scouts in service, but "there is no longer any necessity for the employment of scouts nor is there any appropriation on hand from which to pay them." In his closing remarks, Crook thanked the scouts for their "excellent behaviour" and their "soldierlike conduct and discipline" during the campaign.[158]

The scouts were officially discharged on April 28, 1877.[159] Before they set out from Sidney, Major North wrote to General Sheridan with a special request. His scouts had a herd of 250 ponies, 100 of which had been captured in the Dull Knife fight. Because they preferred to march home rather than travel by train, they would receive only subsistence rather than the forty cents per pony per day for travel expenses. North insisted that his men should be treated like all other enlisted men. North wrote to Sheridan on April 13, 1877, "Are not my men the same as other regularly enlisted and honorably discharged soldiers—entitled to 'travel pay' and rations or commutation of rations[?]"[160]

Later that month the scouts departed from Sidney.[161] They traveled to Julesburg, Colorado, and then by railroad to Ogallala, Nebraska, where they crossed the Platte River. The trip was not without incidents. The night after they crossed the Platte the horses stampeded during a terrible storm. It took the scouts several days to round up most of them. Unfortunately, not all the scouts were able to recover their horses. Echo Hawk, Wichita Blaine, and a few others were forced to follow the scouts on foot. They fell behind and never caught up. As a result, they never received their official discharge papers, which caused them much difficulty later when they applied for pensions.[162] Reportedly this group stole six horses near Grand Island, Nebraska, sometime during their return march.[163]

While Echo Hawk, Blaine, and the others searched for their horses, Major North and the main body of the scouts traveled to Fort McPherson. After drawing rations there, they went into camp. Shortly thereafter a local sheriff and a farmer rode into camp, charging the Pawnees with killing a cow. Although they claimed they had nothing to do with the shooting, the Pawnees, who were eager to get home, paid the farmer for the animal. Frank North did not want to pay for the dead cow at all, for he feared that more settlers would file false claims. Later, Pawnee Puk oot (listed on the muster rolls as Pau ree puck oot, or "Old Horn") confessed to North that he had shot the cow.[164]

Misfortune struck when the scouts arrived at Hays, Kansas, on May 19. Unlike the warm welcome the scouts had received at Sidney, the reception at Hays was inhospitable. When some of the men went into town, one of them, Tah wah chuh e hod de ("Red Willow"), was shot by a marshal. He died of his injuries a few days later at the military hospital at Fort Hays. Major North and his brother had some difficulty restraining their men after the incident. They sent some of their sergeants into town to bring back the more hot-headed young warriors. In the aftermath of the shooting, the local newspaper wrote that "as to the necessity of shooting the Indian we shall not venture an opinion . . . but our citizens certainly owe Major North a debt of gratitude for holding the revengeful and bloodthirsty red skins in check."[165]

At Arkansas City, Kansas, the North brothers said good-bye to their scouts. Major North was suffering from a severe asthma attack, and his brother thought it best for them to board a train at Arkansas City and return home. The scouts arrived at their reservation shortly thereafter. Although they received a warm welcome from their friends and relatives, the newly appointed agent, Charles H. Searing, was less thrilled with the arrival of the scouts. He arrested the five who had been accused of stealing horses near Grand Island. The men were sent to the guardhouse at Fort Reno, Indian Territory, for sixty days. Searing also confiscated two of the stolen horses, which he would keep until their owners came for them. Apparently, the theft of a few horses was a greater offense than the murder of an Indian. The Pawnees accused of stealing the horses were imprisoned immediately, whereas the man who shot Tah wah chuh e hod de was not jailed until he shot and killed a white man a few weeks later. But the agent was perhaps most troubled by the Interior Department's decision to remove Dull Knife's Cheyennes to Indian Territory. He feared that the Cheyennes might seek revenge against the Pawnees for their role in the Powder River expedition.[166]

The Dull Knife Battle was a significant event in the "Great Sioux War" of 1876. Although it was the only victory in Crook's Powder River expedition, it broke the resistance of the Northern Cheyennes. Furthermore, as historian Jerome A. Greene has pointed out, it effectively dissolved the Sioux-Cheyenne alliance and helped to persuade many of the resisting Sioux to give up their arms as well. On a psychological level, as historian

Lessing H. Nohl Jr. observed, Crook's campaign had shown the Northern Cheyennes that "neither remote strongholds nor Arctic temperatures" would offer safety. "To a people accustomed to semi-hibernation during the cold months, this was a demoralizing realization." Wherever the hostiles went, the soldiers of the United States Army and their Indian allies would find them.[167]

CHAPTER 8

Homecoming

The Powder River campaign marked the last time the Pawnee scouts operated together in an all-Indian unit. After returning to their reservation in Indian Territory, the Pawnees began the difficult process of rebuilding their lives. Most took up farming; others looked for work in surrounding areas.

A handful of men occasionally found employment as scouts for the army. Harry Coons served on various occasions as an army scout between 1877 and 1886. Upon his return from the Powder River campaign, during which he had served as a first sergeant, Coons enlisted at Fort Supply, Indian Territory. He joined Captain William C. Hemphill in the search for Dull Knife and Little Wolf's band of Northern Cheyennes, who in September 1878 left their reservation to return to their homeland in the north. Coons was stationed at Fort Reno, Indian Territory, for several years. Apart from acting as a scout and guide, he carried mail and dispatches to posts in the territory and acted as an interpreter for other Indians when called upon by his officers. When off duty, he studied law. He gained the respect of many officers and fellow soldiers. One of his officers wrote that Coons's work in the performance of his duties had "always been characterized [by] zeal, fidelity, capacity and excellent judgment." Unfortunately, his health declined, and in 1886 he received an honorable discharge from the army. Afterward he served as chief of police at the Pawnee reservation, his main task being to guard the borders of the reservation against outlaws and bootleggers. He continued to study law and was admitted to the bar in 1896. He died on August 11, 1899.[1]

Ralph Weeks ("Little Warrior") served as a scout in Colorado during the Ute rebellion of 1879. On one occasion, Weeks and a Chawi boy were scouting on the plains east of the Rocky Mountains when they discovered a small enemy camp. Disguising themselves as wolves, they entered the camp at night and took a small herd of mules. The mules had previously been stolen from a government train, and Weeks and the other scout received $50 each for recovering the animals. During the same campaign, Weeks persuaded a group of Utes to surrender. Following his discharge after the Ute war, Weeks moved back to the Pawnee reservation. He was one of the Indians who joined Buffalo Bill's Wild West Show.[2]

When the Utes took up arms against the United States in 1879, Frank North expected he would be asked to organize the Pawnee battalion again. The order never came. Instead, he remained at the ranch he operated with his business partner, William F. Cody. In 1882 he was elected a member of the Nebraska state legislature, and the following year he joined Buffalo Bill's celebrated Wild West Show. But during one of the performances, he suffered a severe injury when his horse slipped. The injury may have exacerbated his already delicate physical condition. While working for the show, North contracted pneumonia, and on March 14, 1885, only four days after his forty-fifth birthday, he died at his home in Columbus, Nebraska. He was buried three days later.[3]

Some of the remaining white officers were also followed by misfortune. Joseph McFadden, who had been appointed the first commander of the scouts in 1864, died of unknown causes on November 12 of that same year, shortly after the first Pawnee company was disbanded.[4] Edward W. Arnold, one of the captains of the scout company that helped guard the Union Pacific Railroad in 1867, reportedly died on October 11, 1879.[5] After leaving the scouts, William N. Harvey, who had served with the scouts between 1865 and 1870, changed his name to Nicholas C. Creede and for some years found great success in the mining business in Colorado. Suffering from poor health, however, he moved to California in 1893, where, on July 13, 1897, he committed suicide.[6] Tragedy also followed James Murie, who, following his service with the scouts in 1869, began to suffer from mental illness. In 1888 he was admitted to the veterans' home in Grand Island, Nebraska, where he died on December 26, 1910.[7]

Other officers of the battalion fared better. After leaving the scouts, Fred Matthews, a first lieutenant in 1867, joined Buffalo Bill's Wild West Show as a stagecoach driver. He lived until 1890, when he died on Christmas Day at the age of fifty-nine.[8] Charles E. Morse, a captain with scout Company C in 1867, died in Columbus on October 14, 1908, at age sixty-nine. George Lehman, who had served as a sergeant during the Republican River expedition of 1869, died on June 12, 1918, at the age of seventy.[9] After his career as an officer of the Pawnee scouts, Gustavus G. Becher became a real estate dealer in Columbus and was elected to the Nebraska state legislature in 1895. He died on October 8, 1918, at the age of seventy-four.[10] Frank North's brother-in-law, Sylvanus E. Cushing, became first a farmer and then a businessman in Columbus. He eventually moved to Wenatchee, Washington, where he died on October 1, 1904. His remains were apparently returned to Columbus, where they were interred in the family grave at the Columbus Cemetery.[11] Luther North died at age eighty-nine, on April 18, 1935, at Columbus, Nebraska. All these men were buried in the cemetery in their hometown of Columbus, Nebraska.

The Pawnee scouts, meanwhile, faced the difficult task of adjusting to life in Indian Territory. Like Ralph Weeks, a number of other former scouts joined Buffalo Bill's Wild West Show and later Pawnee Bill's Wild West Show. William Cody first hired Pawnees during the 1878–79 season. Frank North, who was Cody's business partner at the North-Cody Ranch in Nebraska, probably used his influence with the tribe to recruit men for the shows. Over the next few years North helped supply Cody's show with more Pawnees. In 1883 Cody persuaded North to join the show himself. He relied on North to organize and discipline the performers for the acts. North "can handle Indians better than any man living," Cody wrote to his business partner William F. ("Doc") Carver. That first season, thirty-six Pawnees joined the show with Major North. In some of Buffalo Bill's performances, the Pawnees were to act as "hostile" Indians, holding up stagecoaches and "massacring" settlers. According to one story, while they were at Colville, Nebraska, the Pawnees got carried away during a dress rehearsal of an attack on the Deadwood stagecoach. After the rehearsal nearly ended in disaster, with some performers suffering injuries, Frank North reportedly told Cody that Cody needed not him and his Pawnees but some old men, a few old horses, and a "hack driver." Cody could "fix them up with all the paint and feathers on the market" and create a "show of illusion not realism." At Cody's insistence, however, the Pawnees and North stayed. The Pawnees enjoyed the work. "We were glad to earn a little money and be off the reservation," said Wichita Blaine, a former scout who joined Buffalo Bill's Wild West Show. The Pawnees even made friends with some of the Sioux Indians in the show.[12]

Those who joined the Wild West Shows were fortunate. They had a chance to see the world and earn some badly needed money for their families at home. For the majority of the Pawnee people, however, the outlook was bleak. Diseases such as malaria and consumption, together with poor diet and water, inadequate housing, and the effects of the climate, wrought havoc on them. Although mortality rates fell after the first three years in Indian Territory, they still exceeded birth rates. Pawnee population figures continued to decline steadily. In 1901 they reached their nadir when only 629 people remained. Many died long before their time. Among them were many former scouts.[13]

Perhaps the story of Abraham Lincoln, veteran of the Dull Knife fight, is typical. After the 1876 campaign, Lincoln worked in the Pawnee Agency blacksmith shop. His wife, Hattie, died in the spring of 1885 while giving birth to their second child, William. The baby was adopted that same day by Echo Hawk and his two wives, Susan and Choorix, who were Lincoln's cousins. Lincoln himself died not long afterward, on October 8, 1885.[14]

The scouts who survived the epidemic of death watched helplessly as spouses, children, and other relatives succumbed. Scout Billy Osborne, for example, lost two wives and six of his seven children. By 1913, Echo Hawk had lost two wives and seven of his fourteen natural and adopted children. By 1904, Roam Chief had lost three wives and seven of his eleven children. Walking Sun lost no fewer than four wives during the early years in Oklahoma, and according to a questionnaire he filled out in 1923, all twelve of his children had died.[15]

Many of the surviving scouts remarried women much younger than they were. Such marriages were not only perfectly acceptable in Pawnee culture, in which proven warriors made preferable marriage partners, but also necessary as the number of eligible (unrelated) partners declined as a result of heavy mortality. After losing his first wife, former scout Leading Fox married a woman twenty-six years younger than he. She was only in her mid-teens at the time of their wedding. Other scouts, such as Billy Osborne and John Buffalo, also married women considerably younger than they.[16]

Rather than investing money and effort in saving the Pawnee people from disease and death, the federal government embarked on a disastrous policy of eradicating Pawnee cultural practices. Beginning in the 1880s the government prevented the Pawnee people from conducting religious ceremonies and social events, wrested political power from the hands of the chiefs and medicine men, and broke up the old tribal and band structures through the allotment policy. This last policy forced families to abandon their village communities and settle on individual, 160-acre allotments. What remained of the land after allotment was to be sold to white settlers. The Pawnees stubbornly resisted the sale of their surplus land. When the Jerome Commission arrived at the agency in 1892 to strong-arm the Pawnees into selling their land, the commissioners reminded them of what had happened to western tribes who had refused to sell their land. These tribes had been forced onto allotments, and their surplus land had been acquired at the government price. This tactic did not impress the Pawnee delegates in the council. White Eagle chastised the commissioners for trying to frighten the Pawnees into selling the land: "You should not try to scare us—talking about the western Indians," he said. "We *helped* you put them on reservations."[17] Other former scouts also spoke out against allotment. Unfortunately, their appeal to the government to honor its debts to the Pawnee people was in vain. In the end, the Pawnee chiefs had no option but to sell their surplus land at $1.25 an acre.

Soon after the allotment agreement was signed, much of the Pawnee reservation was opened to white settlers. The arrival of these newcomers, which began in 1893, created new pressures. Settlers often accused the Pawnees of stealing, and they also introduced liquor into the area. Some settlers showed little respect for the Pawnee people, and violence occasionally ensued. One day a white man in charge of some covered wagons threatened to cut the barbed wire that enclosed Echo Hawk's garden, in order to pass through with his caravan. Despite Echo Hawk's repeated warnings, the man stubbornly continued. In the altercation that followed, Echo Hawk shot the trespasser with a Winchester rifle.[18] Furthermore, few Pawnees had any experience with handling money and quickly became indebted to white bankers and store owners. Although government agents tried to help families manage their funds, some people, such as former scout Roam Chief, were forced to sell land to pay off debts.[19]

Sickness, death, and government policies demoralized the Pawnee people. By 1890, most of the priests who had knowledge of the old bundle ceremonies had passed away, taking with them their knowledge of the ceremonies. As people sank deeper into poverty, social problems such as alcohol abuse, domestic violence, and even suicide (a hitherto unknown phenomenon among the Pawnees) became more common. Many Pawnees believed these crises were the results of the disappearance of the bundle complex.

Desperation gave birth to the Ghost Dance religion, which mixed Christian and native traditions. The Pawnee Ghost Dance was introduced by a young Kitkahahki named Frank White, not to be confused with the former scout of the same name. In 1891 White had met the Northern Arapaho Ghost Dance prophet Sitting Bull while visiting the Wichita Agency. Within a year, nearly two-thirds of the Pawnee people regularly attended White's dances. They danced until exhaustion, when they would fall into trance. In their visions they saw deceased relatives, and upon regaining consciousness they brought back messages from the world of the dead. The Ghost Dance allowed the people to find strength and hope through spiritual communion with the dead. Although agents tried to suppress it because it threatened the government's "civilization program," for several years the Ghost Dance not only offered comfort and solace but also was a creative force that enabled the Pawnees to revive some of their traditional ceremonies and societies.

Many former scouts joined the Ghost Dance movement, which continued despite Frank White's death in 1893 and bans by reservation agents.[20] Among the former scouts who found comfort in the Ghost Dance was Wichita Blaine, veteran of the 1876 campaign. During one of the dances Blaine saw his two dead children. "In my heart I knew they were where Tirawahat is," he told his grandson years later, and "all my sorrows left." Blaine eventually became a leader in the movement and composed several Ghost Dance songs himself.[21] The Skiris developed their own version of the Ghost Dance, as opposed to the South Band version. Ghost Dance leaders among the Skiris included Good Eagle, who, like Wichita Blaine, was a former scout.[22]

Despite the resistance of the Pawnee people, the wheels of the government's "civilization program" ground on. As a matter of survival, many of the scouts urged their children to adopt the ways of the white man and attend the white man's schools. Except for Ralph J. Weeks and Harry Coons, few of the scouts themselves ever attended school. Most never learned to read, write, or even speak English. They signed official documents with thumb marks. Some of the scouts now began to attend church services at the nearby Baptist mission, although attending Christian services did not mean that the Pawnees completely relinquished their own traditions and beliefs. Indeed, many people were comfortable attending church services in the morning and Indian ceremonies in the afternoon. Quite a few old scouts joined the Pawnee medicine lodge societies and performed old ceremonies. Many scouts, including Red Sun, Lone Chief, and John Louwalk, acted as informants for George Dorsey and James Murie when these men collected Pawnee traditional and mythological stories.[23] Even if many Pawnees were now willing to adopt new ways, this did not mean that they were also prepared to relinquish old ones.

Economic conditions on the reservation improved somewhat after the turn of the twentieth century. Those who had survived the onslaught of disease and death began the transition to post-allotment life. They raised their own food and leased remaining land to white farmers and ranchers. Some former scouts did well. They built houses and sent their children to schools. A few earned extra income from oil and gas leases after 1914. Josie Howell, who had enlisted as a scout because it was his "only chance to show his bravery," for years operated the government mill on the reservation after the tribe moved to Indian Territory. He was considered to be among the most "industrious" Pawnees.[24] Simond Adams cultivated twenty-six acres of land and leased the rest of his allotment to farmers and ranchers. He also owned some cattle and a large flock of poultry and received some supplemental income from oil and gas royalties.[25] By 1916, Echo Hawk owned three horses, some poultry, and farm machinery and received additional income from oil, grazing, and farm leases. In 1916 he sold some land and had a new house built. According to the Indian agent, he and his wife, Carrie, were quite "independent."[26] By 1922, Rush Roberts owned a spacious house eleven miles northeast of the town of Pawnee, Oklahoma. For a time he and his wife, Lou, had worked at the Santa Fe Indian School in New Mexico, where their children attended school. All his children went on to secondary schools. In 1923 the Pawnee

Agency superintendent wrote that Roberts's family owned considerable assets and income and that much of the money went to the education of his children.[27]

Not all scouts did so well. Many struggled to survive and were destitute as a result of old age and failing health. Unable to afford a house, Robert Taylor lived in a tent until about 1914.[28] John Buffalo was seventy-six in 1912, nearly blind, and almost helpless from old age. In 1913 the agent reported that Buffalo had only $57.63 remaining in his account.[29] Others were dogged by bad luck. John Box, for example, worked hard to build a successful farming operation, but a tornado destroyed his farm in 1915, prompting him to vow that he would never follow the white man's ways again.[30]

As they grew older, the surviving scouts came to occupy positions of leadership in the tribe. They took their place in the councils and acted as spokesmen for the tribe in its dealings with the government. On such occasions they did not hesitate to remind government agents that they had served as scouts and that their people therefore deserved to be treated better. Because of their position of authority in the tribe, the government also appointed some of the old scouts as tribal judges and police officers. Although these officials were instructed to implement the government's civilization program, they often looked the other way when people staged their ceremonies and medicine "doings."[31]

Many of the scouts were well-known and highly regarded Indian doctors. High Eagle and Wichita Blaine, for example, were Buffalo Doctors. Another former scout, Captain Jim (also known as Young Bull), was the head of the Buffalo Doctor Society and reportedly an expert at treating broken bones.[32] Among many other doctors were Good Eagle, John Buffalo, Brave Chief, Dog Chief, Eli Shotwell, and White Eagle. Once a year the doctors from the various societies gathered for the Medicine Lodge ceremony, to perform dances and compete with each other in sleight-of-hand performances. The doctors' societies faded in the late 1920s as the younger generations showed little interest in continuing them.[33]

One of the more disgraceful episodes in the history of the Pawnee scouts was the government's handling of veterans' pensions. Not only did veterans of the Indian wars receive smaller pension allowances than

Civil War and Spanish-American War veterans, but the seminal Pension Act of March 4, 1917, also failed to recognize some of the campaigns in which Pawnee scouts had served.[34]

Several scouts filed for invalid pensions as early as 1892 and 1893. In their applications, many complained of ailments that they linked to the hardships and dangers of their military service. Their claims were handled by P. J. Meurer, an attorney from Arkansas City, Kansas, and county clerk Charles M. Hill. Unfortunately, the large number of invalid pension claims raised the suspicions of federal officials. In 1895 a grand jury indicted Meurer and Hill for reportedly filing false affidavits. The next year the cases were heard in the district court at the town of Pawnee, Indian/Oklahoma Territory. According to a newspaper report, the judge had considerable trouble getting the Pawnees to testify. Apparently, the cases were dismissed "for want of jurisdiction."[35] It appears that as a result of the controversial claims case, few pensions, if any, were awarded.

The failure to secure pensions in 1893 temporarily put a stop to further pension applications. In the mid-1910s, however, several Pawnees again sought to be compensated for their military service. Sadly, bureaucratic red tape, poor documentation, and, especially, complications arising from the scouts' practice of changing their names over the course of their lives made the application process long and difficult. In most cases it took many years before applicants were finally awarded pensions. Not infrequently, the applicant died before the process was completed.

Typical was the case of John Box, a veteran of the Summit Springs battle. Box's actual name was Fox, but it had been changed to Box through a clerical error several years earlier. Box had served as a scout under the name Red Fox. In 1915 he first applied for a pension. This claim was rejected on the grounds that his service as an Indian scout was not rendered in a war covered by any existing pension law. When the law was changed in March 1917 to include a number of Indian conflicts, Box tried again. He filed his claim in the summer of 1918 together with several other veterans, including Billy Osborne, Roam Chief, Leading Fox, Echo Hawk, High Eagle, and Ruling His Sun. Officials in the Pension Office again rejected his claim, because they found no conclusive evidence that he had been in the Republican River campaign of 1869.

In December 1919 Box traveled to Washington, D.C., together with Walking Sun, to address the issue of the scouts' pensions with Acting Pension Commissioner E. C. Tieman. They were accompanied by James Murie, who acted as their interpreter. Box and Walking Sun gave the commissioner a detailed description of their service against Tall Bull's Dog Soldiers and their role in the Summit Springs battle. They further stated that Robert Taylor, Leading Fox, High Eagle, Billy Osborne, and Eli Shotwell had also served in this campaign. Although their depositions were not put on paper, Commissioner Tieman was willing to accept their account as true and instructed his officers to reexamine these cases. In January 1920 Box's claim was finally approved, and he was awarded a small pension of $20 a month. The Pension Office accepted June 24, 1918, the day Box filed his claim, as the starting date for his pension and issued him a check for $690 to cover this period. Because of Box's and Walking Sun's testimonies, the Pension Office also reexamined the claims of other scouts.[36]

Other scouts who, after a lengthy process, were able to obtain pensions were John Buffalo,[37] Walking Sun,[38] Billy Osborne,[39] High Eagle,[40] Leading Fox,[41] William Riding In,[42] Wichita Blaine, Simond Adams, Rush Roberts, Robert Taylor, Echo Hawk,[43] and Eli Shotwell.[44]

An exceptional case was that of Ruling His Sun, who had served in 1868 and had been present in the battle on Mud Creek on July 30 of that year. He first applied for an invalid's pension in 1893, claiming that he had "contracted Rheumatism [and] lameness off Back from Exposure." The claim was rejected when the Pension Office could find no record of his enlistment in the records of the Adjutant General's Office. In June 1918 Ruling His Sun tried again. Unfortunately, he had lost the discharge papers that proved his enlistment in 1868. Complicating matters was the fact that he was known under several names during the course of his life. Again the Pension Office rejected his claim when it found no record of his service.

Over the next years, Ruling His Sun presented affidavits and statements from various people, including Luther North, in support of his claim. Time and again his applications were rejected. One of the problems was that his service in 1868 was not covered by the Pension Act of March 4, 1917. In 1923, U.S. Congressman E. B. Howard wrote to the Pension Office on behalf of Ruling His Sun. In response, the Pension Office suggested that

Howard propose an amendment to the Pension Act. Howard did not go this far but in 1924 pushed through House Resolution 4283, which stated that Ruling His Sun "should be regarded as an Indian war soldier, and it is therefore recommended that he be granted a pension of $20 per month." On December 8, 1924, Congress enacted the resolution into law.

Although Ruling His Sun now received a pension, the Pension Office had not formally recognized that he had served in 1868. When the new Pension Act of March 3, 1927, raised pension allowances from $20 to $50, the Pension Office excluded Ruling His Sun. That year, Ruling His Sun filed a new claim in order to get an increase in pension payment. To investigate his claim, the Pension Office sent special examiner T. Quinn Jones to interview Ruling His Sun and several other scouts in April 1928. The interviews lasted about six hours. In his report to the Pension Office, written a few days after the interviews, Jones concluded: "Undoubtedly this man served and it would hardly seem fair to reject his claim because his name could not positively be identified by reason of some slight misinterpretation in the syllables." As a result of Jones's investigation, Ruling His Sun's pension was raised to $50 a month.[45]

Although pension money was a welcome addition to their incomes, the scouts also saw it as formal recognition of their sacrifices. For this reason, Walking Sun wrote the Pension Office in September 1920, asking if it was possible to obtain a "scout button in recognition of his service as a scout." Attorney Edwin R. McNeill, of Pawnee, Oklahoma, wrote that Walking Sun desired "to have this as soon as possible, and also proper soldier buttons for his vest, and, also, his coat, so that he can wear them at whatever time he sees fit to do so." The Pension Office responded that they did not have buttons of this kind and forwarded the request to the Office of Indian Affairs. That office, however, did not issue such buttons or medals either.[46]

As the scouts advanced in years, many of them began to suffer from the long-term effects of wounds, injuries, and ailments resulting from exposure and other hardships endured during their military service. For example, Peter Wood, Billy Osborne, and Good Eagle suffered from injuries they incurred during the Republican River campaign in 1869. Walking Sun developed "catarrh of [the] head," a recurring infection of the nasal passages, which he blamed on exposure to the weather during his service.

In addition to having a deformed face resulting from a fall off his horse while a scout, High Eagle contracted severe lung problems during his service, which effectively amounted to the loss of one lung. Others, such as Leading Fox and Ruling His Sun, blamed their rheumatism on exposure during their service.

Many of the scouts also suffered from cataracts and other eye ailments. Robert Taylor and Wichita Blaine were completely blind at the end of their lives and therefore completely dependent on others. Taylor had lost one eye in an accident and usually wore a patch or a scarf over it. When his other eye began to fail, his children and grandchildren looked after him. Because Pawnee children were taught that it was impolite to draw attention to someone's physical ailments, they never asked him how he lost his eye.[47]

One by one, the remaining old scouts passed away. Good Eagle died in 1915, Captain Jim in 1916, John Buffalo in 1920, Eli Shotwell in 1922, Echo Hawk in 1924, John Box in 1925, Billy Osborne and Walking Sun in 1927, Ruling His Sun in 1928, High Eagle in 1929, Robert Taylor in 1930, and William Riding In in 1933. Several of these men were in their late nineties at the time of their death. Ruling His Sun was reportedly around 103 when he passed away. Unlike other scouts, he refused to adopt the white man's appearance and until his death wore the scalp lock and roached hairstyle and the traditional clothing of the Pawnees. According to a local newspaper article, he "steadfastly refused to adopt the white man's customs and as little of his clothing as possible."[48] In 1925 he had attended a ceremony at Trenton, Nebraska, to commemorate the tragedy at Massacre Canyon. One of his wives and one of his children had died in the fight. According to a newspaper report, it was only "with difficulty" that Ruling His Sun could be restrained from attacking several Sioux veterans of the battle who were also in attendance.[49]

Rush Roberts, the last of the Pawnee scouts, died on March 10, 1958. He, too, was nearly one hundred years old at the time of his death. Roberts had been born on November 30, 1859. Both his father, Fancy Eagle, and grandfather, Sitting Eagle, had been highly regarded doctors. Roberts was a survivor of the slaughter at Massacre Canyon in 1873 and had joined the scouts in 1876. After his return from the Powder River campaign he married three sisters, daughters of Kah he kee (translated as "Almighty Chieftain"). He had fifteen children, of whom only seven survived. His son George served in World War I as a member of the Coast Guard Artillery Corps. On February 22, 1904, Roberts was elected a subchief and later served for many years as president of the Pawnee tribal council.[50] The news of his death was announced in newspapers and magazines all over the country, including *Time* magazine.[51]

The passing of the scouts marked the end of an era. Although they had first and foremost fought for their own people, the scouts had been the first Pawnees to fight as allies of the United States. They had served loyally and had always been victorious. Their stories and adventures became the stuff of legend among the Pawnee people, who continue to honor them as true American patriots. The valor of these men appealed to many of the younger people, who soon followed in their footsteps in the service of the U.S. military. Ever since, young Pawnee people have tried to live up to the ideal warrior image established by the scouts.[52]

One of the first of the post-scout warriors was William Pollock, the son of a Kitkahahki warrior. Pollock was born in Nebraska in 1872. After attending the Pawnee reservation boarding school, he enrolled at Haskell Indian Institute in Lawrence, Kansas, where he excelled as a musician and artist. Some of his paintings were exhibited at the Smithsonian Institution in Washington, D.C. After his return to the Pawnee reservation, he became a deputy sheriff. On the eve of the Spanish-American War, he enlisted in the First United States Volunteer Cavalry under Colonel Leonard Wood and Lieutenant Colonel Theodore Roosevelt. The First Volunteer Cavalry soon achieved fame as the "Rough Riders." Pollock saw his service in the tradition of his Pawnee ancestors. "In the memory of our brave fathers," he wrote to a friend shortly before he embarked with the troops for Cuba, "I will try and be like one of them who used to stand single-handed against the foe." Pollock was present at the battles of Las Guasimas, San Juan, and Kettle Hill and the capture of Santiago de Cuba. Theodore Roosevelt said of him that he was one of the "gamest fighters and best soldiers in the regiment." According to Roosevelt, Pollock was always "leading in the charges and always being nearest the enemy." A fellow soldier in Company D recalled how Pollock, like the scouts of old, took off his shirt during one battle. After the war he returned to Pawnee, but shortly after his arrival he contracted pneumonia and died on March 2, 1899. He was buried with full military honors at the cemetery north of the town of Pawnee.[53]

Several Pawnees served along the Texas-Mexico border during the border crisis of 1916. Walter Keys, Thomas Hand, Harry Richard, Jacob Leader, and Frank Young Eagle all served in Company E of the First Oklahoma Infantry. Their company was stationed near San Benito, Texas, to prevent Pancho Villa's raiders from again crossing the border into the United States after their deadly attack on the village of Columbus, New Mexico, earlier that year.[54]

Some fifty Pawnees served during World War I. They were Alex Adams, Joe Ameelyonee, Louis Bayhylle, Arthur Coons, Burress Curley Chief, Harold Curley Chief, Harry Coons Jr., Henry Chapman, Emmett Carrion, Alex Eagle, George Echo Hawk, Elmer Echo Hawk, Joe Esau, Ben Gover, Thomas Hand, Will Justice, Walter Keyes, Jacob Leader, Warren Leader, James Little Sun, Paul Little Eagle, Herbert Morris, Elmo Matlock, Edgar Moore, Lawrence Murie, Wallace Murie, James Mannington, Henry Murie, James Moses, Walter Norman, Johnathan New Rider, Samuel Osborne, Harry Richards, Frank Riding In, Charlie Riding Up, George Roberts, John Spotted Horse Chief, Delbert Spotted Horse Chief, James Sun Eagle, Elmer Sun Eagle, Dick Smith, Julius Smith, John Smith, Jobie Taylor, George Taylor, Grant White, Henry White, Charley Wilson, Ernest Wichita, Frank Young Eagle, and Moses Yellow Horse. Of these men, nearly forty served on the battlefields of France.[55]

Upon their return to Pawnee, Oklahoma, they received a glorious welcome. Frances Densmore, who studied and analyzed Indian music, attended a celebration for the returning Pawnee doughboys on June 6 and 7, 1919. The first day's dance was reserved for Pawnees alone. The next day, white visitors were invited to attend. Old war songs were sung with new words mentioning airplanes and submarines. The veterans were presented with horses and other gifts. One of the returning soldiers brought a German helmet from the battlefield and gave it to his mother, who carried the helmet on a scalp pole. "The young man who gave it to his mother," Densmore wrote, "acted in accordance with an old Indian custom in which scalps were handed over to the women, in whose defense the warriors had gone forth."[56]

After World War I, the Pawnee tribe began to honor its veterans in an annual war dance celebration. The dances were held on Armistice Day, November 11. At the dance, the Pawnees paid special tribute to the aging scouts of the Indian wars. The celebration was held in the South Roundhouse, ten miles south of the town of Pawnee. The Roundhouse was a larger wooden version of an old Pawnee earth lodge. It had a smoke hole at the top of the ceiling, and its door faced east, according to old Pawnee custom, "to greet the morning star." The Roundhouse was always crowded during the Armistice Day celebrations. Brummett Echohawk witnessed the celebrations as a young boy:

> On the west side, and facing east, were the Chiefs and Veterans. There, too, was the American flag attached to a fresh-cut willow pole. Seated next to the flag, the place of honor, were the old Scouts. They wore buckskin leggings trimmed with scalps; broadcloth breechcloths; moccasins with fine beadwork; bear claw necklaces; Presidential medallions. Their braids were wrapped in otter hides. A few still wore the old-time scalp lock with an eagle feather. In earlier times, the scalp lock was painted red and dressed to stand upright as a challenge for the enemy to come take it. They wore paint on their faces. Paint of family colors and paint to signify something holy. The paint was set at the corners of the eyes and at the part of the hair.
> They were proud men . . . warriors who had worn United States Cavalry blue.[57]

Brummett Echohawk soon got the opportunity to represent the Pawnees in the uniform of the United States Army himself. During World War II, he and many other Pawnee men and women served in U.S. armed forces. Pawnee men fought in all theaters of the war: in the Atlantic, the Pacific, North Africa, Europe, and Southeast Asia. The tribe, meanwhile, supported its warriors from the home front. In June 1942 the Pawnees danced in tribute to the men and women in the service. Others worked in war-related industries. Many Pawnee women volunteered and worked as nurses or in other supportive positions. Several Pawnees received medals for bravery. Del Ray Echo Hawk, for example, received the Distinguished Flying Cross, the Soldier's Medal, and the Purple Heart. Charles Harris received the Air Medal. Other Pawnees who received the Purple Heart were Levi Horsechief, Lawrence Good Fox Jr., Thomas Chapman Jr.,

Andrew Roberts, Jacob Moses, Jesse Howell, William Harris Jr., Lloyd Yellowhorse, Brummett Echohawk, George Little Sun, Floyd Rice, Leonard Leading Fox, Chauncey Matlock, Philip Gover, Grant Gover, and David Woods. After being taken prisoner in the Philippines, Alexander Mathews survived the Bataan death march and spent several years as a Japanese prisoner of war. Some, sadly, such as Grant Gover, Charles Harris, George and William Coons, and Eugene Peters (a Pawnee-Otoe), did not return. Those who did received a hero's welcome in Pawnee, Oklahoma.[58]

In 1946 the Pawnee Nation organized its first annual Pawnee Homecoming to honor members of the tribe who had fought in American wars. Rush Roberts (Ah re kah rard), the last surviving scout of Major North's battalion, was the guest of honor during this celebration. The Pawnee Homecoming Powwow has been held ever since. Since World War II, Pawnee Indians have served in every major war of the United States. Pawnee soldiers fought in Korea, Vietnam, and, more recently, the Gulf War. They, too, are honored every year at the Pawnee Homecoming Powwow, which is held during the first week of July. Not coincidentally, the Pawnee Homecoming Powwow coincides with the Fourth of July Independence Day celebration. A large part of the ceremony is still devoted to the Pawnee scouts. Today, virtually all Pawnees trace their ancestry back to one or more scouts and are proud of the tribe's long-standing tradition of service in the United States Army.

Conclusion

Although high-ranking officers such as George Crook, William T. Sherman, and Christopher C. Augur believed that enlisting American Indians in the U.S. Army might have a "civilizing" effect on them, the primary purpose of the Pawnee scouts was to assist the army in the military conquest of the American West. In theory, military service exposed the scouts to Euro-American values of discipline and authority. Through their interaction with white officers and soldiers, it was believed, the scouts would also master the English language and possibly acquire other practical skills. Once they returned to their reservations, they could put these skills to work in their own communities.

But military service did not transform the Pawnees into "acculturated" soldiers. Acculturation was only a secondary consideration. The army hoped to use the Pawnees' skills as trailers, guides, and warriors in its military operations against the hostile tribes of the Great Plains. Despite pontifications by Crook, Sherman, and Augur, the army did little to effect the acculturation of the scouts. Rather than fundamentally changing the Pawnees, their service as scouts reinforced their traditional war-related practices.

Scout service allowed the Pawnees, equipped with weapons supplied by the U.S. government, to exact revenge on their Sioux and Cheyenne enemies—and to be paid for it. The Pawnees were not "duped" into fighting against people of their own race by the American government, as has sometimes been charged. They welcomed the invitation to join the United States in a military alliance against common foes. Their enlistment was a wise strategic policy. By allying themselves with the U.S. Army, the scouts were able to take the war away from their settlements and move it deep into the territory of their enemies. They helped to put the Sioux and the Cheyennes on the defensive.

But they enlisted for personal reasons as well. Some hoped to avenge the death of a loved one. Others hoped to gain war honors. Throughout the existence of the Pawnee battalion, scouts counted coups on their enemies, changed their names after performing brave deeds, and celebrated their victories in scalp dances. During their service the scouts also captured many horses, which earned them economic status within the tribe. After the tribe was removed to Indian Territory, many men joined to escape poverty and disease on the Pawnee reservation.

Exposure to the "civilizing" influences of white soldiers remained limited. Although small detachments of scouts occasionally accompanied white troops, most of the time they remained part of an all-Indian—indeed, all-Pawnee—unit. The boundaries between Indian and white remained essentially intact. Even during military campaigns, contact between the scouts and the troops was limited. Cultural boundaries often separated the Pawnees from the white troops. Their refusal to drink alcohol, for example, prevented many scouts from interacting with white soldiers. At the same time, many white soldiers were suspicious of, if not openly hostile toward, all Indians, even friendly ones such as the Pawnees.

Frank North, too, had to observe certain intratribal boundaries within the scouts organization. Usually the battalion consisted of separate companies or platoons, each composed of members of one of the bands of the tribe. Each unit, whether Chawi, Kitkahahki, Pitahawirata, or Skiri, had its own officers. Thus, traditional tribal divisions were observed at all times. This situation led to problems when General Samuel R. Curtis appointed Joseph McFadden to command the scouts in 1864. Through his marriage to a Pawnee woman, McFadden was associated with his wife's band, and scouts who were members of the other bands did not feel compelled to obey his orders. This delicate problem was skirted with the selection of Frank North as McFadden's lieutenant. North was not identified with a particular band and was therefore more acceptable as a leader.[1]

The military's decision to place nonmilitary personnel in charge of the Pawnee scouts demonstrates a lack of concern about educating and "civilizing" the scouts. Both Joseph McFadden and Frank North were

CONCLUSION

civilians when they were appointed to lead the scouts. McFadden had married into the tribe, and North had been employed at the Pawnee Agency. Both spoke fluent Pawnee. Although McFadden had some previous military experience (he had served under General William S. Harney at Ash Hollow, Nebraska Territory, in 1855), his selection was based principally on his association with the tribe. Almost none of the men whom Frank North later appointed had any previous military experience. The only exception was North's brother, Luther, who had served briefly with the Union cavalry during the Civil War. Because of their limited military experience, North and his staff leaned heavily on the experience of their men.

Much has been written about Frank North's leadership of the Pawnee battalion. Clearly he was an important figure among the scouts, who gave him the honorary title Pani Leshar ("Pawnee Chief"). Part of North's success might have stemmed from his personality. He was a stern but fair leader whose bravery won the Pawnees' respect. His ability to speak the Pawnee langauge greatly facilitated his effectiveness. But the key to understanding North's influence lies in his connection with the army, which allowed him to serve as a mediator between the army and the Pawnee leadership. Appointed by the army, North supplied the Pawnees with guns, horses, and ammunition. In return, the Pawnees accepted him as a war leader, and his battalion as a war party.

North's authority may have had not only a material basis, but also a supernatural one. Because North miraculously escaped death on several occasions, many scouts were convinced that he was under the protection of Tiiraawaahat. Because of his diverse qualifications, many Pawnees, especially those in search of war honors and economic status, wished to join his battalion. Pawnee tradition gave North, as leader of the war party, the authority to discipline his men when they disobeyed his orders. Thus, as historian Thomas Dunlay has pointed out, although North was not a Pawnee Indian by birth, the hierarchical structure of Pawnee society "may well have created a mental niche into which the Pawnees could fit him."[2]

Still, the Pawnees accepted North's authority only conditionally. As soon as he overstepped his authority, the scouts did not hesitate to correct him. They would accept punishment, but only if it was deserved, and only if the form of punishment was fitting. When North attempted to punish a few scouts too harshly in 1867, a number of scouts simply left and returned to their reservation. The army, recognizing the importance of continuing Pawnee support, wisely refrained from pursuing the matter. Junior officers wielded even less authority. Their main role appears to have been that of intermediaries between the scouts and other army units in the field.

North's authority was limited even on the field of battle. Although Luther North usually depicted his brother as leading the charge, it appears that the scouts themselves generally took the initiative. On more than one occasion they urged Frank North to push ahead in order to overtake a hostile party in a surprise attack. Their phenomenal endurance made possible such lengthy ventures deep into hostile territory. The Pawnees also insisted on using their own tactics. The element of surprise was crucial in their operations. While they scouted the land, they wore disguises to avoid detection by the enemy. During the Plum Creek battle in 1867, they deceived Turkey Leg's band of Cheyennes by pretending to be white troops. According to one account, they used horses to lure enemy raiders into ambushes during the 1865 campaign. The scouts preferred to go into battle almost naked. Not only did the heavy army uniforms hamper their movements, but the risk of infection increased when bullets carried pieces of cloth into wounds. The scouts' first target was always their opponents' horse herd. Capturing the horses not only added to their own wealth but also prevented their enemies from escaping.

Understanding his limits as the leader of a Pawnee war party, Frank North did little to change the ways of the men under his command. He rarely drilled his scouts and did so only when ordered to by his superior officers. He did not believe that drills were useful for the men who had been hired as scouts. Indeed, it appears that North himself adopted many of the scouts' customs. He sang with them during their celebrations, and when his men bestowed honors upon him, he reciprocated the honor by presenting gifts to them. The influence of the Pawnee warrior tradition on the North brothers became evident in 1876 when, during a confrontation with some Sioux scouts, they began to sing a Pawnee war song signifying their readiness to fight until death.

Like the leader of a traditional Pawnee war party, North divided the spoils of war among his men after a successful campaign. Whether he was aware of the practice or not, by distributing captured horses among his men he fulfilled one of the functions of the leader of a war party. As a war leader he had the right to keep a large part of the spoils to himself, but he usually gave most of the plunder away. Thus North ensured the trust and loyalty of his men for future campaigns.

During the expeditions and campaigns, the scouts continued to place their faith in Tiiraawaahat. They carried their personal medicine bundles into battle and carefully observed the proper rituals and taboos to secure the blessing and protection of the supernatural. Frank North did not discourage these practices, partly because the scouts would not have accepted his interference and perhaps also because he recognized that confident scouts made better fighters. Each scout prepared for battle with his own customs. Usually these routines involved prayers, bundle rituals, the singing of war songs, or face painting.

Even though they served under the banner of the United States, the Pawnees continued the practice of scalping. Although regular officers often spoke disapprovingly of this custom, Frank North did not stop the practice and most likely could not have done so. The Pawnees displayed the scalps they took during battle whenever they returned from a successful mission. Although Luther North adamantly denied that the Pawnees mutilated the corpses of their slain enemies while serving as scouts, the fact remains that this behavior was not uncommon. It must be understood within the context of Plains Indian warfare and culture. Like other Plains Indians, the Pawnees were not accustomed to taking prisoners and often killed enemy men, women, and children indiscriminately. Although officers and enlisted men often accused their Indian allies of extreme cruelty, the army's record during this period was hardly better. White soldiers, too, frequently took scalps and mutilated the remains of fallen Indians. Perhaps their actions are in fact more disturbing because, unlike Plains Indians, they lacked the cultural framework that validated such behavior. Instead, Euro-Americans reinvented scalping within the entrepreneurial spirit of the time and subsequently turned the practice into a profitable business by issuing scalp bounties.[3]

The Pawnee battalion, then, had all the characteristics of a Pawnee war party. This did not mean that the Pawnees felt no pride in wearing the uniform of the United States. On the contrary, as scouts for the Great Father, they felt like equals of the whites. Unlike the agents back at the reservation, the army treated them like men, not children. They saw themselves not as dupes of a greater power but as allies of a foreign nation that fought a common enemy. Although they wore the uniform of the United States Cavalry, they never ceased to be Pawnees.

Notes

FOREWORD

1. Reeder, "Wolf Men of the Plains," 352.
2. Ibid., v.
3. Ibid.
4. Blaine, *Some Things Are Not Forgotten*, 169.
5. Quoted in Fletcher, *Hako*, 27.

INTRODUCTION

1. Report by Brevet Major General Christopher C. Augur, Headquarters Department of the Platte, Omaha, Nebraska, September 30, 1867, *Annual Report of the Secretary of War*, House Exec. Doc. 1, 40th Congress, 2nd Session, Serial Set 1324 (Washington, D.C.: Government Printing Office, 1867), 59–60.

2. Report of General William T. Sherman, Headquarters Military Division of the Missouri, St. Louis, Mo., October 1, 1867, *Annual Report of the Secretary of War*, House Exec. Doc. 1, 40th Congress, 2nd Session, Serial Set 1324 (Washington, D.C.: Government Printing Office, 1867), 37–38. General George Crook, who commanded the Pawnee scouts during the Powder River Expedition of 1876, also believed that military service had a positive effect on Indians: "One thing is certain, [military service] is the entering wedge by which the tribal organization is broken up, making way for civilizing and Christianizing influences. As a soldier the Indian wears the uniform, draws rations and pay, and is in all respects on an equal footing with a white man. It demonstrates to his simple mind in the most positive manner that we have no prejudice against him on account of his race, and that while he behaves himself he will be treated the same as a white man. Returning to his tribe after this service he is enabled to see beyond the old superstition that has governed his people, and thinks and decides for himself." General George Crook to General Philip H. Sheridan, October 30, 1876, published in the *New York Herald*, November 10, 1876.

3. Frank Joshua North was the second son of Jane Almira Townley and Thomas Jefferson North. The two married in January 1837 in New York State and soon moved to Ohio, where their oldest son, James E. North, was born in September 1838. Frank North was born on March 10, 1840, and his brother Luther Hedden North, on March 6, 1846. Jane North gave birth to two more children, both girls, while the family still lived in Ohio. In 1856 Thomas North moved the family to Iowa, and later that year to Nebraska. While in charge of a surveying group west of Omaha in 1857, Thomas was caught in a severe storm and froze to death. In the spring of 1859 the remaining members of the family finally settled in Columbus, Nebraska. In 1861 Frank was appointed clerk and interpreter at the Pawnee Agency. In August 1864 he helped organize the Pawnee scouts and, although suffering from asthma, was commissioned a lieutenant. During his next enlistment he was appointed with the rank of major. On December 25, 1865, he married Mary L. Smith. The couple had one child, Stella, born in 1870. From 1871 to 1876, while the Pawnee battalion was inactive, Frank served as post guide and interpreter at Fort Russell and Sidney Barracks. After the Pawnee battalion was permanently dismantled in 1877, he went into business with William F. ("Buffalo Bill") Cody and started the Cody-North Ranch on the North Platte River, Nebraska. In 1882 he sold his interest in the ranch and was elected to the Nebraska legislature on the Democratic Party ticket. In 1883 his wife died, and the following year he joined Buffalo Bill's Wild West Show, together with a number of Pawnees. During a show in Hartford, Connecticut, he was severely injured but survived. In 1885, however, he fell ill while traveling to Omaha on business for the show. He was taken home to Columbus, where he died of "congestion of the lungs" on March 14, 1885. He was buried at Columbus, Nebraska, on March 17, 1885. Luther H. North, who served for many years with the scouts together with his brother, died on April 18, 1935, and was also buried at Columbus. "Memorial Leaves Inscribed to the Memory of Major Frank J. North, and Respectfully Dedicated to His Mother, Mrs. Jane A. North, by One Who Admired the Son and Reveres the Mother" (pamphlet, probably by Luther North; n.p.: n.p., 1885), Major Frank J. North Collection, RG 2321 (formerly MS 0448), Nebraska State Historical Society, Lincoln (hereafter cited as "Frank North Collection"), Box 2, Folder 2; Bruce, *Fighting Norths*, 141; "Frank North," *Forest and Stream*, March 19, 1885, 141.

4. Douglas R. Parks, American Indian Studies Research Institute, Indiana University, personal communication, February 29, 2008.

5. Grinnell, *Two Great Scouts;* Bruce, *Fighting Norths;* Danker, *Man of the Plains;* Wilson, *Frank J. North;* O'Donnell, *Luther North.*

6. Hyde, *Pawnee Indians*, 272–73.

7. The best general treatment on Native American scouts remains Dunlay's excellent study, *Wolves for the Blue Soldiers*. The Pawnee scouts are covered in chapter 9 of that book. Other instructive works include Smits, "'Fighting Fire with Fire'"; Downey and Jacobson, *Red Bluecoats;* and Danker, "North Brothers."

CHAPTER 1

1. Grinnell, *Pawnee Hero Stories*, 45–47.
2. Ibid., 47.
3. Smith, "War Complex of the Plains Indians." For an excellent study of the effects of horses and guns on Plains Indian tactics, see Secoy, *Changing Military Patterns*. Also useful, even though they describe the effects of new technologies on the military tactics of eastern tribes, are Starkey, *European and Native American Warfare*, and Malone, *Skulking Way of War*.
4. For a brief but excellent introduction to Pawnee culture, see Parks, "Pawnee." The classic work on Pawnee culture and ethnography is Weltfish, *Lost Universe*.
5. For detailed descriptions of bundles and bundle ceremonies, see Murie, *Ceremonies of the Pawnee*. For an excellent discussion of Skiri Pawnee cosmology and the Skiri bundle complex, see Chamberlain, *When Stars Came Down to Earth*.
6. For decades historians and anthropologists have debated the causes of Plains Indian warfare, and the relevant literature is extensive. For a general overview of Plains warfare, see Robarchek, "Plains Warfare." Other useful studies include Biolsi, "Ecological and Cultural Factors"; Newcomb, "Re-Examination of the Causes"; Jablow, *Cheyenne in Plains Indian Trade Relations*; Mishkin, *Rank and Warfare*; Holder, *The Hoe and the Horse*; Smith, "War Complex of the Plains Indians"; Parks and DeMallie, "Plains Indian Warfare"; and Schneiders, *Big Sky Rivers*. For studies of warfare in aboriginal societies around the world, see Ferguson and Farragher, *Anthropology of War*. An older but influential study is Turney-High, *Primitive War*.
7. Roger C. Echo-Hawk, personal communication, April 18, 2008. Nineteenth-century Pawnee military culture had its antecedents in an earlier age. This appears to be especially the case with the Skiri Pawnees; the historical and ethnographic record of the South Band Pawnees is less detailed. Skiri Pawnee myths recorded in the late nineteenth and early twentieth centuries suggest that martial values had been sanctioned by the sacred powers. Skiri ceremonies make numerous references to warfare. Of course it is possible that such changes merely reflect nineteenth-century realities.
8. John Brown Dunbar, writing in 1880, seems to disagree on this point: "In common with all Indians, the Pawnees were afraid of death to an extreme degree, and therefore, personal exposure or peril was most anxiously avoided as long as possible. Hence much of their warfare partook in some measure of cheap bravado, to the partial suppression of earnest purpose to win victory by sheer courage." Dunbar, "Pawnee Indians," 334. Frances Densmore, on the other hand, who visited the Pawnees in Oklahoma in 1919 and 1920, recorded the following song, which exemplifies the attitude that it is better to die young than live to an old age and become a burden to others: *I ra i ra i ra i i ra ru te ratu hura wiu ra ku*

ri kux ta ratuku ("He comes. It hurts to use a cane. It becomes painful to pick it up.") This song originally belonged to a brave man who lived to an advanced age. It relates to the struggles of an old man now dependent upon others to look after him. Warriors sang the song in battle "when they were all tired out and so nearly beaten that even their hair was disheveled." Sometimes they sang it as they drove their enemies away from their village, and it was also used in the scalp dances that followed the return of a successful war party. Densmore, *Pawnee Music*, 49–50.

9. Weltfish, *Caddoan Texts*, 18.

10. Densmore, *Pawnee Music*, 89–90.

11. According to Pawnee theology, all persons, good or bad, brave or cowardly, would be reunited in the afterlife. But there was apparently also a social division in this afterlife. Dunbar, "Pawnee Indians," 742.

12. Densmore, *Pawnee Music*, 62–63. See also Densmore, "Communication with the Dead."

13. Densmore also related the story of a song with the following lyrics: "My dear child, stop crying. Yonder there, in the expanse of the heavens, is where power dwells." A father composed the song to sing for his son, to soothe him after his mother died. The son learned the song and, after he grew up, made it into a war dance. Densmore, *Pawnee Music*, 112–13.

14. James, *Account of an Expedition*, 438–39.

15. Murray, *Travels in North America*, 286. For the effects of the horse on Pawnee culture, see Mishkin, *Rank and Warfare*, 14–18; Secoy, *Changing Military Patterns;* Ewers, *Plains Indian History*, 207; and Blaine, *Pawnee Passage*, 49–54. The importance of the horse in Pawnee society is further illustrated by a statement by Samuel Allis, missionary to the Pawnees in the 1840s and 1850s, who wrote that "more broils, jealousy, and family quarrels [were] caused by horses than all other troubles combined. The horse frequently causes separation between man and wife, sometimes for life." Allis, "Forty Years among the Indians," 140.

16. Echohawk, "Pawnee Scouts," 12. In Pawnee tradition, the eagle is a creature of the high heavens. It is closest to Tiraawaahat, and because of this special closeness to the celestial powers, its feathers are considered powerful objects. According to Pawnee scholar Roger C. Echo-Hawk, eagle "feathers and references to eagles in naming [ceremonies] serve to express the human aspiration to be trustfully religious and prayerful, and to have one's prayers heard and to receive celestial blessings." Roger C. Echo-Hawk, personal communication, April 21, 2008.

17. "Fighting Norths and Pawnee Scouts," June 1931, 18.

18. Irving, *Indian Sketches*, 126–27, 177.

19. Holliday, *On the Plains in '65*, 16.

20. Gilmore, *Uses of Plants*, 28, 46, 81.

21. Murray, *Travels*, 286; Ewers, *Plains Indian History*, 208–209; Hyde, *Pawnee Indians*, 195; Murie, "Pawnee Indian Societies"; Grinnell, *Pawnee Hero Stories*, 142–60.

NOTES TO PAGES 19–20   251

22. Irving, *A Tour on the Prairies*, 67. Irving believed that Deshetres exaggerated the Pawnees' skills as archers, but other observers confirm Deshetres' story. John K. Townsend, who traveled through Pawnee territory in 1834, witnessed the way a Pawnee arrow shot clear through the carcass of an antelope "and then skimmed to a great distance over the plain." Townsend, *Narrative of a Journey*, 165.

23. Murray also claimed that the Pawnees in 1835 were not well trained in the proper care of their guns: "Having but lately become acquainted with the use of fire-arms, [they] soon destroy them, by examining, firing off powder, and other follies. Some they gamble away; and all that they do not either lose or spoil, they exchange with the Haitans [possibly the Comanches] and other predatory tribes in the West and South for horses; so that when the pay-day returns, very few efficient guns are to be found in the Pawnee village." Despite this observation, one should keep in mind that the "refined" Englishman Murray was not very sympathetic toward the Pawnees, whom he considered a "dirty" people. Furthermore, the guns with which the United States provided the Indians might not have been of good quality. Murray, *Travels*, 269, 381.

24. Dunbar, "Pawnee Indians," 277–79.

25. Murray, *Travels*, 316–17.

26. Parks, "Pawnee," 534. In his memoir, George P. Belden left a detailed description of the manufacture of bows and arrows. According to Belden, each tribe made its arrows differently. The Pawnees used medium points and used elk sinew to attach the arrowheads to the shafts. During the 1860s it became increasingly difficult to identify tribes by their arrows: "Many tribes trade and exchange arrows, while others pick up and keep all the arrows they find. It is a practice among the Pawnees, to carefully collect all the arrows of their enemies and keep them to shoot them again, or trade, while many wily Indians, when they wish to attack the whites, or commit an outrage, purposely use arrows belonging to other tribes. To find a white man dead, with a Pawnee arrow sticking in him, is no longer, as in former days, evidence that a Pawnee killed him, for, most likely, the deed was done by a Cheyenne or Sioux, and the blame thus sought to be thrown on the poor Pawnees." Belden, *Belden, White Chief*, 107.

27. Dunbar, "Pawnee Indians," 749–51.

28. Jones, *Poison Arrows*, 13.

29. James, *Account*, 133–34.

30. Edwin James made the following observation in 1820: "Before the entrance to some of the lodges were small frames, like painter's easels, supporting each a shield, and generally a large painted cylindrical case of skin, prepared like parchment, in which a war dress is deposited. James, "James's Account of S. H. Long's Expedition," 164.

31. Dunbar, "Pawnee Indians," 336. Pawnee scout Echo Hawk preferred to carry a bow and arrows rather than the single-shot, muzzle-loading guns that were issued to him when he enlisted in Frank North's battalion. Dog Chief, another Pawnee

scout, always carried a brass tomahawk into battle. Such weapons were useful additions to the warrior's arsenal. Echohawk, "Pawnee Scouts," 11–12.

32. Dunbar, "Pawnee Indians," 263.

33. Murray, *Travels*, 456.

34. George A. Dorsey related the story of a poor man who sought the blessing of a "stone man" (a meteorite) and became a successful warrior and prominent man in the tribe. Dorsey, "Pawnee Personal Medicine Shrine."

35. Murie, "Pawnee Indian Societies," 639.

36. Grinnell, "Pawnee Mythology," 116.

37. Sometimes this spirit revealed itself in visions and dreams. Usually, however, an individual learned the identity of his guardian spirit when a doctor, who had the power of the same animal, was able to cure him when he was ill. After learning the identity of the spirit, the young man joined the doctor's lodge of his guardian to learn about its secrets. Parks, "Pawnee," 537.

38. According to Densmore, when going into battle, Pawnee warriors sang war songs such as "My whole trust is in mother corn." Densmore, *Pawnee Music*, 92. According to Dunbar, Pawnee warriors spent much time on their appearance. "The full-dress toilet of a young brave was a matter of serious and protracted study . . . No devotee of fashion ever labored more assiduously to produce striking results in dress than some of these Pawnee braves." Warriors shaved their heads closely, except for the scalp lock. The beard and eyebrows were carefully pulled out, and face paint was an important part of the toilet. "After killing an enemy the lower part of the face might be painted black." Dunbar, "Pawnee Indians," 268–69. In 1836, Samuel Allis described some of the charms and spirits to which the Pawnees appealed for power (spelling and typography as in the original): "They often hold conversation with animals such as wildcats, woolves, bears, etc. that these animals are brave in fighting, is the reason why they have their skins, claws, bones etc in there medecine bundles. There braves value a string of the bears claws verry highly they often give a horse for them, and were them in time of war to prevent the balls, and arrows hitting them. The grey eagle is also sacred with them, they skin them with the fetherson which they were as a head dress in time of war which is also a preserver of life, they tie one or more eagles feathers on there boos, quivers, shields, warspears etc which they consider notonly neat, but more aspecially as a safeguard and token of bravery. Some of there braves have told me they have ben alone surrounded by there enemies who were shooting at them from evry side, and the balls & arrows didnot hit them because they had on plenty of bears claws, eagles fethers etc. and in relating the same story have told me they were in a dangerous situation, but it seemed to be the Lords will that they should live longer, and it was thrue his goodness that they were yet alive, but this acknowledgment was selfish and did not come from the hart." Wedel, *Dunbar-Allis Letters*, 707–708.

39. Humfreville, *Twenty Years among Our Savage Indians*, 373.

40. Gilmore, *Uses of Plants*, 10.

41. Murie, "Pawnee Indian Societies," 558–60; Dorsey and Murie, "Pawnee: Society and Religion," 238–51.

42. The lances guarded over the entire tribe and, according to some, had the power to attract buffalo. Hence, they had to be carefully protected. Murie, "Pawnee Indian Societies," 558–78.

43. Saxe, "Reveries upon the Art of War," 241–42.

44. Murie, "Pawnee Indian Societies," 579–94. According to George Bird Grinnell, the Young Dog society received most of its power through a "medicine dance" that had been introduced to it by an Arikara Indian. During this dance (a variant of the "Sun Dance") the dancers appealed to the almighty to take pity on them and bless them with protection and power in battle. Grinnell, "Young Dog's Dance."

45. Murie, "Pawnee Indian Societies," 558–78.

46. James, *Account*, 133–34.

47. Dunbar, "Pawnee Indians," 260–61.

48. Ibid., 335. According to Murray, the Pawnees approached the buffalo during their summer hunt in three parallel columns, led by the chief of the hunt in the center. Murray also wrote that during the hunt, "not a man was allowed to leave the ranks; and the discipline seemed as strict as among regular troops on a march." Murray, *Travels*, 379.

49. For an excellent discussion of the effects of the horse on Plains Indian warfare, see Ewers, *Horse in Blackfoot Indian Culture*, esp. 194–99.

50. Dunbar, "Pawnee Indians," 335.

51. Murie, "Pawnee Indian Societies," 596–97; Gregg, "Commerce of the Prairies," 90, 207.

52. According to Dunbar, the Pawnees' enemies gave a different interpretation of the wolf emblem. To them it signified cowardice. The name Skidi is derived from the word *ski-rik-i*, or wolf, and the proper pronunciation of "Skidi" is actually "Ski-ri." Dunbar, "Pawnee Indians," 259. According to Grinnell, the "Cheyennes, Wichitas and Comanches all testify that they call the Pawnees Wolves because they prowl like wolves; because, too, they have the endurance of wolves, and can travel all day, and dance all night, and can make long journeys, living on the carcasses they find on their way, or on no food at all." Grinnell, *Pawnee Hero Stories*, 246.

53. The leader of the war party was entitled to wear a special war dress, which consisted of an otter skin (which was split in the middle and worn over the shoulders, with the head hanging over his back), the skin of a swift hawk, a dried ear of corn, and flint arrowheads encircled by sweet grass. Parks, "Pawnee," 528.

54. Murie, "Pawnee Indian Societies," 595–96. Migrants along the Oregon Trail recalled that the Pawnees imitated the howls of wolves or the sounds of wild turkeys to disguise their approach. Mattes, *Great Platte River Road*, 158. While crossing the Great Plains in 1846, William Clayton, a Mormon pioneer and member of Brigham

Young's advance party to the Great Salt Lake, witnessed a Pawnee horse-raiding party in operation. One day a guard in Clayton's camp saw something move in the grass at the foot of a high mole. The guard proceeded toward it, thinking it was a wolf. When he came within "twelve to fourteen rods" of it, he stooped to shoot at the supposed wolf. "The moment he elevated his rifle, fifteen Indians sprang to their feet all naked except the breech cloth, and armed with rifles and bows and arrows. Each man having a rifle slung on his back, and his bow strung tight in his hand and about twenty arrows." Billington, *William Clayton's Journal*, 109.

55. Lopez, *Of Wolves and Men*, 112. For an interesting discussion of the role of wolf symbolism in Plains Indian warfare, see Comba, "Wolf Warriors." Comba shows that the various coyote, fox, and dog societies among Plains Indian groups were related to wolf societies. He argues that by adopting wolf power, warriors also adopted wild, dangerous, destructive, and therefore potentially antisocial behavior. The challenge was to avoid becoming "*too* wild, lest they lose their humanity and endanger the continuity of normal social life" (47). Apart from the obvious wolf symbolism (endurance, tenacity, stealth, cooperation, etc.), I have so far discovered no resemblance between wolf-hunting tactics and Pawnee war tactics. For discussions of wolf (hunting) behavior, see Mech, *The Wolf*; Carbyn, *Buffalo Wolf*; Carbyn, Oosenbrug, and Arrions, *Wolves, Bison*; Allen, "How Wolves Kill"; and Steinhart, *The Company of Wolves*, chapter 3.

56. Blaine, *Pawnee Passage*, 110. Edwin James tells of a leader of a Kitkahahki war party who carried a war whistle around his neck. James, *Account*, 133.

57. Pattie, *Personal Narrative*, 47.

58. Van de Logt, "Powers of the Heavens." For a detailed description of a scalp sacrifice, see Murie, *Ceremonies of the Pawnee*, vol. 1, *The Skiri*, 136–54. Witnessing a "scalp dance" in 1824, James O. Pattie wrote that during the dance the women could exact "revenge" on the scalp. According to Pattie, the Pawnees raised a tall pole, on the top of which they attached the scalps they had taken in the last battle. The dance, in which the warriors sang of their deeds, lasted three days. At the end of the dance, the men took the pole down and gave the scalps to the women, whose turn it was to vent their anger at the scalps. They kicked the scalps about and threw them around until they, too, ceased "in the apparent satisfaction of gratified revenge." Pattie, "Personal Narrative," 44.

59. Maximilian, "Travels in the Interior of North America," 326.

60. Murie wrote that coups were of no particular importance because they did not qualify a man for public service. Only consecrations of buffalo meat, wildcat skins, and so forth, could do so. For important services a person would have to have four or more consecration ceremonies to his credit. Murie, "Pawnee Indian Societies," 640.

61. Smith, "War Complex," 426–34. According to Smith, the object was not simply to kill the enemy but to humiliate him. See also Grinnell, "Coup and Scalp."

62. Cooke, *Scenes and Adventures*, 110–11.

63. Murie, "Pawnee Indian Societies," 596–97.
64. Fletcher, "Pawnee Ritual Used When Changing a Man's Name."
65. Murie, "Pawnee Indian Societies," 597.
66. Murray, *Travels*, 329–33.
67. Murie, "Pawnee Indian Societies," 598–99. Edwin James, who accompanied Stephen H. Long on his journey to the West in 1819–20, told the story of an old Minnetarie (Hidatsa) warrior who, as a youth, had been captured by the Skiris as he was trying to steal some of their horses. The Skiris flogged him, thrust a stick up his anus, and sent him off with the stick "depending like a tail." James also related the story of the Omaha Chief Mot-tschu-jinga (Little Grizzly Bear), who was captured and subjected to a humiliating torture. The Skiris flogged him, cut off his hair, broke his pipe, forced him to drink urine mixed with bison gall, and drove him from their village without food. He later returned with his warriors and burned a Pawnee village in revenge. These stories seem to be exceptions, because the Pawnees seldom allowed adult male captives to live very long. James, "James's Account," 88, 98.
68. Following the "homecoming" ceremony was a "wolf" dance, in which all young men who wished to join the next war party danced while the old men, according to Murie, sat around and ridiculed their ardor. Murie, "Pawnee Indian Societies," 597.
69. Cooke, *Scenes and Adventures*, 110–11.
70. James, "James's Account," 149, 208–209.
71. Echo-Hawk, "Pawnee Mortuary Traditions," 91.
72. Murray, *Travels*, 439. Father Pierre-Jean DeSmet described the burial of a Pawnee brave who had been killed during a running fight with some Arapahos in 1851: "The Pawnees were returning with their dead and wounded and all the stolen horses. On their return to camp, nothing was heard but cries of sorrow, rage and despair, with threats and vociferations against their enemies. It was a harrowing scene. The deceased warrior was decorated and painted with all the marks of distinction of a great brave, and loaded with his finest ornaments. They placed him in the grave amid the acclamations and lamentations of the whole tribe." Chittenden and Richardson, *Life, Letters and Travels of Father Pierre-Jean DeSmet*, vol. 2, 722. DeSmet also described Pawnee graves: "As we went on, we saw here and there the solitary burial places of the Pawnees; probably those of some chiefs or warriors who had fallen in combat with their hereditary foes, the Sioux, Cheyennes or Osages. These tombs were adorned with buffalo skulls painted red; the body is put, in a sitting position, into a little cabin made of reeds and branches of trees, strongly interwoven to keep the wolves out. The face is daubed with vermillion, the body is covered with its finest war-ornaments, and beside it one sees provisions of every kind, dried meat, tobacco, powder and lead, gun, bow and arrows. For several years the families will come back every spring to renew these provisions. Their idea is that the soul hovers for a long time about the spot where the body reposes, before taking its flight to the land of souls." Ibid., vol. 1, 205.

73. Quoted in Ewers, *Plains Indian History*, 204.
74. Parks, "Pawnee," 520; Hyde, *Pawnee Indians*, 223–29.
75. White, "Winning of the West"; Calloway, "Inter-Tribal Balance of Power."
76. James, *Account*, 362–64.
77. Dorsey, "How the Pawnee Captured the Cheyenne Medicine Arrows."
78. Hyde, *Pawnee Indians*, 179, 181–82.
79. Cheney, *Sioux Winter Count*, 26. According to the Swift Bear and High Hawk winter counts, the Sioux and their allies killed one hundred Skiris that year. Cohen, "Even in Those Days Pictures Were Important," 31; Curtis, "High Hawk's Winter Count," 175.
80. Higginbotham, "Wind-Roan Bear Winter Count," 21; Wedel, *Dunbar-Allis Letters*, 656–60; Roger Echo-Hawk, personal communication, April 25, 2008.
81. Hyde, *Pawnee Indians*, 223–29.
82. By 1820 the Pawnee chiefs seemed to be duly impressed with the power of the United States. Edwin James described a speech made by "Tarrarecawaho," a Chawi chief who had visited Governor Clarke at St. Louis the year before, to Major Benjamin O'Fallon. "When he tells you that he is a chief, he speaks truly; when he says that his soldiers appear like the grass in the spring, in place of those who die, he speaks truly; you, my nation, are like the fly in strength, just so easily can this mighty nation crush you between their fingers." James, *Account*, 353.
83. The literature on the Morning Star ceremony of the Skiri Pawnees is extensive. The most detailed description is in Murie, *Ceremonies of the Pawnee*, vol. 1, *The Skiri*, 114–36. Other descriptions include Dorsey, "Skidi Rite of Human Sacrifice"; Grinnell, *Pawnee Hero Stories*, 362–69; Linton, "Origin of the Skidi Pawnee Sacrifice to the Morning Star"; Linton, *Sacrifice to the Morning Star by the Skidi Pawnee*; Ross, *Das Menschenopfer der Skidi-Pawnee*; Jones, "John Dougherty and the Pawnee Rite of Human Sacrifice"; Thurman, "A Case of Historical Mythology"; Thurman, "Skidi Pawnee Morning Star Sacrifice of 1827"; Thurman, "Timing of the Skidi-Pawnee Morning Star Sacrifice"; Chittenden and Richardson, *Travels of Father DeSmet*, vol. 3, 976–88; Wissler and Spinden, "Pawnee Human Sacrifice to the Morning Star"; Duke, "Morning Star Ceremony of the Skiri Pawnee"; and Densmore, *Pawnee Music*, 18–24.
84. Kappler, *Indian Affairs*, vol. 2, *Treaties*, 259.
85. Ibid., 416–18.
86. Dunbar began his work among the Chawis while Allis went to live among the Skiris. Under pressure from Sioux attacks, Dunbar and Allis decided to abandon the mission in 1844. They left the area, an option the Pawnees did not have. Overall, the missionary effort was not very successful. During the ten years in which Dunbar and Allis operated among the Pawnees, warfare only increased, diseases further decimated the tribe, and poverty was rampant. Apart from a relatively successful inoculation program, the missionaries were unable to bring

much relief to the Pawnees, who, at this time, needed guns more than they needed God. Hyde, *Pawnee Indians*, 191; Wedel, *Dunbar-Allis Letters*, vii–xvii, 656–60, 730–31, 684.

87. Dodge, "Report on the Expedition of Dragoons"; Pelzer, "Captain Ford's Journal."

88. Chittenden and Richardson, *Travels of Father DeSmet*, vol. 2, 687–88. Densmore claimed that the name of the boy who killed Alight On The Clouds was "Carrying-the-shield." Densmore, *Pawnee Music*, 59–60.

89. The constant threat of enemy attacks forced the Pawnees to keep sentinels posted around camp during the night. Oehler and Smith, *Description of a Journey*, 25–26.

90. Mattes, *Great Platte River Road*, 156–58; Parkman, *Oregon Trail*, 57–58.

91. The land cession treaty of 1857 apparently did not satisfy the settlers, who called for the removal of the tribe to Indian Territory. In 1859, shortly after the tribe had left on its annual buffalo hunt, a Pawnee village burned down under suspicious circumstances, destroying not only the Indians' homes but also their provisions. Although the newspapers claimed the fire was set by the Sioux, the destitute Pawnees believed it had been the work of white settlers. When some angry warriors plundered a few homesteads in retaliation, the governor of the Territory of Nebraska responded by sending a force of dragoons and militia in pursuit. Although the Pawnees could have eradicated the poorly trained American command easily, the chiefs decided to settle the "Pawnee War" without bloodshed. They quickly sued for peace and promised to pay for the damages. Undoubtedly they wanted to avoid antagonizing the only nation that was not hostile toward them. Hyde, *Pawnee Indians*, 241–48.

92. In 1862, while the main body of the tribe was on its annual hunt, a Sioux force of six hundred men attacked the people who had stayed behind. Among these was a young Pawnee warrior named Crooked Hand. Crooked Hand and several other young warriors defended their village heroically, eventually driving the Sioux away. Although he was suffering from some illness at the time, Crooked Hand single-handedly killed six enemies. Hyde, *Pawnee Indians*, 224, 253–55. Crooked Hand's son, Dog Chief (also known as Simond Adams), later served as a U.S. Indian scout in 1870 and 1876.

93. Until the mid-1860s, American officials mainly called upon the goodwill of the powerful nomadic tribes to cease their raids against the sedentary nations. In 1860, for example, Captain Alfred Sully, whose defensive measures at the Pawnee village had proved totally inadequate, sent an officer to Fort Laramie to sue for peace on behalf of the Pawnees. The Sioux showed no interest, and their actions showed their determination to drive the Pawnees away from the Loup River altogether. Hyde, *Pawnee Indians*, 250–51.

94. Ewers, "Intertribal Warfare."

CHAPTER 2

1. White, "Winning of the West," 342; Calloway, "Inter-Tribal Balance of Power."

2. For a detailed history of the effects of the Colorado gold rush on Indian-white relations, see West, *Contested Plains*.

3. Utley, *Frontiersmen in Blue*, 60.

4. Among the forts along the Oregon and California Trails on the central plains were Fort Kearny (in operation from 1848 to 1871; not to be confused with another post of the same name located on the Missouri River south of Lincoln, Nebraska, which was in existence from 1846 to 1848), Fort Laramie (1849–90), Fort Fetterman ((1867–82), Fort Sidney (also known as Sidney Barracks, 1867–94), Fort Sedgwick (1864–71), Fort McPherson (1863–80), Fort Atkinson (1850–54), Fort Dodge (1865–82), Fort Larned (1859–78), and Fort Hays (1865–89). Prucha, *Guide to Military Posts*, 44–45.

5. Utley, *Indian Frontier*, chapter 2.

6. Utley, *Frontiersmen*, 19. For an excellent discussion of the problems hampering the army's mission, see Wooster, *The Military and United States Indian Policy*. See also Ball, *Army Regulars on the Western Frontier*.

7. Before 1854, a cavalry man received $8 a month. Foot soldiers and artillery men received $7, whereas company sergeants earned $13 a month. After 1854, monthly wages were raised to $12 for the cavalry, $11 for infantry and artillery men, and $17 for sergeants. Soldiers who reenlisted received more per month than first-time recruits. Utley, *Frontiersmen*, 36. For a classic treatment of soldier life in the Indian Wars, see Rickey, *Forty Miles a Day*.

8. Humfreville, *Twenty Years*, 57. Humfreville, who served in the Eleventh Ohio Cavalry, first met the Pawnee scouts during the Curtis and Mitchell campaign against the Cheyennes in August 1864.

9. The quoted line in this paragraph is from Rickey, *Forty Miles A Day*, 230. See also Hoig, *Sand Creek Massacre*.

10. Utley, *Frontiersmen*, 32–33.

11. Wooster, *United States Indian Policy*, 111–112, 213. Other useful studies include Gates, "Indians and Insurrectos," and Simmons, "Indian Wars and U.S. Military Thought."

12. Wooster, *United States Indian Policy*, 5–6.

13. According to Philippe Regis de Trobriand, an army officer who analyzed Indian warfare in his journals, the Indian mode of warfare terrified American soldiers: "Many of the new soldiers, thoroughly frightened by ridiculous reports and absurd commentaries on the Indians, have become accustomed to considering them so dangerous that they think more of avoiding them than of fighting them." De Trobriand became an advocate for the use of Indian scouts and allies in the military campaigns of the West. Kane, *Military Life in Dakota*, 60. In his memoir,

Captain J. Lee Humfreville recalled his anxiety in battle: "When the battle opened there was always great uneasiness even among the most hardened campaigners. I know that I was always frightened from the time the engagement opened until it was finished, for the Indians generally outnumbered us not less than two to one. Once wounded and left on the field, there was nothing in store for a white man but torture and death. The thought of such a fate added terror to my distress, though, at the same time, it nerved me to desperation." Humfreville, *Twenty Years*, 58.

14. Utley, *Frontier Regulars*, 45–53.

15. Dunlay, *Wolves for the Blue Soldiers*, chapter 1; Hauptman, *Between Two Fires*; George Washington to John Robinson, April 7, 1756, George Washington Papers, 1741–1799, Library of Congress, http://memory.loc.gov/ammem/gwhtml/gwhome.html.

16. For an excellent history of Sumner's campaign, see Chalfant, *Cheyennes and Horse Soldiers*.

17. According to Percival Lowe and Robert Morris Peck, who served in the expedition, the name of the Pawnee chief meant "Speck-in-the-eye." Chalfant, *Cheyennes*, 110–11.

18. Ibid., 156–60. According to Lieutenant David S. Stanley, the Pawnees "took us pretty straight to [the Cheyennes]." Stanley, *Personal Memoirs*, 43. They took the command to the Cheyennes with little consideration of the train of six-mule wagons that carried the provisions. Hence, Sumner was forced to send most of the wagons back to Fort Laramie. According to one witness, the Pawnee guides were the only ones who knew anything of the country. *New York Times*, October 15, 1857.

19. According to George Bird Grinnell, the two medicine men were named "Ice" (later assuming the name Ho tua'hwo ko ma is, or White Bull) and "Dark" (Ah no kit'). Grinnell, *Fighting Cheyennes*, 117. See also Berthrong, *Southern Cheyennes*, 140. According to George Bent, Grey Beard was an influential medicine man of the southern Cheyennes, and White Bull (or Ice) was a medicine man of the northern Cheyennes. Hyde, *Life of George Bent*, 102–104.

20. Peck, "Recollections of Early Times in Kansas Territory." Chalfant gives a slightly different rendition of Sumner's words to Lieutenant Stanley. Chalfant, *Cheyennes*, 189–92.

21. Peck, "Recollections," 499.

22. Ibid.

23. Chalfant, *Cheyennes*, 208.

24. Ibid, 227. According to Robert Peck, Sumner discharged the Pawnees because of their conduct during and immediately after the battle, when they tried to buy the Cheyenne captive from him. Peck wrote that the Pawnees left for their village the morning after the battle. Peck, "Recollections," 499. Although it may be true that Sumner was unhappy about the Pawnees' conduct, he did not officially

discharge them. It appears that he wanted them to guide Foote's command back to Fort Kearny.

25. Chalfant, *Cheyennes*, 273.

26. Ibid., 276–79; *Chicago Daily Tribune*, September 14, 1857.

27. Chalfant, *Cheyennes*, 285, 290. In the weeks following the battle of the Solomon, some debate arose over Sumner's decision to engage the Indians with the cavalry only, and to charge them with sabers. Critics argued that Sumner should have waited for the infantry, which was only several miles behind. They also believed the saber charge had needlessly endangered the troops. *New York Times*, October 15, 1857.

28. The chiefs and headmen signed the treaty on September 24, 1857. Congress ratified it on March 31 of the following year. Kappler, *Indian Affairs*, vol. 2, *Treaties*, 767.

29. The army's attitudes toward Indian soldiers changed little over the next decades, despite the contributions of the Pawnees and other auxiliaries. According to Paul Beck, most officers continued to see Indians as inferior beings. They came to accept them into American society only "as second-class citizens, much as Black Americans had been." Beck, "Military Officers' Views of Indian Scouts."

30. *Annual Report of the Commissioner of Indian Affairs*, 1860, 92 (hereafter cited as *ARCIA*).

31. *ARCIA*, 1862, 122.

32. U.S. Department of War, *War of the Rebellion*, Series 1, vol. 13, 645 (hereafter cited as *War of the Rebellion*).

33. Ibid.

34. Utley, *Frontiersmen*, 261–99; McDermott, *Circle of Fire*, 1–14. For a discussion of the Indian war in Colorado in 1864, see Hoig, *Sand Creek Massacre*.

35. General Curtis headed the Department of Kansas, which was subdivided into the District of Colorado (under John M. Chivington) and the District of Nebraska (under Brigadier General Robert B. Mitchell). Samuel Ryan Curtis (1805–66) was a West Point graduate from New York State. He served as colonel of the Third Ohio Infantry during the Mexican War and later practiced law in Iowa. At the outbreak of the Civil War he became colonel of the Second Iowa Infantry. In 1862 he advanced to the rank of major general, commanding the Department of Missouri, before taking over command of the Department of Kansas in 1864. Robert Byington Mitchell (1823–82) moved in 1855 from Ohio to Kansas. During the Civil War he served as colonel of the Second Kansas Volunteer Infantry before being promoted to brigadier general. He assumed command of the District of Nebraska early in 1864. In 1865 President Andrew Johnson appointed him governor of the Territory of New Mexico. See Danker, *Man of the Plains*, 29, 30.

36. Becher, *Massacre along the Medicine Road*, 304. During the Civil War, several Indian regiments served in the Union and Confederate armies. Major-General James G. Blunt, commander of the District of the Frontier, a subdivision of Curtis's

department, commanded three regiments of "Indian Home Guards." On March 27, 1864, Blunt wrote Curtis that the "Indian soldiers are excellent horsemen, and well fitted for scouting and all kinds of mounted service. As they are likely to be used to protect the Indian country against the operations of guerrillas and raiders, it is almost indispensable that they should be mounted, as our force here is very small, and therefore should be made as effective as possible. The Indians are willing to re-enlist for three years, as regular volunteers, if they can be reorganized as mounted troops." Perhaps Blunt's use of Indian auxiliaries from the "Five Tribes"—the Creeks, Cherokees, Choctaws, Chickasaws, and Seminoles—inspired Curtis to experiment with the enlistment of the Pawnees. *War of the Rebellion*, Series 1, vol. 34, part 2, 755.

37. Of course it is possible that Mitchell enlisted the Pawnees on instructions from Curtis, who was his superior as commander of the Department of Kansas. But so far the historical records have not produced such an order. For a brief biographical sketch of Ware, see John D. McDermott's introduction to Ware, *Indian War of 1864*, xi–xix.

38. In May 1864 Mitchell had visited the Pawnee Agency. It is possible that the Pawnee chiefs addressed to him the issue of Sioux depredations. *War of the Rebellion*, Series 1, vol. 34, part 3, 711. According to George Bent, some Oglalas under Bad Wound and Whistler had joined Spotted Tail near Cottonwood Creek in order to avoid trouble with the Americans. Hyde, *Life of George Bent*, 137.

39. Luther North denied that Frank North accompanied Mitchell's troops in charge of the Pawnees. In a letter to Robert Bruce, Luther commented, "I have said several times before that Ware never saw Frank in his life. . . . if Mitchell ever had a council with the sioux and Pawnees I never heard of it nor did Frank. . . . I hope that as far as the Norths are concerned you wont quote Eugene Ware [because] he didnt know the Norths and what he thought of the Pawnee scouts doesnt make any difference to me." Luther North to Robert Bruce, November 6, 1931, and December 8, 1931, Robert Bruce "Fighting Norths and Pawnee Scouts Papers," Department of Special Collections, McFarlin Library, University of Tulsa, Oklahoma (hereafter cited as "Robert Bruce Papers"), Box 1, Folder 4. It is possible, however, that a number of Pawnees accompanied Mitchell's command in July. On June 26 Mitchell was in Omaha when he received word that a group of hostile Indians had attacked and killed four Pawnees who were cutting hay at the agency. The next day Mitchell started in pursuit of the raiders. Some Pawnees might have joined his command while he paused at the Pawnee Agency. Whether Frank North was also present is unclear from the records. Perhaps he was not. Ware might have confused him with another man. *War of the Rebellion*, Series 1, vol. 34, part 4, 567. It appears that Mitchell indeed met with a group of Indians, possibly Spotted Tail's Brulés. On the morning of July 19, Mitchell wrote Curtis from Fort Cottonwood that the "Indians are moving down the [Platte] valley toward Julesburg in force. I am leaving here this morning with two companies of Cavalry and one

section of artillery to meet them." *War of the Rebellion*, Series 1, vol. 41, part 2, 276. Unfortunately, there are no records that relate details of the meeting between Mitchell and the Brulés that afternoon.

40. Ware, *Indian War*. See also Grinnell, *Fighting Cheyennes*, 151–52, and Hyde, *Life of George Bent*, 137–38.

41. Ware, *Indian War*, 156–65. According to George Bent, the meeting was held in June 1864. It appears, however, that Bent was not present himself. He might have heard about the events at the meeting from the Sioux. It is also possible that Bent's version was based on Ware's memoir. In his letters to George Hyde, Bent actually cited Ware's book. Hyde, *Life of George Bent*, 174.

42. Mitchell's troops began the march to Fort Laramie on July 20, 1864, and arrived at the post seven days later. Several of his companies patrolled the area. By August 8 Mitchell had returned to Julesburg, Colorado Territory. See correspondence between Mitchell and Curtis in *War of the Rebellion*, Series 1, vol. 41, part 2, 302, 429, 462–63, 612–13.

43. Ware, *Indian War*, 157–95.

44. Ibid., 188.

45. Ibid., 210.

46. Utley, *Frontiersmen*, 289.

47. On August 9, 1864, U.S. Collector Horace Everett, of Council Bluffs, Iowa, wrote Curtis that he had received word that "the Pawnees are very anxious to join our troops in an expedition against [the Cheyennes], but that their offer is refused on the ground that it is against the policy of the Government to arm one tribe against another. The Omahas also would be glad to join us. Do you think that in these times of the nation's trial such mawkish sentimentalities should cease? These two tribes could furnish at least 2,000 warriors. . . . Pray, if you can, influence the War Department to authorize the employment of these Indians. They will eventually fight on the one side or the other. Why not make and keep them our friends?" *War of the Rebellion*, Series 1, vol. 41, part 2, 626–27. See also Heape, "Pawnee-United States Relations," 297.

48. Here again the exact order of events is somewhat unclear. Hyde states that Curtis came up from Kansas and had a council with the chiefs of the Pawnee tribe. A letter from Agent Lushbaugh seems to confirm this, and nothing in Luther North's account seems to contradict it. Grinnell implies that Frank North first accompanied the general to Fort Kearney and then returned to the agency to enlist the men. Hyde, *Pawnee Indians*, 269; Agent Benjamin F. Lushbaugh to W. M. Albin, superintendent of Indian affairs, September 30, 1864, *ARCIA* 1864, 383; Danker, *Man of the Plains*, 29; Grinnell, *Two Great Scouts*, 71.

49. In a letter to his own department on August 25, 1864, Curtis wrote: "Joseph McFadden, having reported with seventy-six Pawnee Indians, is hereby appointed to act as captain of scouts at $5 a day and rations, commencing on the 20th day of this month. He will also be entitled to rations in kind. Indians will be

NOTES TO PAGES 54–58   263

paid as scouts at the rates paid soldiers while they are in actual service." *War of the Rebellion*, Series 1, vol. 41, part 2, 864. See also Grinnell, *Two Great Scouts*, 71.

50. *War of the Rebellion*, Series 1, vol. 41, part 3, 36; vol. 41, part 1, 243–47; vol. 48, part 1, 1040–41.

51. *War of the Rebellion*, Series 1, vol. 41, part 3, 257.

52. Grinnell, *Two Great Scouts*, 72–73. See also Becher, *Massacre*, 306–10.

53. Becher, *Massacre*, 309.

54. *War of the Rebellion*, Series 1, vol. 41, part 1, 243.

55. Ibid. Alfred E. Sorenson, whose history of the Pawnee battalion was based on information from Frank North himself, gave a different explanation for McFadden's lack of authority: "McFadden, as a great many other white men had done, had degraded himself by marrying a squaw, by whom he had several children, and, in 1858, he had adopted the Indian style of dress, wearing a blanket and breech-cloth, and in every other respect living like an Indian. As a rule, when the Indians find a white man—a superior being—lowering himself in this way, they lose all respect for him. And so it was in McFadden's case, and this was the explanation of his lack of control over the Pawnees." Sorenson, "Quarter of a Century on the Frontier." Another copy of this manuscript is in the Bancroft Library, Berkeley, California. Sorenson's manuscript also appeared in a slightly different form as a serial in the *Platte County (Nebraska) Times* in 1896 and 1897, under the title "Life of Major Frank North, the Famous Pawnee Scout."

CHAPTER 3

1. On September 16, 1864, Curtis reached his headquarters at Fort Leavenworth, Kansas. There he found a letter from Governor Saunders of the Territory of Nebraska, wanting to know whether Curtis intended to take the Pawnee Indians with him against Confederate General Sterling Price. Curtis responded in a letter of September 17: "In answer to your inquiry as to taking Indians as militia, think it better not. I am authorized to take them as U.S. scouts for a year on same terms as other Federal cavalry." *War of the Rebellion*, Series 1, vol. 41, part 3, 236.

2. Grinnell, *Two Great Scouts*, 74. For the names of the scouts recruited in the fall of 1864, see National Archives and Records Administration (NARA), Compiled Service Records of Volunteer Union Soldiers in Organizations from the Territory of Nebraska, National Archives Microfilm Publications, M1787 (hereafter cited as NARA, Compiled Service Records), Rolls 42 and 43.

3. Sorenson, "Quarter of a Century," 70.

4. Grinnell, *Two Great Scouts*, 77–79.

5. Ibid., 79.

6. Sorenson, "Quarter of a Century," 71. According to George Bird Grinnell, all thirty-five men of Lieutenant Small's company deserted. Grinnell, *Two Great Scouts*, 79. This seems to be inaccurate. The official rolls list six men who deserted

before muster. However, it appears that the muster rolls mistakenly list "Giving-up-his-seat" as one of the deserters. Patrick, *Report of John R. Patrick*, 205–209. See also NARA, Compiled Service Records, Rolls 42 and 43. As always, the names have been translated by the mustering officer only imperfectly. The rumor that the Pawnees would be sent south was not a complete fabrication. As shown by the September letter from Governor Saunders to General Curtis, referred to in note 1, this chapter, there was some discussion about using the Indians as auxiliaries against the Confederate armies. Baptiste Bayhylle's ancestry is not quite clear. According to some traditions, he was of French or Mexican (Spanish) ancestry and spent his early youth in St. Louis before moving to Pawnee territory in the 1850s. During his life, some Pawnees referred to him disparagingly as "the Mexican." He reportedly served as agency interpreter with a half-brother named Frank Deteyr in 1859. Deteyr was killed by the Sioux in 1861, and Bayhylle continued to serve as interpreter. Brummett Echohawk translated Bayhylle's Pawnee name as "One Whom The Great Spirit Shines Down Upon." Echohawk, "Pawnee Scouts," 12. More recently, Bayhylle's descendents translated his name as "Chief They All Look To." Bayhylle was born around 1829 and died on October 25, 1897. According to the label on a photograph taken by William H. Jackson, Bayhylle claimed to have scouted for Lieutenant Colonel George Armstrong Custer. Roger C. Echo-Hawk, personal communication, 25 April 2008.

7. James Murie (1843–1910), after immigrating to the United States, moved to Nebraska, where he married a Skiri Pawnee woman whose English name became Anna Murie. Murie served for several years as an officer of the Pawnee battalion, first as a second lieutenant and later as captain. In April 1869 he reenlisted with the scouts, but during the summer of that year he suffered what appeared to be sunstroke but turned out later to be mental illness, "superinduced by the exposure of the several Indian campaigns." By 1871 he had been admitted to an institution for the mentally ill, and Anna Murie and her three children went to live with her brother. The Nebraska legislature that year approved a resolution to provide relief for Murie and his family. One of the Muries' children, James Rolfe Murie (1862–1921), later wrote several important works on Pawnee society and culture. Although the son would publicly state that his father died when he was struck by lightning while scouting with the Pawnee battalion, Captain Murie in fact spent his last years in Grand Island, Nebraska, where, in 1888, at the age of forty-five, he was moved to the Soldiers and Sailors Home. He died there on December 26, 1910, and was buried in the Nebraska Veterans Cemetery at Grand Island. Parks, "James Murie, Pawnee Ethnographer"; U.S. Senate, "Resolution of the Legislature of Nebraska"; James Murie, letter published in *Southern Workman* (March 1880); "James Murie," Old West Grave Sites, www.dimensional.com/~sgrimm/james_murie.htm.

8. Danker, *Man of the Plains*, 32.

9. William N. Harvey (1843–97) was born near Fort Wayne, Indiana. He met Frank North in Columbus, Nebraska, and in 1864 enlisted with the Pawnee scouts. According to the muster rolls, he had previously been a brick maker. Luther North described him as a "quiet, low spoken and very pleasant fellow, and somewhat eccentric," as well as a "crack rifle shot." Harvey reenlisted several times, serving with the scouts until 1870. *Forest and Stream* magazine later described him as "a good scout, though rather too lazy for any use." After his service with the scouts, Harvey reportedly changed his name to Nicholas C. Creede and moved to Colorado, where he made a fortune in the mining business. The town of Creede, in southwestern Colorado, was named after him. In the 1890s, several newspapers, including the *New York Sun* and the *Los Angeles Times*, ran stories written by Cy Warman supposedly based on the life and scout service of "Nat" Creede. In 1893, suffering poor health from his years on the plains, he moved to California. In January 1897 he separated from his wife, and a few months later, on July 13, 1897, he committed suicide by taking an overdose of morphine. He was a multimillionaire at the time of his death. *New York Times*, July 14, 1897; *Los Angeles Times*, September 5, 1897; *Forest and Stream*, July 1896, 1; Danker, *Man of the Plains*, 54–55, 65, 111–12, 151; NARA, Compiled Service Records, Roll 42.

10. Grinnell, *Two Great Scouts*, 80.

11. Halaas and Masich, "Cheyenne Dog Soldier Ledger Book," 84.

12. NARA, Compiled Service Records, Roll 43.

13. Letter from "M," February 26, 1865, *Nebraska Republican*, March 3, 1865, quoted in McDermott, *Circle of Fire*, 50.

14. Grinnell, *Two Great Scouts*, 80.

15. U.S. Department of War, Returns from U.S. Military Posts, 1800–1916, Microfilm M617 (Washington, D.C.: National Archives Microfilm Publications, 1965) (hereafter cited as NARA, Returns from Military Posts), Roll 565, "Fort Kearny, Nebraska,", February 28, 1865. According to Grinnell, Lieutenant Small was accompanied by forty men. Grinnell, *Two Great Scouts*, 80.

16. Grinnell, *Two Great Scouts*, 81.

17. See Hoig, *Sand Creek Massacre*.

18. Utley, *Frontiersmen*, 300–302.

19. NARA, Returns from Military Posts, Roll 565, "Fort Kearny," March 31, 1865; NARA, Compiled Service Records, Rolls 42 and 43. The exact date of Tuck oo wa ter roo's death is unclear. According to one document he died on March 20, whereas in another he is listed as having died on March 24, 1865. In 1868 *The Ladies' Repository* published a story featuring a Pawnee Indian by the name of Tuck oo wa ter oo. It is unclear whether the story is fiction or based on fact. It was written by a Mr. G. Lame, military clerk in General Robert B. Mitchell's headquarters, and tells the story of Tuck oo wa ter oo's involvement in the liberation of a number of Omaha women who had been captured by the Sioux. Tuck oo wa

ter-oo, also known as "Doctor Jim," is described there as being a brother of a Pawnee priest. After freeing the Omaha women, he married one of them. Lame, "Tuck-oo-wa-ter-oo."

20. NARA, Compiled Service Records, Roll 42.

21. Ibid., Rolls 42 and 43. During one patrol with Lieutenant Nance's company of the First Nebraska Veteran Volunteers, the Pawnee scouts observed some of Nance's men cut down a telegraph post and chop it up into firewood. The scouts alerted Captain North, who told his men that "they should not look on the act as an example, and that it was decidedly wrong." North reported the vandalism to Colonel C. H. McNally, commander of Fort Rankin. Frank North to Colonel C. H. McNally, May 22, 1865, Alan W. Farley Collection, Box 4, Folder 35, Western History Collections, University of Oklahoma, Norman.

22. NARA, Compiled Service Records, Roll 43.

23. Ibid., Roll 42.

24. Utley, *Frontiersmen*, 303; Hewett, *Supplement*, part 2, "Record of Events," vol. 39, serial no. 51, 21–22. According to the post returns from Fort Sedgwick (Rankin), the Pawnees remained at the post until June 1865. NARA, Returns from Military Posts, Roll 1144, "Fort Sedgwick, Colorado," March–June 1865. According to some reports, a few weeks before the arrival of the scouts, several Indians had been hung at Fort Laramie. They had been accused of involvement in raids against overland migrants and the abduction of several white women. Among the Indians hanged were Two Face, Blackfoot, and Big or Old Crow. The commander of Fort Laramie ordered that the bodies be left hanging as an example to other "bad Indians." According to one account, the Pawnee scouts cut down the dead Indians and buried them shortly after their arrival at the fort. Jensen, *Settler and Soldier Interviews of Eli S. Ricker*, 318–19, 410, 425–26. See also Becher, *Massacre*, 372–73, 377.

25. Major General Grenville M. Dodge to Major General John Pope, quoted in McDermott, *Circle of Fire*, 46–47.

26. Utley, *Frontiersmen*, 304–306. The District of the Plains embraced the former Districts of Utah, Colorado, and Nebraska. Its headquarters were at Denver, Colorado Territory. On March 30, Connor assumed command of the new district.

27. Brigadier General Connor has been the subject of two biographies: Rogers, *Soldiers of the Overland* (1938), and Madsen, *Glory Hunter* (1990). See also Keenan, *Encyclopedia of American Indian Wars*, 51.

28. Hafen and Hafen, *Powder River Campaigns*, 28–31. This work offers the most complete account of the campaign. For a brief description, see Hampton, "The Powder River Expedition 1865."

29. Hafen and Hafen, *Powder River Campaigns*, 25.

30. Ibid.

31. Ibid., 25–26. The Omaha and Winnebago scouts were under the command of Captain Edwin R. Nash, First Lieutenant Michael Evans, and Second Lieutenant Gavin Mitchell, brother of General Robert B. Mitchell. Patrick, *Report*, 209.

32. The campaign was further delayed because of the struggle between war and peace factions in the administration in Washington. The indecision there allowed the hostile bands to continue their raids against American targets. On June 14, 1865, some Sioux killed Captain William D. Fouts and three soldiers of the Seventh Iowa Cavalry. On July 26, Indians attacked a small detachment of the Eleventh Kansas Cavalry under Lieutenant Caspar W. Collins near Platte Bridge Station, Wyoming. Collins and four of his men died during the attack. Utley, *Frontiersmen*, 318–20; Hafen and Hafen, *Powder River Campaigns*, 36–37, 42.

33. Hafen and Hafen, *Powder River Campaigns*, 36–37, 42.

34. Ibid., 43.

35. Connor did not reach Fort Laramie until late June or early July. The Pawnee scouts accompanied him as he made his way from Julesburg, Colorado, to Fort Laramie. Hewett, *Supplement*, 22. According to John McDermott, the scouts did not join Connor's column until August 1, at La Bonte's Ford, Wyoming Territory. McDermott, *Circle of Fire*, 104.

36. "Diary of Capt. B. F. Rockafellow, Sixth Michigan Cavalry," in Hafen and Hafen, *Powder River Campaigns*, 175, 179, 180.

37. Palmer, *Powder River Indian Expedition*, 14. Luther North claimed that Palmer was not present during the campaign. Although Palmer's account contains a number of inaccuracies, there is too little evidence to suggest that he was not a member of Connor's campaign. Luther North to Robert Bruce, July 15, 1928, Robert Bruce Papers, Box 1, Folder 3.

38. "Diary of Capt. B. F. Rockafellow," 179.

39. Hyde, *Life of George Bent*, 206.

40. "Diary of Capt. B. F. Rockafellow," 180. According to Hervey Johnson, of Company G, Eleventh Ohio Cavalry, Connor's dispatches informed the soldiers at Platte Bridge Station that the general had reached the Powder River safely and had begun construction of the fort. Unrau, *Tending the Talking Wire*, 278.

41. McDermott, *Circle of Fire*, 107.

42. Burnett, "Fincelius G. Burnett with the Connor Expedition," According to the Sorenson account, North dismounted two of his scouts, placed them at the head of the column, and told them that "if they lost the trail it would be the peril of their lives." This statement, however, seems somewhat out of character.

43. Grinnell, *Two Great Scouts*, 89–92. Grinnell states that the Pawnees killed twenty-six Cheyennes, but General Connor's report of August 19 mentions twenty-four Indians killed. Another account comes from Captain Henry E. Palmer, who served in Connor's expedition. According to Palmer, some "twenty-four scalps were taken, twenty-four horses captured, and quite an amount of other plunder, such as saddles, fancy horse-trappings and Indian fixtures generally." Palmer, *Powder River Indian Expedition*, 18. Guide Finn Burnett was clearly off the mark when he wrote that the Pawnees killed about forty-two Cheyennes. Although Burnett claimed to have been present at the fight, his is perhaps the least reliable version of it. Burnett

was eighty-seven when he wrote his memoir, "History of the Western Division of the Powder River Expedition," reprinted as "Fincelius G. Burnett with the Connor Expedition," in Hafen and Hafen, *Powder River Campaigns*. According to General Grenville Dodge, this particular group of Cheyennes had attacked and murdered a party of American soldiers a few weeks earlier. On the body of a dead Cheyenne the Pawnees discovered a diary belonging to one of the American soldiers. The diary contained drawings, made by the Cheyennes, that explained where they had been and what they had done over the past weeks. Dodge, *Battle of Atlanta*, 88–89. Cheyenne mixed-blood George Bent claimed that only five people were killed. Hyde, *Life of George Bent*, 203, 227, 228. Another possible source describing this fight was discovered in the so-called Little Shield Ledger, in which one episode depicts a fight between Cheyennes and Pawnee scouts in a ravine. Coleman, "Blinded by the Sun," 34–35.

44. McDermott, *Circle of Fire*, 107, 221.
45. "Diary of Capt. B. F. Rockafellow," 181.
46. Sorenson, "Quarter of a Century," 83.
47. Connor to Dodge, August 19, 1865, in Hafen and Hafen, *Powder River Campaigns*, 46.
48. "Diary of Capt. B. F. Rockafellow," 182.
49. Palmer, *Powder River Indian Expedition*, 19.
50. Grinnell, *Two Great Scouts*, 93–94. According to John Box, Frank North received his name from a Skiri, which would have made him a member of the Skiri band. Luther North believed his brother had received his name from a Chawi, making him a member of that band. Frank North, however, never identified himself with one band in particular. Bruce, *Pawnee Naming Ceremonial*, 10.
51. Grinnell, *Two Great Scouts*, 93–94; Patrick, *Report*, 207. According to the muster rolls, Little Ears enrolled on January 12, 1865, and was officially mustered in the next day. His enlistment papers list him as being twenty-five years of age, five feet nine inches tall, and a trapper of profession. Frank North filled out his death certificate. NARA, Compiled Service Records, Roll 42. The exact location of Little Ears's grave is unknown. He was buried near Fort Connor (later renamed Fort Reno) and may well have been the first soldier buried in the post cemetery there. It is unclear whether he was buried like a regular soldier or whether it was a traditional Pawnee interment. After Fort Reno was abandoned in 1868, its cemetery was no longer maintained and allowed to become dilapidated. Eventually the remains of the people buried there were exhumed and reburied at Custer National Cemetery, Montana, in 1911. Among the reinterred remains were those of seven "unknowns." It is possible that Little Ears was among these. It is also possible that his remains are still buried somewhere else in the Fort Reno area. John A. Doerner, chief historian, Little Bighorn Battlefield National Monument, Crow Agency, Montana, personal communication, January 28, 2008.

52. Grinnell, *Two Great Scouts*, 97–99; Palmer, *Powder River Indian Expedition*, 19; *Chicago Daily Tribune*, September 15, 1865. Finn Burnett reported North's narrow escape this way: "Major North while scouting near the Crazy Woman's Fork of the Powder River with his Pawnees, ran into a war party, which they chased through the hills. The major in the chase became separated from his men and ran into a bunch of hostiles, who killed his horse, and [he] was doing his best to stand them off. When he had about given up hope, one of his Pawnees, Bob White, a sergeant and one of his scouts [the muster rolls list White as a wagoner], came to him. Frank told Bob to hurry and bring some of the other scouts to his relief. Bob, instead of obeying, jumped off his horse and lay down beside Frank saying: 'Me heap brave, me no run, you and me killem plenty Sioux, that better.' They were having a warm time when found and relieved by some of his scouts." Burnett, "Burnett with the Connor Expedition," 208–209. Again there are questions about the accuracy of the report, because Burnett placed this incident before the fight of August 16. All other sources indicate that this event took place on August 19. Gene Weltfish, Pawnee Field Notes, Summer 1938, n.p., Gene Weltfish Collection, American Indian Studies Research Institute, Indiana University, Bloomington (hereafter cited as Weltfish, Pawnee Field Notes).

53. "Diary of Capt. B. F. Rockafellow," 183.

54. Ibid., 184; Grinnell, *Two Great Scouts*, 100–102.

55. David, *Finn Burnett*, 72, 76; Burnett, "Burnett with the Connor Expedition." Burnett later wrote to Robert Bruce: "I had the honor of being with [the Pawnee scouts] in several engagements, and give them credit for being as cool and brave under all conditions as any man with whom I have ever been engaged. A monument should be erected at the old Pawnee Agency on the Loup River, Nebraska, in memory of Major Frank North and his Pawnee Scouts." Fincelius G. Burnett to Robert Bruce, February 19, 1929, Robert Bruce Papers, Box 1, Folder 1.

56. "Diary of Capt. B. F. Rockafellow," 184; Palmer, *Powder River Indian Expedition*, 19; *Chicago Daily Tribune*, September 15, 1865.

57. Hampton, "Powder River Expedition," 12.

58. Among these scouts were La tah cots oo kah toos ("The Eagle Of The Valley"), Ler roo suck (Koo) cosh ("Hunts The Enemy"), Li re/he coots ("The Brave"), Se gule kah wah de ("Wandering Sun"), Tah cha rux oo kah tah we ("Wounded Man"), Tah Kah ("White"), Ta we ah re shah ("Chief Of All"), Ta we li hereis ("A Shield"), Te kit ta lah we le or Te kit te we lah we re ("The Great Spirit Sees Me"), Tit tah e wits ("Brave Man" no. 2), Tit ta wa war de ("Going With The War Party"), and Wit te de root kah wah ("I Am The Bravest"). I have been unable to ascertain their exact instructions. It seems likely that they carried mail or escorted a supply train. In any event, these scouts apparently remained in service, because later that summer two of them, Ta we li hereis ("A Shield") and Tah Kah ("White"), served as guides for Major General Dodge. NARA, Compiled Service Records, Roll 43.

59. Luther North to George Bird Grinnell, published in *Forest and Stream* March 30, 1901, 244; McDermott, *Circle of Fire*, 108.

60. Palmer, *Powder River Indian Expedition*, 24. Grinnell claims that ten Pawnees accompanied North on this scout. Grinnell, *Two Great Scouts*, 105.

61. General Connor's report of the Tongue River battle can be found in Rogers, *Soldiers of the Overland*, 198–99, and in Hafen and Hafen, *Powder River Campaigns*, 46–48. Palmer claimed that 250 white troops were present in Connor's party. Palmer, *Powder River Indian Expedition*, 25; Grinnell, *Two Great Scouts*, 106–107; McDermott, *Circle of Fire*, 111.

62. Grinnell, *Fighting Cheyennes*, 210–11. According to McDermott's sources, Chief Black Bear was absent at the time, fighting some Crow Indians. He had left Medicine Man in charge. McDermott, *Circle of Fire*, 112.

63. Palmer, *Powder River Indian Expedition*, 26–28. According to Connor's report, the attack started at 7:30 in the morning. Hafen and Hafen, *Powder River Campaigns*, 46.

64. McDermott cites a letter written by Luther North claiming that Frank North and fifteen Pawnees continued the charge with Connor and ultimately rescued him when the Arapahos launched their counterattack. Only Lieutenant Small and Murie's scouts remained behind to loot the village. No other sources support this claim, however, and it is significant that Luther did not mention it in his memoir, *Man of the Plains*. It also seems unlikely that this occurred because Connor later chastised the Pawnees for abandoning the charge in order to look for plunder. McDermott, *Circle of Fire*, 113.

65. According to Palmer, the soldiers also placed some of their dead comrades on the giant stakes, to prevent the Indians from mutilating the bodies. Palmer, *Powder River Indian Expedition*, 28–29.

66. Ibid., 31.

67. Hafen and Hafen, *Powder River Campaigns*, 46–48, 213. According to Palmer, two U.S. soldiers died during the battle, as well as three or four of North's Indian scouts. Palmer was clearly mistaken in this last claim, for no such casualties appear on the muster rolls. Palmer also stated that a Pawnee scout had found a little Indian boy. When asked what he was going to do with the child, the Pawnee answered, "Don't know; kill him, mebby." According to Palmer, the soldiers saved the boy. Palmer, *Powder River Indian Expedition*, 31; Grinnell, *Two Great Scouts*, 108–109; Patrick, *Report*, 210. In a letter to Gordon W. Lillie ("Pawnee Bill"), dated November 15, 1928, Luther North wrote that Black Bear's camp consisted of 184 lodges and that the troops killed about 150 Arapahos. Gordon W. Lillie Papers, Box 12, Folder 3, Western History Collections, University of Oklahoma, Norman (hereafter cited as "Lillie Papers").

68. Hafen and Hafen, *Powder River Campaigns*, 47; Grinnell, *Two Great Scouts*, 110–11. According to Luther North's letter cited by McDermott (see n. 64, this chapter), Connor awarded spoils to Chief Little Priest and three other Winnebagos,

as well as Frank North and fifteen Pawnee scouts. This claim, however, appears to be false. McDermott, *Circle of Fire*, 116.

69. Flavius Vegetius Renatus, "Military Institutions of the Romans," 172.

70. Hafen and Hafen, *Powder River Campaigns*, 47; Palmer, *Powder River Indian Expedition*, 34.

71. Halaas and Masich, "Cheyenne Ledger Book," 83–84.

72. Rogers, *Soldiers of the Overland*, 212; Palmer, *Powder River Indian Expedition*, 36.

73. Accompanying Cole's command was Major Lyman G. Bennett, who joined the column as engineer and cartographer on July 4. The Pawnee guides reportedly called him "Pohote the Willa" or "Hill Climber," because he often climbed hills to make observations for his maps. McDermott, *Circle of Fire*, 129.

74. Cole reported twelve men killed and two missing from his command. Walker lost one man killed and four wounded. Cole estimated that the Indians lost 200 to 500 warriors during the skirmishes. These numbers were a gross exaggeration, probably an attempt to polish up his awful record for the expedition. Walker's report was more to the truth: "as to the number of Indians killed in our long fight with them I cannot say as we killed one," he wrote. According to Grinnell, only one Indian, "Black Whetstone, an old Sioux, was killed during the fights." Grinnell, *Fighting Cheyennes*, 214; Hampton, "Powder River Expedition," 9–12.

75. According to McDermott, Thomas and the scouts discovered the camp on September 15. McDermott, *Circle of Fire*, 137.

76. Ibid., 234. The citation for Thomas's Congressional Medal of Honor reads: "Thomas, Charles L., Rank and organization: Sergeant, Company E, 11th Ohio Cavalry. Place and date: At Powder River Expedition Dakota territory, 17 September 1865. Entered service at: ———. Birth: Philadelphia, Pa. Date of issue: 24 August 1894. Citation: Carried a message through a country infested with hostile Indians and saved the life of a comrade en route."

77. Palmer, *Powder River Indian Expedition*, 40–41. According to Grinnell and Sorenson, about thirty-five of Cole and Walker's soldiers perished as a result of exhaustion and starvation. It appears that this number is incorrect. Grinnell, *Two Great Scouts*, 118–23; McDermott, *Circle of Fire*, 140.

78. Madsen, *Glory Hunter*, 153.

79. Grinnell, *Two Great Scouts*, 123–25. The Pawnee scouts returned to Fort Kearny in October 1865. Frank North and Second Lieutenant James Murie proceeded with their men to the Pawnee Agency. Lieutenant Charles Small remained at Fort Kearny. In December 1865 and January 1866 Murie was sent on scouts with some of the men to Plum Creek. The Pawnees were mustered out of service in April 1866. NARA, Returns from Military Posts, Roll 565, "Fort Kearny," October 1865–April 1866.

80. Utley, *Frontiersmen*, 332. According to Burnett, General Connor was pleased with the performance of his troops, including the Pawnees, during the campaign: "General Connor was a brave commander of men, fearless and discreet, never

asking a man to go where he would not lead. His men loved him; he despised disobedience and cowardice. There were three regiments under his command in 1865; he loved these men—the Second Colorado, the Second California and the Eleventh Ohio. I have heard him say that with these three regiments and ninety Pawnee scouts under Major Frank North, he could whip all of the Indians on the plains, and I believe that he could have done it." Fincelius G. Burnett, quoted in Hebart and Brininstool, *Bozeman Trail*, 261.

81. Lang, *Loyal West Virginia* 231–32.

82. Holliday, *On the Plains*, 73–74.

83. Frank North did not accompany his men to Fort Kearny. A few weeks earlier, on December 24, 1865, he had married Mary Louise Smith (1845–1883) in Columbus, Nebraska. Danker, *Man of the Plains*, 37.

84. Ibid., 38–39, 42. Frenchman Creek was also known as Frenchman's Fork and Whiteman's Fork.

85. *Omaha Republican*, January 29, 1888. The Pawnees continued to demand payment for their services in 1864. On May 3, Superintendent E. B. Taylor wrote to the commissioner of Indian affairs, "These Pawnees rendered valuable service to the war department, and should be paid." One week later, Pawnee Agent D. H. Wheeler, who had taken office on July 10, 1865, granted permission to two men named Robert Moreland and Daniel Taylor to take nine Kitkahahki Pawnees to Washington, where they could address their grievances in person. When they arrived in the East, however, Moreland abandoned the Pawnees, who were sent back to Nebraska at great expense. The Pawnees never received their pay, and Agent Wheeler was dismissed for granting Moreland permission to take the Pawnees off their reservation without formal authorization from the Indian Office. U.S. Bureau of Indian Affairs, *Letters Received by the Office of Indian Affairs, 1824–1881*, D 100, M 234 (hereafter cited as *Letters Received*), Roll 660.

86. The records do not show in which hospital White was treated. NARA, Compiled Service Records, Roll 43.

87. Ordway, "Reminiscences," 152–55. See also McReynolds, *Thirty Years on the Frontier*, 209–12.

CHAPTER 4

1. Bryant, "Entering the Global Economy." For a complete history of the Union Pacific Railroad, see Bain, *Empire Express*.

2. Dodge's relations with the Pawnees were not always cordial. The first Pawnee Indian he ever saw tried to steal his horse while he was on a surveying mission near the Elkhorn River in 1853. According to Dodge's memoirs, at one point the Pawnees believed he had poisoned one of their chiefs, "Ish-got-up." The Pawnees forced him to drink his own "medicine." When nothing happened,

the Pawnees decided to release him. During the mid-1850s relations between the Pawnees and the white settlers grew increasingly worse. In July 1855 rumor spread that Pawnees and Omahas had murdered a number of settlers. Alarmed at these rumors, Dodge took his wife and young daughter and moved to Omaha. Hirshson, *Grenville M. Dodge*, 19–21.

3. Umatilla Gregory, introduction to Dodge, *How We Built the Union Pacific Railway*.

4. Agent Benjamin Lushbaugh to Commissioner William P. Dole, December 17, 1864, *Letters Received*, Roll 660.

5. Seymour, *Incidents of a Trip*, 86–90; Bain, *Empire Express*, 266, 290–93. A detailed but bigoted account of the performance staged by the Pawnees appeared under the title "The Great Pacific Railroad Excursion," *Chicago Tribune*, October 29, 1866.

6. Dodge, *How We Built the Union Pacific*, 15, 18.

7. Sherman to Dodge, January 18, 1867, quoted in Athearn, "General Sherman and the Western Railroads," 44.

8. Ibid., 41.

9. Utley, *Frontier Regulars*, 11.

10. "An Act to increase and fix the Military Peace Establishment," 332.

11. C. C. Augur to Commissioner L. V. Bogy, February 27, 1867, *Letters Received*, Roll 660.

12. National Archives and Records Administration, Records Relating to Military Service, Record Group 94, "Register of Enlistments in the United States Army, 1798–1914," Microfilm Publications M233, Roll 70 (hereafter cited as Register of Enlistments), vol. 150, "1866–1873, Indian Scouts."

13. According to Luther North, a "Commissioner Lee" was first lieutenant of Company A, Isaac Davis was first lieutenant of Company B, and Fred Matthews was first lieutenant of Company C. It appears that North was wrong. For the exact composition of the officers of the Pawnee companies, see NARA, Returns from Military Posts, Roll 565, "Fort Kearny," March 1867. Donald Danker provides brief biographies of some of the officers of the battalion. Captain Charles E. Morse (1839–1908) was born in New York State. In the 1840s his family moved to Illinois. Around 1859 Morse went to California, but he returned and settled in Columbus, where he met Frank North. In 1868 he married Alphonsene North. Fred Matthews (1832–1890) was born in Canada. Between 1864 and 1866 he drove a stagecoach line from Columbus. Like Frank North, he joined Buffalo Bill's Wild West Show. In his act he drove the stagecoach that came under "attack" by Indians. Gustavus G. Becher (1844–1918) was born in Pilsen, Bohemia. The Becher family moved to the United States in 1847 and in 1856 settled in Columbus. After his career as an officer of the Pawnee scouts, Becher became a real estate dealer in Columbus. In 1895 he was elected to the Nebraska state legislature.

Captain Edward W. Arnold (1831–1916) was a long-time friend of the North family. In 1873 he, too, was elected to the Nebraska state legislature. Danker, *Man of the Plains*, 11ff., 49-50; Grinnell, *Two Great Scouts*, 138–39.

14. Grinnell, *Two Great Scouts*, 139–40; Danker, *Man of the Plains*, 51–52. Initially, the newspapers reported that three scalps were taken, but later reports stated that only one Sioux was killed. *New York Times*, June 5, 8, and 11, 1867.

15. Bruce, *Fighting Norths*, 26–27. For biographical information on Baptiste Bayhylle, see chapter 3, n. 6.

16. According to other sources, the Indian Bayhylle killed was the brother of Red Cloud.

17. *New York Times*, June 17, 1867. Apparently this report inspired one Denver citizen to offer $10 bounties for the scalps of hostile Indians, and the citizens of Central City created a fund of $5,000 to pay $25 apiece for "scalps brought to them with the ears on." *New York Times*, June 22, 1867.

18. Danker, *Man of the Plains*, 52–53. Many of the Spencer rifles were not new but had been used before, and some were defective. Luther North carefully inspected each gun and returned the defective ones for working rifles. He related how General William Hensley Emory (1811–77), who commanded the fort at this time, became irritated at his close inspection of the rifles. When Emory tried to demonstrate that there was nothing wrong with the guns, the rifle exploded in his hands. The general almost lost an eye in this incident.

19. Danker, *Man of the Plains*, 54; Luther H. North to Gordon W. Lillie, November 15, 1928, Lillie Papers, Box 12, Folder 3.

20. According to Luther North, the Pawnees killed four Arapahos. Bruce, *Fighting Norths*, 26–28, 56. According to Grinnell, however, the Pawnees killed two Arapahos and captured only two mules and one pony. Grinnell, *Two Great Scouts*, 143. Other sources also list only two Arapaho deaths. See Webb, *Chronological List of Engagements*, 30. According to Webb, the scouts who engaged the Arapahos belonged to Company C, Pawnee Scouts. This company was composed of Skiris under Captain Charles Morse. After arriving at Fort Laramie, North's companies traveled to Granite Canyon and Fort Sanders. According to Luther North, an Arapaho named Little Crow was at Fort Sanders complaining about the raid. He was threatening to kill Frank North just as North appeared on the horizon. Instead of following up on his threat, Little Crow fled in panic. Danker, *Man of the Plains*, 53–54, 72. Charles Morse's name "Big Chief" is from Luther North to Robert Bruce, February 1, 1932, Robert Bruce Papers, Box 1, Folder 5.

21. In June 1867 Captain Arnold's company of scouts, for example, was stationed at Fort Sedgwick, Colorado Territory. According to the post returns he patrolled the area around "[Lodge] Pole Creek." NARA, Returns from Military Posts, Roll 1144, "Fort Sedgwick, Colorado," March–June 1865.

22. Thomas O'Donnell manuscript, MS 0698, Nebraska State Historical Society, Lincoln, Nebraska, 7–8.

23. Unfortunately, Scovill did not write down this description until 1924, when it was published in *Adventure* magazine. Consequently, it is impossible to determine with accuracy when the events he described took place. E. T. Scovill, letter published in *Adventure*, January 20, 1924, 178. A slightly edited version of Scoville's letter appeared in the *Los Angeles Times*, March 30, 1924.

24. Thomas O'Donnell manuscript, 7–8.

25. Seymour, *Reminiscence of the Union Pacific Railroad*, 11–28.

26. Ibid., 28–33.

27. It appears that Seymour's party was in no serious danger after the Pawnees abandoned it. In his reports to Colonel Augur, Seymour greatly exaggerated the danger his party was in, as well as his heroic role in guiding the party back to camp. In his memoirs he even referred to the event as the "Great Indian Battle of July 11." Seymour's dramatic report of the incident received a quick response from Colonel Augur's office on July 15, 1867. In the letter the general commended Seymour and Hurd for their "ability and coolness," and he promoted Seymour to "Brevet Major General" for his "distinguished gallantry, in observing the enemy through his field glass," and Hurd to "Brevet Brigadier General" for "gallant and meritorious service during the war." The letter also promoted the near hind mule to "Brevet Horse." Ibid., 35–41; Dodge, *How We Built the Union Pacific*, 135.

28. Thomas O'Donnell manuscript, 8–9.

29. Little is known about Private William F. Hynes. He enlisted in May 1866 in Philadelphia and was assigned to Company E, Second Cavalry. He spent most of his three years in the service along the Oregon and Bozeman Trails. His memoir of his years in the army, *Soldiers of the Frontier* (1943), offers valuable insights into the life of an ordinary cavalryman as well as the lives of some of the Indian people he encountered. Unlike many other people of his generation, Hynes was an admirer of Indian people and surprisingly sympathetic toward them. He was also critical of the army's policies toward Indian people. In May 1869 he was honorably discharged from service. The story of a duel between the Pawnee scout and a Sioux Indian appears in chapter 16 of his memoir. Hynes, *Soldiers of the Frontier*, 129–38.

30. Ibid.
31. Ibid.
32. Ibid.
33. Ibid.
34. Ibid.
35. Ibid.
36. Ibid.

37. Dodge, *Our Wild Indians*, 456–58. See also Dodge, *Plains of the Great West and Their Inhabitants*, 383–85.

38. Hafen and Hafen, *Diaries of William Henry Jackson*, 200–201.

39. W. H. Jackson to Robert Bruce, May 2, 1931, in Bruce, *Fighting Norths*, 28.

40. Jackson, *Descriptive Catalogue*; Chronister, "Pawnee Men."

41. E. T. Scovill, letter published in *Adventure,* January 20, 1924, 178.

42. Hyde, *Life of George Bent,* 272–73, 276–77. John Stands In Timber, a Cheyenne tribal historian, also relates the story of the Plum Creek massacre. See Liberty and Stands In Timber, *Cheyenne Memories,* 173–76.

43. Thompson's account appeared first in the *St. Louis Democrat,* August 8, 1867, and was reprinted in the *New York Times,* August 19, 1867. The author of the article was probably Henry M. Stanley, who also left an account of the Plum Creek massacre in his memoir, *My Early Travels and Adventures in America and Africa,* 173–83. Stanley later achieved fame as an explorer in Africa, where he located the missionary and explorer Dr. David Livingston.

44. Stanley, *Early Travels,* 173–83 According to Porcupine, a Cheyenne who was present during the massacre, there were indeed two trains. After the first train derailed, the second train stopped, and five men climbed out. Possibly the men saw the Indians, because this second train soon backed away. According to Grinnell, Thompson's scalp, preserved in alcohol, was later stored in the Omaha Public Library Museum. Grinnell, *Fighting Cheyennes,* 264–68.

45. North's and Murie's reports of the battle at Plum Creek were published in the *New York Times,* August 25, 1867. For another account of the battle, see the *Chicago Daily Tribune,* August 25, 1867. Russ Czaplewski published a number of these accounts in *Captive of the Cheyenne,* 112–27.

46. Hyde, *Life of George Bent,* 277.

47. Dodge, *Our Wild Indians,* 442–44. Dodge stated that there were no losses on the side of the Pawnees, but that appears to be incorrect. According to one report, the Pawnees lost one horse killed and five wounded. Bruce, *Fighting Norths,* 30. According to Luther North, his brother was present during the Plum Creek battle. Luther North to Robert Bruce, May 17, 1928, Robert Bruce Papers, Box 1, Folder 3.

48. Dodge, *Our Wild Indians,* 443; Stanley, *Early Travels,* 183. It is doubtful that Murie and Davis made serious attempts to restrain their men from mutilating the bodies of their enemies.

49. *New York Times,* August 25, 1867. According to Grinnell, the little girl's name was Island Woman, a name she might have received because of her daring escape while crossing the Platte. Grinnell, *Fighting Cheyennes,* 268.

50. The Cheyenne boy later received the name "Pawnee" because of his capture by the scouts. Grinnell, *Fighting Cheyennes,* 268. The government officials present were Generals Sherman, Harney, Terry, Augur, and Sanborn, Commissioner of Indian Affairs N. G. Taylor, Colonel Tappan, and Senator Henderson. Spotted Tail, Man Afraid Of His Horses, Man That Walks Under The Ground, Pawnee Killer, Standing Elk, Spotted Bear, Black Deer, Turkey Leg, Cut Nose, Whistler, Big Mouth, Cold Feet, Cold Face, Crazy Lodge, and others represented the Sioux and the Cheyennes. The white captives were one seventeen-year-old and two nineteen-year-old girls, a pair of six-year-old twin boys, and a baby. Grinnell,

Fighting Cheyennes, 268–69. According to Luther North, the name of two of the girls was Martin, but Donald Danker wrote that North was mistaken, and the two girls were actually daughters of Peter Campbell, who owned a farm near present-day Doniphan, Nebraska. The two girls and their twin brothers had been captured on July 24, 1867. Danker, *Man of the Plains*, 61. In a letter to Robert Bruce, Luther North wrote that the woman prisoner was Turkey Leg's wife. Bruce, *Fighting Norths*, 30.

51. Sun Tzu, *Art of War*, 66, 84.

52. *Chicago Daily Tribune* (deriving the news item from an Omaha newspaper), August 22, 1867.

53. *New York Times*, September 2, 1867.

54. Grinnell is not quite clear what the purpose of the paymaster's mission was. Perhaps he was bringing gifts to be distributed to the Indians in order to appease them, or perhaps it was an attempt to induce them to attend the Fort Laramie peace council. Grinnell, *Two Great Scouts*, 148.

55. Bruce, *Fighting Norths*, 28–29. In his autobiography, Luther North stated that the Sioux numbered about 100 Indians. Danker, *Man of the Plains*, 61–62.

56. Bain, *Empire Express*, 409–10. According to Grinnell, one of the travelers was Oakes Ames, but Bain wrote that the excursionist was Oliver Ames, brother of the congressman. Grinnell, *Two Great Scouts*, 148–50. For another description of Co rux ah kah wah de's feat, see Bruce, *Fighting Norths*, 19. Traveling Bear's name is sometimes spelled Corux a kah wadde.

57. The name Takuwutiru does not appear on any of the muster rolls, possibly because it was adopted later. Weltfish, Pawnee Field Notes.

58. Danker, "North Brothers," 79; Dunlay, *Wolves for the Blue Soldiers*, 156; testimonies by Ruling His Sun and High Eagle, April 11, 1928, Ruling His Sun Pension File, National Archives and Records Administration, Records of the Veterans Administration (VA), Record Group 15.7.4, "Pension and Bounty Land Warrant Application Files" (hereafter cited as "VA Records, Pension Application Files"). For the names of the men who left, see Register of Enlistments, vol. 150, "1866–1873, Indian Scouts." The original muster rolls state that Pe-ah-tah-wuck-oo died near the Black Hills. The Pawnee scouts, however, never served near the Black Hills of South Dakota in 1867. In a letter to Robert Bruce, Luther North explained that the hills near present-day Laramie, Wyoming, were called the Black Hills in the 1860s. They were later renamed "Laramie Hills" to distinguish them from the Black Hills of South Dakota. Bruce, *Fighting Norths*, 27. The *Chicago Daily Tribune*, November 3, 1867, reported that "sixty Pawnee scouts stationed near Cheyenne mutinied on Thursday. They came down the Union pacific Railroad to Columbus, and have gone to the Pawnee reservation."

59. Report by Brevet Major General Christopher C. Augur, Headquarters Department of the Platte, Omaha, Nebraska, September 30, 1867, *Annual Report of the Secretary of War*, House Exec. Doc. 1, 40th Congress, 2nd Session, Serial Set

1324 (Washington, D.C.: Government Printing Office, 1867), 59–60; Report of Lieutenant General William T. Sherman, Headquarters Military Division of the Missouri, St. Louis, Mo., October 1, 1867, *Annual Report of the Secretary of War*, House Exec. Doc. 1, 40th Congress, 2nd Session, Serial Set 1324 (Washington, D.C.: Government Printing Office, 1867), 37–38. See also Bruce, *Fighting Norths*, 10.

60. Grinnell, *Two Great Scouts*, 153; Danker, *Man of the Plains*, 65.

61. From the Register of Enlistments for 1868, I have ascertained that 96 Pawnees were enlisted. Adding the two company captains and two first lieutenants brings the total number of enlisted men to exactly 100. "Register of Enlistments," vol. 150, "1866–1873, Indian Scouts."

62. Although he is now generally known as Ruling His Sun, his name is more accurately translated as "Ruling His Son." He received this name after moving to Oklahoma, but he did not know who gave him the name. Before his name was changed to Fox Chief, he was known as Le sah roo ka roo ("Is He The Chief?"). Testimony by Ruling His Sun, April 11, 1928, Ruling His Sun Pension File, VA Records, Pension Application Files.

63. Danker, *Man of the Plains*, 65–66; Grinnell, *Two Great Scouts*, 153.

64. Register of Enlistments, vol. 150, "1866–1873, Indian Scouts," n.p.

65. Pawnee historian Mark Evarts told Gene Weltfish in 1935 that the Chawi chief Pitaresaru had asked the commanding officer at Fort Kearny to look after his people. Pitaresaru was referring to the people who had stayed behind on the reservation, but his words were incorrectly translated, and Major North was ordered to escort the Pawnees on their hunting expedition. Weltfish, Pawnee Field Notes, n.p.

66. Aldrich, "Diary of a Twenty Days' Sport"; Hall, "Last Great Buffalo Hunt"; Francis Wayland Dunn diary, entries covering July 24–August 15, 1868, Francis W. Dunn Papers, Bentley Historical Library, University of Michigan, Ann Arbor. Sumner Oaks was the son of George D. Oaks, who owned the St. Charles Hotel in Omaha. Danker, "Journal of an Indian Fighter," 94 n. 15. Some discrepancies exist between Aldrich's description and the Dunn diary concerning the exact dates of the expedition. I have kept the dates given in the Dunn diary.

67. Francis Dunn diary, entry for July 24, 1868.

68. Aldrich, "Diary."

69. Francis Dunn diary, entry for July 25, 1868.

70. Aldrich, "Diary."

71. Francis Dunn diary, entry for July 26, 1868; Aldrich, "Diary."

72. Aldrich, "Diary."

73. Francis Dunn diary, entry for July 30, 1868; Aldrich, "Diary"; Bruce, *Fighting Norths*, 32–33. For the involvement of White Eagle, Billy Osborne, and Noted Fox, see Gene Weltfish, "Some Stories about Major North's Pawnee Scouts: As Reported to Gene Weltfish by Mark Evarts," unpublished paper, Gene Weltfish Papers, American Indian Studies Research Institute, Indiana University, Bloomington. According

to Grinnell, the Sioux belonged to Spotted Tail's band. Grinnell, *Two Great Scouts*, 154–55. The name of the scout who went for help is from Luther H. North to Gordon W. Lillie, November 15, 1928, Lillie Papers, Box 12, Folder 3. William Henry Jackson, who photographed this man in the 1860s or 1870s, said that his Pawnee name was La roo ra shar roo cosh. Jackson, *Descriptive Catalogue*, 66. However, the muster rolls for 1868 do not bear this name. Register of Enlistments, vol. 150, "1866–1873, Indian Scouts."

74. Francis Dunn diary, entry for July 25, 1868.

75. Elsewhere Luther North claimed that the battle lasted six hours. Luther H. North to Gordon W. Lillie, November 15, 1928, Lillie Papers, Box 12, Folder 3.

76. Aldrich, "Diary."

77. Testimony by Ruling His Sun, April 11, 1928, Ruling His Sun Pension File, VA Records, Pension Application Files.

78. Dunn gave a slightly different account: "One Indian was shot while coming towards [North's] squad. They shot his horse + then ran up behind [and] one of them, jumped off and struck him with his whip, Counting Coo, they call it to strike a man before he is shot, then shot him with a revolver and scalped him in as many seconds as the thing could be told. Frank thought if he had resisted at all they might have saved him but he had nothing but bow + arrows. All the Indians had taken off their saddles for the hunt and a good many of them exchanged their carbines for bows + arrows because they were lighter. The Pawnees wouldn't go near him after he was scalped. No good they say wouldn't even see if he was alive. They think a scalped man will turn into some kind of animal." Francis Dunn diary, entry for July 30, 1868.

79. Records compiled from the Register of Enlistments, vol. 150, "1866–1873, Indian Scouts."

80. Aldrich, "Diary."

81. Francis Dunn diary, entry for July 31 and August 1, 1868.

82. Aldrich, "Diary"; Francis Dunn diary, entry for August 7 and 8, 1868.

83. Danker, *Man of the Plains*, 65; "Pawnee against Sioux: A Graphic Sketch of Mr. Warman's 'On the Plains in the Sixties,'" *Los Angeles Times*, May 3, 1896, 13. The *New York Times*, July 31, 1868, reported that Lieutenant "Howley" was injured in the fight. The name of the Pawnee who died is from Register of Enlistments, vol. 150, "1866–1873, Indian Scouts," n.p. It is unclear where Loo law we luck oo la it was buried, but it seems likely that he was taken back to Wood River for burial there.

84. *Omaha Weekly Herald*, September 2, 1868.

85. Special Order 51, September 2, 1870, Frank North Collection, Box 1, S2-F1.

86. Webb, *Chronological List*, 40.

87. Grinnell, *Two Great Scouts*, 156–57. There appear to be no official reports about this fight in the military records, nor did Luther North mention it in his memoirs. It is possible that Grinnell was actually describing Lieutenant Harvey's

fight with the Yanktons near Wood River on July 28—the fight in which Loo law we luck oo la it was mortally wounded. Another possibility is that this is the same fight described by Private William F. Hynes, which took place in the summer of 1867. Hynes, *Soldiers of the Frontier,* 130–38.

88. F.M.D., "A Presbyterian Minister after Buffalo," *New York Evangelist,* November 12, 1868, 2.

89. Among the officers were Colonel Litchfield, Major Russell, Captain Coates, Major Noyes, Captain Spalding, and Lieutenant O'Brien.

90. Townshend, *Ten Thousand Miles of Travel,* 94–96.

91. Ibid., 96–97, 115–16.

92. Ibid., 112.

93. Ibid., 114–15.

94. Ibid., 113–14.

95. Ibid., 120–21.

96. Ibid., 130.

97. Ibid., 144.

98. Testimony by Ruling His Sun, April 11, 1928, Ruling His Sun Pension File, VA Records, Pension Application Files. Unfortunately, Le tah kuts kee le pah kee's name does not appear on the muster roll for that year. He might have enlisted under a name different from the one given by Ruling His Sun.

99. Register of Enlistments, vol. 150, "1866–1873, Indian Scouts," n.p.; Grinnell, *Two Great Scouts,* 157.

CHAPTER 5

1. Frank North had married Mary Louise Smith on December 25, 1865. Danker, "Journal," 91–101.

2. White, "Indian Raids on the Kansas Frontier," 370. For a good overview of the events leading up to the Republican River campaign, see Broome, *Dog Soldier Justice,* 7–33, 45–55, 89–106.

3. Riding In, "Six Pawnee Crania," 102–104.

4. Ibid., 110.

5. Leckie, *Buffalo Soldiers,* 44. Captain Byrne's report and Charles Martin's testimony can be found in *Letters Received,* Roll 660. See also *New York Times,* March 19 and 21, 1869.

6. Riding In, "Six Pawnee Crania," 105–106. General Alfred Sully defended the soldiers' conduct: "Perhaps the death of these Indians is to be regretted as they are considered as friendly, but they justly deserved their fate and the officer and his men deserve great praise for their forbearance on the occasion. There are other small parties of Pawnees in this section. I have troops out trying to hunt them up and if found they will be justly dealt with. I would respectfully suggest the propriety of keeping these friendly Indians on their reservations, if this is

NOTES TO PAGES 112–17   281

[impracticable] that I be notified when parties leave—their agent and the chiefs know very well, when parties leave their villages on foot with lariats, that they are on a marauding expedition." *Letters Received*, Roll 660.

7. Register of Enlistments, vol. 150, "1866–1873, Indian Scouts," n.p. Fort McPherson was established in 1863. It underwent several name changes—Cantonment McKean, Post of Cottonwood, and Fort Cottonwood—before receiving its final name in 1866, when it was named after Brigadier General James B. McPherson, who had been killed at the battle for Atlanta on July 22, 1864. Frazer, *Forts of the West*, 88. For the Pawnee name, see Billy Osborne's deposition in support of Leading Fox's pension application, September 4, 1923, Leading Fox Pension File, VA Records, Pension Application Files.

8. Danker, "Journal," 101.

9. Danker, *Man of the Plains*, 96–99.

10. Ibid.; Holmes, *Fort McPherson*, 34.

11. Whaley to Denman, March 22, 1869, *Letters Received*, Roll 660. According to the Register of Enlistments, one of the scouts, Te-na-se-pa ("Bow") deserted on March 6, possibly in protest of the murder of the discharged Pawnees earlier that year.

12. Denman to Commissioner Taylor, April 1, 1869, *Letters Received*, Roll 660.

13. Riding In, "Six Pawnee Crania," 106–109; "Generations Later, Remains Reburied, 100 Indians Gather at Genoa Cemetery," *Omaha World-Herald*, 6 September 1995.

14. Riding In, "Six Pawnee Crania," 111. The Register of Enlistments states that the Pawnees were mustered in on April 23, whereas North's diary says they were not officially mustered in until the next day. It is reasonable to assume that Lieutenant Litchfield, who mustered the Indians in, recorded April 23 so that the Indians would be paid for the extra day. Register of Enlistments, vol. 150, "1866–1873, Indian Scouts," n.p.; Danker, "Journal," 118–19.

15. Danker, "Journal," 120. During most of this time Frank North traveled back and forth to his home in Columbus. During his absences Captain Luther North and Captain Sylvanus E. Cushing were in charge of the two companies.

16. High Eagle, Invalid's Pension Application, August 3, 1893, and April 4, 1894, High Eagle Pension File, VA Records, Pension Application Files.

17. Danker, *Man of the Plains*, 99–101. Frank North did not mentioned this incident in the diary he kept for 1869, nor was it included in the Sorenson manuscript, "Quarter of a Century on the Frontier." North was indeed with the scouts on the North Platte River on May 14 and 15, 1869. He is also known for his great modesty in reporting his own exploits, even in his personal writings. It is unlikely that Luther North invented this incident to raise the stature of his older brother (as he was apt to do on occasion). It seems more plausible that the event occurred at some other time and was mistakenly reported by Luther North as having happened in 1869.

18. Testimony by Ruling His Sun, April 11, 1928, Ruling His Sun Pension File, VA Records, Pension Application Files. Ruling His Sun said he was a scout at this

time, although elsewhere he stated that he was mustered out in 1868 and did not reenlist. The discrepancy might be explained Ruling His Sun's failing memory and the passage of time. He might have heard the story and believed it took place while he was in the service. Or perhaps this event took place in 1868 after all, and it was indeed Luther North who got the date wrong.

19. Weltfish, "Some Stories about Major North's Pawnee Scouts," Weltfish Papers.

20. Danker, "Journal," 125.

21. Among the casualties of the fight were six soldiers, including Lieutenant Frederick H. Beecher, after whom the island in the river was thereafter named. Several Cheyennes, including chief Roman Nose, also perished in the battle. Berthrong, *Southern Cheyennes*, 310–14; Grinnell, *Fighting Cheyennes*, 277–92; Broome, *Dog Soldier Justice*, 35–44.

22. Berthrong provided the following description of the Cheyenne Dog Soldiers: "The Dog Soldiers, also called the 'Dog Men,' were unquestionably 'the most important, distinct, and aggressive of all the warrior societies.' Comprising half of the Cheyenne warriors, the Dog Soldiers controlled the whole tribe. But the constant recurrence of the Dog Soldiers' exploits in the white man's records, especially during the wars on the Plains, can only be explained by the observers' unfamiliarity with the total organization of the Cheyenne warrior societies. The Dog Soldiers became numerically the most important of the societies in the early part of the nineteenth century. Sometime before 1850 all adult male members of the Flexed Leg band joined the Dog Soldiers, and they became a band within the tribe, camping together in the tribal camp circle. The Dog Soldiers were not governed by the usual band chiefs but by their own military chiefs. For these reasons the Dog Soldiers had greater cohesion and strength than other bands and soldier societies." Berthrong, *Southern Cheyennes*, 68.

23. For an excellent biography of Philip Henry Sheridan (1831–88), see Hutton, *Phil Sheridan*.

24. Broome, *Dog Soldier Justice*, 57–70. For an excellent account of the Washita Battle and its implications, see Greene, *Washita*.

25. Camp Supply, at the confluence of Wolf Creek and the North Fork of the Canadian River, was established on November 8, 1868. The name was changed to Fort Supply on December 30, 1878. It was abandoned in 1895. Prucha, *Guide to Military Posts*, 110.

26. White, "Indian Raids," 373; Weingardt, *Sound the Charge*, 23.

27. Eugene Asa Carr (1830–1910) was born in New York and graduated from West Point in 1850. He joined General William S. Harney's campaign against the Sioux in 1854. During the Civil War he won a Medal of Honor at Pea Ridge and was assigned to the Fifth Cavalry. During the 1870s he served in Arizona and was in command of troops at Cibecue Creek when a number of Apache scouts suddenly turned on the troops. Several troopers died in this incident, and the

military command censured Carr for failing to take appropriate precautions. In 1879 he assumed command of the Sixth Cavalry, which served in New Mexico and on the Pine Ridge Reservation during the Indian "uprising" at Wounded Knee. In 1893 he retired. He died in Washington, D.C., in 1910. Keenan, *Encyclopedia of American Indian Wars, 1492–1890*, 37. For a complete biography of Carr, see King, *War Eagle*.

28. Broome, *Dog Soldier Justice*, 71–88; Price, *Across the Continent with the Fifth Cavalry*, 134–35; "Record of Engagements with Hostile Indians within the Military Division of the Missouri from 1868 to 1882, Lieutenant-General P. H. Sheridan, Commanding," reprinted in Peters, *Indian Battles and Skirmishes*, 20.

29. White, "Indian Raids," 373–78. For a detailed treatment of the depredations by the Cheyennes, particularly the Spillman Creek raid and the capture of Susanna Alderice, see Broome, *Dog Soldier Justice*, 89–106.

30. White, "Indian Raids," 380–84.

31. King, "Republican River Expedition," 31–32.

32. The order was issued through Assistant Adjutant General George D. Ruggles on June 7, 1869. Weingardt, *Sound the Charge*, 73–74.

33. Other officers on the expedition were (Brevet) Majors Thomas E. Maley, Gustavus E. Urban, Leicester Walker, and John B. Babcock; Captains Jeremiah C. Denney, George F. Price, Robert Sweatman, Philip Dwyer, John H. Kane, Edward M. Hayes, and William H. Brown; and Lieutenant Charles B. Brady. King, "Republican River Expedition," 33–34; King, *War Eagle*, 100–101.

34. James E. Welch left an account of the Republican River expedition in a letter to his friend Colonel Henry O. Clark, of Vermont. The letter, which was sent from Edith, Coke County, Texas, on June 16, 1891, was first published in Brady, *Indian Fights and Fighters*, 173–79. A part of Welch's account was also reprinted in Weingardt, *Sound the Charge*, 111–14. Unfortunately, there are many inaccuracies in this account. Weingardt even questioned whether Welch was actually present during the expedition. But because Carr believed his expedition was hopelessly undermanned, he might indeed have allowed Welch and others to join the command as volunteers without pay.

35. Sorenson, "Quarter of a Century."

36. Cody, *Autobiography of Buffalo Bill*, 183.

37. Register of Enlistments, vol. 150, "1866–1873, Indian Scouts," n.p.; Danker, "Journal," 129–30.

38. Apart from the Pawnee scouts, civilian scouts, and wagon train, the column consisted of troops A, C, E, F, G, I, L, and M of the Fifth Cavalry. Many of these companies were undermanned. The entire column consisted of about 475 men. Broome, *Dog Soldier Justice*, 148.

39. King, "Republican River Expedition," 35–37.

40. Werner, *Summit Springs Battle*, 73–74.

41. King, "Republican River Expedition," 37; Werner, *Summit Springs*, 73–74.

42. Danker, *Man of the Plains*, 106–107. According to Luther North, William Cody was the first to start the pursuit of the hostiles, because his horse was still saddled and nearby. In his autobiography Cody gave a slightly different rendition: "My horse was close at hand. Mounting him bareback, I galloped after the mule herd, which had been stampeded. I supposed that I would be the first man on the scene. But I found I was mistaken. The Pawnee scouts, unlike regular soldiers, had not waited for the formality of orders from their officers. Jumping their ponies bareback and putting ropes in the animals' mouths, they had hurried to the place from which the shots came and got there before I did." Cody, *Autobiography*, 184.

43. Danker, *Man of the Plains*, 108.

44. In his autobiography, *Man of the Plains*, 108, North claimed he was arrested for his insubordination. But in a letter to his uncle Jacob C. North on November 28, 1874, he wrote that he was not.

45. Danker, "Journal," 132.

46. Report of Major Carr to Brigadier General George Ruggles, June 30, 1869, in Werner, *Summit Springs*, 73–74.

47. Near the Beaver River the command stumbled upon the battlefield where Carr's troops had fought the Indians on May 15. The men found a good deal of property scattered around, as well as some ponies. The Indians had not returned to recover any of their property. From the remains left at the site, the Pawnees determined that these had been northern Indians. The troops also found the bones of three U.S. soldiers of the Fifth Cavalry who had perished in the fight, and they buried the remains in a simple ceremony. Report of Major Carr to Brigadier General George Ruggles, June 30, 1869, in Werner, *Summit Springs*, 77.

48. In his diary of the march, Frank North wrote on June 21, 1869, that "nothing of importance occurred except some fun riding one of our bucking horses. it threw Wallace 3 times. finally a lieut. rode it." Sam Wallace, according to Donald Danker, was first sergeant of Company B, "Pawnee Scouts." Danker, "Journal," 133.

49. Cody, *Autobiography*, 186.

50. Danker, "Journal," 133; Danker, *Man of the Plains*, 110.

51. Danker, "Journal," 134; Danker, *Man of the Plains*, 110.

52. Report of Major Carr to Brigadier General George Ruggles, June 30, 1869, in Werner, *Summit Springs*, 78.

53. Danker, "Journal," 135, 136.

54. King, "Republican River Expedition," 47.

55. Report of Major Carr to Brigadier General George Ruggles, June 30, 1869, in Werner, *Summit Springs*, 76.

56. Danker, "Journal," 137. Also see Danker's footnote on the same page.

57. According to Major North's diary, two white men joined the Pawnees on their scout. Only one returned. It is not unlikely that the man who disappeared seized the opportunity to desert. Danker, "Journal," 136.

58. Broome, *Dog Soldier Justice*, 155.

59. Werner, *Summit Springs*, 61; King, "Republican River Expedition," 48. According to George Bent, Howling Magpie had been wounded in a previous fight with the scouts. However, none of the official documents or personal writings of those present during the campaign relates any skirmish with Cheyennes before July 5. Hyde, *Life of George Bent*, 330–31.

60. Letter published in the *New York Times*, July 26, 1869, and the *Army and Navy Journal*, July 31, 1869, 791. I have been unable to determine the identity of the author of this letter. It was written near Fort Sedgwick on July 14, 1869, and was addressed to a friend of the author's in St. Louis.

61. Danker, "Journal," 137. Among the returning scouts were Gus Becher, Barclay White, and Sam Wallace.

62. Werner, *Summit Springs*, 62.

63. According to George F. Price, Corporal Kyle and his men were surrounded by thirteen Sioux warriors. The soldiers succeeded in killing three Indians. Price, *Across the Continent*, 22. According to the official records of engagements, however, Kyle's party only wounded two Indians before returning to camp. Corporal Kyle was later awarded a Congressional Medal of Honor for his actions. Jeff Broome, who spelled the corporal's name "Kile," wrote that he was later killed by Wild Bill Hickok. Broome, *Dog Soldier Justice*, 156–59.

64. George Bent provided an interesting account of the raid from the Cheyenne perspective. Hyde, *Life of George Bent*, 329–30.

65. Danker, "Journal," 138; Werner, *Summit Springs*, 62; Danker, *Man of the Plains*, 111.

66. King, "Republican River Expedition," 50–51; Werner, *Summit Spring*, 63. According to George Bent's account, an advance party of Pawnee scouts discovered two old Cheyenne men and one woman following the trail of the main village. The Pawnees killed all three. Again, no additional information in the official records corroborates this claim. Hyde, *Life of George Bent*, 331.

67. Hyde, *Life of George Bent*, 331–32; King, "Republican River Expedition," 67; Price, *Across the Continent*, 140.

68. The command was composed of men of the companies A, C, D, E, G, and H, Fifth Cavalry, and men from companies A, B, and C of the Pawnee scouts. Company M stayed behind, together with the remaining soldiers and Pawnees, to escort the wagon train. Broome, *Dog Soldier Justice*, 161; Price, *Across the Continent*, 137.

69. Report of Major Carr to Brigadier General George Ruggles, July 20, 1869, in Werner, *Summit Springs*, 63; King, "Republican River Expedition," 53.

70. According to Luther North, they found three trails, each leading in a different direction. Carr divided the command into three detachments: Royall and Cody took the right-hand trail, toward the northeast; Carr followed the left-hand trail, toward the northwest, with five or six scouts under Sergeant Sam Wallace; and Major North took thirty-five scouts on the middle trail, leading straight north.

When Frank North's men had traveled about fifteen miles they were overtaken by a Pawnee scout from Carr's detachment with orders to join the general as quickly as possible, because he had discovered the Cheyenne village. Danker, *Man of the Plains*, 113. Broome wrote that Royall's command consisted of companies E and G and two companies of Pawnee scouts, as well as William Cody. Carr, meanwhile took companies A, C, D, and H and one company of Pawnees along the main trail. Broome, *Dog Soldier Justice*, 161–62.

71. Report of Major Carr to Brigadier General Ruggles, July 20, 1869, in Werner, *Summit Springs*, 63–64; Brady, *Indian Fights*, 174–75.

72. Price, *Across the Continent*, 138 and Appendix 6, "Company Officers of the Fifth Cavalry," 605–17. Company M was still with the wagon train. Major Crittenden commanded the front line. Although Lieutenant George H. Price was generally regarded as the regimental historian, there are some problems with his account. Captain Samuel S. Sumner wrote that the Pawnees were on the left, nearest to the village, while companies C, H, A, G, and K were on the right. Letter by Captain Samuel Sumner, *Army and Navy Journal*, August 7, 1869, 802, reprinted in Weingardt, *Sound the Charge*, 90–91. According to Lester Walker's account, reprinted in Weingardt, *Sound the Charge*, 108–10, Captain Maley commanded the right column while Sumner, North, and the Pawnee scouts were on the left, and Walker's own command was situated in the center. Both Price's and Walker's accounts were written long after the battle, whereas Sumner's account was written only days afterward and may be the most accurate. Sumner, however, listed company K as one of the units present at the battle, but Company K was not present during the expedition at all.

73. According to Broome, the charge was started at 2:00 P.M. Broome, *Dog Soldier Justice*, 164. On June 6, 1929, Clarence Reckmeyer, Robert H. Bruce, and Luther North visited the Summit Springs battle site. According to Reckmeyer in 1929, the site was located about twelve miles south and five miles east of Sterling, Colorado, on Section 1, Township 5 North, Range 52 West. Reckmeyer, "Battle of Summit Springs," 211.

74. Danker, *Man of the Plains*, 115.

75. Testimony by Leading Fox, September 4, 1923, Leading Fox Pension File, VA Records, Pension Application Files.

76. Letter by Captain Samuel Sumner, *Army and Navy Journal*, August 7, 1869, 802, reprinted in Weingardt, *Sound the Charge*, 90–91.

77. Price, *Across the Continent*, 139.

78. Hyde, *Life of George Bent*, 333.

79. Brady, *Indian Fights*, 176.

80. Report of Major Carr to Brigadier General George Ruggles, July 20, 1869, in Werner, *Summit Springs*, 65.

81. Hyde, *Life of George Bent*, 334.

82. Danker, *Man of the Plains*, 117.

83. Russell, *Lives and Legends of Buffalo Bill*, 130–32, 138–48, 449. Luther North expressed his disapproval of Cody's claims on several occasions. See, for example, Brininstool, *Fighting Indian Warriors*, 228–29.

84. Brady, *Indian Fights*, 177.

85. Carr made this statement in a letter of recommendation for McGrath. The letter is printed in Rickey, *Forty Miles a Day*, 64. It should be pointed out, however, that Carr also credited Buffalo Bill with shooting the Cheyenne chief.

86. Hyde, *Life of George Bent*, 333.

87. Broome, *Dog Soldier Justice*, 169.

88. Tomblin, "Years Take Their Toll of Pawnee Scouts," 134; Reckmeyer, "Battle of Summit Springs," 217. Luther North was apparently unaware that Tall Bull had been scalped. In a letter to Gordon W. Lillie in 1929 he stated: "I saw in an Omaha paper where a couple of Pawnee women were quarreling over a scalp taken at Summit Springs now the only chief that was killed there was Tall Bull he was killed by Frank and when I last saw him he wasn't scalped if Horsefeathers or any other Indian scalped him they went back and done it after night for I saw him about sundown or perhaps a little before." Luther H. North to Gordon W. Lillie, February 11, 1929, Lillie Papers, Box 12, Folder 4.

89. Welch observed that after the fight "we found we had one hundred and seventeen prisoners, four squaws, and fifteen children. They were turned over to the Pawnees." Welch believed the Pawnees had killed the prisoners. Clearly, he was in error. He exaggerated the number of prisoners, and they were never handed over to the Pawnees. Perhaps Welch wanted to emphasize his opinion of Indians. In his account he made the following personal observation: "I think it just as impossible to make a civilized man of the Indian as it would be to make a shepherd dog of a wolf, or a manly man of a dude. They do not in my opinion possess a single trait that elevates a man above a brute. They are treacherous, cowardly, and ungrateful, Cooper to the contrary notwithstanding." Brady, *Indian Fights*, 178.

90. According to Reckmeyer, Sergeant Traveling Bear was also known as "Big George," because he was over six feet tall. Traveling Bear died at the hands of Sioux at Massacre Canyon, Nebraska, on August 6, 1873. Reckmeyer, "Battle of Summit Springs," 215.

91. Report of Major Carr to Brigadier General George Ruggles, July 20, 1869, in Werner, *Summit Springs*, 66.

92. Ibid.

93. Ibid., 66, 69–70.

94. Broome, *Dog Soldier Justice*, 179–82; Weingardt, *Sound the Charge*, 53–55.

95. Billy Osborne, Application for Invalid's Pension, August 3, 1893, Billy Osborne Pension File, VA Records, Pension Application Files. The exact circumstances under which Osborne received his injuries are unknown. It is possible that he actually received his injuries while chasing hostile Indians in the weeks after the battle.

96. Nora White Good Eagle, deposition in support of her application for a widow's pension, December 15, 1932, Nora White Good Eagle Pension File, VA Records, Pension Application Files.

97. Roger C. Echo-Hawk, personal communication, April 25, 2008, based on interviews conducted with High Eagle by Marion N. Tomblin around 1929.

98. King, "Republican River Expedition," 58–59; Danker, "Journal," 140–41.

99. Report of Major Carr to Brigadier General George Ruggles, July 20, 1869, in Werner, *Summit Springs*, 62, 66.

100. U.S. Senate, Committee on Veterans' Affairs, *Medal of Honor Recipients*, 284.

101. Luther North blamed the confusion on the fact that the two men had similar names. Danker, *Man of the Plains*, 120.

102. Broome, *Dog Soldier Justice*, 157–58.

103. Cody, *Autobiography*, 195.

104. King, *War Eagle*, 119.

105. Fisher, "The Royall and Duncan Pursuits," 297; Price, *Across the Continent*, 141.

106. Wishart, "Death of Edward McMurtry." See also Riding In, "United States v. Yellow Sun." Luther North recalled that Blue Hawk, a Kitkahahki, had served with him in 1867. "He was a fine man, but unfortunate," Luther wrote. Luther North to Robert Bruce, February 9, 1929, Robert Bruce Papers, Box 1, Folder 1.

107. Fisher, "Royall and Duncan Pursuits," 297; Peters, *Indian Battles*, 23.

108. Fisher, "Royall and Duncan Pursuits," 298. After rejoining his battalion, Major North gave Luther North and James Murie passes to return home and placed Sylvanus E. Cushing and Gustavus Becher in charge of their companies. The reason for their resignation is unclear. Luther North claimed he resigned after a dispute with Major Carr, but Carr was no longer present. James Murie had been seriously ill during the previous campaign, and it seems plausible that he wanted to return home to recuperate. Danker, "Journal," 146n.

109. Danker, "Journal," 146–48; Register of Enlistments, vol. 150, "1866–1873, Indian Scouts," n.p.

110. Cody, *Autobiography*, 196–97. For the story of the destruction of the giants by Tiiraawaahat, see Dorsey, *Traditions of the Skidi Pawnee*, 23–24.

111. Danker, "Journal," 150–55.

112. Peters, *Indian Battles*, 24. Price claimed that two companies of the Second Cavalry were present in the Duncan pursuit and listed Company E instead of Company C as one of the units present during the expedition. Price, *Across the Continent*, 141.

113. Danker, "Journal," 155 (see also 155n).

114. Cody, *Autobiography*, 207.

115. Fisher, "Royall and Duncan Pursuits," 300–301; Danker, "Journal," 158.

116. Fisher, "Royall and Duncan Pursuits," 301; Danker, "Journal," 158.

117. Fisher, "Royall and Duncan Pursuits," 301–302; Danker, "Journal," 160 and 160n.
118. Fisher, "Royall and Duncan Pursuits," 303–304; Danker, "Journal," 162.
119. Fisher, "Royall and Duncan Pursuits," 304–305; Danker, "Journal," 165–67.
120. Register of Enlistments, vol. 150, "1866–1873, Indian Scouts," n.p.
121. Reckmeyer, "Battle of Summit Springs," 219–20. A slightly different version of this text can be found in Weingardt, *Sound the Charge*, 87.
122. Weingardt, *Sound the Charge*, 88. The original "Joint Resolution of the Nebraska State Legislature, 1870," is on display in the State Building (the capitol) in Lincoln, Nebraska. Copies of the resolution can be found in the Frank North Collection.
123. Filipiak, "Battle of Summit Springs."
124. White, "Indian Raids," 387–88.

CHAPTER 6

1. Other denominations did not receive appointments until 1870. Milner, *With Good Intentions*.
2. Ibid., 38.
3. Uh-sah-wuck-oo-led-ee-hoor is the spelling according to Luther North in Danker, *Man of the Plains*, 138. In other places Big Spotted Horse's name is spelled Esaue-Kedadeho. Pratt, *Battlefield and Classroom*, 78. Contrary to what is often claimed, this is not the Pawnee who is buried at Fort McPherson National Cemetery. The name was reportedly common among the Pawnees. This Big Spotted Horse was a noted warrior and a highly successful horse raider. In 1852, when he was fifteen, he reportedly killed the noted Cheyenne warrior Alight On The Clouds, who tried to count coup on him but did not expect the boy to be left-handed and was shot in the eye with an arrow. "Left Hand" was another name by which Big Spotted Horse was known. Although held in high regard, he was not a chief. He spent considerable time among the Wichitas in Indian Territory. In 1873 he was the first Pawnee to leave Nebraska and settle in Oklahoma. His departure caused a rift in the Pawnee tribe. Others eventually followed his example. Big Spotted Horse served as a U.S. Army scout during the Red River war and was appointed with the rank of sergeant. He received praise from Captain Richard Henry Pratt, with whom he served at the time. As a result of dramatic depopulation among the Pawnees, Big Spotted Horse, the principal advocate of removal to Indian Territory, became the most hated man on the reservation. The scorn of his fellow tribesmen became so intolerable that he asked the agent for permission to relocate to the Wichita Agency. When the agent denied his request, he ran away. According to Hyde, Big Spotted Horse was killed by Texas cowboys when he attempted steal a horse, but Hyde appears to have been mistaken. There

is more compelling evidence that Big Spotted Horse was murdered in Caldwell, Kansas. According to Echo Hawk family traditions, the murder occurred when Big Spotted Horse and his family were on their way back to Nebraska, after they had determined that they did not like Oklahoma. The incident was recorded in the local newspaper, the *Caldwell Journal*. Roger Echo-Hawk, personal communication, April 25, 2008; Hyde, *Pawnee Indians*, 234–35, 297–301, 316–19, 335, 360; Shirley, *Pawnee Bill*, 93–94.

4. The exact number of horses captured is unclear. According to Luther North the Pawnees brought in about 150 horses, but in a letter to Lieutenant General Philip Sheridan, Major General J. M. Schofield wrote that the Pawnees had captured 240 animals. Schofield to Sheridan, January 17, 1870, *Letters Received*, Roll 661.

5. Lieutenant General Sheridan to Brevet Major General C. C. Augur, [January 19] 1870, *Letters Received*, Roll 661.

6. Augur to Sheridan, March 17, 1870, *Letters Received*, Roll 661.

7. Superintendent Janney to Commissioner of Indian Affairs Ely S. Parker, April 22, 1870, *Letters Received*, Roll 661; Milner, *Good Intentions*, 39. During the march to Fort Harker the scouts also met the brother of Susanna Alderice, the captive who had been killed during the battle of Summit Springs. Danker, *Man of the Plains*, 139–42. For Luther North's recollections of Nick Coots, see Bruce, *Fighting Norths*, 33.

8. Danker, *Man of the Plains*, 143–46. Luther North received $112 for his services as guide and interpreter during the march to Fort Harker. Janney to Parker, September 18, 1870, *Letters Received*, Roll 661.

9. Troth to Janney, May 21, 1870, Janney to Parker, June 22, 1870, and Agent DeWit C. Poole of the Whetstone Agency to Janney, June 28, 1870, *Letters Received*, Roll 661.

10. Janney to Parker, February 17, 1870, *Letters Received*, Roll 661.

11. Poole, *Among the Sioux*, 58–63, 125, 128–32.

12. Hyde, *Pawnee Indians*, 302; Dunlay, *Wolves for the Blue Soldiers*, 153. Samuel Allis, a missionary to the Pawnees in the 1840s and 1850s, complained that Pawnee boys quickly forgot everything they learned in school after they turned sixteen: "Although Indian children make good progress in reading, and especially in writing, it does them little good, as they leave the school and forget all they have learned, particularly the boys, for it is difficult to keep them in school after they are some sixteen years old. At that age they commence going to war. They establish their character as braves by stealing horses and killing their enemies." Allis, "Forty Years," 159.

13. Pope to Sherman, June 2, 1870, *Letters Received*, Roll 661.

14. On May 31 Agent Troth reported that the Pawnees and the neighboring whites did not get along well. In order to prevent difficulties between Indians and whites, Troth asked the authorities of Platte County "to arrest as vagrants all Indians found off this Reservation without a pass and lodge them in jail and let

me know and I will send for them." Janney approved of Troth's measure and on June 23 wrote to Commissioner Parker that the Pawnees were allowed to travel freely to Omaha by train "in such numbers as to be troublesome, [and] the mayor of Omaha has complained to me about it." Janney instructed Troth to send two chiefs and two "policemen" to Omaha to gather up the Pawnees in Omaha and Council Bluffs. On June 30 Janney reported that the Pawnees had returned to the agency. "An effort will be made," Janney wrote to Parker, "to keep them at home hereafter." Troth to Janney, May 31, 1870, Janney to Parker, June 23, 1870, and Janney to Parker, June 30, 1870, *Letters Received*, Roll 661.

15. A copy of Hammond's letter to Oakes Ames was sent to the Office of Indian Affairs, June 27, 1870, *Letters Received*, Roll 661.

16. For a good biography of Marsh, see Schuchert and LeVene, *O. C. Marsh*. Harry Degen Ziegler also published an account of Marsh's expedition, in the *New York Weekly Herald*, 24 December 1870.

17. Reiger, *Passing of the Great West*, 32–33.

18. Betts, "Yale College Expedition of 1870," 663; Reiger, *Passing of the Great West*, 33–34; Price, *Across the Continent*, 614; Holmes, *Fort McPherson*, 42.

19. Betts, "Yale College Expedition," 663; Reiger, *Passing of the Great West*, 34.

20. According to Schuchert and LeVene, the proper spelling of the names of the two scouts was Tuck-he-ge-louhs and La-oodle-sock. Schuchert and LeVene, *O. C. Marsh*, 102. The Register of Enlistments of the Pawnee Indian scouts for 1870 lists two Indians named Tuck-it-te-louks ("Alone To War") and La-hoo-re-sock ("Head Warrior"), respectively. Register of Enlistments, vol. 150, "1866–1873, Indian Scouts," n.p.

21. Reiger, *Passing of the Great West*, 35–36.

22. Betts, "Yale College Expedition," 664–65.

23. Frank North to O. C. Marsh, January 5, 1871; copy in Robert Bruce Papers, Box 1, Folder 2.

24. Betts, "Yale College Expedition," 664; Grinnell, "Pawnee Mythology," 121–22.

25. See also Grinnell, "Old-Time Bone Hunt."

26. Betts, "Yale College Expedition," 666; Reiger, *Passing of the Great West*, 35.

27. Reiger, *Passing of the Great West*, 36.

28. Betts, "Yale College Expedition," 666.

29. A copy of the muster roll of Company A, Pawnee Scouts, 1870, can be found in the Robert Bruce Papers, Box 2, Folder 9. See also Weltfish, Pawnee Field Notes.

30. Special Order 51, Headquarters District of the Republican; copy in Robert Bruce Papers, Box 2, Folder 9. See also Holmes, *Fort McPherson*, 42, and NARA, Returns from Military Posts, Roll 708, "Fort McPherson, Nebraska," September 1870.

31. During one hunt, William Cody and Luther North played a prank on one of the English guests, pretending that a nearby group of scouts was in fact enemy

Indians about to attack. The visitor panicked and fled in terror, not stopping until he reached the camp. Cody, *Life of Hon. William F. Cody*, 290–91; Danker, *Man of the Plains*, 147–48.

32. Danker, *Man of the Plains*, 149–50.

33. Register of Enlistments, vol. 150, "1866–1873, Indian Scouts," n.p. Major Benjamin Alvord, paymaster, paid the scouts at McPherson. NARA, Returns from Military Posts, Roll 708, "Fort McPherson, Nebraska," December 1870.

34. Janney to Parker, February 23, 1871, *Letters Received*, Roll 661.

35. Janney to Parker, February 23, March 2, April 11, and April 24, 1871, *Letters Received*, Roll 661; Wishart, *Unspeakable Sadness*, 192–93.

36. Troth to Janney, September 8, 1871, *ARCIA* 1871, 453.

37. White to Walker, March 29, 1872, *Letters Received*, Roll 661.

38. Barnett to Walker, June 20, 1872, A. A. Porter (Barnett's lawyer) to Walker, July 3, 1870, and Barnett to General Porter, Secretary of President Grant, July 18, 1872, *Letters Received*, Roll 661.

39. White to Walker, December 5, 1872, *Letters Received*, Roll 661. In 1872 the Office of Indian Affairs also received its first pension requests from widows of deceased scouts. In September that year, several Pawnee women whose husbands had died while serving as scouts in the army wrote to the Department of the Interior requesting pension benefits. Stah roo kah wah har's husband, Tuck oo wu to roo ("The Man That Strikes The Enemy"), Second Sergeant in Company A, had died at Fort Kearney on March 20, 1865. Chuck ih tah ra shah applied for a pension as the widow of Ow wih toosh ("First To Run"), a corporal in Company A, who had died of consumption at Julesburg, Colorado Territory, on June 20, 1865. Stah roo's husband, Private Kah hah liens ("Little Ears"), had died of an accidental gunshot wound during Connor's campaign, on August 18, 1865. For Stah roo kah wah [hoo], the request came too late. A month after the Pension Office received her application, she, too, had died. Commissioner [J. A. Barth/Barker?] of the Pension Office of the Department of the Interior to the Commissioner of Indian Affairs, September 2, September 5, and September 13, 1872, and Agent Troth to Superintendent White, October 8, 1872, *Letters Received*, Roll 661.

40. Riley, "Battle of Massacre Canyon," 224.

41. Ibid., 225–30. Luther North and George Bird Grinnell left excellent accounts of the summer hunt of 1872. See Danker, *Man of the Plains*, 170–73; Reiger, *Passing of the Great West*, 57–72; and Grinnell, "Buffalo Hunt with the Pawnees."

42. Although some sources spell his name Ku ruks ra wa ri, it appears that this Traveling Bear is the same man as Co rux ah kah wah de, who was present at the battle of Summit Springs in 1869.

43. Riley, "Dr. David Franklin Powell," 163.

44. The battle of Massacre Canyon has been the subject of a number of works. Riley, "Battle of Massacre Canyon," presents a good overview. Blaine and Blaine,

"Pa-re-su A-ri-ra-ke," adds the Pawnee perspective and provides a different account of the event. Trail Agent John W. Williamson published his memoir of the event under the title *The Battle of Massacre Canyon: The Unfortunate Ending of the Last Buffalo Hunt of the Pawnees*. Unfortunately, Williamson's account, written half a century after the fact, contains many errors and discrepancies. In 1935 *Nebraska History Magazine* (vol. 16) devoted an entire issue to the battle (Sheldon, "Massacre Canyon Number"). The issue includes official accounts, correspondence, a historical overview by Addison E. Sheldon, and a discussion of the dedication of the Massacre Canyon Memorial in 1930. See also "The Fighting Norths and Pawnee Scouts," *Motor Travel*, September and October 1931, 16–18.

45. Hyde, *Pawnee Indians*, 316.

46. For good discussions surrounding the circumstances of Pawnee removal, see Blaine, *Pawnee Passage*; White, *Roots of Dependency*; and Wishart, *Unspeakable Sadness*, 174–202.

47. Blaine, *Pawnee Passage*, 215ff.

48. According to George Hyde, Big Spotted Horse had gone to live with the Wichitas in 1870. He returned to the Pawnee Agency in 1872 and appeared to be the ringleader in favor of removal to Indian Territory. Perhaps Burgess agreed to let him leave the reservation because he considered him a troublemaker. In the spring of 1870 Big Spotted Horse had been responsible for stealing a large number of horses from the Cheyennes. Hyde, *Pawnee Indians*, 316.

49. In other sources Pitalesharo is sometimes spelled Pitaresaru.

50. Blaine, *Pawnee Passage*, 217–18; Milner, *Good Intentions*, 69–70.

51. Blaine, *Pawnee Passage*, 218–33.

52. White to commissioner of Indian affairs, May 4, 1874, *Letters Received*, Roll 663. On April 28, 1874, Lieutenant Colonel George A. Woodward, Fourteenth Infantry, had requested four Pawnee scouts, and General E. O. C. Ord passed the request on to the Office of Indian Affairs. The letter cited was Superintendent White's response. See also Milner, *Good Intentions*, 71.

53. The command consisted of Companies B and D, Second Cavalry; Companies F, H, and M, Third Cavalry; Company H, Fourth Infantry; Company D, Thirteenth Infantry; 4 Pawnee scouts; 2 guides (William Cody and Tom Sun); 6 unidentified scouts; 20 packers; 30 teamsters; 1 ambulance; 28 wagons; and 70 pack mules. The total command consisted of 15 officers, 343 troopers, and 58 hired civilians. Mills, *Big Horn Expedition*, 3–5. According to Mills's memoirs, these Sioux had entered the parade grounds at Forts Fetterman and Steele and killed several soldiers. Mills, *My Story*, 155.

54. Mills, *Big Horn Expedition*, 4–5, 11. At this time the Third Cavalry was stationed at Fort McPherson, Nebraska. See Holmes, *Fort McPherson*, 53.

55. Mills, *Big Horn Expedition*, 5–15.

56. Haley, *Buffalo War*, chapters 1–3. In 1875 General Philip Sheridan appeared before the Texas legislature to defend the slaughter of the buffalo by white hunters.

Although overhunting had been the cause of the Red River war, Sheridan opposed proposals in Texas calling for the preservation of the buffalo. According to Sheridan, the buffalo hunters had "done more in the last two years to settle the vexed Indian question than the entire regular army has done in the past thirty years. They are destroying the Indians' commissary. . . . Send them powder and lead, if you will; but, for the sake of lasting peace, let them kill, skin, and sell until the buffaloes are exterminated. Then your prairies can be covered with speckled cattle and the festive cowboy, who follows the hunter as a second forerunner of an advanced civilization." Quoted in Haley, *Buffalo War*, 25.

57. Ibid., chapters 3–6; Leckie, *Buffalo Soldiers*, 116–17.

58. Haley, *Buffalo War*, chapter 7; Leckie, *Buffalo Soldiers*, 124.

59. Haley, *Buffalo War*, chapter 8; Leckie, *Buffalo Soldiers*, 123. Some eyewitness accounts and reports of the Anadarko fight can be found in *Letters Received*, Roll 929 (Wichita Agency), frames 1415–1432.

60. Leckie, *Buffalo Soldiers*, 130. Reeder; "Wolf Men," 320–21.

61. Augur to Sheridan, September 13, 1874, *Letters Received*, M 234, Roll 929 (Wichita Agency), frames 1437–1439.

62. Leckie, *Buffalo Soldiers*, 130. According to Reeder, company F was part of the command instead of company K. Reeder, "Wolf Men," 321. In a letter to his wife, Lieutenant Richard H. Pratt wrote, "[Wish] you could have seen me at the head of my forty braves, as I marched through the post this morning. I have organized and equipped my command in a manner eminently satisfactory (to myself) and must say I am not without pride in it. Think of a command of forty only two of whom can understand their commander, and in which five nationalities are represented!" Richard H. Pratt to his wife, September 9, 1874, [Grant] Foreman Collection, Box 33, Folder 17, Oklahoma Historical Society, Oklahoma City.

63. Pratt to his wife, September 23, 1874, Foreman Collection, Box 33, Folder 17.

64. Davidson's report of the march can be found in Taylor, *Indian Campaign on the Staked Plains*, 69–73. See also Leckie, *Buffalo Soldiers*, 130–31.

65. Hutton, *Phil Sheridan*, 253–54.

66. Register of Enlistments, vol. 151, "1866–1873, Indian Scouts," n.p. Apart from the Pawnees, Pratt's company consisted of "31 Wichitas, . . . 14 Tawankanas, 10 Wacoes, 5 Kechies, 2 Caddoes, 2 Delawares, 1 Arapaho, 1 Shawnee, 1 Comanche and 5 white men." Lieutenant R. H. Pratt to Acting Assistant Adjutant General, November 29, 1874, in Taylor, *Indian Campaign*, 121. See also Reeder, "Wolf Men," 322. Michael L. Tate states that at least half the scouts were Kiowas and Comanches. Tate, "Indian Scouting Detachments," 219–21.

67. Hutton, *Phil Sheridan*, 253–54.

68. According to an article by Lieutenant Pratt, his scouts also served as a personal body guard while he camped near a Kiowa village under Chief Big Bow.

Although Big Bow had pledged to surrender, Pratt was not entirely certain whether he was acting in good faith. See Pratt, "Some Indian Experiences," 214–16.

69. Taylor, *Indian Campaign*, 122; Reeder, "Wolf Men," 323; Haley, *Buffalo War*, chapter 13. According to Leckie, Carpenter captured only 45 Kiowas and 50 horses. Leckie, *Buffalo Soldiers*, 131–32.

70. Taylor, *Indian Campaign*, 122–24.

71. Reeder, "Wolf Men," 325–26.

72. Pratt, *Battlefield and Classroom*, 78–79. Davidson's fondness for liquor was well known. Big Spotted Horse's conduct during the expeditions seems to contrast with that implied in Pratt's report of December 3, 1874. According to that report, Pratt had obtained some evidence showing that Big Spotted Horse had been involved in the murder of a citizen on the Washita River in August. It appears that the charges were dropped, for there are no documents available that indicate that Big Spotted Horse was subjected to a formal investigation. Taylor, *Indian Campaign*, 134.

CHAPTER 7

1. Pawnee removal took place in several stages. On October 10, 1874, about forty lodges set out for the Wichita Agency. Two weeks later a large group led by John W. Williamson followed. These people joined the Pawnees under Big Spotted Horse, who had migrated to the Wichita Agency the previous year. Only a small faction remained at the Pawnee Agency in Nebraska. The Pawnees stayed with the Wichitas until June 1875, when they moved onto their new reservation on Black Bear Creek. The remaining Pawnees in Nebraska joined them there later that year. Although the land was good, the sudden change of climate, the hardships of removal, and the lack of adequate housing, subsistence, and medical facilities placed an enormous strain on the health of the people. Mortality rates exceeded birth rates until the early 1900s, when the Pawnee population had declined to seven hundred souls. Blaine, *Pawnee Passage*, chapter 10; Wishart, *Unspeakable Sadness*, 196–202. In "The Dispossession of the Pawnees," Wishart argued that the Pawnees migrated to Indian Territory to preserve Pawnee tribalism. According to Wishart, the pressures at the original Pawnee reservation in Nebraska threatened to destroy Pawnee unity.

2. For an excellent study of the Black Hills expedition, see Jackson, *Custer's Gold*. For Grinnell's and North's experiences during the expedition, see Reiger, *Passing of the Great West*, and Danker, *Man of the Plains*, 179–93.

3. There are several good books on the Great Sioux War, including Benson, *Black Hills War*, and Gray, *Centennial Campaign*. Utley provides a brief but fairly complete account of the war in his classic work *Frontier Regulars*, chapters 14 and 15. The following account of the war is based largely on Robinson's more recent history, *A Good Year to Die*.

4. For biographies of George Crook (1828–90), see Schmitt, *General George Crook*, and Robinson, *General Crook and the Western Frontier*.

5. Robinson, *Good Year to Die*, 193. Perhaps the best treatment of the Custer battle is Gray, *Custer's Last Campaign*. For a controversial interpretation from the perspective of the Northern Cheyennes in the battle, see Marquis, *Keep the Last Bullet for Yourself*. For the Arikara account of the battle, see Libby, *Arikara Narrative of Custer's Campaign*.

6. Robinson, *Good Year to Die*, 216, 224.

7. The act is reproduced in *ARCIA*, 1877, 225. On August 19, 1876, the *Chicago Daily Tribune* reported that the commissioner of Indian affairs had "given permission to Gen. Sheridan to raise 1,000 Pawnee scouts for the Sioux war." This report was wrong in that the act did not specify the tribal affiliation of the scouts.

8. Sheridan believed that Indian scouts made poor allies because they did "not possess stability or tenacity of purpose." In the mid-1880s he would declare that it would be unwise to recruit a military force from "a race so distinctive from that governing this country." Nevertheless, always the pragmatist, Sheridan was willing to set aside his own convictions to create the best possible army on such short notice to deal with the crisis situation in the war of 1876. Hutton, *Phil Sheridan*, 366.

9. *Army and Navy Journal*, August 19, 1876, 22; Greene, *Morning Star Dawn*, 14–16.

10. The letter of instruction is in the Frank North Collection, Box 1, S1-F1.

11. Danker, *Man of the Plains*, 195–97. According to Bruce, the Pawnees were recruited on September 3 and were officially mustered in on September 18, 1876. Captain Pollock, however, entered September 3 as the official date of enlistment on the muster rolls. Bruce, *Fighting Norths*, 44. Sorenson provided a slightly different version of events in "Life of Major Frank North," December 19, 1896.

12. Danker, *Man of the Plains*, 197–98.

13. Sorenson, "Life of Major North," December 19, 1896. Garland Blaine related the tradition of Frank North's visit to his grandfather's lodge on the Pawnee reservation: "A former United States Army Pawnee Scout, Leading with the Bear was ill when Maj. Frank North and Capt. Luther North went to the Pawnee agency in 1876 to seek men to fight the Cheyennes. Effie [Garland Blaine's grandmother] remembered she was outside the tipi one day and saw a man coming on foot. He may have been leading a horse. She said he was not very tall, and he looked sick—his skin was yellow and his eyes were big. Because all the men were absent, she ran inside. The man came to the tipi and said in perfect Pawnee, 'My child, is this where —— lives?' He gave a name that Effie did not recognize for a minute. She had not heard her father called that for many years. She raised the tipi flap and replied, 'Yes, you can come inside and see my father.' Her father looked up, saw the man, and cried out, 'Here he stands. Pari resaru [Pawnee Chief] has come.' He had given him that name after a battle some years before. North called him by his old Pawnee Scout name. Effie's father [stood] up, they

clasped hands, put their chests together, and patted each other. Each felt bad to see the other not looking well. Her father said, 'You do not look well, Grandfather.' 'I do not feel well,' North replied, 'but I have come to see the Scouts who are still living. I have also come to recruit some men to go and fight your enemies.' They talked for awhile and her father asked him to stay for supper. 'I cooked the meal, and they ate,' Effie remembered. 'Afterward he thanked me and turned to my father saying, "you are getting heavy [old]. It is good to know you are still here and your children can see you. Have a strong mind and think good thoughts. Don't weaken, look to God. He is the one who's in charge of us."' Father then talked to him in the same manner, and they said goodbye. He said he was going back to the agency, and he did." Blaine, *Some Things Are Not Forgotten*, 9–10.

14. Hyde, *Pawnee Indians*, 339–40. See also Smits, "'Fighting Fire with Fire,'" 103.

15. Sorenson, "Life of Major North," December 19, 1896.

16. Grinnell, quoted in Smits, "'Fighting Fire with Fire,'" 100. See also Grinnell, *Pawnee Hero Stories*, 399.

17. Rush Roberts to Don Rickey, August 1954, Don J. Rickey Jr. Collection, Denver Public Library, Denver, Colorado. See also Downey and Jacobson, *Red Bluecoats*, 41.

18. Rush Roberts to Robert Bruce, July 24, 1929. See also "Pawnee Trails and Trailers" (September 1929), 9; Bruce, *Fighting Norths*, 57.

19. Blaine, *Some Things*, 10.

20. Walking Sun affidavit in support of Wichita Blaine's pension application, May 22, 1919, Walking Sun Pension File, VA Records, Pension Application Files.

21. The proper spelling of Leading Chief's name is Raahirasuureesaaru' ("In The Lead In A Chiefly Manner"). William R. Anderson, American Indian Studies Research Institute, Indiana University, Bloomington, personal communication, February 16, 2008.

22. Bourke, *Mackenzie's Last Fight with the Cheyennes*, 14.

23. Roger C. Echo-Hawk, personal communication, 25 April 2008.

24. Blaine, *Some Things*, 6.

25. Luther North to Robert Bruce, August 25, 1929, printed in "Pawnee Trails and Trailers," September 1929, 11. See also Bruce, *Fighting Norths*, 43.

26. Blaine, *Some Things*, 11.

27. In his memoirs and correspondence, Luther North liked to recall an incident during the trip to Sidney Barracks. While in camp, he suggested singing an old war song commemorating a glorious battle in which the Pawnees defeated the Ponca Indians, who had come to their village under the false pretense of peace. When Luther made the suggestion, all became quiet in the camp. Li Heris oo la shar (Frank White), one of the headmen, came over and told North that there was a Ponca with the battalion who had married a Pawnee woman and was now a full member of the tribe. Li Heris oo la shar explained that the men did not wish

to offend their friend by singing the Ponca song. Bruce, *Fighting Norths*, 42; Danker, *Man of the Plains*, 200–201.

28. Blaine, *Some Things*, 54–55.

29. Danker, *Man of the Plains*, 201; "Register of Enlistments, vol. 150, "1866–1873, Indian Scouts," n.p.; "Pawnee Trails and Trailers," October 1929, 16, 17; Bruce, *Fighting Norths*, 44; *Sidney (Nebraska) Telegraph*, September 23, 1876, and October 14, 1876.

30. Frank North diary, 1876–77, Frank North Collection, Box 1, S3-F1 (hereafter cited as "Frank North diary"), 89; *Sidney Telegraph*, September 30, 1876.

31. Frank North diary, 89; Register of Enlistments, vol. 150, "1866–1873, Indian Scouts," n.p. According to one source, the bodies of at least two of these scouts were buried at Sidney Barracks military cemetery. They were reportedly exhumed and reinterred, with full military honors, at Fort McPherson National Cemetery in 1922. A search of the Fort McPherson National Cemetery database revealed four graves of unknown Indian scouts. It is possible that the remains of the two Pawnee scouts are among them. The only "identified" Pawnee buried there was called Spotted Horse. According to historian Paul D. Riley, Spotted Horse was killed near Elm Creek on August 14, 1862, by Brulé Sioux. He was originally buried at Fort Kearny, Nebraska, but in November 1873 his remains were reinterred at the Fort McPherson cemetery. Riley, "David Franklin Powell," 169. See also "Spotted Horse's Medal," *New York Times*, May 3, 1896. The claim brought forth by some authors that the Pawnee buried at Fort McPherson was the famous Big Spotted Horse is probably false. Big Spotted Horse was murdered in Kansas in 1883. In 1875, another Pawnee with the name Spotted Horse died near Bunker Hill, Kansas, en route from Nebraska to the new reservation in Indian Territory. According to John Williamson, who escorted the Pawnees to Oklahoma, this Pawnee wished to mourn at the grave of his brother, who had been killed there by Sioux a few years before. Spotted Horse apparently developed pneumonia after staying at his brother's grave overnight. He was buried in the Bunker Hill Cemetery, Kansas. Materials and correspondence concerning the identity of the Pawnee buried at Fort McPherson were provided by the Department of Veterans Affairs, Fort McPherson National Cemetery, Maxwell, Nebraska, June 2005.

32. Greene, "Surrounding of Red Cloud."

33. *Army and Navy Journal*, October 21, 1876, 166.

34. Kime, *Powder River Expedition Journals of Colonel Dodge*, entry for November 16, 1876.

35. Robinson, *Good Year to Die*, 257–58. For biographies of Mackenzie, see Pierce, *Most Promising Young Officer*, and Robinson, *Bad Hand*.

36. Prucha, *Guide to Military Posts*, 102.

37. Hedren, *Fort Laramie*, 155.

38. George Crook to P. H. Sheridan, October 2, 1876, in "Military Reports on the Red Cloud–Red Leaf Surround," *Nebraska History* 15 (October-December 1934), 292.

39. Greene, "Surrounding of Red Cloud," 70–71. For an eyewitness account of these events, see Ricker, "The Surround of Red Cloud and Red Leaf," and Paul, *Nebraska Indian Wars Reader*, 157–60.

40. There is some confusion about the number of Pawnees who were present at the surrounds. According to some accounts, Mackenzie and Gordon each had twenty-four Pawnees at his disposal. Major North's diary, however, speaks of forty-two scouts. Frank North diary, entry for October 22, 1876; Greene, "Surrounding of Red Cloud," 71; Danker, *Man of the Plains*, 201–203. Sorenson gave a slightly different account of the surrounding of the Sioux villages in "Life of Major North," December 19 and 26, 1896, and January 2, 1897.

41. Greene, "Surrounding of Red Cloud," 71–72.

42. Ibid., 72.

43. Danker, *Man of the Plains*, 203–204.

44. Luther North to Elmo S. Watson, December 6, 1934, Elmo Scott Watson Papers, Newberry Library, Chicago, Illinois.

45. Greene, "Surrounding of Red Cloud," 73. The position of "Chief of all Sioux" did not exist among the Lakotas, but Red Cloud had been so designated by white officials. In a letter of October 25, Sheridan instructed Crook to "Go right on disarming and dismounting every Indian connected with the Red Cloud Agency; and if Spotted Tail and his Indians do not come up squarely, dismount and disarm them. There must be no halfway work in this matter. All Indians out there must be on our side without question or else on the side of the hostiles. We cannot any longer afford to use so much of our forces guarding Indians alleged to be friendly when they are really hostile." On October 30, Crook responded: "The other bands not disarmed, known as the Arapahoes, Loafers, and Cut-off Sioux, have been loyal to us, and to have disarmed them with the others would simply have arrayed the white man against the Indian and placed the loyal and the disloyal on the same footing." "Military Reports on the Red Cloud–Red Leaf Surround," 294.

46. Ricker, "Surround of Red Cloud and Red Leaf"; Paul, *Nebraska Indian Wars Reader*, 160.

47. Luther North claimed that only twenty scouts accompanied Major North, but most other sources speak of forty to fifty scouts. Jerry Roche, a newspaper correspondent from New York, was with the soldiers transporting supplies to Camp Robinson when the Pawnees suddenly appeared. He published a lively account of the episode in the *New York Herald*, November 4, 1876.

48. Greene, "Surrounding of Red Cloud," 73–74; Danker, *Man of the Plains*, 206.

49. Hedren, *Fort Laramie,* 195.

50. *New York Herald,* November 10, 1876; *Army and Navy Journal,* November 18, 1876, 229; Greene, *Morning Star Dawn,* 28–29.

51. Wheeler, *Buffalo Days,* 125–26. Bruce provides a fairly detailed list of the Sioux and Arapaho scouts present in Crook's command. See "Pawnee Trails and Trailers," March 1930, 17; "A Day with the 'Fighting Cheyennes,'" April 1930, 19.

52. Grinnell, *Fighting Cheyennes,* 369.

53. Robinson, *Good Year to Die,* 284–85.

54. Wheeler, *Buffalo Days,* 127.

55. Ibid., 122.

56. Frank North diary, entry for October 31 and November 1, 1876.

57. Bourke, *Mackenzie's Last Fight,* 7.

58. Clark, *Indian Sign Language,* 5. See also Hutton, *Phil Sheridan,* 341–42.

59. Henry H. Bellas, quoted in Greene, *Battles and Skirmishes,* 173.

60. Grinnell, *Two Great Scouts,* 256–57.

61. Although Crook was at times a brilliant tactician, he often failed to communicate his plans to his officers. To many of his staff members, he appeared sometimes erratic. His orders were often vague and broad, and they frequently puzzled his officers. Robinson, *Good Year to Die,* 56–57; Danker, *Man of the Plains,* 207.

62. "Fighting Norths and Pawnee Scouts," April 1931, 17.

63. Bourke, *Mackenzie's Last Fight,* 8. See also Greene, *Battles and Skirmishes,* 175.

64. Robinson, *Good Year to Die,* 284–85. The name of Cantonment Reno was later changed to Fort McKinney, after Lieutenant John McKinney, who died in the Dull Knife battle. The post was abandoned on November 7, 1894. Prucha, *Guide to Military Posts,* 89. See also Greene, *Morning Star Dawn,* 72–75.

65. Frank North diary, n.p.

66. Bruce, *Fighting Norths,* 57.

67. Frank North diary, n.p.

68. Dodge, *Our Wild Indians,* 464.

69. On November 7 Crook held a council with the Sioux, Arapahos, and Cheyenne scouts. At this meeting Three Bears, Fast Thunder (both Sioux), and Sharp Nose called for the good treatment of their people back at the agencies. They also demanded that they be given some of the horses the Pawnees had been driving. Crook agreed. "Our Indian Allies: Crook's Talk with His Red Soldiers," *New York Herald,* November 16, 1876; Danker, *Man of the Plains,* 208–10.

70. Sorenson, "Life of Major North," January 2, 1896; Bourke, *Mackenzie's Last Fight,* 12; Bourke, *On the Border With Crook,* 392. The Register of Enlistments spells the latter man's name Us sak kish oo kah lah, but Bourke spelled it U-sanky-su-cola.

71. Sorenson, "Life of Major North," January 9, 1896.

72. Bourke, *Mackenzie's Last Fight,* 11–12; "Our Indian Allies: Crook's Talk with His Red Soldiers," *New York Herald,* November 16, 1876.

73. Bourke, *Mackenzie's Last Fight,* 12.

74. John G. Bourke's diary entry, quoted in Smith, *Sagebrush Soldier*, 57.

75. Sorenson, "Life of Major North," January 9, 1896; Danker, *Man of the Plains*, 210-11.

76. *New York Herald*, November 27, 1876; *Army and Navy Journal*, December 2, 1876, 270.

77. Bourke, *Mackenzie's Last Fight*,, 13. According to William Garnett, Lakota interpreter, the Sioux had up to this point not associated with the Pawnees. During the march to Fort Reno the two groups had camped apart. Only one Lakota scout, Joe Bush, reportedly would visit the Pawnees. It is unclear whether Bush had some connection with the Pawnees. In any event, after Crook's council "all the tribes entered into the most cordial and sociable relations, and approved and cemented the conciliation by exchange of presents, some of these being valuable horses." Jensen, *Indian Interviews of Eli S. Ricker, 1903-1919*, 25. Grinnell wrote that the Pawnees and the other scouts also engaged in hand games. On one occasion the Pawnees were playing against some Cheyenne scouts, and the Pawnees lost several horses until they discovered that one of the Cheyennes was cheating. Instead of holding the hand-game bone in one of his hands, he hid it in his robe. At one point in the game, two Pawnees sprang forward and grabbed the Cheyenne's wrists before he could drop the bone into one of his hands. The matter was resolved peacefully when the Cheyennes returned all the horses they had won. Grinnell, *Story of the Indian*, 28.

78. Robinson, *Good Year to Die*, 287-88; Greene, *Morning Star Dawn*, 82-84.

79. Luther North to Robert Bruce, December 4, 1929, Robert Bruce Papers, Box 1, Folder 1.

80. Mackenzie's column consisted of the various companies of the Third, Fourth, and Fifth Cavalries under Captain Mauck and Major Gordon, the Pawnee scouts under Major North and Captain Cushing, the Shoshone scouts under Tom Cosgrove and Walter S. Schuyler, the remaining scouts under Lieutenants William P. Clark and Hayden DeLany, a number of volunteers and white scouts under Lieutenants James Allison and James M. Jones, and a pack train consisting of 250 mules. Greene, *Morning Star Dawn*, 85.

81. Greene, *Battles and Skirmishes*, 175.

82. Wheeler, *Buffalo Days*, 130.

83. Smith, *Sagebrush Soldier*, 61-64.

84. Greene, *Morning Star Dawn*, 95-96.

85. The exact location of this narrow pass, where the troops could travel only in single file, is in dispute. Most authors seem to believe it was the narrow passage between Fraker Mountain and Fraker Mountain Rock, a piece of the mountain that had broken off a long time ago. Ken and Cheri Graves, who own the land where the Dull Knife battle took place and know it better than anyone else, believe the canyon described by Luther North and others was in fact located farther north and suggest that it might have been "Rock Hanson Red Draw."

86. Danker, *Man of the Plains*, 211–12.
87. Grinnell, *Fighting Cheyennes*, chapter 27; Greene, *Morning Star Dawn*, 92.
88. Danker, *Man of the Plains*, 212–13. This canyon would be the gap between Fraker Mountain and Fraker Rock, on the east side of the valley. There the Pawnees left their saddles, horse gear, and other equipment that they would not need during the fight. In the evening, after the battle, they returned to get their saddles but found that the straps and cinches had been cut to pieces. Luther North suspected that the Sioux and Cheyenne scouts, who were riding up behind them, were responsible for the vandalism. "Fighting Norths and Pawnee Scouts," June 1931, 19.
89. "Fighting Norths and Pawnee Scouts," May 1931, 23.
90. "A Day with the 'Fighting Cheyennes,'" February 1931, 22.
91. Blaine, *Some Things*, 6.
92. Smith, *Sagebrush Soldier*, 66.
93. In an interview with Eli S. Ricker on December 7, 1905, William L. Judkins gave a different order of the charge. He said that the Sioux were placed first in the column, followed by the Cheyennes, Shoshones, and Pawnees, respectively. Behind the Pawnees came companies M and D of the Fourth Cavalry. The reason for this arrangement, according to Judkins, was that "the use of Indians as soldiers under white commanders was an uncertain experiment." In 1876 Judkins was a member of Company D, Fourth Cavalry. Jensen, *Settler and Soldier Interviews*, 298.
94. *Army and Navy Journal*, December 9, 1876, 286.
95. Bourke, *Mackenzie's Last Fight*, 29–30.
96. Greene, *Battles and Skirmishes*, 177. In a letter to Robert Bruce, Luther North denied that there was a Pawnee who played a flute at the time of the attack: "There was no flageolets in our company some of the Sioux or Shoshone scouts may have had small bone whistles but I doubt it the only flageolets I ever heard was among the Santee Sioux and Winnebagoe when I was in the 2nd Nebr. Cavalry in 1863. medicine men were often great warriors Traveling Bear was a medicine man I think we had only one with us in 1876 all writers seem to want to get something out of the ordinary when writing of the scouts Col Wheeler tells of Frank calling his men with a whistle. he gave them orders as any officer would his soldiers he never carried a whistle in his life. the Santee Sioux and Winnebago Indians used flageolets to serenade there sweethearts I never heard of their use in war and I am quite sure there were none used in the Dull Knife fight. in fact I never heard of the Brulle or Ogalala Sioux use them anywhere but they may have." Luther North to Robert Bruce, January 7, 1930, Robert Bruce Papers, Box 1, Folder 4.
97. Grinnell, *Fighting Cheyennes*, 370–74; Nohl, "Mackenzie against Dull Knife," 88; Greene, *Morning Star Dawn*, 90.
98. After visiting the battle site under the guidance of Cheri Graves of the Red Fork Ranch in July 2005, I believe the Shoshone scouts were quite able to spread a

deadly fire into the camp. Such long-range fire, however, especially when vision was obscured by smoke from the guns, was dangerous for the troops and scouts charging the village. But even if Luther North's claim is correct, the psychological effect of the appearance of the Shoshone scouts on the Cheyennes must have been considerable. Thus, although not engaged in hand-to-hand fighting, the Shoshones made an important contribution to the battle.

99. Danker, *Man of the Plains*, 213–14.

100. Ibid., 214.

101. Greene, *Battles and Skirmishes*, 120.

102. Grinnell, *Fighting Cheyennes*, 364.

103. Luther North to George Bird Grinnell, February 14, 1877, published in *Forest and Stream*, May 10, 1877, 212.

104. Wheeler, *Buffalo Days*, 133.

105. Danker, *Man of the Plains*, 214.

106. Grinnell, *Pawnee Hero Stories*, 74–75. Ralph Weeks was one of Grinnell's Pawnee informants. According to Jerry Roche, correspondent for the *New York Herald*, McKinney lived for another twenty minutes after being shot. As he fell from his horse, mortally wounded, he supposedly cried out, "Get back from this place, you are ambushed," and then exclaimed, "Oh! my poor mother! Tell her! Tell her!" *New York Herald*, December 1 and 11, 1876. According to the Cheyenne account, as recorded by Grinnell, Tall Bull (not to be confused with the Dog Soldier chief), Walking Whirlwind, Burns Red (In The Sun), Walking Calf, Hawks Visit, and Four Spirits were among the Cheyennes killed by the soldiers. Scabby, Curly, and Two Bulls were injured. Scabby died of his wounds two days later. Grinnell, *Fighting Cheyennes*, 365.

107. Wheeler, *Buffalo Days*, 136.

108. Greene, *Lakota and Cheyenne*, 114. For excellent accounts of the battle from the Cheyennes' perspective, see Grinnell, *Fighting Cheyennes*, 359–82, and Liberty and Stands In Timber, *Cheyenne Memories*, 214–19.

109. *New York Herald*, December 11, 1876.

110. In 1879 Little Bear accompanied a small group of Pawnee hunters on a buffalo hunt in Indian Territory. During this expedition he mentioned his service in the scouts to an officer of a small army detachment that escorted the group. Clark, "Pawnee Buffalo Hunt," 390.

111. Buecker, "Journals of James S. McClellan," 29. In a letter to Robert Bruce, McClellan later wrote, "I still remember that the Pawnee had a wide grin on his face at the thought of outwitting me in the matter of the coup." "Pawnee Trails and Trailers," March 1930, 20. McClellan later returned to the place where he had killed the Cheyenne and found one of the white scouts scalping the Indian. Obviously, scalping was not merely an Indian custom. Perhaps the white scout took the scalp as a morbid souvenir or to trade it to Indians for other valuables. Luther North, however, in a letter to Bruce on March 24, 1930, emphatically denied

McClellan's report that the Pawnees mutilated bodies, except for the taking of scalps. He called McClellan a "Lyar" and even expressed doubt that McClellan was present during the fight. "Things like this make me pretty mad. I wouldn't believe this man under oath. you must see he is lying when he says [in his account] that the Crow [Indians] were there. you can quote me as you like." Robert Bruce Papers, Box 1, Folder 4.

112. Danker, *Man of the Plains*, 215–16; *New York Herald*, December 1 and 11, 1876. Greene wrote that the Shoshone scout had been shot by the Pawnees. Greene, *Morning Star Dawn*, 157.

113. Grinnell, *Fighting Cheyennes*, 367.

114. Danker, *Man of the Plains*, 216–17.

115. Frank North diary, n.p.

116. After a difficult, eleven-day march, the Cheyennes reached Crazy Horse's camp, where they were fed. Greene, *Lakota and Cheyenne*, 114.

117. Luther North, quoted in Danker, "North Brothers," 83.

118. In 1877 the Northern Cheyennes were removed to the Darlington Agency, Indian Territory, to live with the Southern Cheyennes. Unhappy with the conditions in Oklahoma and longing to return to the Powder River country, Chiefs Dull Knife and Little Wolf led their people on an exodus north. For a history of this epic journey see Monnet, *Tell Them We Are Going Home*.

119. Smith, *Sagebrush Soldier*, 77.

120. Bourke, *Mackenzie's Last Fight*, 39.

121. *New York Herald*, December 11, 1876; Wheeler, *Buffalo Days*, 144–45.

122. Bourke, *Mackenzie's Last Fight*, 35.

123. "Fighting Norths and Pawnee Scouts," April 1931, 17.

124. North to Grinnell, February 14, 1877, published in *Forest and Stream*, May 10, 1877, 212.

125. Green estimated about 120 Cheyenne casualties, of whom 40 were killed. Greene, *Morning Star Dawn*, 140.

126. The loss of the men, particularly Lieutenant McKinney, weighed heavily on Colonel Mackenzie, who believed the attack had been a great failure. The outcome of the battle, indeed, caused him deep emotional depression. It was one of the symptoms of his approaching insanity. Robinson, *Good Year to Die*, 301–303.

127. *New York Herald*, December 11, 1876; Greene, *Morning Star Dawn*, 115. Information on High Eagle's wound comes from Roger C. Echo-Hawk, personal communication, 25 April 2008, based on interviews conducted with High Eagle by Marion N. Tomblin around 1929.

128. *Army and Navy Journal*, December 2, 1876, 270.

129. In his diary, Major North recorded that "the Gen. [Mackenzie's brevet rank] thinks we got enough [plunder] out of the village to make up for [the] loss in [our own] horses. The sioux [scouts] had a regular Knock down over their division.

the Gen. gave each of my fine men that were in scout an extra pony each and one to Peter [Headman] for one he had killed in the fight." The sources do not reveal exactly how the distribution of horses and other spoils took place. Undoubtedly, the distribution of the spoils followed a certain protocol, and North would have had to determine who would receive the most prized items. Obviously, those who were most deserving because of their particular contributions on the field of battle went first. In other instances, distribution might not have been so easy. North probably observed protocol by first honoring the most esteemed men in the battalion (chiefs, head soldiers, noncommissioned officers, etc.). Li Heris oo la shar ("Leading Chief," or Frank White), for example, received two horses, whereas most other scouts received only one. It appears that White received the extra horse because of his status as one of the leading men among the Pawnee scouts. The other Pawnees who received an extra horse were rewarded for exceptional bravery. Grinnell, *Two Great Scouts*, 275. According to William Garnett, the Sioux interpreter, Mackenzie gave first pick to the Sioux and Arapaho scouts who had discovered the village, next to the Sioux and Arapaho scouts who had captured the Cheyenne Indian a few days earlier, then to the Shoshone and Pawnee scouts who had been in the skirmish with the retreating Cheyennes, followed by Garnett and another group of Sioux scouts who had been sent back to Crook while the battle with the Cheyennes was going on. Finally, "one scout from each tribe was sent to take a horse." Jensen, *Indian Interviews*, 38.

130. "Pawnee Trails and Trailers," February 1930, 18–19; Luther North to Robert Bruce, December 4, 1929, Robert Bruce Papers, Box 1, Folder 1; Greene, *Morning Star Dawn*, 161. According to Grinnell, there were only three Cheyennes in the party that surprised the Pawnees. Two Moon (the younger), Yellow Eagle, and Turtle Road were the ones who recaptured the horses. Grinnell, *Fighting Cheyennes*, 381–82.

131. Bourke, *Mackenzie's Last Fight*, 42.

132. Walter R. Echo-Hawk, personal communication, December 20, 2004. Brummett Echohawk explained that the name really means "A Warrior Whose Deeds Are Echoed." Echohawk, "Pawnee Scouts," 12. Another free translation would be "Hawk, Whose Deeds They Are Echoing." According to Roger Echo-Hawk, the term "hawk" reflects the male aspiration to be successful in all endeavors of life, not just in warfare. Roger Echo-Hawk, *Children of the Seven Brothers*, 23–24.

133. Smith, *Sagebrush Soldier*, 93–94.

134. Richard Irving Dodge diary, November 30 and December 20, 1876, in Kime, *Powder River Journals*, 99, 133. In his published memoirs, Dodge described this event in more detail, but he exaggerated it somewhat to achieve a more dramatic effect. See Dodge, *Our Wild Indians*, 514–15. Dodge had met Frank White ten years earlier during some "scrapes" with the Sioux. See Dodge, *Plains of North America*, 326–27.

135. Nohl, "Mackenzie against Dull Knife."
136. Smith, *Sagebrush Soldier*, 94; Buecker, "Journals of James S. McClellan," 29.
137. James S. McClellan's reminiscences in "A Day with the 'Fighting Cheyennes,'" September 1930, 10.
138. Robinson, *Good Year to Die*, 302.
139. Danker, *Man of the Plains*, 218–19.
140. Robinson, *Good Year to Die*, 305–306; Greene, *Morning Star Dawn*, 166–74.
141. Luther North to Robert Bruce, March 24, 1930, Robert Bruce Papers, Box 1, Folder 4.
142. Frank North diary, entry for December 15 and 16, 1876. On Monday, December 18, North wrote in his diary: "The Indians had a big day today. first the Skeedes danced to the Chowes and got seven or eight horses. Then the Chowes went to the Arrapahoes and danced and got twelve horses. Ralph [Weeks] got 3 + Frank [White] 2."
143. Frank North diary, entry for December 24, 1876.
144. Kime, *Powder River Journals*, 133. In his memoir, Dodge described this event in more detail: "One day I was sitting in my tent when I heard the terrible war-whoop, accompanied by a rattling succession of shots, and, rushing out, I saw a long line of Indians in skirmishing order, advancing at a run over a hill to the Pawnee camp. I could see that the Pawnees, though in commotion, did not appear to be alarmed, and as there was no excitement at headquarters, I presumed the demonstration to be a ceremony of some kind. Getting my hat and overcoat, I made for the scene of action, but when I arrived the dance was already under full headway. The Sioux, the most cunning of all the Plains tribes, taking advantage of the near approach of separation, had determined to add another to the terrible blows they had in late years dealt the Pawnees by giving them a 'begging dance.' The Sioux were almost as numerous as the Pawnees, and the dance did not cease till every rascally dancer had hugged almost every individual Pawnee, and thus secured from him a liberal present. The head chief of the Pawnee, a great friend of mine, known as Frank [White, who was actually not a chief at all], but whose name I never could master, literally stripped himself, giving to the Sioux chief a war-bonnet and dress, for which to my knowledge, he had refused one hundred dollars. The unfortunate Pawnees were left almost in 'puris naturalibus.' The next day I met Frank, and remonstrated with him for his own and his people's foolishness in tamely submitting to be so swindled. He admitted everything, said he knew the Sioux had done it purposely, and from hostile feeling, but that it was the 'Indian road,' and that he and his people would have been disgraced among all the Indians, had they not given as they did. His only hope was that General Crook would delay his return march for a few days, in which case it was the intention of the Pawnees to give a return 'begging dance' to the Sioux, in the hope of at least getting some of their things back. He did not expect to get all back, for he said, 'The Sioux always were mean, stingy, cunning, and underhanded,

while the Pawnees are well known for their generosity and open-handedness.'" Dodge, *Our Wild Indians*, 368–69.

145. Danker, *Man of the Plains*, 224.
146. Bourke, *Mackenzie's Last Fight*, 48.
147. Greene, *Morning Star Dawn*, 182.
148. Frank North diary, entry for January 20, 1877.
149. Danker, *Man of the Plains*, 227.
150. Frank North diary, entry for January 21, 1877.
151. Buecker and Paul, "Pawnee Scouts," 19; Buecker, "Letters of Caroline Frey Winne," 32.
152. Bruce, *Fighting Norths*, 55. In a letter to Robert Bruce, Luther North wrote that the men had "quite a lot of fun and if McClellan got any glory out of it I am glad of it." He added that the battle "wasn't much like a real battle." North to Bruce, December 30, 1930, Robert Bruce Papers, Box 1, Folder 4.
153. *Sidney Telegraph*, March 10, 1877.
154. *Omaha Daily Republican*, March 10, 1877, 4; Thomas R. Buecker, curator, Fort Robinson Museum, Crawford, Nebraska, personal communication, July 2005.
155. Buecker, "Letters of Caroline Frey Winne," 30.
156. Gilbert, "Big Hawk Chief," 36–38.
157. Luther North to Robert Bruce, October 23, 1928, Robert Bruce Papers, Box 1, Folder 1.
158. Crook's original letter with instructions is in the Frank North Collection, Box 1, S1–F1.
159. Register of Enlistments, vol. 150, "1866–1873, Indian Scouts," n.p.
160. North to Sheridan, April 13, 1877, Frank North Collection, Box 1, S1–F1.
161. *Frank Leslie's Illustrated Magazine* published an illustration and a brief report on the Pawnee scouts in Sidney. "Some of these dark warriors present themselves on the platform [at Sidney Station], buried in blue army coats three sizes too large, with their long, shaggy hair blowing in their faces.... Now, nothing more alarming than a Pawnee Scout is to be seen. Glancing at one of these warriors, it is difficult to imagine them a kin race to the strong, fierce foes of eight years ago." Clipping furnished by Thomas R. Buecker, Fort Robinson Museum, Crawford, Nebraska.
162. Rush Roberts and Walking Sun affidavits in support of Echo Hawk's pension application, April 18, 1921, Echo Hawk Pension File, VA Records, Pension Application Files. See also Wichita Blaine's affidavit in support of his pension claim, May 22, 1919, a copy of which is in Walking Sun Pension File, VA Records, Pension Application Files.
163. *ARCIA*, 1877, 95–96.
164. Danker, *Man of the Plains*, 229–31.
165. Ibid., 231–32. Agent Charles H. Searing reported to Commissioner of Indian Affairs Hayt: "While the scouts were at Hays City, Kans. en route home, after

being mustered out, a white man, who erroneously thought one of them was trying to break into his store, shot at him several times, inflicting wounds from which he died in the post-hospital at Fort Hays. I am informed the civil authorities will investigate the case at the term of their court held in October. Meanwhile the man who shot him shot another man shortly after, and is now in jail for that offense, and will probably go to the penitentiary for it." *ARCIA*, 1877, 95–96.

166. *ARCIA*, 1877, 95–96.

167. Greene, *Morning Star Dawn*, 187; Nohl, "Mackenzie against Dull Knife," 92.

CHAPTER 8

1. Harry Coons was born in 1856. As a boy he attended school at the Pawnee Agency, and in 1876 he joined the scouts in Crook's winter campaign against the Sioux and Cheyennes. According to some reports, his health problems stemmed from the demanding marches during that campaign. "The Scout Harry Coons, who served with the Norths," Robert Bruce Papers, Box 2, Folder 10; Reeder, "Wolf Men," 350–51. For a history of the Dull Knife escape, see Monnet, *Tell Them We Are Going Home*. Shortly after Coons's death, *Forest and Stream* published a letter he had sent to the magazine in which he described a visit to the old Pawnee country in Nebraska in 1894. *Forest and Stream*, September 23, 1899, 244.

2. Grinnell, *Pawnee Hero Stories*, 70–73, 79–82.

3. *Columbus (Nebraska) Democrat*, March 21, 1885; *New York Times*, August 1, 1884, and March 16, 1885.

4. NEGenWeb Project, "Platte County, Nebraska Veterans: Indian, Mexican, Spanish-American and Peace-Time through 1969," www.rootsweb.com/~neplatte/miscwars.html.

5. NEGenWeb Project, "Platte County, Nebraska Civil Veterans," www.rootsweb.com/~neplatte/civil.html.

6. *New York Times*, July 14, 1897; *Los Angeles Times*, September 5, 1897; *Forest and Stream*, July 1896, 1.

7. U.S. Senate, "Resolution of the Legislature of Nebraska."

8. Kenneth Martin and Bob Morrison, "Civil War Veterans Buried in Nebraska," Nebraska State Historical Society, Lincoln, Nebraska. According to Danker, Matthews was born in 1831. Danker, *Man of the Plains*, 49. However, Matthews's headstone at the Columbus Cemetery gives 1832 as his year of birth.

9. Danker was uncertain about Morse's birthdate. Danker, *Man of the Plains*, 49. Morse's headstone at the Columbus Cemetery says he was born on September 6, 1839. George Lehman was born on January 6, 1848.

10. Danker, *Man of the Plains*, 50. According to Danker, Becher died in 1913. Becher's headstone at the Columbus Cemetery, however, gives 1918 as the year of his death.

11. Bruce, *Fighting Norths*, 40. Cushing's headstone spells his first name "Sylvenus."

12. Kasson, *Buffalo Bill's Wild West*, 168–70; Moses, *Wild West Shows*, 23; Shirley, *Pawnee Bill*; Blaine, *Some Things*, 168.

13. Parks, "Pawnee," 543; Lesser, *Pawnee Ghost Dance Hand Game*, 33–42; Blaine, *Some Things*, chapter 2.

14. Roger C. Echo-Hawk, personal communication, 25 April 2008.

15. Billy Osborne, Echo Hawk, Roam Chief, and Walking Sun Pension Files, VA Records, Pension Application Files; Roger C. Echo-Hawk, personal communication, 25 April 2008.

16. Leading Fox, John Buffalo, and Billy Osborne Pension Files, VA Records, Pension Application Files.

17. White Eagle, quoted in Blaine, *Some Things*, 44.

18. On another occasion, Echo Hawk and a few other Pawnees chased some white men who had stolen some horses and mules belonging to the Pawnees. They intercepted the horse thieves on the Cimarron River south of the Pawnee Agency, and a gun battle ensued in which the Pawnees were victorious. Echohawk, "Brummett Echohawk Tells the Pawnee Story," 19, 23.

19. Blaine, *Some Things*, 86–97.

20. Although many former scouts joined the movement, a few did not. Among these were the so-called mixed-bloods Baptiste Bayhylle and Harry Coons. Frank White publicly denounced these men and others for their criticism of the Ghost Dance and their adherence to the white man's churches. Lesser, *Ghost Dance Hand Game*, 62.

21. Blaine, *Some Things*, 59–60.

22. Lesser, *Ghost Dance Hand Game*, 82.

23. Dorsey, *Traditions of the Skidi Pawnee*; Dorsey, *Pawnee Mythology*; Dorsey and Murie, "The Pawnee"; Murie, *Ceremonies of the Pawnee*.

24. Weltfish, Pawnee Field Notes.

25. Simond Adams, Pawnee Agency, Individual Indian Agency Files, Oklahoma Historical Society, Oklahoma City (hereafter cited as "OHS").

26. Echo Hawk, Pawnee Agency, Individual Indian Agency Files, OHS.

27. Rush Roberts, Pawnee Agency, Individual Indian Agency Files, OHS.

28. Robert Taylor, Pawnee Agency, Individual Indian Agency Files, OHS.

29. John Buffalo, Pawnee Agency, Individual Indian Agency Files, OHS.

30. Blaine, *Some Things*, 49–50; John Box, Pawnee Agency, Individual Indian Agency Files, OHS.

31. Blaine, *Some Things*, 14.

32. Ibid., 149, 190–205.

33. Dorsey and Murie, "The Pawnee," n.p.

34. For a brief but good overview of Indian Wars pensions and veterans organizations and their struggles to obtain pensions, see Greene, *Indian War Veterans*, xv–xlii.

35. *El Reno (Oklahoma) News*, November 20, 1896.

36. In 1923 Box appealed to the Pension Office for an increase in his pension, stating that another scout by the name of La tah cots tah kah ("White Eagle," Box's brother) was receiving $72 per month. This time the Pension Office instructed special examiner N. H. Nicholson to travel to Pawnee, Oklahoma, and conduct interviews with Box and several other scouts to investigate the matter. Nicholson arrived in September 1923 and interviewed Box, Robert Taylor, High Eagle, Billy Osborne, and Leading Fox. Their testimonies provide important insights into the scouts' military service. Unfortunately, Box's testimony did not sway the Pension Office. In May 1925 the office informed Box's attorney that "this bureau is unable to afford him [Box] any further relief." It explained that La tah cots tah kah was entitled to $72 a month because he had served more than ninety days during the Civil War and required the "aid and assistance of another person." John Box Pension File, VA Records, Pension Application Files.

37. John Buffalo was one of the first of the scouts to apply for a pension. He filed his first claim in 1892 but never heard back from the Pension Office. He filed a new claim in June 1918, and this time it was approved with surprising speed. Buffalo, however, did not get to enjoy his modest pension of $20 per month for long. He died on February 10, 1920. John Buffalo Pension File, VA Records, Pension Application Files.

38. Walking Sun first applied for an invalid's pension in 1893 for ailments resulting from his service as a scout. His complaints were examined by Dr. L. G. Poe in April 1894. On the basis of Poe's findings and the fact that Walking Sun's name did not appear in the muster rolls, the Pension Office rejected the claim. In July 1918 Walking Sun applied again. His case dragged on until December 1919, when he accompanied John Box to meet with Acting Pension Commissioner E. C. Tieman. The commissioner accepted their statements and instructed his office to reexamine the case. In January 1920 Walking Sun's claim was approved, and a check for $690 was issued in his name. In 1923 Walking Sun filed yet another claim, this time for his services during the Red River war of 1874. Not surprisingly, this claim was rejected, on the grounds that he was already receiving a pension. In 1927, however, his pension was increased from $20 to $50 a month under the provisions of the Pension Act of March 3, 1927. Walking Sun Pension File, VA Records, Pension Application Files.

39. Billy Osborne first applied for an invalid's pension in 1893 for injuries sustained in the Summit Springs battle. The claim was rejected because there was no documentation of his injuries and a physician who examined him in 1895 found no evidence of an injury. A second application, filed in June 1918, this time for a regular pension, was initially rejected also but was approved in January 1920 after John Box's visit to the Pension Office. Billy Osborne Pension File, VA Records, Pension Application Files.

40. High Eagle applied for an invalid's pension in 1893 for injuries sustained during the Summit Springs battle. Although examination by a physician showed

severe injuries to his face and lungs, the claim was rejected for lack of documentation. In June 1918 he applied for a regular "survivor's pension." This claim was approved in January 1920, following John Box's visit to the Pension Office in 1919. High Eagle Pension File, VA Records, Pension Application Files.

41. Leading Fox first applied for a pension in July 1893, claiming that he suffered from "sore eyes" and "rheumatism from exposure while in line of his duty." The claim was rejected the next year because his Pawnee name was not on any of the muster rolls. In June 1918 he filed a new claim, but it was again rejected. Leading Fox's claim was reopened after John Box's testimony, but this time the Pension Office rejected his claim because the name he had given ("Red Fox") was identical to the name under which John Box had once served. Despite statements by Leading Fox and other scouts explaining that Leading Fox had adopted the name after John Box had taken another, the Pension Office refused to award his claim. However, it agreed to send special examiner N. H. Nicholson to conduct interviews to establish Leading Fox's correct identity. In October 1923 the Pension Office finally approved Leading Fox's claim and issued him a check for $1,580. Until his death on October 10, 1926, he received $20 per month. Leading Fox Pension File, VA Records, Pension Application Files.

42. On March 3, 1923, Riding In filed a pension application in Anadarko, Caddo County, Oklahoma. He claimed a pension based on his service in Lieutenant Richard H. Pratt's command during the Red River war in 1874. His claim was eventually awarded. At the time of his death on September 18, 1933, he was receiving a pension of $45 per month.

43. Echo Hawk also applied for a pension in June 1918, for his service in 1876. Unfortunately, he had never received his discharge papers, having been one of the scouts who fell behind after his horse had stampeded on the journey back. Several scouts filed affidavits in support of his claim, which was not accepted until April 1923. Echo Hawk Pension File, VA Records, Pension Application Files.

44. Eli Shotwell's first application for a pension, in September 1915, was rejected, but a second one, filed in July 1918, was approved. At the time of his death on October 1, 1922, Shotwell was receiving $20 a month. Eli Shotwell Pension File, VA Records, Pension Application Files.

45. Ruling His Sun Pension File, VA Records, Pension Application Files.

46. Walking Sun Pension File, VA Records, Pension Application Files.

47. Walters, *Talking Indian*, 153–54.

48. *Pawnee (Oklahoma) Courier-Dispatch and Times-Democrat*, October 4, 1928. See also Lillie, "Oklahoma Has Lost Oldest, Most Picturesque Character."

49. *New York Times*, October 4, 1928.

50. "Pawnee Trails and Trailers," July 1929, 5–6; Bruce, *Fighting Norths*, 63–64.

51. *Time*, March 24, 1958.

52. For a perceptive study of the effect of the "warrior ideal" on later Native American men and women serving in the U.S. armed forces, see Barsh, "War and the Reconfiguring of American Indian Society."

53. In November 1899 the citizens of Pawnee erected a monument at the site of Pollock's grave to memorialize his service as well as that of seven other Spanish-American War veterans from Pawnee. Theodore Roosevelt, who mentioned Pollock on several occasions in his war memoirs as well as in public, wrote after the funeral that Pollock "conferred honor by his conduct not only upon the Pawnee tribe, but on the American army and nation." Reeder, "Wolf Men," 367–71; Roosevelt, *Rough Riders;* Finney, "William Pollock."

54. Reeder, "Wolf Men," 371–72. See also Houston, "Oklahoma National Guard on the Mexican Border."

55. Pawnee Agency records, Roll PA 44, "Military Relations and Affairs," Indian Archives Division, Oklahoma Historical Society Microfilm Publications (Oklahoma City, 1978), frame 0048. For an excellent overview of the contributions of American Indians in World War I, see Britten, *American Indians in World War I.* See also Chastaine, *Story of the 36th,* and Wise, *Red Man in the New World Drama.*

56. Densmore, "Songs of Indian Soldiers during the World War." For a detailed discussion of the Pawnees' contributions during World War I, see Reeder, "Wolf Men," 372–80. Another dance was held in August 1920. The festivities included parades, speeches, and dances. During the parade, the old scouts were dressed in "war bonnets and bright blankets." Too old to ride horses, they joined the parade in automobiles. Among the speakers that day was scout Rush Roberts, who reminded the people that "the government had called upon the Pawnees to aid in quieting the other tribes and in helping to bring about peaceful relations between the Indians and whites." "Pawnee Dances Honor Indians Soldiers," *Daily Oklahoman* (Oklahoma City), August 20, 1920.

57. Echohawk, "Pawnee Scouts," 10.

58. Hale, "Uncle Sam's Warriors." For excellent histories of the Indian experience in World War II, see Bernstein, *American Indians and World War II,* and Townsend, *World War II and the American Indian.*

CHAPTER 9

1. According to Luther North, his brother received the name Skiri Tah Kah ("White Wolf") from the Chawis, making him nominally a member of that band. According to John Box, a Pawnee Indian, North received his name from the Skiris, which would have made him a member of the Skiri band. Major North himself never claimed membership in any particular band. The men in his command during the 1865 campaign gave him the name Pani Leshar ("Pawnee Chief"), a generic title indicating a position superordinate to the individual bands. Bruce, *Pawnee Naming Ceremonial,* 10.

2. Dunlay, *Wolves for the Blue Soldiers*, 151.

3. For an excellent discussion of European-Indian warfare as a cultural conflict, see Abler, "Scalping, Torture, Cannibalism, and Rape."

Bibliography

ARCHIVAL COLLECTIONS

American Indian Studies Research Institute, Indiana University, Bloomington
  Alexander Lesser Collection
  Gene Weltfish Collection
Bentley Library, University of Michigan, Ann Arbor
  Francis W. Dunn Papers
Denver Public Library, Denver, Colorado
  Don Rickey Jr. Collection
National Archives and Records Administration (NARA), Washington, D.C
  Compiled Service Records of Volunteer Union Soldiers in Organizations from the Territory of Nebraska, National Archives Microfilm Publications, M1787, Rolls 42 and 43
  Records of the Office Indian Affairs, Record Group 75
  Records of the Veterans Administration, Record Group 15.7.4, "Pension and Bounty Land Warrant Application Files": Adams, Simond; Blaine, Wichita; Box, John; Buffalo, John; Captain Jim; Coons, Harry; Echo Hawk; Fancy Eagle; Good Eagle; Hand, Alex; High Eagle; Hopkins, Robert; Leading Fox; Lel la hoo ris ah la shar; Osborne, Billy; Riding In, William; Roam Chief; Roberts, Rush; Ruling His Sun; Running Wolf; Shotwell, Eli; Taylor, Robert; Walking Sun; White, Frank
  Records Relating to Military Service, Record Group 94, Register of Enlistments in the United States Army, 1798–1914, vols. 150–51, Indian Scouts, 1866–77, Microfilm Publications M233, Rolls 70–71
  U.S. Department of War, Returns from U.S. Military Posts, 1800–1916, Microfilm 617, National Archives Microfilm Publications, 1965
    Fort Fetterman, Wyoming, July 1867–April 1882 (Roll 365)
    Fort Kearny, Nebraska, January 1861–May 1871 (Roll 565)
    Fort Laramie, Wyoming, January 1861–December 1876 (Roll 596)
    Fort McKinney, Wyoming, October 1876–December 1887 (Roll 703)

Fort McPherson, Nebraska, January 1866–December 1872 and January 1873–May 1880 (Rolls 708 and 709)
Fort Reno, Wyoming, September 1865–August 1868 (Roll 1002)
Fort Sedgwick, Colorado, November 1864–May 1871 (Roll 1144)
Sidney Barracks, Nebraska, October 1870–December 1881 (Roll 1171)

Nebraska State Historical Society, Lincoln, Nebraska
    Luther Hedden North Collection
    Major Frank J. North Collection
    RG 500, U.S. War Department Records, 1768–1947
    RG 503, Fort McPherson, Nebraska
    RG 505, Fort Kearny, Nebraska
    RG 518, Fort Sidney, Nebraska
    Ruby E. Wilson Collection
    Thomas O'Donnell manuscript

Newberry Library, Chicago, Illinois
    Elmo Scott Watson Papers

Oklahoma Historical Society, Oklahoma City
    Grant Foreman Collection
    Indian Pioneer History Collection
    Oklahoma WPA Oral History Interviews Collection
    Pawnee Agency, Individual Indian Agency Files

State Historical Society of North Dakota, Bismarck
    Charles Lemon Hall Collection

University of Tulsa, Oklahoma, Department of Special Collections, McFarlin Library
    Robert Bruce "Fighting Norths and Pawnee Scouts" Papers

Western History Collections, University of Oklahoma, Norman
    Alan W. Farley Collection
    Alice Marriott Collection
    Gordon W. Lillie ("Pawnee Bill") Papers
    Gordon W. Lillie Photograph Collection
    Indian War Veterans Collection
    Karl and Iva Schmitt Collection

NEWSPAPERS

The Answer (Pawnee, Oklahoma)
Army and Navy Journal (New York), 1864–77
Atoka Indian Citizen (Atoka, Oklahoma)
Atoka Vindicator (Atoka, Oklahoma)
Cheyenne Transporter (Oklahoma)
Chicago Tribune

Daily Oklahoman (Oklahoma City)
Edmond Sun-Democrat (Edmond, Oklahoma)
El Reno News (El Reno, Oklahoma)
Guthrie Daily Leader (Guthrie, Oklahoma)
Los Angeles Times
New York Evangelist
New York Times
New York Weekly Herald
Omaha Republican (Omaha, Nebraska)
Omaha Weekly (Omaha, Nebraska)
Omaha World-Herald (Omaha, Nebraska)
Pawnee Daily News (Pawnee, Oklahoma)
Pawnee Q County Republican (Pawnee, Oklahoma)
Pawnee Republican (Pawnee, Oklahoma)
Pawnee Scout (Pawnee, Oklahoma)
Platte County Times (Columbus, Nebraska)
Stillwater Gazette (Stillwater, Oklahoma)
St. Louis Democrat (St. Louis, Missouri)
Tulsa Daily World (Tulsa, Oklahoma)
Vinita Indian Chieftain (Vinita, Oklahoma)
Washington Post

BOOKS, ARTICLES, AND OTHER PUBLISHED AND UNPUBLISHED WORKS

Abler, Thomas S. "Scalping, Torture, Cannibalism, and Rape: An Ethnohistorical Analysis of Conflicting Cultural Values in War." *Anthropologica* 34, no. 1 (1992): 3–20.

"An Act to Increase and Fix the Military Peace Establishment of the United States." *United States Statutes at Large*, vol. 8, *Public Acts of the Thirty-ninth Congress, Session 1*, chapter 299. Washington, D.C.

Aldrich, J. J. "Diary of a Twenty Days' Sport." *Omaha (Nebraska) Weekly Herald*, August 19 and 26 and September 2, 1868.

Allen, Durwood L. "How Wolves Kill." *Natural History*, May 1979, 46–50.

Allis, Samuel. "Forty Years among the Indians and on the Eastern Borders of Nebraska." *Transactions and Reports of the Nebraska State Historical Society* 2 (1887): 133–66.

Anderson, Harry H., ed. *Indian Campaigns: Sketches of Cavalry Service in Arizona and on the Northern Plains, by Captain Charles King*. Fort Collins, Colo.: Old Army Press, 1984.

Annual Reports of the Commissioner of Indian Affairs. Washington, D.C.: Government Printing Office, 1860, 1862, 1864, 1871, and 1877.

Athearn, Robert G. "General Sherman and the Western Railroads." *Pacific Historical Review* 24, no. 1 (1955): 39–48.

———. *William Tecumseh Sherman and the Settlement of the West*. Norman: University of Oklahoma Press, 1995.

Bain, David H. *Empire Express: Building the First Transcontinental Railroad*. New York: Penguin Putnam, 1999.

Ball, Durwood. *Army Regulars on the Western Frontier, 1848–1861*. Norman: University of Oklahoma Press, 2001.

Barsh, Russell L. "War and the Reconfiguring of American Indian Society." *Journal of American Studies* 35, no. 3 (2001): 371–410.

Bassett, Samuel C. "The Sioux Pawnee War." *Nebraska History* 5, no. 2 (1922): 30.

Becher, Ronald. *Massacre along the Medicine Road: A Social History of the Indian War of 1864 in Nebraska Territory*. Caldwell, Idaho: Caxton Press, 1999.

Beck, Paul N. "Military Officers' Views of Indian Scouts 1865–1890." *Military History of the West* 23, no. 1 (1993): 1–19.

Belden, George P. *Belden, the White Chief; or, Twelve Years among the Wild Indians of the Plains*. Edited by General James S. Brisbin. Cincinnati, Ohio: C. F. Vent, 1871. Reprint, Athens: Ohio University Press, 1974.

Benson, Douglas S. *The Black Hills War: A History of the Conflict with Sioux Indians, 1876–1877*. Chicago: D. S. Benson, 1983.

Bernstein, Alison R. *American Indians and World War II: Toward a New Era in Indian Affairs*. Norman: University of Oklahoma Press, 1991.

Berthrong, Donald J. *The Southern Cheyennes*. Norman: University of Oklahoma Press, 1963.

Betts, Charles W. "The Yale Expedition of 1870." *Harper's New Monthly Magazine*, October 1871, 641–71.

Billington, Ray Allen, ed. *William Clayton's Journal: A Daily Record of the Journey of the Original Company of "Mormon" Pioneers from Nauvoo, Illinois, to the Valley of the Great Salt Lake*. New York: Arno Press, 1973.

Biolsi, Thomas. "Ecological and Cultural Factors in Plains Indian Warfare." In *Warfare, Culture, and Environment*, edited by R. Brian Ferguson, 141–68. Orlando, Fla.: Academic Press, 1984.

Blaine, Garland J., and Martha Royce Blaine. "Pa-re-su A-ri-ra-ke: The Hunters that Were Massacred." *Nebraska History* 58, no. 3 (1977): 342–58.

Blaine, Martha Royce. *Pawnee Passage, 1870–1875*. Norman: University of Oklahoma Press, 1990.

———. *Some Things Are Not Forgotten: A Pawnee Family Remembers*. Lincoln: University of Nebraska Press, 1997.

Boughter, Judith A. *The Pawnee Nation: An Annotated Research Bibliography*. Lanham, Md.: Scarecrow Press, 2004.

Bourke, John G. *Mackenzie's Last Fight with the Cheyennes: A Winter Campaign in Wyoming and Montana*. New York: Argonaut Press, 1966.

———. *On the Border with Crook*. Columbus, Ohio: Long's College Book Company, 1950.
Brady, Cyrus T., ed. *Indian Fights and Fighters*. Lincoln: University of Nebraska Press, 1971.
Brininstool, E. A. *Fighting Indian Warriors: True Tales of the Wild Frontiers*. Harrisburg, Pa.: Stackpole, 1953. Reprint, New York: Indian Head Books, 1995.
Britten, Thomas A. *American Indians in World War I: At Home and at War*. Albuquerque: University of New Mexico Press, 1997.
Broome, Jeff. *Dog Soldier Justice: The Ordeal of Susanna Alderice in the Kansas Indian War*. Lincoln, Kans.: Lincoln County Historical Society, 2003.
Bruce, Robert. *The Fighting Norths and Pawnee Scouts: Narratives and Reminiscences of Military Service on the Old Frontier*. New York: Privately published, 1932.
———. *Pawnee Naming Ceremonial: Near Pawnee Oklahoma, Armistice Day, November 11, 1932, the Naming of Wyo-La-Shar*. New York: Privately published, 1933.
Bryant, Keith L., Jr. "Entering the Global Economy." In *The Oxford History of the American West*, edited by Clyde A. Milner II, Carol A. O'Connor, and Martha A. Sandweiss, 213–24. New York: Oxford University Press, 1994.
Buecker, Thomas R., ed. "The Journals of James S. McClellan, 1st Sgt., Company H, 3rd Cavalry." *Annals of Wyoming* 57, no. 1 (1985): 21–34.
———, ed. "Letters of Caroline Frey Winne from Sidney Barracks and Fort McPherson, Nebraska, 1874–1878." *Nebraska History* 62, no. 1 (1981): 1–46.
———, and R. Eli Paul. "The Pawnee Scouts: Auxiliary Troops in the U.S. Cavalry, 1864–1877." *Military Images* 7, no. 1 (1985): 16–19.
Burnett, Fincelius G. "History of the Western Division of the Powder River Expedition." *Annals of Wyoming* 8, no. 3 (1932): 569–79. Reprinted as "Fincelius G. Burnett with the Connor Expedition" in *Powder River Campaigns and Sawyers Expedition of 1865: A Documentary Account Comprising Official Reports, Diaries, Contemporary Newspaper Accounts, and Personal Narratives*, edited by LeRoy R. Hafen and Ann W. Hafen. Glendale, Calif.: Arthur H. Clark, 1961.
Burnham, Philip. "Unlikely Recruits: Indians Scouting for America." *MHQ: Quarterly Journal of Military History* 11, no. 3 (1999): 78–85.
Calloway, Colin G. "Army Allies or Tribal Survival? The 'Other Indians' in the 1876 Campaign." In *Legacy: New Perspectives on the Battle of the Little Bighorn*, edited by Charles E. Rankin, 63–81. Helena, Mont.: Montana Historical Society Press, 1996.
———. "The Inter-Tribal Balance of Power on the Great Plains, 1760–1850." *Journal of American Studies* 16, no. 1 (1982): 25–47.
Carbyn, Lu N. *The Buffalo Wolf: Predators, Prey, and the Politics of Nature*. Washington, D.C.: Smithsonian Books, 2003.
———, S. M. Oosenbrug, and D. W. Arrions. *Wolves, Bison . . . and the Dynamics Related to the Peace-Athabasca Delta in Canada's Wood Buffalo National Park*. Edmonton: University of Alberta, 1993.

Chalfant, William Y. *Cheyennes and Horse Soldiers: The 1857 Expedition and the Battle of Solomon's Fork.* Norman: University of Oklahoma Press, 1989.

Chamberlain, Von D. *When Stars Came Down to Earth: Cosmology of the Skidi Pawnee Indians of North America.* Los Altos, Calif.: Ballena Press, 1982.

Chastaine, Ben H. *Story of the 36th: The Experiences of the 36th Division in the World War.* Oklahoma City, Okla.: n.p., 1920.

Cheney, Roberta C. *Sioux Winter Count: A 131-Year Calendar of Events.* Happy Camp, Calif.: Naturegraph, 1998.

Chittenden, Hiram M., and Alfred Talbot Richardson, eds. *Life, Letters and Travels of Father Pierre-Jean DeSmet, S.J., 1801–1873.* 4 vols. New York: Klaus Reprint, 1969.

Chronister, Allen. "Pawnee Men, Late 1860s and Early 1870s." *Whispering Wind* 35, no. 4 (2006): 20–24.

Clark, Joseph S. "A Pawnee Buffalo Hunt." *Chronicles of Oklahoma* 20, no. 4 (1942): 387–95.

Clark, William Philo. *The Indian Sign Language.* Lincoln: University of Nebraska Press, 1982.

Clausewitz, Carl von. *On War.* Edited and translated by Michael Howard and Peter Paret, with a commentary by Bernard Brodie. Princeton, N.J.: Princeton University Press, 1984.

Clendenen, Clarence C. *Blood on the Border: The United States Army and the Mexican Irregulars.* New York: Macmillan, 1969.

Cody, William F. *An Autobiography of Buffalo Bill.* New York: Farrar and Rinehart, 1920.

Cohen, Lucy Kramer. "Even in Those Days Pictures Were Important." *Indians at Work* 9, no. 5 (January 1942): 18–21; 9, no. 6 (February 1942), 30–31; 9, no. 7 (March 1942), 29–30.

Coleman, Winfield. "Blinded by the Sun: Shamanism and Warfare in the Little Shield Ledger." *European Review of Native American Studies* 18, no. 1 (2004): 31–39.

Comba, Enrico. "Wolf Warriors and Dog Feasts: Animal Metaphors in Plains Military Societies." *European Review of Native American Studies* 5, no. 2 (1991): 41–48.

Cooke, Philip St. George. *Scenes and Adventures in the Army, or, Romance of Military Life.* Philadelphia: Lindsay and Blakiston, 1857. Reprint, New York: Arno Press, 1973.

Curtis, Edward S. "High Hawk's Winter Count." In *The North American Indian,* vol. 3, by Edward S. Curtis, 159–82. Edited by Frederick Webb Hodge. New York: Johnson Reprint, 1970.

Czaplewski, Russ. *Captive of the Cheyenne: The Story of Nancy Jane Morton and the Plum Creek Massacre.* Kearney, Neb.: Baby Biplane Books, 1994.

Danker, Donald F., ed. "Journal of an Indian Fighter, 1869: Diary of Frank J. North." *Nebraska History* 39, no. 2 (1958): 87–177.

———, ed. *Man of the Plains: Recollections of Luther North, 1856–1882*. Lincoln: University of Nebraska Press, 1961.

———. "The North Brothers and the Pawnee Scouts." In *The Nebraska Indian Wars Reader, 1865–1877*, edited by R. Eli Paul, 73–87. Lincoln: University of Nebraska Press, 1998. Originally published in *Nebraska History* 42 (September 1961): 161–78.

David, Robert B. *Finn Burnett, Frontiersman: The Life and Adventures of an Indian Fighter, Mail Coach Driver, Miner, Pioneer Cattleman, Participant in the Powder River Expedition, Survivor of the Hay Field Fight, Associate of Jim Bridger and Chief Washakie*. Glendale, Calif.: Arthur H. Clark, 1937.

"A Day with the 'Fighting Cheyennes.'" *Motor Travel*, April 1930–February 1931.

Densmore, Frances. "Communication with the Dead as Practised by the American Indians." *Man* 50 (April 1950): 40–41.

———. *Pawnee Music*. Washington, D.C.: Government Printing Office, 1929.

———. "The Songs of Indian Soldiers during the World War." *Musical Quarterly* 20 (October 1934): 419–25.

Dodge, Grenville M. *The Battle of Atlanta and Other Campaigns*. Council Bluffs, Iowa: Monarch Printing, 1911. Reprint, Denver, Colo.: Sage Books, 1965.

———. *How We Built the Union Pacific Railway and Other Railway Papers and Addresses*. Denver, Colo.: Sage Books, 1965.

Dodge, Henry. "Report on the Expedition of Dragoons, under Colonel Henry Dodge, to the Rocky Mountains in 1835." In *American State Papers: Military Affairs* 6: 130–46. Washington, D.C.: Government Printing Office, 1861. Reprint, Buffalo, N.Y.: William S. Hein, 1998.

Dodge, Richard Irving. *The Plains of the Great West and Their Inhabitants: Being a Description of the Plains, Game, Indians, &c. of the Great North American Desert*. Edited by Wayne R. Kime. New York: G. P. Putnam's Sons, 1877. Reprinted under the title *The Plains of North America and Their Inhabitants*. Newark: University of Delaware Press, 1989.

Dodge, Richard Irving. *Our Wild Indians: Thirty-Three Years' Personal Experience among the Red Men of the Great West*. Hartford, Conn.: A. D. Worthington, 1883.

Dorsey, George A. "How the Pawnee Captured the Cheyenne Medicine Arrows." *American Anthropologist* 5, no. 4 (1903): 644–58.

———. *The Pawnee Mythology*. Lincoln: University of Nebraska Press, 1997.

———. "A Pawnee Personal Medicine Shrine." *American Anthropologist* 7, no. 3 (1905): 496–98.

———. "The Skidi Rite of Human Sacrifice." *Proceedings of the 15th International Congress of Americanists*, part 2 (1906): 65–70.

———. *Traditions of the Skidi Pawnee*. New York: Kraus Reprint, 1969.

———, and James R. Murie. "The Pawnee: Society and Religion of the Skidi Pawnee." Unpublished manuscript, Field Museum Library Archives, Chicago, Illinois, n.d. Copy at the American Indian Studies Research Institute, Indiana University, Bloomington.

Downey, Fairfax, and Jacques Noel Jacobson Jr. *The Red Bluecoats: The Indian Scouts, U.S. Army*. Fort Collins, Colo.: Old Army Press, 1973.

Duke, Philip, ed. "The Morning Star Ceremony of the Skiri Pawnee as Described by Alfred C. Haddon." *Plains Anthropologist* 34, no. 125 (1989): 103–203.

Dunbar, John Brown. "The Pawnee Indians." *Magazine of American History* 4 (April 1880): 241–81; 5 (November 1880): 320–45; and 8 (1882): 734–56.

Dunlay, Thomas W. *Wolves for the Blue Soldiers: Indian Scouts and Auxiliaries with the United States Army, 1860–1890*. Lincoln: University of Nebraska Press, 1982.

Echohawk, Brummett. "Brummett Echohawk Tells the Pawnee Story: Indian Artist Recounts Tribal History from Time of Earth Lodges to That of Boarding Schools and Itchy Uniforms." *Westerners Brand Book* 14, no. 3 (1957): 17–19, 22–23.

———. "Pawnee Scouts." *Oklahoma Today* 27 (1977): 9–12.

Echo-Hawk, Roger C. "Children of the Seven Brothers: Two Centuries of Echo Hawk Family History." Manuscript. 1998.

———. "Pawnee Mortuary Traditions." *American Indian Culture and Research Journal* 16 (1992): 77–99.

Ewers, John C. *The Horse in Blackfoot Indian Culture: With Comparative Material from Other Western Tribes*. Bulletin of the Bureau of American Ethnology 159. Washington, D.C.: Smithsonian Institution.

———. "Intertribal Warfare as the Precursor of Indian-White Warfare on the Northern Great Plains." In *Plains Indian History and Culture: Essays on Continuity and Change*, by John C. Ewers, 166–79. Norman: University of Oklahoma Press, 1997.

———. *Plains Indian History and Culture: Essays on Continuity and Change*. Norman: University of Oklahoma Press, 1997.

Ferguson, R. Brian, and Leslie E. Farragher, eds. *The Anthropology of War: A Bibliography*. New York: Guggenheim Foundation, 1988.

"The Fighting Norths and Pawnee Scouts." *Motor Travel*, March–December 1931.

Filipiak, Jack D. "The Battle of Summit Springs." *Colorado Magazine* 41 (1964): 343–54.

Finney, Frank F. "William Pollock: Pawnee Indian, Artist and Rough Rider." *Chronicles of Oklahoma* 33, no. 4 (1955): 509–11.

Fisher, John R. "The Royall and Duncan Pursuits: Aftermath of the Battle of Summit Springs, 1869." *Nebraska History* 50, no. 3 (Fall 1969): 292–308.

Flavius Vegetius Renatus. "The Military Institutions of the Romans." In *Roots of Strategy: The 5 Greatest Military Classics of All Time*, edited by Thomas R. Phillips, 65–175. New York: MJF Books, n.d.

Fletcher, Alice C. "Giving Thanks: A Pawnee Ceremony." *Journal of American Folk-Lore* 13, no. 51 (1900): 261–66.

———. *The Hako: Song, Pipe, and Unity in a Pawnee Calumet Ceremony*. Lincoln: University of Nebraska Press, 1996.

———. "A Pawnee Ritual Used When Changing a Man's Name." *American Anthropologist* 1, no. 1 (1899): 82–97.
———. "Pawnee Star Lore." *Journal of American Folk-Lore* 16, no. 60 (1903): 10–15.
———. "Star Cult among the Pawnee: A Preliminary Report." *American Anthropologist* 4, no. 4 (1902): 730–36.
Flores, Dan. "Bison Ecology and Bison Diplomacy: The Southern Plains from 1800 to 1850." *Journal of American History* 78, no. 2 (1991): 465–85.
Frazer, Robert W. *Forts of the West: Military Forts and Presidios and Posts Commonly Called Forts West of the Mississippi River to 1898.* Norman: University of Oklahoma Press, 1988.
Garavaglia, Louis A., and Charles G. Worman. *Firearms of the American West, 1866–1894.* Niwot, Colo.: University Press of Colorado, 1997.
Gates, John M. "Indians and Insurrectos: The U.S. Army's Experience with Insurgency." *Parameters: Journal of the U.S. Army War College* 8, no. 1 (1983): 59–68.
Gilbert, Bill. "Big Hawk Chief, a Pawnee Runner: Was He the Fastest Man in the World?" *American West* 21, no. 4 (1984): 36–38.
Gilmore, Melvin R. *Uses of Plants by the Indians of the Missouri River Region: Enlarged Edition with New Illustrations by Bellamy Parks Jansen.* Lincoln: University of Nebraska Press, 1991.
Gray, John S. *Centennial Campaign: The Sioux War of 1876.* Fort Collins, Colo.: Old Army Press, 1976.
———. *Custer's Last Campaign: Mitch Boyer and the Little Bighorn Reconstructed.* Lincoln: University of Nebraska Press, 1991.
Greene, Jerome A., ed. *Battles and Skirmishes of the Great Sioux War, 1876–1877: The Military View.* Norman: University of Oklahoma Press, 1993.
———. *Indian War Veterans: Memories of Army Life and Campaigns in the West, 1864–1898.* New York: Savas Beatie, 2007.
———, ed. *Lakota and Cheyenne: Indian Views of the Great Sioux War, 1876–1877.* Norman: University of Oklahoma Press, 1994.
———. *Morning Star Dawn: The Powder River Expedition and the Northern Cheyennes, 1876.* Norman: University of Oklahoma Press, 2003.
———. "The Surrounding of Red Cloud and Red Leaf, 1876: A Preemptive Maneuver of the Great Sioux War." *Nebraska History* 82, no. 2 (2001): 69–70.
———. *Washita: The U.S. Army and the Southern Cheyennes, 1867–1869.* Norman: University of Oklahoma Press, 2004.
Gregg, Josiah. *Commerce of the Prairies, or, The Journal of a Santa Fe? trader: During Eight Expeditions across the Great Western Prairies, and a Residence of Nearly Nine Years in Northern Mexico.* New York: H. G. Langley, 1844. Reprinted as vol. 20 of *Early Western Travels, 1748–1846,* edited by Reuben Gold Thwaites. Cleveland, Ohio: Arthur H. Clark, 1905.
Grenier, John. *The First Way of War: American War Making on the Frontier.* New York: Cambridge University Press, 2005.

Grinnell, George Bird [writing as "Ornis"]. "Buffalo Hunt with the Pawnees." *Forest and Stream*, December 25, 1873, 1–2.

———. *The Cheyenne Indians: Their History and Ways of Life*. New York: Cooper Square Publishers, 1962.

———. "Coup and Scalp among the Plains Indians." *American Anthropologist* 12, no. 2 (1910): 296–310.

———. *The Fighting Cheyennes*. Norman: University of Oklahoma Press, 1977.

———. "Marriage among the Pawnees." *American Anthropologist* 4, no. 3 (July 1891): 275–81.

———. "An Old-Time Bone Hunt." *Natural History* 23 (1923): 329–36.

———. *Pawnee, Blackfoot and Cheyenne: History and Folklore of the Plains from the Writings of George Bird Grinnell*. Selected and with an introduction by Dee Brown. New York: Charles Scribner's Sons, 1961.

———. *Pawnee Hero Stories and Folk-Tales: With Notes on the Origin, Customs and Character of the Pawnee People*. Lincoln: University of Nebraska Press, 1961.

———. "Pawnee Mythology." *Journal of American Folk-Lore* 6, no. 21 (1893): 113–30.

———. "A Pawnee Star Myth." *Journal of American Folk-Lore* 7, no. 26 (1894): 197–200.

———. *The Story of the Indian*. New York: D. Appleton, 1908.

———. *Two Great Scouts and Their Pawnee Battalion: The Experiences of Frank J. North and Luther H. North, Pioneers in the Great West, 1856–1882, and Their Defence of the Building of the Union Pacific Railroad*. Cleveland, Ohio: Arthur H. Clark, 1928. Reprint, Lincoln: University of Nebraska Press, 1973.

———. "Two Pawnian Tribal Names." *American Anthropologist* 4, no. 2 (April 1891): 197–99.

———. "The Young Dog's Dance." *Journal of American Folk-Lore* 4, no. 15 (1891): 307–13.

Hafen, LeRoy R., and Ann W. Hafen, eds. *The Diaries of William Henry Jackson: Frontier Photographer*. Glendale, Calif.: Arthur H. Clark, 1959.

———, eds. *Powder River Campaigns and Sawyers Expedition of 1865: A Documentary Account Comprising Official Reports, Diaries, Contemporary Newspaper Accounts, and Personal Narratives*. Glendale, Calif.: Arthur H. Clark, 1961.

Halaas, David F., and Andrew E. Masich. "The Cheyenne Dog Soldier Ledger Book: The Rope that Ties Memory to Truth." In *People of the Buffalo*, vol. 1, *The Plains Indians of North America: Military Art, Warfare and Change. Essays in Honor of John C. Ewers*, edited by Colin F. Taylor and Hugh A. Dempsey, 83–96. Wyk auf Foehr, Germany: Tatanka Press, 2003.

Hale, Duane K. "Uncle Sam's Warriors: American Indians in World War II." *Chronicles of Oklahoma* 69, no. 4 (1991–92): 408–29.

Haley, James L. *The Buffalo War: The History of the Red River Indian Uprising in 1874*. Norman: University of Oklahoma Press, 1985.

Hall, Edith Thompson. "The Last Great Buffalo Hunt." *Chicago Tribune*, April 11, 1965.
Hampton, H. D. "The Powder River Expedition 1865." *Montana: The Magazine of History* 14, no. 4 (1964): 2-15.
Hauptman, Laurence M. *Between Two Fires: American Indians in the Civil War.* New York: Free Press, 1996.
Hazen, Rueben W. *History of the Pawnee Indians.* Fremont, Neb.: Fremont Tribune, 1893.
Heape, Roger Kent. "Pawnee-United States Relations from 1803 to 1875." Ph.D. dissertation, St. Louis University, Missouri, 1982.
Hebart, Grace Raymond, and E. A. Brininstool. *The Bozeman Trail: Historical Accounts of the Blazing of the Overland Routes into the Northwest, and the Fights with Red Cloud's Warriors.* Cleveland, Ohio: Arthur H. Clark, 1922.
Hedren, Paul L. *Fort Laramie and the Great Sioux War.* Norman: University of Oklahoma Press, 1988.
Hewett, Janet B., ed. *Supplement to the Official Records of the Union and Confederate Armies.* Wilmington, N.C.: Broadfoot Publishing, 1996.
Higginbotham, N. A. "The Wind-Roan Bear Winter Count." *Plains Anthropologist* 26, no. 91 (1981): 1-42.
Hirshson, Stanley P. *Grenville M. Dodge: Soldier, Politician, Railroad Engineer.* Bloomington: Indiana University Press, 1967.
Hoebel, E. Adamson. *The Cheyennes: Indians of the Great Plains.* New York: Holt, 1960.
Hoig, Stan. *The Sand Creek Massacre.* Norman: University of Oklahoma Press, 1961.
Holder, Preston. *The Hoe and the Horse on the Plains: A Study of Cultural Development among North American Indians.* Lincoln: University of Nebraska Press, 1991.
Holliday, George H. *On the Plains in '65.* N.p., 1883.
Holmes, Louis A. *Fort McPherson, Nebraska: Guardian of the Tracks and Trails.* Lincoln, Neb.: Johnsen Publishing, 1963.
Houston, Donald E. "The Oklahoma National Guard on the Mexican Border, 1916." *Chronicles of Oklahoma* 53, no. 4 (1975-76): 447-62.
Humfreville, J. Lee. *Twenty Years among Our Savage Indians.* Hartford, Conn.: Hartford Publishing Company, 1897.
Hutton, Paul A. *Phil Sheridan and His Army.* Norman: University of Oklahoma Press, 1999.
Hyde, George E., ed. *Life of George Bent Written from His Letters.* Norman: University of Oklahoma Press, 1967.
―――. *The Pawnee Indians.* Norman: University of Oklahoma Press, 1974.
Hynes, William Francis. *Soldiers of the Frontier.* Denver, Colo.: N.p., 1943.
"Interview with Luther H. North, April 21, 1917, Regarding the Battle of Summit Springs." In *Camp on Custer: Transcribing the Custer Myth*, edited by Bruce R. Liddic and Paul Harbaugh, 163-82. Spokane, Wash.: Arthur H. Clark, 1995.

"Interview of Mr. F. G. Burnett, Veteran Indian Fighter of Lander, Wyoming, by Mrs. T. S. Taliaferro, Jr., at Rock Springs, Wyoming, on July Seventh, 1931." Manuscript copy, Albertson's Library, Boise State University, Boise, Idaho.

Irving, John Treat. *Indian Sketches, Taken during an Expedition to the Pawnee Tribes*. Edited by John Francis McDermott. Norman: University of Oklahoma Press, 1955.

Irving, Washington. *A Tour on the Prairies*. Edited by John Francis McDermott. Norman: University of Oklahoma Press, 1956.

Jablow, Joseph. *The Cheyenne in Plains Indian Trade Relations, 1795–1840*. Lincoln: University of Nebraska Press, 1994.

Jackson, Donald D. *Custer's Gold: The United States Cavalry Expedition of 1874*. New Haven, Conn.: Yale University Press, 1966. Reprint, Lincoln: University of Nebraska Press, 1972.

Jackson, William H. *Descriptive Catalogue of Photographs of North American Indians*. Washington, D.C.: Government Printing Office, 1877.

Jacobson, Jacques Noel, Jr. "The Uniform of the Indian Scouts." *Military Collector and Historian* 26, no. 3 (1974): 137–44.

Jacques, E. P. "Reminiscences of Major North." *Forest and Stream*, July 31, 1897, 82–83.

James, Edwin. *Account of an Expedition from Pittsburgh to the Rocky Mountains, Performed in the Years 1819 and '20*, vol. 1. Philadelphia: H. C. Carey and I. Lea, 1823.

———. *James's Account of S. H. Long's Expedition, 1819–1820*. Reprinted as vol. 15 of *Early Western Travels, 1748–1846*, edited by Reuben Gold Thwaites. Cleveland, Ohio: Arthur H. Clark, 1905.

Jensen, Richard E., ed. *The Indian Interviews of Eli S. Ricker, 1903–1919*. Lincoln: University of Nebraska Press, 2005.

———, ed. *The Settler and Soldier Interviews of Eli S. Ricker, 1903–1919*. Lincoln: University of Nebraska Press, 2005.

Jones, David E. *Poison Arrows: North American Indian Hunting and Warfare*. Austin: University of Texas Press, 2007.

Jones, Dorothy V. "John Dougherty and the Pawnee Rite of Human Sacrifice: April 1827." *Missouri Historical Review* 63, no. 3 (1969): 293–316.

Kane, Lucille M., ed. and trans. *Military Life in Dakota: The Journal of Philippe Regis de Trobriand*. St. Paul, Minn.: Alvord Memorial Commission, 1951.

Kappler, Charles J., comp. and ed. *Indian Affairs: Laws and Treaties*, vol. 2, *Treaties*. Washington, D.C.: Government Printing Office, 1904.

Karol, Joseph S., ed. *Red Horse Owner's Winter Count: The Oglala Sioux, 1786–1968*. Martin, S.D.: Booster Publishing, 1969.

Kasson, Joy S. *Buffalo Bill's Wild West: Celebrity, Memory, and Popular History*. New York: Hill and Wang, 2000.

Keenan, Jerry. *Encyclopedia of American Indian Wars, 1492–1890*. Santa Barbara, Calif.: ABC-CLIO, 1997.

Kime, Wayne R., ed. *The Powder River Expedition Journals of Colonel Richard Irving Dodge*. Norman: University of Oklahoma Press, 1997.
King, James T. "The Republican River Expedition, June–July, 1869." *Nebraska History* 41 (September 1960): 165–99, (December 1960): 281–97. Reprinted in *The Nebraska Indian Wars Reader, 1865–1877*, edited by R. Eli Paul, 31–70. Lincoln: University of Nebraska Press, 1998.
———. *War Eagle: A Life of General Eugene A. Carr*. Lincoln: University of Nebraska Press, 1963.
Lame, G. "Tuck-oo-wa-ter-oo." *The Ladies Repository: A Monthly Periodical, Devoted to Literature, Arts, and Religion* 2, no. 1 (1868): 25–27.
Lang, Theodore F. *Loyal West Virginia from 1861 to 1865*. Baltimore, Md.: Deutsch Publishing, 1895.
Leckie, William H. *The Buffalo Soldiers: A Narrative of the Negro Cavalry in the West*. Norman: University of Oklahoma Press, 1967.
Lesser, Alexander. "Cultural Significance of the Ghost Dance." *American Anthropologist* 35, no. 1 (1933): 108–15.
———. *The Pawnee Ghost Dance Hand Game: Ghost Dance Revival and Ethnic Identity*. Lincoln: University of Nebraska Press, 1996.
Liberty, Margot, and John Stands In Timber. *Cheyenne Memories*. New Haven, Conn.: Yale University Press, 1998 [1967].
Libby, Orin G. *The Arikara Narrative of Custer's Campaign and the Battle of the Little Bighorn*. Norman: University of Oklahoma Press, 1998.
Lillie, Gordon W. "Oklahoma Has Lost Oldest, Most Picturesque Character in Death of Pawnee Chief." In *Oklahoma Yesterday—Today—Tomorrow*, edited by Lerona R. Morris, 91–92. Guthrie, Okla.: Co-operative Publishing Company, 1930.
Linton, Ralph. "The Origin of the Skidi Pawnee Sacrifice to the Morning Star." *American Anthropologist* 28, no. 3 (1926): 457–66.
———. *The Sacrifice to the Morning Star by the Skidi Pawnee*. Chicago: Field Museum of Natural History, 1922.
Lopez, Barry H. *Of Wolves and Men*. New York: Charles Scribner's Sons, 1978.
Madson, Brigham D. *Glory Hunter: A Biography of Patrick Edward Connor*. Salt Lake City: University of Utah Press, 1990.
Malone, Patrick M. *The Skulking Way of War: Technology and Tactics among the New England Indians*. Baltimore, Md.: Johns Hopkins University Press, 1993.
Marquis, Thomas B. *Keep the Last Bullet for Yourself: The True Story of Custer's Last Stand*. Algonac, Mich.: Reference Publications, 1976.
Martin, Kenneth, and Bob Morrison. "Civil War Veterans Buried in Nebraska." Manuscript (list). Lincoln: Nebraska State Historical Society.
Mattes, Merrill J. *The Great Platte River Road: The Covered Wagon Mainline via Fort Kearny to Fort Laramie*. Nebraska State Historical Society Publications 25. Lincoln, 1969.

Maximilian, Prince of Wied. *Travels in the Interior of North America, 1832–1834*. Reprinted as vol. 22 of *Early Western Travels, 1748–1846*, edited by Reuben Gold Thwaites. Cleveland, Ohio: Arthur H. Clark, 1906.

McDermott, John D. *Circle of Fire: The Indian War of 1865*. Mechanicsburg, Penn.: Stackpole, 2003.

McReynolds, Robert. *Thirty Years on the Frontier*. Colorado Springs, Colo.: El Paso Publishing, 1906.

Mech, L. David. *The Wolf: The Ecology and Behavior of an Endangered Species*. Minneapolis: University of Minnesota Press, 1981.

"Military Reports on the Red Cloud–Red Leaf Surround." *Nebraska History* 15, no. 4 (1934): 291–95.

Mills, Anson B. *Big Horn Expedition: August 15 to September 30, 1874*. Independence Rock, Wyoming Territory: N.p., 1874.

——. *My Story*. Washington, D.C.: Self-published, 1918.

Milner, Clyde A., II. *With Good Intentions: Quaker Work among the Pawnees, Otos, and Omahas in the 1870s*. Lincoln: University of Nebraska Press, 1982.

Mishkin, Bernard. *Rank and Warfare among the Plains Indians*. New York: J. J. Augustin, 1940.

Monnet, John H. *Tell Them We Are Going Home: The Odyssey of the Northern Cheyennes*. Norman: University of Oklahoma Press, 2001.

Moses, L. G. *Wild West Shows and the Images of American Indians, 1883–1933*. Albuquerque: University of New Mexico Press, 1996.

Murie, James R. *Ceremonies of the Pawnee*. 2 vols. Edited by Douglas R. Parks. Washington, D.C.: Smithsonian Institution, 1981.

——. "Pawnee Indian Societies." *Anthropological Papers of the American Museum of Natural History* 11, part 7 (1914): 545–644. New York.

Murray, Charles Augustus. *Travels in North America during the Years 1834, 1835, 1836: Including a Summer Residence with the Pawnee Tribe of Indians and a Visit to Cuba and the Azore Islands*. London: Richard Bentley, 1839. Reprint, New York: Da Capo Press, 1974.

Newcomb, William W., Jr. "A Re-Examination of the Causes of Plains Warfare." *American Anthropologist* 52, no. 3 (1950): 317–30.

Nohl, Lessing H., Jr. "Mackenzie against Dull Knife: Breaking the Northern Cheyennes in 1876." In *Probing the American West: Papers from the Santa Fe Conference*, edited by K. Ross Toole et al., 86–92. Santa Fe: Museum of New Mexico Press, 1962.

"North Brothers Memorial Number." *Nebraska History* 15, no. 4 (1934): 258–314.

O'Donnell, Jeff. *Luther North, Frontier Scout*. Lincoln, Neb.: J. and L. Lee, 1995.

Oehler, Gottlieb F., and David Z. Smith. *Description of a Journey and a Visit to the Pawnee Indians*. Fairfield, Wash.: Ye Galleon Press, 1974.

Ordway, Edward. "Reminiscences." *Annals of Wyoming* 5, no. 4 (1929): 149–60.

Palmer, H. E. "History of the Powder River Expedition of 1865." In *Transactions and Reports of the Nebraska State Historical Society*, vol. 2, 197–229. Lincoln, Neb.: State Journal Company, 1887.

———. *The Powder River Indian Expedition, 1865*. Omaha, Neb.: Republican Company, 1887.

Parkman, Francis. *The Oregon Trail: Sketches of Prairie and Rocky Mountain Life*. New York: Modern Library, 1949.

Patrick, John R. *Report of John R. Patrick, Adjutant-General of Nebraska, to the Governor of the State of Nebraska, January 1, 1871*. Des Moines, Iowa: Mills and Company, 1871.

Pattie, James Ohio. *The Personal Narrative of James O. Pattie*. Reprinted as vol. 18 of *Early Western Travels, 1748–1846*, edited by Reuben Gold Thwaites. Cleveland, Ohio: Arthur H. Clark, 1905.

Paul, R. Eli, ed. *The Nebraska Indian Wars Reader, 1865–1877*. Lincoln: University of Nebraska Press, 1998.

Parks, Douglas R. "James Murie, Pawnee Ethnographer." In *American Indian Intellectuals of the Nineteenth and Early Twentieth Centuries*, edited by Margot Liberty, 86–104. Norman: University of Oklahoma Press, 2002.

———. "Pawnee." In *Handbook of North American Indians*, vol. 13, *Plains*, edited by Raymond J. DeMallie, 515–47. Washington, D.C.: Smithsonian Institution, 2001.

———, and Raymond J. DeMallie. "Plains Indian Warfare." In *The People of the Buffalo*, vol. 1, *The Plains Indians of North America: Military Art, Warfare and Change. Essays in Honor of John C. Ewers*, eds. Colin F. Taylor and Hugh A. Dempsey, 66–76. Wyck auf Foehr, Germany: Tatanka Press, 2004.

"Pawnee Trails and Trailers." *Motor Travel*, March 1929, 10–13; April 1929, 11–14; May 1929, 11–14; June 1929, 8–11; July 1929, 5–7; August 1929, 17–20; September 1929, 9–13; October 1929, 16–19; December 1929, 16–18; January 1930, 20–21; February 1930, 17–20; March 1930, 17–20.

Peck, Robert Morris. "Recollections of Early Times in Kansas Territory: From the Standpoint of a Regular Cavalryman." *Kansas Historical Society Collections* 8 (1903–1904): 484–507. Reprinted in *Relations with the Indians of the Plains, 1857–1861*, edited by LeRoy R. Hafen and Ann W. Hafen, 97–140. Glendale, Calif.: Arthur H. Clark, 1959.

Pelzer, Louis, ed. "Captain Ford's Journal of an Expedition to the Rocky Mountains." *Mississippi Valley Historical Review* 12, no. 4 (1926): 550–79.

Peters, Joseph P., comp. *Indian Battles and Skirmishes on the American Frontier, 1790–1898*. New York: Argonaut Press, 1966.

Pierce, Michael D. *The Most Promising Young Officer: A Life of Ranald Slidell Mackenzie*. Norman: University of Oklahoma Press, 1993.

Poole, D. C. *Among the Sioux of Dakota: Eighteen Months' Experience as an Indian Agent, 1869–70*. St. Paul: Minnesota Historical Society Press, 1988.

Pratt, Richard Henry. *Battlefield and Classroom: Four Decades with the American Indian*. New Haven, Conn.: Yale University Press, 1964.

———. "Some Indian Experiences." *Cavalry Journal* 16 (October 1905): 200–217.
Price, George F. *Across the Continent with the Fifth Cavalry.* New York: Antiquarian Press, 1959.
Prucha, Francis Paul. *A Guide to the Military Posts of the United States, 1789–1895.* Madison: State Historical Society of Wisconsin, 1964.
Reckmeyer, Clarence. "The Battle of Summit Springs." *Colorado Magazine* 6 (November 1929): 211–20.
Reeder, William S., Jr. "Wolf Men of the Plains: Pawnee Indian Warriors, Past and Present." Ph.D. dissertation, Kansas State University, 2001.
Reiger, John F., ed. *The Passing of the Great West: Selected Papers of George Bird Grinnell.* New York: Winchester Press, 1972.
Ricker, Eli S. "The Surround of Red Cloud and Red Leaf: Interview of William Garnett." *Nebraska History* 15, no. 4 (1934): 288–91. Reprinted in *The Nebraska Indian Wars Reader, 1865–1877*, edited by R. Eli Paul, 157–60. Lincoln: University of Nebraska Press, 1998.
Rickey, Don, Jr. *Forty Miles a Day on Beans and Hay: The Enlisted Soldier Fighting the Indian Wars.* Norman: University of Oklahoma Press, 1963.
Riding In, James T. "Keepers of Tirawahut's Covenant: The Development and Destruction of Pawnee Culture." Ph.D. dissertation, University of California, Los Angeles, 1991.
———. "Six Pawnee Crania: Historical and Contemporary Issues Associated with the Massacre and Decapitation of Pawnee Indians in 1869." *American Indian Culture and Research Journal* 16 (1992): 101–19.
———. "The United States v. Yellow Sun et al. (The Pawnee People): A Case Study of Institutional and Societal Racism and U.S. Justice in Nebraska from the 1850s to 1870s." *Wicazo Sa Review* 17, no. 1 (2002): 13–41.
Riley, Paul D. "The Battle of Massacre Canyon." *Nebraska History* 54, no. 2 (1973): 221–50.
———. "Dr. David Franklin Powell and Fort McPherson." *Nebraska History* 51, no. 2 (1970): 152–70.
Robarchek, Clayton A. "Plains Warfare and the Anthropology of War." In *Skeletal Biology in the Great Plains: Migration, Warfare, Health, and Subsistence*, eds. Douglas W. Owsley and Richard L. Jantz, 307–16. Washington, D.C.: Smithsonian Institution Press, 1994.
Robinson, Charles M., III. *Bad Hand: A Biography of General Ranald S. Mackenzie.* Austin, Tex.: State House Press, 1993.
———. *General Crook and the Western Frontier.* Norman: University of Oklahoma Press, 2001.
———. *A Good Year to Die: The Story of the Great Sioux War.* New York: Random House, 1995.
Rogers, Fred B. *Soldiers of the Overland.* San Francisco: Grabhorn Press, 1938.
Roosevelt, Theodore. *The Rough Riders.* New York: C. Scribner's Sons, 1899. Reprint, Dallas, Tex.: Taylor Publishing, 1997.

Ross, Sonja Brigitte. *Das Menschenopfer der Skidi-Pawnee.* Bonn, Germany: Holos Verlag, 1989.
Roster of Nebraska Volunteers from 1861-1869. Adjutant General's Office, State of Nebraska. Hastings, Neb.: Wigton and Evans, 1888.
Russell, Don, Jr. *The Lives and Legends of Buffalo Bill.* Norman: University of Oklahoma Press, 1960.
Saxe, Maurice de. "My Reveries upon the Art of War." In *Roots of Strategy: The 5 Greatest Military Classics of All Time,* edited by Thomas R. Phillips, 176-300. New York: MJF Books, n.d.
Schmitt, Martin F., ed. *General George Crook: His Autobiography.* Norman: University of Oklahoma Press, 1946.
Schneiders, Robert Kelly. *Big Sky Rivers: The Yellowstone and Upper Missouri.* Lawrence: University Press of Kansas, 2003.
Schuchert, Charles, and Clara Mae LeVene. *O. C. Marsh, Pioneer in Paleontology.* New Haven, Conn.: Yale University Press, 1940.
Secoy, Raymond F. *Changing Military Patterns on the Great Plains: 17th Century through Early 19th Century.* New York: J. J. Augustin, 1953. Reprint, Lincoln: University of Nebraska Press, 1992.
Seymour, Silas. *Incidents of a Trip through the Great Platte Valley, to the Rocky Mountains and Laramie Plains, in the Fall of 1866, with a Synoptical Statement of the Various Pacific Railroads, and an Account of the Great Union Pacific Railroad Excursion to the One Hundredth Meridian of Longitude.* New York: D. Van Nostrand, 1867.
———. *A Reminiscence of the Union Pacific Railroad, Containing Some Account of the Discovery of the Eastern Base of the Rocky Mountains and of the Great Indian Battle of July 11, 1867.* Quebec, Canada: A. Cote, 1873.
Sheldon, Addison E., ed. "Massacre Canyon Number: Last Inter-Tribal Indian Battle in America." *Nebraska History* 16, no. 3 (1935): 130-84.
———. "The North Brothers and the Pawnee Nation." *Nebraska History* 15, no. 4 (1935): 297-304.
Shirley, Glenn. *Pawnee Bill: A Biography of Major Gordon W. Lillie, White Chief of the Pawnees, Wild West Showman, Last of the Land Boomers.* Albuquerque: University of New Mexico Press, 1958. Reprint, Lincoln: University of Nebraska Press, 1965.
Simmons, Clyde R. "The Indian Wars and U.S. Military Thought, 1865-1890." *Parameters* 22, no. 1 (1992): 60-72.
Skelton, William B. "Army Officers' Attitudes toward Indians, 1830-1860." *Pacific Northwest Quarterly* 67, no. 3 (1976): 113-24.
Smith, Marian W. "The War Complex of the Plains Indians." *Proceedings of the American Philosophical Society* 78, no. 3 (1938): 425-60.
Smith, Sherry L. *Sagebrush Soldier: Private William Earl Smith's View of the Sioux War of 1876.* Norman: University of Oklahoma Press, 1989.
Smits, David D. "'Fighting Fire with Fire': The Frontier Army's Use of Indian Scouts and Allies in the TransMississippi Campaigns, 1860-1890." *American Indian Culture and Research Journal* 22 (1998): 73-116.

Sorenson, Alfred E. "Life of Major Frank North, the Famous Pawnee Scout." *Platte County (Nebraska) Times*, May 1896–January 1897.

———. "A Quarter of a Century on the Frontier, or, The Adventures of Major Frank North, the 'White Chief of the Pawnees.' The Story of His life as Told by Himself and Written by Alfred Sorenson." Manuscript, Nebraska State Historical Society, Lincoln, Nebraska, Frank North Collection, RG 2321 (formerly MS 0448), Box 1, S4–F1.

Speelman, Margaret. "The Last of His Line—A Pawnee." In *Oklahoma Yesterday—Today—Tomorrow*, edited by Lerona R. Morris, 95–97. Guthrie, OK: Co-operative Publishing Company, 1930.

Stanley, David S. *Personal Memoirs of Major-General D. S. Stanley, U.S.A.* Cambridge, Mass.: Harvard University Press, 1917.

Stanley, Henry M. *My Early Travels and Adventures in America and Africa.* London: Duckworth, 2001.

Starkey, Armstrong. *European and Native American Warfare, 1675–1815.* Norman: University of Oklahoma Press, 1998.

Steinhart, Peter. *The Company of Wolves.* New York: Alfred A. Knopf, 1995.

Sun Tzu. *The Art of War.* Translated and with an introduction by Samuel B. Griffith. New York: Oxford University Press, 1971.

Tate, Michael L. "Apache Scouts, Police, and Judges as Agents of Acculturation, 1865–1920." Ph.D. dissertation, University of Toledo, 1974.

———. "Indian Scouting Detachments in the Red River War, 1874–1875." *Red River Valley Historical Review* 3, no. 2 (1978): 202–26.

Taylor, Joe F., ed. *The Indian Campaign on the Staked Plains, 1874–1875: Military Correspondence from War Department Adjutant General's Office File 2815–1874.* Canyon, Tex.: Panhandle-Plains Historical Society, 1962.

Thurman, Melburn D. "A Case of Historical Mythology: The Skidi Pawnee Morning Star Sacrifice of 1833." *Plains Anthropologist* 15, no. 50, part 1 (1970): 309–11.

———. "The Skidi Pawnee Morning Star Sacrifice of 1827." *Nebraska History* 51, no. 3 (1970): 268–80.

———. "The Timing of the Skidi-Pawnee Morning Star Sacrifice." *Ethnohistory* 30, no. 3 (1983): 155–63.

Tomblin, Marion. "Years Take Their Toll of Pawnee Scouts." In *Oklahoma Yesterday—Today—Tomorrow*, edited by Lerona R. Morris, 132–36. Guthrie, OK: Co-operative Publishing Company, 1930.

Townsend, John K. *Narrative of a Journey across the Rocky Mountains.* Reprinted in *Early Western Travels, 1748–1846*, vol. 21, edited by Reuben Gold Thwaites, 113–369. Cleveland, Ohio: Arthur H. Clark, 1905.

Townsend, Kenneth W. *World War II and the American Indian.* Albuquerque: University of New Mexico Press, 2000.

Townshend, F. Trench. *Ten Thousand Miles of Travel, Sport, and Adventure.* London: Hurst and Blackett, 1869.

Turney-High, Harry H. *Primitive War: Its Practice and Concepts.* Columbia: University of South Carolina Press, 1949.

Unrau, William E., ed. *Tending the Talking Wire: A Buck Soldier's View of Indian Country, 1863–1866.* Salt Lake City: University of Utah Press, 1979.

U.S. Department of War. *The War of the Rebellion: A Compilation of the Official Records of the Union and Confederate Armies.* Washington, D.C.: Government Printing Office, 1880–1901.

U.S. Senate. "Resolution of the Legislature of Nebraska asking Relief for Captain James Murrie [sic]." Senate Miscellaneous Document 52, April 15, 1871, 42nd Congress, 1st Session (1871), Serial Set vol. 1467.

———, Committee on Veterans' Affairs. *Medal of Honor Recipients, 1863–1973: "In the Name of the Congress of the United States."* Washington, D.C.: Government Printing Office, 1973.

Utley, Robert M. *Frontier Regulars: The United States Army and the Indian, 1866–1891.* Lincoln: University of Nebraska Press, 1974.

———. *Frontiersmen in Blue: The United States Army and the Indian, 1848–1865.* New York: Macmillan, 1967.

———. *The Indian Frontier of the American West, 1846–1890.* Albuquerque: University of New Mexico Press, 1984.

van de Logt, Mark. "'The Powers of the Heavens Shall Eat of My Smoke': The Significance of Scalping in Pawnee Warfare." *Journal of Military History* 72, no. 1 (2008): 71–104.

Walters, Anna L. *Talking Indian: Reflections on Survival and Writing.* Ithaca, N.Y.: Firebrand Books, 1992.

Ware, Eugene F. *The Indian War of 1864, Being a Fragment of the Early History of Kansas, Nebraska, Colorado and Wyoming.* Topeka, Kans.: Crane, 1911. Reprint, Lincoln: University of Nebraska Press, 1994.

Watson, Elmo Scott. "The Battle of Summit Springs." *Chicago Westerners Brand Book* 7, no. 7 (1950): 49–51.

Webb, George W., comp. *Chronological List of Engagements between the Regular Army of the United States and Various Tribes of Hostile Indians which Occurred during the Years 1790 to 1898, Inclusive.* New York: AMS Press, 1976.

Wedel, Waldo R., ed. *The Dunbar-Allis Letters on the Pawnee.* New York: Garland, 1985.

Weigley, Russell F. *The American Way of War: A History of United States Military Strategy and Policy.* Bloomington: Indiana University Press, 1977.

Weingardt, Richard. *Sound the Charge: The Western Frontier, Spillman Creek to Summit Springs.* Englewood, Colo.: Jacqueline Enterprises, 1978.

Weltfish, Gene. *Caddoan Texts: Pawnee, South Band Dialect.* New York: G. E. Stechert, 1937.

———. *The Lost Universe: Pawnee Life and Culture.* Lincoln: University of Nebraska Press, 1977.

Werner, Fred H. *The Dull Knife Battle*. Greeley, Colo.: Werner Publications, 1981.
———. *The Summit Springs Battle, July 11, 1869*. Greeley, Colo.: Werner Publications, 1991.
West, Elliott. *The Contested Plains: Indians, Goldseekers, and the Rush to Colorado*. Lawrence: University Press of Kansas, 1998.
Wheeler, Homer W. *Buffalo Days: Forty Years in the Old West. The Personal Narrative of a Cattleman, Indian Fighter and Army Officer*. Indianapolis: Bobbs-Merrill, 1925.
White, Lonnie J. "Indian Raids on the Kansas Frontier, 1869." *Kansas Historical Quarterly* 38, no. 4 (1972): 369–88.
White, Richard. "The Cultural Landscape of the Pawnees." *Great Plains Quarterly* 2, no. 1 (1982): 31–40.
———. *The Roots of Dependency: Subsistence, Environment and Social Change among the Choctaws, Pawnees and Navajos*. Lincoln: University of Nebraska Press, 1983.
———. "The Winning of the West: The Expansion of the Western Sioux in the Eighteenth and Nineteenth Centuries." *Journal of American History* 65 (1978): 319–43.
Williamson, John W. *The Battle of Massacre Canyon: The Unfortunate Ending of the Last Buffalo Hunt of the Pawnees*. Trenton, Neb.: Republican Leader, 1922.
Wilson, Ruby E. *Frank J. North: Pawnee Scout Commander and Pioneer*. Athens, Ohio: Swallow Press, 1984.
Wise, Jennings C. *The Red Man in the New World Drama*. Washington, D.C.: N.p., 1931.
Wishart, David J. "The Death of Edward McMurtry." *Great Plains Quarterly* 19, no. 1 (1999): 5–21.
———. "The Dispossession of the Pawnee." *Annals of the Association of American Geographers* 69, no. 3 (1979): 382–401.
———. *An Unspeakable Sadness: The Dispossession of the Nebraska Indians*. Lincoln: University of Nebraska Press, 1994.
Wissler, Clark. *The American Indian*. New York: Oxford University Press, 1922.
———, and Herbert J. Spinden. "The Pawnee Human Sacrifice to the Morning Star." *American Museum Journal* 16 (1916): 48–55.
Wooster, Robert. *The Military and United States Indian Policy, 1865–1903*. New Haven, Conn.: Yale University Press, 1988.

Index

Page numbers in italics refer to illustrations.

Acculturation, 161–62, 241
Act Concerning the Employment of Indian Scouts (1876), 189, 296n7
Adams, Simond (Us sah kip pe di la shah—"Dog Chief"), 129, 192, 231, 232, 234, 251–52n31
Alcoholism, 161, 230
Alderice, Susanna, 119, 132
Aldrich, John J., 101, 102, 103
Alight On the Clouds, 34
Allis, Samuel, 34, 250n15, 252n38, 256–57n86, 290n12
A Man That Left His Enemy Lying In The Water (La roo ra shar roo cosh), *147*
Ames, Oliver, 98, 277n56
Animal symbolism, 14, 20, 252n38; bear, 20, 252n38; eagle, 17, 20, 250n16, 252n38; wolf, 20, 25–26, 254n55, 255n68
Anti-Indian prejudice: and Mulberry Creek killings, 111–12, 114, 280–81n6; by U.S. officials, 43, 48, 53, 55–56, 196, 202, 260n29, 287n89
Apache Indians, 14, 32
Arapaho Indians, 14; alliance with Cheyenne and Sioux, 60; as Pawnee enemy, 4, 7, 33, 36, 158; as U.S. Army scouts, 201, 204, 205, 207, 211, 213, 215, 216–17, 219; U.S. attacks on, 71–72, 87, 274n20; white settlers and, 49–50
Army and Navy Journal, 195, 216
Arnold, Edward W., 84, 226, 274n13
Ash Hollow massacre (1855), 43–44
A Shield (Tah we li hereis), 61
Augur, Christopher Columbus, 83, 89, 106, 158–59, 275n27; on "civilizing" function of scouts, 3, 161, 241; on enlistment of scouts, 84, 100, 162, 170, 180; pleased with scouts, 97, 99

Bad Wound, 60
Bailey, G. M., 78
Ballard, Charles T., 164
Barclay, George D., 125, 138
Barnett, Sidney, 171–72
Bates, Alfred E., 113
Bayhylle, Baptiste, 58, 85, 87, *147*, 309n20; biographical information, 264n6
Bear (Co rux), 115–16
Bear River massacre (1863), 62
Bears, 20, 252n38
Beaver Creek battle (1869), 119
Beaver Dam, 207

335

Becher, Gustavus G., 85, 100, 101, 107, 125, 288n108; biographical information, 227, 273–74n13, 308n10
Beecher, Frederick H., 282n21
Beecher's Island battle (1869), 118, 282n21
Belden, George P., 251n26
Bellas, Henry H., 202, 210
Bennett, Lyman G., 271n73
Bent, George, 65, 262n41, 268n43
Benton, Thomas Hart, 80
Berthrong, Donald J., 282n22
Best One Of All (La hoor a sac), 165, 167–68, 291n20
Betts, Charles Wyllys, 164, 165, 167, 168
Big Gip, 130
Big Hawk Chief, 221
Big Red Meat, 178, 179, 184
Big Spotted Horse (Uh sah wuck oo led ee hoor), 34–35, 158, 177–78, 179, 183; biographical information, 289–90n3, 298n31; motive for enlisting, 180; moves to Indian territory, 175–76, 289n3, 293n48; praised by Pratt, 184–85, 295n72
Big Tree, 178
Bird, 201
Black Bear, 71
Black Coal, 200
Black Hairy Dog, 208, 210
Black Kettle, 119
Black Moon, 130
Black Mouse, 201
Black Wolf, 29
Blaine, Effie, 16
Blaine, Wichita, 193, 209, 222; joins scouts, 191–92; later life, 227–28, 230, 232, 234, 236
Blickensderfer, Jacob, Jr., 88
Blown Away, 201
Blue Hawk (Coo towy goots oo ter a oos), 135, *143*
Blunt, James G., 260–61n36

Bourke, John G., 192, 202, 205, 217; on Pawnee scouts, 203, 210, 214, 215, 219
Bowers, Brookes, 94
Box, John, 110, *155*, 232, 236; pension request by, 233–34, 310n36
Box, John (Red Fox), 129
Boy Chief, 160
Bozeman, John M., 49
Bozeman Trail, 76
Brave Chief (La sah root e cha ris), 100, *153*, 232
Brave Wolf, 73–74
Bridger, Jim, 70
Broome, Jeff, 134
Brown, Albert, 63–64
Brown, William H., 138
Brulé Sioux. *See* Sioux, Broulé
Buell, George P., 179
Buffalo: Pawnee hunts of, 65, 101–102, 104, 107–108, 124, 169–70, 173, 253n48; settlers' overhunting of, 33, 158, 174, 178, 293–94n56
Buffalo, John, *155*, 228, 232; pension and death, 234, 236, 310n37
Buffalo Doctor Society, 232
Bundles: sacred, 13, 14, 20, 21, 174, 230; war, 25, 30, 192–93, 245
Burgess, William, 173, 175, 293n48
Burnett, Fincelius ("Finn"), 66, 68, 69, 72, 267–68n43, 269n52, 269n55
Bush, Joe, 301n77
Bushnell, Charles, 98
Byrne, Edward, 111, 112

Captain Jim (Young Bull), *155*, 232, 236
Carpenter, Louis H., 184
Carr, Eugene Asa, 109, 123, 124, 126–27, 134, 169; biographical information, 282–83n27; and Marsh scientific expedition, 164; on Pawnee scouts, 120, 123, 125, 131; on shortages of men and

INDEX

equipment, 120, 283n34; and Summit Springs battle, 127–28, 129, 131, 133
Carter, T. J., 88
Carver, William F. ("Doc"), 227
Chandler, Zachariah, 188
Changing Bear, 200
Cheyenne: alliance with Sioux, 60, 223; attacks on settlers, 106, 110–11, 119; Custer campaign against, 118–19; in Great Sioux War, 186–87, 189, 207–16, 223–24; as Pawnee enemy, 14, 32–33, 34, 35–36, 158, 241–42; in Plum Creek battle, 95–97, 244, 276n47; Powder River expedition against (1865), 60, 62–63, 65–67, 68–69, 77–78; at Red Cloud and Spotted Tail agencies, 196–97; in Red River war, 178, 179, 184; Republican River expedition against, 118, 119, 122, 125–26, 129–33, 135, 282n21, 286nn72–73; resist confinement to reservation, 39; Sand Creek massacre against, 41, 60, 82; Turkey Leg band of, 93–97; and Union Pacific Railroad, 82; as U.S. Army scouts, 201, 204, 301n77; U.S. campaign against (1857), 43–47, 260n27; war against in Colorado (1864), 49–50
Chivington, John M., 50, 60
Cholera, 32
Christianity, 230, 231
"Civilizing" of Indians, 3, 39, 158, 161–62, 230–31, 241, 242, 247n2
Civil War, 41; Indian scouts in, 43, 260–61n36
Clark, William Philo, 201, 202, 203, 204
Clayton, William, 253–54n54
Coal Bear, 208
Cody, William F. ("Buffalo Bill"), 165, 166, 176, 291–92n31; as buffalo hunter, 124, 169; claims by, 130, 287n83; as Frank North business partner, 226, 227–28, 248n3; in Republican River expedition, 120, 121, 128, 134–35, 137, 284n42; Wild West Show of, 140, 172, 226, 227–28
Cole, Nelson, 63, 74, 75, 271n74
Collins, Caspar W., 267n32
Colorado, 33, 38, 39; war against Cheyenne (1864), 49–50
Comanche Fox (Ke wuck oo lar lih tah), 58
Comanche Indians, 14, 37, 50; as Pawnee enemies, 32, 111, 180; in Red River war, 178–79, 184, 196
Comba, Enrico, 254n55
Coming Around With The Herd (Tuc ca rix te ta ru pe row), *143*
Congressional Medal of Honor: to Charles Thomas, 75, 271n76; to John Kyle, 285n63; to Mad Bear and Traveling Bear, 133–34
Connelll, John, 179
Connor, Patrick Edward, 75, 82; biographical information, 62; depredations against Indians by, 62–63, 64; on Pawnee scouts, 72, 271–72n80; in Powder River campaign (1965), 65, 70, 71–75
Cooke, Philip St. George, 28, 30, 83
Coons, Harry, 225, 231, 308n1, 309n20
Co roox ah kah, 101
Co rux tah kah tah, 136
Cosgrove, Tom, 201, 203
Coup counting: in Pawnee martial tradition, 4, 27–28, 254nn60–61; by Pawnee scouts, 85–86, 211, 213
Crazy Horse, 47, 187–88, 189, 194, 207
Crittenden, Eugene W., 120
Crook, George, 43; indecisive and erratic orders by, 202–203, 218, 300n61; and Indian scouts, 195–96, 204, 205, 222, 241, 247n2; in Powder River campaign (1876–77), 188, 195, 197, 199, 200, 202–203, 299n45; as skilled tactician, 195–96, 300n61

Crooked Hand, 257n92
Crow Indians, 201, 270n62
Crow Split Nose, 210
Curly Chief, 193
Curtis, Samuel R., 53–55; biographical information on, 260n35; and Pawnee scouts, 50, 53, 57, 242, 262–63nn48–49, 263n1
Cushing, Sylvanus E., 169; in 1869 campaign, 115, 123, 281n15, 288n108; in 1876–77 campaign, 194, 198, 219; later life, 227, 308n11
Custer, George Armstrong, 118–19, 187, 188; at battle of Little Bighorn, 189

Dances: "begging," 219, 306–307n144; Sun Dance, 44, 178, 253n44; war, 30, 86, 92, 194, 217, 219–20, 221, 253n44, 255n68
Daughterty, William E., 138
Davidson, John W. "Black Jack," 179–80, 182–83, 185, 295n72
Davis, Isaac, 84, 95
Davis, Jefferson, 44, 80
Delaney, Hayden, 201
Denman, H. B., 114
Denney, Jeremiah C., 122
Densmore, Frances, 16, 238, 249–50n8, 250n13, 252n38
Denver, James W., 47
Deshetres, Antoine, 18–19
DeSmet, Pierre Jean, 255n72
Dillon, Sidney, 98
Dodge, Grenville M., 62, 268n43; biographical information, 81; and Pawnee scouts, 81, 90, 272–73n2
Dodge, Richard Irving: and Indian scouts, 92–93, 96, 196, 203–204, 306n144; in Powder River campaign (1876-77), 200, 201–202, 217
Dog Soldiers (Hotamitaniu), 119, 127, 129–33; about, 118, 282n22
Dorsey, George A., 231, 252n34
Douglas, Stephen A., 80–81

Driving A Herd (Ta caw deex taw see ux), *150*
Duff, John R., 88
Dull Knife, 47, 187–88, 189, 194, 207, 208, 209; surrender of, 214
Dull Knife battle (1876), 207–17; Cheyenne casualties in, 215, 303n106, 304n125; Indian scouts in, 209–10, 215–16, 302n93, 302n96, 302–303n98; Pawnee celebration following, 217, 219–20, 304–305n129; significance of, 223–24; U.S. casualties in, 212, 215–16, 304n126; U.S. military deployment in, 207, 301n80
Dunbar, John Brown, 32, 253n52; as missionary to Pawnee, 34, 256–57n86; on Pawnee military culture, 16, 20, 23–24, 249–50n8, 252n38
Duncan, Thomas, 137, 138, 139
Dunlay, Thomas, 243
Dunn, Francis Wayland, 101, 103, 106, 279n78
Durant, Thomas C., 82, 98
Dwyer, Philip, 138

Eagle Chief (La ta cuts la shar), *141, 153*, 193
Eagles, 17, 20, 250n16, 252n38
Echo Hawk, 17, 192, 222, 251n31; adopts name of, 217; later life, 228, 229, 231, 236, 309n18; pension, 233, 234, 311n43; photo, *152*
Echohawk, Brummett, 239
Echo Hawk, Del Ray, 239
Echo-Hawk, Roger C., 15, 31, 250n16
Elkins, Stephen B., 40
Elting, Oscar, 197
Emory, William Hensley, 274n18
Evans, John, 50
Evans, Michael, 266n31
Evarts, Mark, 117, 278n65
Everett, Horace, 262n47
Ewing, Alexander Hamilton, 164

Fall Leaf, 45
Fast Thunder, 200, 300n69
Fighting Bear (Co rux ta puk), 159
First Man To War (Kit e ka rus oo kah wah), 58
First To Run (Ow it toost), 61, 292n39
Fisher, 201
Fleming, Rufus E., 76–77
Fletcher, Alice C., 28
Floyd, John B., 46
Foote, Rensselaer W., 46, 47
Forsyth, George A., 118
Fouts, William D., 67, 267n32
Fox (Kewuck), 58; changes name to Brave Shield, 85–86
Fox Chief (Ke wuck oo la shar), 104
Frank Leslie's Illustrated Magazine, 307n161
Friday, William, 200
Fryer, B. E., 115

Gambling, 104, 108, 134, 161
Garnett, William, 199
Ghost Dance movement, 230, 309n20
Gibbon, John R., 188
Gillette, Lee P., 59
Gillis, J. L., 48
Gold, 38, 49, 187
Good Eagle (La tah cots too ri ha), 133, 230, 232, 235, 236
Gordon, George A., 197, 198
Grant, Ulysses S., 62, 81, 187, 196; policy toward Indians, 157, 185
Grattan, John L., 43
Great Sioux War (1876–77): causes of, 186–88; Dull Knife battle, 207–17; Indian warriors joining, 195, 197; Little Bighorn battle, 189, 208–209; Rosebud battle, 188–89. *See also* Powder River campaign (1876–77)
Greene, Jerome A., 210, 216, 223
Gregg, Josiah, 24–25
Grey Beard, 45, 259n19
Grinnell, George Bird, 98, 100, 107, 173, 187, 259n19; book by, 5; and Marsh scientific expedition, 164, 165, 167–68; on motivation for joining scouts, 191; on Pawnee military culture, 12, 253n44; on Powder River campaign (1865), 68, 69, 72
Griswold, John Wool, 164
Grouard, Frank, 199, 200, 208

Halleck, H. W., 49
Hammond, Charles L., 220
Hammond, O. G., 162, 163, 169
Hard Robe, 201
Harney, William S., 43
Harper's New Monthly Magazine, 164
Harris, Charles, 239
Harvey, William N., 58, 69, 85, 100, 101, 105; biographical information, 265n9; changes name to Nicholas C. Creede, 226, 265n9
Hawk Chief (Koot tah we coots oo lel la shar), 61
Hayes, Rutherford B., 82
Headman, Peter (Pe isk ee la shar—"Boy Chief"), 159, 183, 213, 216
Hemphill, William C., 225
Henshaw, George, 94
Hicks, Elias, 157
High Eagle, 129, 131, 216; later life, 232, 236; pension fight by, 233, 234, 310–11n40; permanent injury to, 133, 236; photo, *155*
Hill, Charles M., 233
Holliday, George H., 17–18, 77
Horse raids: against other tribes by Pawnee, 158–59, 175, 180, 254n54, 290n4; against Pawnee, 160, 173; in Pawnee martial culture, 15, 23, 24–25
Horses, 133, 134, 198–200, 204, 206; Pawnee, 17–18, 107; and Pawnee cultural traditions, 17, 250n15
Howard, E. B., 234–35
Howell, Josie, 231
Howling Magpie, 125, 285n59

Humfreville, J. Lee, 21, 40–41, 259n13
Hurd, Marshall F., 89, 275n27
Huron Indians, 43
Hyde, George H., 4–5
Hynes, William F., 90, 91, 275n29

I Am The Bravest (Wit te de root kah wah), 60–61
Iowa Indians, 14
Iron Shirt, 178
Iron Teeth, 212, 214
Iroquois Indians, 43
Irving, John Treat, 17, 251n22
Isa-tai, 178

Jackson, William Henry, 93
James, Edwin, 19–20, 30, 251n30, 255n67, 256n82
Janise, Nick (LaJeunesse), 97
Janney, Samuel M., 158, 159, 160, 171, 291n14; against Pawnee scouts, 161, 170
Jerome Commission, 229
Johnson, Andrew, 83, 84
Jones, John B., 179
Jones, T. Quinn, 235
Judkins, William L., 302n93
Julesburg, Colorado, 53, 60, 61

Kansas, 55, 157, 178; attacks by Indians in, 106, 109, 111, 119–20, 140, 178; citizen attacks on Pawnee, 111, 159–60
Karituhuiwu, 117, 118
Kaw Indians, 14
Keller, Alexander, 215
Kendall, C. P., 107
Ke wuck ookah lah, 194
Kidd, James H., 63, 69
Kiowa Indians, 14, 37, 50; as Pawnee enemy, 32, 111, 180; peace council with Pawnees, 174–75; in Red River war, 178–79, 184, 196; as U.S. scouts, 294n66
Kirkwood, Samuel J., 81

Kislingsberry, Fred, 136, 137, 138
Ki wa ku ta hi ra sa, 68
Knife Chief, *153*
Koot tah we coots oo hadde, 104
Kyle, John, 126, 285n63

Last Bull, 210
Lawton, Lieutenant, 209
Leader of Scouts (Tah he rus ke tah), 100
Leading Fox, 228, 233, 234, 236, 311n41
Lehman, George, 125, 138, 227
Like A Fox (Ke wuk o we terah rook), *149*
Lillie, Gordon W. ("Pawnee Bill"), 131
Lincoln, Abraham (scout), 192, 228
Little Bear (Co rux kit e butts), 212, 303n110
Little Bighorn battle (1876), 189, 208–209
Little Bird, 72
Little Crow (Kah kah kit e butts), 61
Little Eagle (La tah cots kit e butts), 58
Little Ears (Kah hah liens), 67–68, 268n51, 292n39
Little Fork, 200
Little Fox (Ke wuck oo kit e butts), 58
Little Grizzly Bear (Mottschujinga), 255n67
Little Hawk, 129
Little Man, 125
Little Priest, 63, 270n68
Little Robe, 119, 158
Little Thunder, 60
Little Wolf, 47, 187–88, 208
Little Wound, 119
Lone Bear, 130
Lone Chief, 11–12, 175, 231
Lone Wolf, 178, 179
Long, Eli, 47
Loo law we luck oo la it, 105, 279n83
Loo ree wah ka we rah rick soo, 116, 117

INDEX 341

Louisiana Purchase, 37
Louwalk, John, 231
Lushbaugh, Benjamin F., 48, 49, 53, 81, 262n48

Mackenzie, Ranald S., 179, 184; and Dull Knife battle, 207, 208, 209, 210–11, 213, 301n80, 304n126; on Indian scouts, 182, 216; military reputation of, 196; in Powder River campaign (1876–77), 195, 196–97, 198, 199, 200, 202, 217–18
Mad Bear (Co rux te chod ish), 125, 126; awarded Medal of Honor, 133
Magee, Henry Wells, 101
Maley, Thomas E., 129
Maman-ti, 178
Man That Left His Enemy Lying In The Water, 103, 279n73
Man That Steals Horses (Kah Deeks), 61
Many Beaver Dams, 210
Marsh, O. C., 163, 164–68
Mason, George, 130–31
Massacre Canyon (1873), 173–74, 175, 236, 292–93n44
Mathews, Alexander, 240
Matthews, Fred, 85, 89–90, 100, 112–13, 121, 171; biographical information, 226–27, 273n13, 308n8
Mauck, Clarence, 198
Maximilian, Prince, 27
McClellan, James S., 213, 220, 303–304n111
McDermott, John, 70
McFadden, Joseph, 226, 262–63n49; relations with Pawnee, 53–54, 55, 242–43, 263n55
McFarland, Alexander, 215
McGrath, Daniel, 131
McKinney, John A., 211–12, 215, 303n106
McMurtry, Edward, 135
McNeill, Edwin R., 235

McPherson, James B., 281n7
Medicine Man, 71
Medicine Water, 178
Mengis, Joseph, 215
Merrill, Lewis, 85, 100
Meurerm O, H, 233
Mexican War, 37, 39
Mexico border crisis (1916), 238
Miles, Nelson A., 179, 195
Mills, Anson, 176–77
Minnesota, 49
Missionaries, 34, 39
Missouri, 54
Missouria Indians, 14, 33
Mitchell, Gavin, 266n31
Mitchell, Robert B., 50–52, 53–55, 261nn38–39; biographical information, 260n35; and Pawnee scouts, 50, 52–53, 55, 57
Montana, 49, 194–95
Mooar, Josiah Wright, 178
Moreland, Robert, 272n85
Morse, Charles E., 87, 100, 106; biographical information, 227, 273n13, 308n9
Mulberry Creek attack (1869), 111–12, 114, 280–81n6
Mullen, Ira, 168
Murie, James R., 84–85, 234; biographical information, 226, 264n7; on Pawnee scouts, 25, 27, 254n60; photo, 155; in Powder River expedition (1865), 58, 69, 271n79; in Republican River expedition, 121, 125
Murie, James Rolfe (son), 155, 264n7
Murray, Charles, 20, 29, 31, 253n48; on Pawnees' weapons, 19, 251n23

Nash, Edwin R., 63, 266n31
Nebraska, 55, 106, 119–20, 157; "Pawnee War" in, 257n91; praises Pawnee scouts, 139–40
Nebraska Republican, 58–59
New Mexico, 179

New York Times, 86
Nicholson, John Reed, 164
Nick Coots ("Bird"), 159, 174
Night Chief (La roo rutk a haw la shar), *147*
Nohl, Lessing H., Jr., 224
North, Frank J., 52, 107, 114, 135, 169, 222, 266n21; biographical information, 53–54, 248n3; as Cody business partner, 226, 227–28, 248n3; commissioned to lead Pawnee scouts, 51, 53, 58; on disciplining and drilling of scouts, 59, 88, 194, 244; divides up war spoils, 67, 134, 244–45; in Dull Knife battle, 208, 211, 212, 214; enlists recruits, 57–58, 100, 112, 115, 121, 168, 189–91; at Fort Kearny, 109, 110; health problems of, 190, 194, 223; horse of, 117–18, 204; and intertribal Pawnee divisions, 242; later years and death, 226, 248n3; leadership authority of, 55, 104–105, 242–44, 312n1; life saved by Pawnee scouts, 77–78, 80, 274n20; and Marsh scientific expedition, 164, 165, 166; names whites only as officers, 168–69; organizes new companies, 54, 57–58, 84–85, 100, 112–13, 121, 161, 168; overemphasis on his role, 4–5; and Pawnee-Sioux scout tensions, 203, 204–205; photo, *144*; in Powder River campaign (1865), 66, 68, 70, 74, 267n42, 269n52, 271n79; praised by State of Nebraska, 139–40; punishments and disciplining by, 98, 125, 193, 201, 243–44; receives Pawnee name, 67, 243, 268n50; in Republican River expedition, 97–98, 107, 116–17, 123, 126, 130, 136, 137–38, 281n17; scouts' customs adopted by, 66, 244; at Sioux-Pawnee peace council, 51, 261n39

North, James E., 100
North, Luther H., 57, 70, 159, 169, 173, 234, 261n39; with Custer's Black Hills expedition, 187; death of, 227, 248n3; in Dull Knife battle, 208, 210, 211, 213, 214, 302n96, 303–304n111; leadership in battalion, 85, 112–13, 281n15; military experience of, 243; on Pawnee military tactics, 17, 37; photo, *145*; on poverty at Pawnee reservation, 190; and Powder River campaign (1876–77), 194, 198, 199, 218, 297n27; receives Pawnee name, 87; recruitment of scouts by, 58, 193; reprimand of, 122–23; and Republican River expedition, 86–87, 103, 105, 124, 274n18; on Summit Springs battle, 127, 129, 130; writes accounts of Pawnee scouts, 4–5, 117
Noted Fox, 102–103
Noyes, Henry E., 112

Oaks, Sumner, 101
O'Donnell, Thomas, 87, 88, 90
Office of Indian Affairs, 99, 172, 185, 235
Oglala Sioux. *See* Sioux, Oglala
O ho a tay, 205
Old Crow, 201
Old Eagle, 200
Omaha Daily Republican, 221
Omaha Indians, 14, 32–33, 262n47
Omaha Weekly Herald, 106
Omohundro, John Burwell ("Texas Jack"), 172
One Who Brings Herds (Tuh cod ix te cah wah), *148*
One Who Strikes The Chiefs First (Tec ta sha cod dic), *147*
Ord, Edward O. C., 176, 177
Osage Indians, 14, 32
Osborne, Billy (Koot tah we coots oo la ri e coots—"Brave Hawk"), 102,

129, 133, 287n95; later life, 228, 235, 236; pension effort, 233, 234, 310n39; photo, *155*
Otoe Indians, 14, 32–33

Pacific Railroad Act (1862), 81
Palmer, Henry E., 71, 72, 267n37, 267n43, 270n67
Panic of 1873, 187
Parker, Ely S., 162
Patterson, J. W., 82
Pattie, James O., 26, 254n58
Pawnee: alliance with U.S., 4, 12, 33–34, 36, 37, 241–42; Chawi band, 13, 23, 28, 33, 84–85, 99, 242, 312n1; "civilizing" and acculturation of, 3, 158, 161–62, 230–31, 241, 242, 247n2; desecretation of bodies of, 115; economic conditions of at turn of century, 231; and Ghost Dance movement, 230; heroic age of, 32; intertribal divisions within, 13, 67–68, 242; Kitkahahki band, 13, 23, 28, 85, 100, 242; Massacre Canyon as turning point for, 173–74; participation in America's wars, 43, 237–40, 260–61n36; peace council with Sioux, 50–52; Pitahawirata band, 13, 23, 28, 85, 99, 242; population decline, 186, 228, 295n1; poverty and disease, 32, 51, 158, 174, 186, 190, 228, 230; removal to Indian Territory, 174–76, 186, 295n1; reservation boundaries, 35; semipermanent towns of, 13; Sioux, Cheyenne, and Arapaho as enemies, 4, 5, 14, 32–33, 35–36, 191, 202, 203–204, 241–42; spiritual demoralization of, 158, 174, 230; territory of in 1800, 13; treaties with U.S., 34, 35, 38, 47–48, 114–15, 257n91, 260n28; and white settlers, 38, 111, 159–60, 174. *See also* Skiri Pawnee

Pawnee Agency, 157, 158; school, 162, 171, 290n12
Pawnee Indians, The (Hyde), 4–5
Pawnee Killer, 60, 94, 119, 127, 134, 135, 137, 161
Pawnee martial traditions and culture: bows and arrows, 18–19, 251n22, 251n26; ceremonial dances, 30, 86, 92, 194, 217, 219–20, 221, 253n44, 255n68; coup counting, 4, 27–28, 85–86, 211, 213, 254nn60–61; cultural richness of, 12–13; death on battlefield, 11–12, 15–16, 31, 249–50n8; discipline, 23; food, 24; funeral and burial of combatant, 30–31, 68, 166, 255n72; guns, 18, 20, 58, 251n23; historical antecedents of, 15, 249n7; homecoming ceremony, 29–30, 240, 255n68; horsemanship, 17–18; horse raids, 15, 23, 24–25, 158–59, 175, 180, 254n54, 290n4; lances, 21–22, 253n42; maneuvers, 24; and manhood, 11, 12; marriage, 228; medicines, 21; men's societies, 21–23, 25; military commanders, 26; name-giving ceremonies, 28–29, 67, 217, 268n50; no taking of prisoners, 26, 131, 212, 245, 287n89; physical endurance, 16, 20, 160, 244; raids as tactic, 6, 24; reasons for going to war, 14–15; reinforced by Pawnee scout battalion, 4, 161–62, 244–45; as runners, 20, 160, 219, 221; sacrifice of enemy prisoners, 34; scalp raids, 15, 23, 25; scalp taking, 4, 15, 23, 26–27, 66, 67, 69, 73, 86, 88, 125–26, 211, 220, 245, 254n58, 279n78; shields, 19–20, 251n30; stealth and surprise, 4, 26, 42, 96–97, 254n54; taking of spoils and trophies, 15, 27, 67, 73, 134, 216, 244–45, 270n68, 304–305n129; temperance, 185; torture of

Pawnee martial traditions and culture (*continued*)
captives, 29, 255n67; U.S. effort to eradicate, 229; war bundles, 25, 30, 192–93, 245; war paint, 93, 128; war parties, 4, 6, 23, 25, 244–45; warriors' dress and appearance, 93, 252n38, 253n53; war songs, 29, 94, 210, 220, 238

Pawnee Puk oot, 222

Pawnee religious beliefs, 13–14; on afterlife, 16, 250n11; animal symbolism, 14, 17, 20, 25–26, 250n16, 252n38, 254n55, 255n68; faith in Tiiraawaahat, 13, 17, 136, 166, 243, 245; guardian spirits, 252n37; role of priests, 13–14; sacred bundles, 13, 14, 20, 21, 174, 230; songs, 16, 250n13, 252n38; on supernatural, 13, 20, 116, 243; taboos, 20–21

Pawnee scout battalion: in 1857 anti-Cheyenne campaign, 43–47, 259n18; casualties in battle, 104, 105, 125, 216, 279n83; as "civilizing" influence, 3, 241, 242, 247n2; commended, 97, 139–40, 182, 184–85, 216, 220–21, 295n72; commissioned and noncommissioned officers, 58, 84–85, 100, 112–13, 121, 168–70; company structure, 54, 57–58, 84–85, 100, 112–13, 121, 161, 168, 200–201; congressional acts on, 84, 189; desertions from, 263–64n6; discipline, 59–60, 87–88, 98–99, 121, 125, 201, 216, 221; drilling and training, 59, 194, 244; in Dull Knife battle, 207, 208, 209, 210–12, 216, 220–21; freelance scouts for Marsh expedition, 163, 164–68; guarding Union Pacific Railroad, 84–109, 168, 169; guns of, 58, 86, 274n17; historical accounts of, 4–5; Indian Office efforts against, 158, 161, 162, 163, 170, 172; initial formation, 48, 49, 50, 57–58; intertribal tensions within, 67–68, 242; military effectiveness of, 5, 97, 244; musterings out, 78, 99, 109, 139, 184, 221–22; "mutiny" of, 98–99; and Pawnee military culture, 4, 97, 241, 242, 244–45; Pawnee term for, 3; payment of, 55, 73, 118, 203, 220, 272n85; in Plum Creek battle, 95–97, 276n47; in Powder River campaign (1865), 60–76; problems with white population, 159–60, 223, 307–308n165; punishment in, 125, 193, 201, 243–44; recruitment, 53, 57–58, 100, 112–13, 121, 168, 180, 183, 189–93, 262n47, 263n1, 278n61, 296n11, 296–97n13; recruitment motivations, 4, 12, 36, 180, 190–91, 241–42; in Red River war, 177, 180–85; reformed in 1876, 189–90; relations with regular troops, 201–202; in Republican River country (1870), 169–70; in Republican River expedition (1869), 121–39; reputation of, 4, 171; saves Cole and Walker columns, 74, 75, 76; skepticism by officers about, 55, 120, 123; in Summit Springs battle, 129–30, 131; tactics, 5, 37, 92–93, 96–97, 244; tensions with Sioux scouts, 201, 203–6, 211, 301n77; uniforms of, 54, 59, 86, 93, 97, 121, 128, 183; veterans pensions of, 7, 232–35, 310–11nn36–44; war party character of, 4, 244–45; and Wild West exhibitions, 171–72; in Wyoming Territory (1864), 52–55, 262n42; in Wyoming Territory (1874), 176–77

Peabody, George, 163

Peace councils: Pawnee and Brulé Sioux (1871), 170–71; Pawnee and Cheyenne (1835), 34; Pawnee and

Kiowas (1873), 174–75; Pawnee and Sioux (1870), 160; Pawnee and Sioux scouts (1876), 204–206, 300n69, 301n77
Pe ah tah wuck oo, 99, 277n58
Peck, Robert M., 45, 46, 55, 259n24
Pensions, veterans', 7, 232–35, 292n39, 310–11nn36–44
Pitalesharo, 175
Pitaresaru, 278n65
Platt, Elivira, 162
Plum Creek battle (1867), 95–97, 244, 276n47
Pollack, William, 237, 312n53
Ponca Indians, 14, 32–33, 297–98n27
Pope, John, 62, 75, 162; rescinds Connor order, 64, 72
Pourier, Baptiste ("Big Bat"), 199, 200
Powder Chief, 130
Powder River campaign (1865), 63–76; balance sheet of, 76; capture of Arapaho horses, 66, 68, 72, 75–76; Cheyenne and U.S. casualties, 66, 72, 267n43, 270n67, 271n74; exhaustion of Cole and Walker columns, 74, 271n77; logistical and weather problems, 64, 73, 74; Pawnee scouts' key role in, 76, 271–72n80; plan for, 63–65; skirmishes and battles: Frenchman's Creek, 77–78; Julesburg, 60; Sussex, 66–67, 267–68n43; Tongue River, 70–72, 270n67
Powder River campaign (1876–77), 200–224; departure of, 202–203; Dull Knife battle, 207–16; effects of inclement weather, 218–19; move on Red Cloud and Red Leaf camps, 197–200; Sheridan's plans for, 195; tensions between Pawnee and Sioux scouts, 201, 203–206, 211, 301n77; troop composition and strength, 200–201. *See also* Great Sioux War

Pratt, Richard Henry, 180, 183–84, 294n62, 294–95n68; praises Pawnee scouts, 182, 184–85
Pretty Voiced Bull, 201
Price, George Frederick, 127, 137
Price, George H., 129, 286n72
Price, William Redwood, 179
Pullman, George M., 82

Quakers, 157–58, 172, 175–76
Quanah Parker, 178

Railroad, transcontinental, 80–83. *See also* Union Pacific Railroad
Rattlesnake (Loots tow oots), *146*
Rawlins, John A., 88
Red Bull, 68
Red Cloud, 82, 160, 188, 197–98; dismissed as "principal chief," 199, 299n45
Red Cloud Agency, 195, 199; census of, 196–97
Red Hawk (Roam Chief), 192
Red Leaf, 197, 198–99
Red River war (1874), 177–85; campaign plan for, 179; role of Pawnee scouts in, 184–85; significance of, 178; skirmishes and battles: Adobe Walls, 179; Andarko, 179; Palo Duro Canyon, 184
Red Sun, 231
Red Willow (Tah wah chuh e hod de), 223, 307–308n165
Reeve, Charles McCormick, 164
Reilly, Bernard, Jr., 164, 166
Republican River expedition (1869), 120–39; Carr on, 120, 133, 283n34; commanders in, 120; composition of, 121–22, 283n38; plagued by problems, 122, 124; significance of, 139; skirmishes and battles: July 5, 125–26, 286n63; July 11 (Summit Springs), 129–33; June 15 (Prairie Dog Creek), 172, 284n42; September 26, 137–38

Revolution, American, 43
Reynolds, Joseph, 188
Rickey, Don, Jr., 40
Riding In, William, 183, 234, 236, 311n42
Roam Chief: pension request by, 233; subsequent life, 228, 229
Roaming Scout (Ki ri ki ri see ra ki wa ri), *154*
Roberts, Rush (Ah re Kah rard), 191, 192, 203; as last living scout, 156, 236, 240; later life, 231–32, 234, 236, 240; photo, *156*
Robinson, Charles M., 189
Robinson, Lieutenant, 220
Roche, Jerry, 206, 212, 214, 299n47, 303n106; on scouts' fighting qualities, 216
Rockafellow, B. F., 65
Rockwell, Charles, 202
Roman Nose, 47, 282n21
Roosevelt, Theodore, 237–38
Royall, William B., 120, 125, 128, 129, 134, 135
Ruggles, George D., 123
Ruling His Sun, 100, 109, 193, 281–82n18; account of 1868 battle, 103–104; and Frank North, 80, 117; later years and death, 236; name changed to, 278n62; pension claim by, 233, 234–35, 277n58
Russell, James Matson, 164
Ryan, Patrick F., 215

Sandas, George, 74
Sand Creek massacre (1864), 41, 60, 82
Santa Fe Trail, 37–38, 62
Sargent, Henry Bradford, 164
Satanta, 178
Saxe, Maurice de, 22
Scalp taking: in Pawnee tradition, 4, 15, 23, 26–27, 254n58; by Pawnee scouts, 66, 67, 69, 73, 86, 88, 125–26, 211, 220, 245, 279n78

Schofield, George W., 184
Schuyler, Walter S., 201
Scott, Winfield, 44
Scovill, E. T., 87–88, 93, 275n23
Searing, Charles H., 223
Sedgwick, John, 44
Seeing Eagle, *155*
Seeing The Horse (Ah roose ah too ta it), 58
Settlers, 119–20; influx of, 37–38; and Pawnee, 35, 159–60, 257n91
Seymour, Silas, 88, 89–90, 275n27
Sharp Nose, 200, 205, 300n69
Shave Head, 125
Sheridan, Philip H., 158–59, 164, 183, 282n23; and Pawnee scouts, 183, 189–90, 221, 296n8; plans military campaigns, 118, 179, 188, 195, 299n45; urges slaughter of buffalo, 293–94n56
Sherman, William T., 81, 83, 164, 187; on Pawnee scouts, 3, 86–87, 99, 161, 241
Shield (Luck tah choo), 100
Shoshone Indians: as U.S. scouts, 201, 203, 205, 209, 210, 213, 215, 217, 302–303n96; U.S. war against, 62
Shot-Throat (Pakixtsaks), 117
Shotwell, Eli (Flying Hawk Whistling), 129, 232, 236; pension effort of, 234, 311n44
Sibley, Henry H., 49
Sidney Telegraph, 220–21
Singing Bear, 201
Sioux: alliance with Cheyenne, 60, 223; armed revolt in Minnesota (1862), 49; attacks on settlements, 110–11; Brulé, 50–51, 60, 85, 94, 138, 158, 170, 173, 188, 197; in Great Sioux War, 186–90, 223–24; Hunkpapa, 189, 194; massacre of Pawnee by, 173–74, 236; Oglala, 60, 82, 85, 88, 135, 137–39, 158, 160, 170, 173, 188, 189, 194, 196, 197, 214; as Pawnee enemy, 14, 32–33,

35–36, 79, 87, 170, 171, 175–76, 191, 203, 241–42, 256n79, 257nn92–93; peace council with Pawnee, 50–52; Powder River campaign against (1865), 62, 63, 65, 69, 74, 79; at Red Cloud and Spotted Tail agencies, 196–97; Republican River expedition against, 107, 116–18; resist confinement to reservation, 39; seizure of skulls of, 166; and Union Pacific Railroad, 82, 85–86, 88–93, 97–98, 102–105; as U.S. Army scouts, 199, 200–201, 203–206, 211, 216, 219, 299n45, 301n77, 305n129, 306–307n144
Sitting Bull, 187–88, 189, 194
Sitting Fox (Ke wuck oo weete), 61
Six Feathers, 200
Skiri Pawnee, 6–7, 13, 21, 23, 33, 34, 230; and Frank North's Pawnee name, 268n50, 312n1; scout company of, 23, 85, 121, 123, 242, 247n20; spiritual beliefs of, 18, 249n7; wolf emblem of, 25, 253n52
Sky Chief (Te low lut sha, Ti ra wa hut Re sa ru), 173, 174; photos, 142, 147
Small, Charles A., 57, 58, 59, 61, 70, 271n79
Smallpox, 32, 33, 51
Smith, Edward P., 188
Smith, James F., 168
Smith, John, 52
Smith, Marian W., 12
Smith, William Earl, 209, 214, 217
Solomon River battle (1857), 45–46, 260n27
Sorenson, Alfred E., 263n55
Spanish-American War, 237–38, 312n53
Spotted Horse, 298n31
Spotted Tail, 50, 60, 160, 188; appointed chief of "loyal" Sioux, 199, 299n45; as master diplomat, 170–71
Spotted Tail Agency, 197, 199

Spotted Wolf, 94
Stanley, David S., 45, 47, 259n18
Stanley, Henry M., 96, 276n43
Stars (Chuck kah), 61
Steadman, C. B., 58
Stone Calf, 178
Stowe, Elias, 138
Stuart, James E. B. ("Jeb"), 47
Stu le kit tah we ait, 194
Sullivan, John, 212, 215
Sully, Alfred, 49, 257n93
Summit Springs battle (1869), 129–33, 286nn72–73; Pawnee participants in, 129, 234; significance of, 140
Sumner, Edwin Vose, 44, 46, 259–60n24, 260n27; on Pawnee scouts, 55
Sumner, Samuel S., 129, 135, 221
Sun, Tom, 176
Sun Chief, 160
Sun Chief (Sa gule ah la shar), 159
Sun Dance, 44, 178, 253n44
Sun Tzu, 97
Sweatman, Robert, 123
Swift Bear, 197

Takuwutiru, 98
Tall Bull (Hotu'a e hka'ash tait), 47, 60, 118, 127; death of, 130–31, 287n88
Tall Wild Cat, 201
Ta ra da ka wa, 44, 45, 46, 48
Taylor, Daniel, 272n85
Taylor, E. B., 272n85
Taylor, Robert (Riding Stolen Horse), 129, 232, 234, 236
Temperance, 185
Terry, Alfred Howe, 188
Tesson, Louis S., 124
Texas, 178, 179
The Buffalo Runner (Lah low we hoo la shar), 60
The Duelist (Tucky tee lous), 165, 167, 291n20

The Great Spirit Sees Me (Te kit ta we lah we re), 60
The Man That Strikes The Enemy (Tuck oo wa ter roo), 60–61, 265–66n19, 292n39
Thomas, Charles L., 74, 75, 271n76
Thomas, Earl D., 164
Thompson, William, 94
Three Bears, 200, 204, 205, 206, 213, 300n69
Thunderbird Lance society, 21–22
Thunder Cloud, 201
Tieman, E. C., 234
Tongue River battle (1865), 70–72, 270n67
Torture, 29, 255n67
Townsend, E. D., 162
Townsend, John K., 251n22
Townshend, F. Trench, 107, 108, 109
Tracks On The Hill (Too re cha hoo ris), 60
Train, George Francis, 98
Traveling Bear (Co rux ah kah wah de), 98, 113–14, 131, 287n90, 302n96; receives Medal of Honor, 133–34; survived Massacre Canyon, 174
Treaties: with Pawnee (1818), 34; with Pawnee (1825), 34; with Pawnee (1833), 34; with Pawnee (1851), 38; with Pawnee (1853), 38; with Pawnee (1857), 35, 47–48, 114–15, 257n91, 260n28; with Plains Tribes (1867), 178; with Sioux (1868), 187
Trobriand, Philippe Regis de, 258n13
Troth, Jacob M., 158, 159, 160, 171, 172, 290–91n14; against Pawnee scout battalion, 161, 170
Truteau, Jean Baptiste, 31
Tup si paw, 205
Turkey Leg, 93–94, 95, 96
Two Crows, 127, 130
Two Strikes, 127

Union Pacific Railroad (UPRR): completion of transcontinental route by, 109; employs Pawnee guards, 162, 163, 168, 169; and Marsh scientific expedition, 164; Pawnees as laborers on, 81–82; photo, *152*; requests U.S. military assistance, 80; Sioux and Cheyenne attacks on, 82–83, 94, 276n44
Union Pacific Railroad protection mission (1867-68), 84–109; skirmishes and battles: Chimney Rock, 91–92; Court House Rock, 107; Granite Canyon, 89–90, 275n27; Lodgepole Creek, 87, 270n20; Mud Creek, 102–104, 279n78; Ogalala, 100–101; Plum Creek, 95–97, 244, 276n47; South Platte River, 86; Wood River, 105, 279n83
U.S. Army: anti-Indian prejudices in, 53, 55–56, 196, 202, 260n29; campaign against Cheyenne (1857), 43–47; campaign against Sioux in Minnesota (1862), 49; campaign against Western Sioux (1863-64), 49; command structure in West, 62; composition of, 40; in Great Sioux War, 187–224; hardships and desertion problem, 40–41; and Indian warrior tactics and skill, 42, 195–96, 258–59n13; massacres of Indians by, 41, 43–44, 62–63; mission to protect Union Pacific Railroad, 84–109; officer corps of, 41; Pawnee alliance with, 4, 12, 33–34, 36, 37, 241–42; pay rates, 40, 258n7; Powder River campaign (1865), 60–76; in Red River war, 177–85; Republican River expedition (1869), 120–39; size of, 39–40, 83–84, 189; strategy and tactics of, 41–43; supply and mobility problems, 42, 43; transcontinental railroad seen as solution for, 83; Western posts and forts, 38, 39, 258n3; Wyoming

expedition (1864), 53–55; Wyoming expedition (1874), 176–77, 293n53
U.S. government: alliance with Pawnee, 4, 12, 33–34, 36, 37, 241–42; "civilization program" toward Indians, 39, 158, 230–31, 232; Grant policy toward Indians, 157; Indian reservation policy, 38–39, 174, 229; limited control of West, 37; and Pawnee veterans' pensions, 7, 232–35, 310–11nn36–44; treaties with Pawnees, 34, 35, 38, 47–48, 114–15, 257n91, 260n28; treaties with Plains Tribes, 178, 187; war and peace factions in, 267n32
Utley, Robert M., 41, 76

Vegetius, 73
Villa, Pancho, 238
Volkmar, William Jefferson, 122, 137

Wade, Benjamin, 82
Wadsworth, James Wolcott, 164, 169
Walker, F. A., 171
Walker, Leicester, 129, 130, 135
Walker, Samuel, 63, 64, 74, 75, 271n74
Walking Sun (Us sa kouht), 192, 228, 234, 235, 236, 310n38
Walking Whirlwind, 34
Wallace, Sam, 125
Wandering Around (Cah we hoo roo), 100
Wandering Eagle (Koot tah we coots oo ter rar re), 58
Wandering Sun (Se gule kah wah de), 69, 76
Ware, Eugene F., 50, 51, 52, 261n39; low opinion of Pawnee scouts, 52–53, 55
War Pipes (Ste tock tah hoo ra rick), 60
War spoils and trophies: in Pawnee martial traditions, 15, 27; Pawnee scouts' taking of, 67, 73, 134, 216, 244–45, 270n68, 304–305n129

Washington, George, 43
Webb, George W., 274n20
Weeks, Ralph J. ("Little Warrior"), 192, 211, 212, 231, 303n106; on Dull Knife battle, 221; later life, 225–26
Weichell, Maria, 119, 132
Welch, James E., 120, 128, 130, 131, 287n89
Weltfish, Gene, 68, 98, 117
Whaley, Charles H., 114
Wheaton, Frank, 75
Wheelan, James N., 138
Wheeler, D. H, 272n85
Wheeler, Homer W., 207, 211, 212, 215
Whistler, 119, 127, 134, 137
White (Tah Kah), 60
White, Barclay, 171, 172, 176
White, Bob, 68, 78, 108, 176
White, Frank (Kitkahahki), 230, 309n20
White, Frank (Li Heris oo la shar—"Leading Chief"), 175, 192, 217, 297–98n27, 305n129; fights off Sioux war party, 92–93, 201–202; at Peace Council with Sioux, 204–206
White, Jay E., 168
White, Lonnie J., 140
White, Samuel, 61
White Bull, 45, 259n19
White Eagle, 102, 229, 232
White Horse (As sau taw ka), 119, *151*, 200
White Man Chief (Chatiks tah kah lah shar), 168
White Wolf, 178
Whitney, Asa, 80
Whitney, Eli, IV, 164
Wichita Agency, 175, 179, 180, 183, 190
Wild Hog, 208
Williamson, John W., 173, 295n1, 298n31

Wolf: as emblem of Skiris, 25, 253n52; symbolism, 20, 25–26, 254n55; wolf dance, 255n68
Wolf With Plenty Of Hair, 130
Woman's Heart, 178
Women: in military service, 239; and Pawnee traditions, 20–21, 29, 238, 254n58
Wood, Peter, 129, 235
Wooster, Robert, 42
World War I, 238, 312n56
World War II, 239–40

Wyoming, 266n24; 1864 military expedition, 53–55; 1874 military expedition, 176–77, 293n53

Yankton Indians, 105
Yellow Bear, 158
Yellow Shirt, 201
Young Chief, *153*
Young Eagle (Le tah kuts kee le pah kee), 109

Ziegler, Harry Degen, 164

www.ingramcontent.com/pod-product-compliance
Lightning Source LLC
Chambersburg PA
CBHW031426160426
43195CB00010BB/633